Critical Thinking: Developing an Effective Worldview

Gary Jason

San Diego State University

WADSWORTH

THOMSON LEARNING ™

Australia • Canada • Mexico • Singapore • Spain • United Kingdom • United States

WADSWORTH

THOMSON LEARNING ™

Philosophy Editor: Peter Adams
Assistant Editor: Kara Kindstrom
Editorial Assistant: Chalida Anusasananan
Marketing Manager: Dave Garrison
Print Buyer: Robert King
Permissions Editor: Stephanie Keough-Hedges

Production Service: Penmarin Books
Copy Editor: Laura Larson
Cover Designer: Annabelle Ison
Cover Printer: Von Hoffmann Graphics
Compositor: Thompson Type
Printer: Von Hoffmann Graphics

ISBN 0-534-57389-4

Wadsworth/Thomson Learning
10 Davis Drive
Belmont, CA 94002-3098
USA

For information about our products, contact us:
Thomson Learning Academic Resource Center
1-800-423-0563
http://www.wadsworth.com

International Headquarters
Thomson Learning
International Division
290 Harbor Drive, 2nd Floor
Stamford, CT 06902-7477
USA

UK/Europe/Middle East/South Africa
Thomson Learning
Berkshire House
168-173 High Holborn
London WCIV 7AA
United Kingdom

Asia
Thomson Learning
60 Albert Street, #15-01
Albert Complex
Singapore 189969

Canada
Nelson Thomson Learning
1120 Birchmount Road
Toronto, Ontario MIK 5G4
Canada

Contents

Preface

To the Instructor

The last decade especially has seen the growth of the critical thinking movement, and the concomitant appearance of a number of texts intended for critical thinking courses. Since this text also is intended for such courses, a few remarks are in order about what topics it covers and why it covers them the way it does.

Let us begin with the overall orientation. At the risk of oversimplification, it seems that critical thinking texts tend to have one of three basic orientations. First, many critical thinking texts are aimed at courses that have a heavy component of composition instruction—typically taught in the English department or in conjunction with the English department. Second, many critical thinking texts are aimed at courses that have a heavy component of rhetoric instruction—typically taught in the speech/communication department. Third, many critical thinking texts are aimed at courses that have a heavy component of informal logic—typically taught in the philosophy department.

My text falls squarely in that third group. I say this with full appreciation of the virtues of the other two approaches. But any author does well to focus on one area if the book is to be of manageable length.

In the domain of informal logic, this text covers much that is standard: the nature of statements, single- and multiple-argument identification, pitfalls of language, definition, truth tables and Venn diagrams, analogy, generalization, causal inference, and informal fallacies. However, the treatment of these topics is decidedly nonstandard. Inductive inference is accorded more coverage than deductive. The material on deduction is presented in two chapters not merely as techniques for determining the validity of given arguments but also for determining the consistency of already held beliefs, and drawing out the consequences of those beliefs, as well as for checking for logical truth. The discussion of pitfalls of language is much more detailed than is usual. Informal fallacies are not presented in isolation but rather are embedded in the discussion of acceptable reasoning. For example, false analogy is discussed *after* the student has a grasp of what correct analogical reasoning is all about. And topics are accompanied by numerous exercises with a realistic orientation, often taken from ordinary sources such as newspapers and magazines.

In addition to the standard topics, this text contains material not commonly found in critical thinking or introductory logic texts. There is a separate chapter on the structure of questions and what counts as acceptable answers to questions of various types. Another chapter discusses topical relevance, wherein fallacies of relevance are discussed from the perspective of logic of questions covered earlier in the chapter on questions. This allows a more adequate discussion of, for example, the fallacies of emotional appeal, because the student is able to see *when* appeals to emotion are relevant and when not. A separate chapter covers observation and testimony, wherein the fallacy of bad appeal to authority is addressed. I present definition as a tool for clarity of thought and expression, but I also discuss taxonomy.

I have wrapped the discussion of these topics around five basic criteria for rational thought: clarity, relevance, consistency, justification, and explanatory and predictive power. This structure allows the student to fit the material discussed into a general framework.

Finally, in the last three chapters of the book, I develop a general model for decision making and apply it to the two areas that characterize our society: consumer choice in a market economy and political choice in a representative democracy. I cover in great detail the psychological mechanisms that can defeat critical thinking, along with a critique of common consumer advertising and political rhetoric.

In keeping with the *informal* logical orientation of this text, I have kept technical matters to a minimum. Truth tables are discussed briefly (without natural deduction rules or truth trees, and Venn diagrams are discussed briefly (without syllogistic or predicate logic). I have deliberately kept mathematics to the very minimum. Of course, there is a trade-off: This approach limits how deeply I can explain, say, the rules governing sampling or the logic of hypothesis testing. But there is much you can say without needing sophisticated mathematics to say it, and as it is, far more material appears in this book than can be covered in one semester.

I have tried to supply a wealth of exercises in each chapter, perhaps more than most instructors will actually use. I do this because I believe that working exercises is the best way for the student to internalize critical thinking skills. In those exercises chosen from real-life writings, I have usually chosen passages from newspapers, popular magazines, and popular books rather than classic philosophical texts. I want students to learn to apply critical thinking skills to ordinary discourse without having to train them in matters best left to an introductory philosophy course.

I have also tried to keep topics modular wherever possible because of the wide diversity of topics covered in critical thinking courses. For example, while some instructors prefer covering some basic deductive logic in their courses, others avoid it like herpes. So I have two chapters on elementary deductive logic (just truth tables and Venn diagrams) that give a nice introduction to the key deductive concepts (validity, consistency, equivalence, entailment, and logical truth). But these chapters can be skipped entirely without loss to the rest of the book. There is of course a trade-off: a small amount of redundancy. I talk about the truth tabular definitions of the Boolean connectives very briefly when discussing types of statements in Chapter 2 and deductive argument forms in Chapter 5, and then review that material in Chapters 9 and 10. Another case of redundancy regards discussion of advertising. In Chapter 6 (in the section on fallacies of ambiguity), Chapter 8 (when discussing fallacies of relevance), and Chapter 12 (in the section on hasty generalization), I discuss fallacious ads. But I devote a separate chapter as well to advertising. Again, this is the price of modularity. Some other modules: Chapters 6 and 7 (on pitfalls of language and the tools for achieving clarity in the expression of thoughts); Chapter 12 and 13 (on inductive generalization, instantiation, and analogy); Chapters 14 and 15 (on causality and explanation); and Chapters 16, 17, and 18 (on decision making in general and consumer and political choice in particular).

Given the wealth of material covered, the text strives for concision wherever possible, without sacrificing essential detail. Also, I have kept the prose level at the lower-division college level, avoiding recondite vocabulary and technical jargon wherever possible but also avoiding a "cutesy" or a dumbed-down "Hey, wow, kids!" style that in my experience students view as condescending. Comprehensiveness of coverage, concreteness and topicality of illustration, and clarity of prose have been my goals.

Sections that are difficult or that involve diagram tools not necessary for comprehending the basic concepts are marked with a plus sign and can be omitted without interrupting the continuity of the material. All even-numbered exercises are answered in the back of the text, and all major terms are defined in the glossary. The odd-numbered exercises are answered in the intructor's manual.

This text contains more material than can be covered in one semester because instructors differ in the topics they prefer, and I want this text to be useful in a wide variety of courses. For those teaching critical thinking/introduction to logic, I suggest covering (in order) Chapters 1, 2, 3, 4, 5, 6, 7, 9, and 10. For those teaching critical thinking/informal fallacies, I suggest covering (in order) Chapters 1, 2, 4, 5, 6, 7, 8, 11, 12, 13, and 14. For those teaching applied critical thinking, I suggest covering (in order) Chapters 1, 2, 4, 5, 6, 8, 11, 12, 13, 14, 15, 16, 17, and 18.

I wish to thank the following professors for reviewing early drafts of this book: Frank Beckwith, Leonard J. Berkowitz, Tom Carroll, George Gale, Steve Giambrone, Bob Ginsberg, Sterling Harwood, William Lawhead, Michael O'Rourke, Anita Silvers, James Slinger, Joseph Tarala, W. Robin White, and Frank C. C. Young. I also wish to thank those who reviewed later drafts of this text: Francis Beckwith, Trinity International University; Istvan Berkeley, University of Louisiana at Lafayette; David Buller, Northern Illinois University; Frank Fair, Sam Houston State (TX); Dr. Tom Feehan, Holy Cross; Keith Korcz, U. of SW Louisiana; Isabel Luengo, Mira Costa College (CA); Michael O'Rourke, University of Idaho; Morton Schagrin, SUNY-Fredonia; and James Slinger, Fresno State. All errors, of course, remain my sole responsibility.

My thanks are due as well to my wife Janice and daughter Irina, for generously letting me spend time on writing that might have been spent with them. I am also grateful to David Goodman, who patiently word-processed endless drafts of this text.

Gary Jason
Department of Philosophy
San Diego State University

Part One   Chapter 1

The Elements of Critical Thinking: Statements, Questions, and Arguments

Critical Thinking: Developing an Effective Worldview

---

1   *Critical Thinking and Mental Models*

People differ from the simplest animals in a number of significant ways. From the perspective of critical thinking, the most significant difference between us and, say, protozoa is that we interact with the world in a fundamentally different way than do the protozoa. With all due respect to protozoa, a protozoan lives by blind action. It interacts with its environment directly—if it bumps into an object, it may try to ingest it. If it is lucky, it finds a tasty morsel. If not, what it ingests is toxic and it dies. On the other hand, while some people live more or less like protozoa, most people interact with the world with the aid of their pictures of it. An intelligent person develops a picture or, more accurately, a **model** of the world as he or she grows and uses that model as a substitute for blind action. For example, a reasonably aware person knows that, under usual conditions, an object falls down when dropped. It is that awareness, rather than the actual experience, that makes a person not want to be thrown from a window.

Human beings, then, unlike the lowest forms of life, do not deal with the world blindly or haphazardly. They use their rationality to create and shape a mental model, a *worldview,* of that world to use as a tool. Now, higher animals besides human beings also develop mental models, but none of these other animals seem (at first glance, anyway) to develop such models in such detail or use them as fully as people do at their most reasonable moments. The mental model you develop is what you use to make choices and take actions, and you develop it over a lifetime of learning—by experiencing things yourself, questioning others, experimenting, observing, and drawing inferences from what you have learned.

Let's use for brevity the handier term for mental model I gave earlier: a worldview. A **worldview** is a set of beliefs about the world or some aspect of it—that is, a group of statements you take to be true about it. As the cognitive psychologist Dietrich Dorner (1996: 41) defines it:

> The totality of such assumptions in an individual's mind—assumptions about
> the simple or complex links and the one-way or reciprocal influences between variables—constitute what we call that individual's "reality model." A reality model
> can be explicit, always available to the individual in a conscious form, or it can be

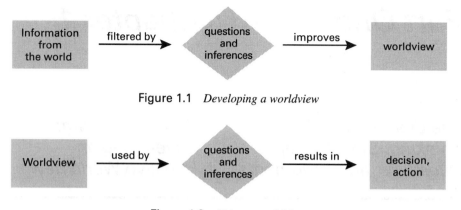

Figure 1.1   *Developing a worldview*

Figure 1.2   *Using a worldview*

implicit, with the individual himself unaware that he is operating on a certain set of assumptions and unable to articulate what those assumptions are. Implicit knowledge is quite common. We usually call it "intuition," and we say of someone who has it, "He has a feel for these things."

Your worldview is not a static thing—it changes continually, with beliefs being added or deleted in the face of experience. You change your worldview by questioning it, other people, and the world around you and by inferring, drawing conclusions from, the information gathered. Moreover, your worldview is not a passive thing—you use it continually, as a tool to help make decisions and take actions. We can summarize these points as Figures 1.1 and 1.2.

In the view of this book, worldviews are tools, tools for surviving and living well. Broadly defined, **critical thinking** means developing an ever better worldview and using it well in all aspects of your life. Looking at Figures 1.1 and 1.2, we see that clearly the heart of critical thinking is the ability to ask fruitful questions and infer or reason well. Or, as we shall say, the essence of critical thinking is questioning and arguing logically. Throughout this text, we will formulate rules for questioning and reasoning well and also discuss common fallacies. Since the term *fallacy* will crop up often in our discussions, let us define it at the outset. A **fallacy** is a mistake in reasoning. It is clear that a critical thinker should want to avoid fallacies.

But what qualities make a worldview, as well as the logic we use to develop and employ it, acceptable? Five qualities come to mind—five criteria of critical thinking—which we will discuss briefly now and explore in detail in the rest of this book. These criteria are clarity, consistency, relevance, justification, and explanatory/predictive power.

2   *Clarity and Consistency*

We said earlier that a worldview consists of a set of statements about the world or some aspect of it. This can mean some part of the physical universe, or the social realm, or the moral world. For example, you probably have developed a worldview of the political system of the United States, of how automobile engines work, and of a million other aspects of our world. Now, focusing just on the worldview itself, we can see that the beliefs in it have to be reasonably clear to be useful. For instance, the statement "The rich don't give my kind no respect" is so unclear as to be useless in, say, predicting how you are going to be treated by people you meet. What does *respect* mean in this regard? And what people count as your "kind"? On the other hand, the statement "Any object released near the surface of the Earth in a vacuum will fall with an acceleration of 32 feet/second^2" is admirably clear, at least to those educated enough to understand the sentence, and hence much more useful as a tool in explaining and predicting how objects will behave if dropped off a cliff.

So clarity is obviously desirable in a worldview. Somewhat less clear is the need for consistency. A group of statements is **consistent** if and only if they can all be true at the same time. (A group of statements is thus **inconsistent** if and only if they cannot all be true at the same time.) Now, could an inconsistent belief system be very useful as a tool?

Consider the following belief system, consisting of my beliefs about dogs:

1. All dogs are unfriendly.
2. Mandy is the dog who lives next door.
3. Mandy is friendly.

Suppose that I have little experience with dogs and that statements 1 to 3 comprise all I know or believe about dogs. My belief system is obviously inconsistent: statements 1 and 2 together imply that Mandy should be unfriendly; but statement 3 contradicts this conclusion. As I walk up to Mandy, what behavior should I expect? My worldview doesn't help me decide, precisely because it *is* inconsistent.

Clarity and consistency, being features of a useful worldview, are essential features of critical thinking.

3 Relevance

Clarity and consistency are concepts that apply to a worldview. But the quality of relevance can be introduced only after we talk about questions a bit.

We said that we modify our worldviews in part by questioning other people and nature, and we apply our worldviews to new situations by "questioning" our worldviews or accessing the information in them. But a major requirement of the logic of questions is **relevance,** the requirement that the information collected be appropriate to the issue at hand.

Consider an example: Suppose you are trying to learn more about dog behavior because you are going to be a mail carrier. You are trying to expand your worldview regarding the canine world. Some key questions you will want to research are these: In what situations do dogs become aggressive? Which breeds of dogs are most inclined to attack? How dangerous are dog attacks, anyway? You decide to go to the library and research these issues.

Clearly, the following books would be irrelevant:

Everything You Ever Wanted to Know about Cats but Were Afraid to Ask
The Way of All Waterfowl
Crime and Punishment

Possibly relevant would be these titles:

> *Breeds of Dogs*
> *Dogs—The Silent Killers*
> *How to Keep Your Dog Happy*

I say "possibly relevant" because determining what precisely is relevant is sometimes tricky: a book such as the last one on keeping a dog happy is relevant to the issue of aggression in dogs if but only if we assume happy dogs are nonaggressive. Background information plays a role in determining relevance.

Critical thinking, then, involves the skill of framing pertinent questions and seeking answers relevant to the question at hand.

4   *Justification and Explanatory/Predictive Power*

We want our worldview models to be reliable and useful. But suppose my belief system about dogs rests solely on what my Uncle Ray has told me about them, and Ray is a barber with no exceptional knowledge of dogs. How reliable would my belief system be? It would not be reliable at all. Now, if my belief system were based on extensive library research, extensive conversations with numerous dog breeders and veterinarians, and also my personal experiences with numerous dogs, my belief system would be much more reliable, because my beliefs would be much better justified.

Being justified in believing a statement involves having evidence for it. Logicians use the term *argument* to refer to a statement together with the justification for it. The logic of inference/argument is thus a useful tool in determining whether beliefs are justified.

Justification is important to the reliability of a belief system. But in addition to being reliable, we want our worldviews to be useful—they are tools after all. A worldview is practically useful if it helps you explain and understand the world around you and if it allows you to predict and control events in the world around you. Succinctly put, we want our belief systems to have explanatory and predictive power.

Perhaps the best examples of predictive and explanatory power come from the history of science. Louis Pasteur, for example, proved to skeptical people the existence of microbes and their role in causing disease. People's mental models of disease were made greatly more useful—we now understand how infections arise, and we can predict and to some extent control infectious disease accordingly.

Prediction and explanation, like justification, involve the logic of inference. So again, logic is crucial to critical thinking, since it helps us make useful mental models.

5   *The Usefulness of Critical Thinking*

Before embarking on our tour of critical thinking, we ought to reflect a bit about the usefulness of what we are about to learn.

I suppose the easiest way to see the value of critical thinking is to point out just how much deceit and humbug surround us. The most obvious area of deceit is the consumer realm. We are bombarded constantly with misleading and illogical ads and sales pitches, in junk mail, on the TV, over the phone, at the front door—everywhere. Someone is always trying to sell us something and will say anything to get the sale. We constantly pass laws to ensure truth in advertising and stop consumer fraud, but the tricksters can create new scams faster than lawmakers can outlaw them. There is no substitute for having a critical mind when deciding what to buy and how to invest.

Also obvious is the amount of deceit in the realm of politics. Many, if not most, politicians and political spokespeople use rhetorical tricks to win elections or get their policies adopted. Even assuming that political sophistry is done either out of ignorance or out of good intentions (politicians often argue that "you can't do good unless you are first elected"), it is clear from the history of the twentieth century that tremendous harm has been done by people duped by persuasive politicians.

Perhaps you are thinking that I have picked too easy a target to make my case: salespeople and politicians. But we needn't stop there. In the general realm of science, for example, we often encounter bunkum—pseudoscience, as it is often called. People claimed to have been abducted by aliens, that the Earth is flat, that apricot pits can cure cancer, that ground-up rhinoceros horn can enhance your sex life—the list is endless. Moreover, such lack of critical thinking is not just confined to the fringes of science. Mainstream scientists are not immune from the same types of bad reasoning as the rest of us are guilty of, as Robert Youngson (1998) amply illustrates in his book *Scientific Blunders: A Brief History of How Wrong Scientists Can Sometimes Be.*

Even in the realm of religion, we need critical thought. Bizarre cults abound, with devotees checking their critical faculties at the door. We only notice them when they make the news (such as the cult in Jonestown, or the Koresh followers in Waco, or the freaks who let loose poison gas in the Tokyo subway), but cults are ever with us.

In short, critical thinking has an important role to play in shielding us from the sophistry that surrounds us.

6   *The Organization of This Book*

The ensuing chapters of this book elaborate the concepts I have briefly sketched here. In the first part, we look at the elements of critical thinking. A worldview is a group of statements, so in Chapter 2 we discuss the nature of statements in detail. We create, modify, and use our worldviews by asking questions and drawing inferences (constructing arguments). Accordingly, Chapter 3 describes questions—their structure and how to answer them appropriately. In Chapters 4 and 5, we define arguments, considering what forms they have and how to identify them in practice.

Chapters 2 through 5 thus involve preliminaries—key definitions and skills concerning statements, questions, and arguments. In the second part of this book, we look at the goals of critical thinking. Chapters 6 through 15 develop the skills necessary to achieve clarity, consistency, relevance, justification, and explanatory/predictive power in our thinking. Chapters 6 and 7 deal with clarity: what pitfalls of language give rise to obscurity, and what logical tools can be employed to help achieve clarity. In Chapter 8, we discuss relevance at length; in particular, we examine the ways in which people fail to bring relevant information to bear on the issue at hand in a discussion. In Chapters 9 and 10, we learn the basics of deductive logic, which is a tool for achieving both consistency and justification.

Chapters 11 through 15 explore inductive logic, the chief tool in exploring justification and explanatory/predictive power. We look at observation and testimony in Chapter 11. In Chapter 12 we discuss generalization and case reasoning—that is, the application of general beliefs to particular cases. We learn about analogical reasoning in Chapter 13, and Chapter 14 covers reasoning about cause and effect. Chapter 15 describes hypothesis and explanation.

The third part of the book invites us to apply the tools we have learned to the world around us. Chapter 16 presents a simple model for decision making. We use this model in Chapter 17 to look at consumer choice and in Chapter 18 to help understand political choice.

You should note a few things. First, all even-numbered problems are answered in the back of the book. Second, every major term is printed in bold print just before it is defined; these terms also are collected in the glossary. Third, we use "scientific footnoting" in the text. That is, when quoting from an article or book, we don't use a footnote that gives the full description of the cited book or article; instead, we refer in the main text to the author, year of publication, and page, if necessary, and then list these works in the bibliography. You will find this approach much easier to read than old-fashioned footnoting.

InfoTrac College Edition

You can locate InfoTrac College Edition articles about this chapter by accessing the InfoTrac College Edition Web site (www.infotrac-college.com/wadsworth/). Using the InfoTrac College Edition subject guide, enter the search terms relevant to this chapter, and then read abstracts for relevant articles.

Chapter 2

Grasping Assertions

---

1   Assertions and Sentences

One of the most basic units of communication is a *statement,* a claim that something is the case. Since this concept will be so important throughout the text, we need to spend a moment to define it carefully.

We must begin by defining *sentence.* A **sentence** is a grammatical string of words in a given language. Sentences fall into several categories: declarative, interrogative, exclamatory, and so on. We use sentences to do all sorts of things: convey information, request information, make jokes, christen babies, and make promises, to name just a few. Of most importance now is the use of sentences to convey information, to "state facts." A **statement** is what is typically asserted using a declarative sentence. Other words for *statement* are *claim* and *proposition.*

A statement can be true or false, depending on whether the information asserted is correct or incorrect. (Hereafter we will abbreviate "true" by *T* and "false" by *F,* and we will call T and F **truth values.**) When we say that any statement is either T or F, we do not mean that the truth or falsity of every statement is known. "There are 14,555,233 mountains on Pluto" is T or F, but nobody yet knows which.

Because statements are the kinds of things that can be T or F, they are quite different from questions and commands. It makes no sense to answer the question "What time is it?" by "I disagree—you're absolutely wrong." Saying the question is wrong (or correct) is strange; questions can be loaded, stupid, based on mistaken assumptions, or misleading—but never T or F. Similarly, it makes no sense to speak of a command as being T or F; one cannot very well reply to the order "Shoot that man!" by saying "Sir, your order is false." Orders can be immoral, inappropriate, or silly, and they can be disobeyed—but they are not T or F.

Somewhat harder to see is the difference between statements and sentences: one usually uses a declarative sentence to make a statement, but that does not mean that the sentence is the statement. The sentence is better viewed as the tool used to make the assertion.

Here are a few points that should clarify the distinction between sentences and statements. First, different English declaratives may be used to make the same claim (statement). For example, the active and passive voice construction "Mary loves John" and

"John is loved by Mary" are used to make the same statement. But they are clearly different sentences: the first has only three words, whereas the second has five.

Of more interest is the fact that statements often are made using nondeclarative sentences. You know of *rhetorical questions,* which are interrogative sentences (such as "Do you really believe that?") used to state claims (here, that the listener is mistaken). But there are rhetorical commands as well: "Get out of here!" and "Take a hike!" express the statement that the listener is wrong, even though a nondeclarative sentence (here, an exclamation) is used.

To clarify even more the point that statements are not sentences, remember that until now we have been dealing solely with English. It should be clear that sentences from different natural languages can be used to make the same claim: "John is rich" and "Juan es rico," for example. Somewhat less obvious is the fact that conventional gestures and noises can express statements as well. A Bronx cheer can be used to deny (emphatically, albeit crudely) another's assertion; so can an obscene gesture.

2 *Statement Forms: Simple and Compound*

Statements can be classified in various ways. We can classify them on the basis of their purpose—that is, on the basis of the questions they answer. Such a classification would group together statements that describe what has occurred, those that ascribe responsibility, those that give an example (exemplify), those that explain, those that classify, those that specify, and so on.

Statements can also be classified by topic: those about politics, those about art, those about science, and so on.

Of most importance for us at the moment is the classification of statements on the basis of structure. We say a statement is **simple** if it contains no other statements as parts or "components." Here are some simple statements:

> Whales are fat.
> Pat is ugly.
> Yoshi is dead.

On the other hand, a statement is **compound** if it does contain one or more statements as components:

> If whales are fat, pigs are skinny. [Components: "Whales are fat," "pigs are skinny"]
> Loni is mean and ugly. [Components: "Loni is mean," "Loni is ugly"]
> I believe that Bonita is a good singer. [Component: "Bonita is a good singer"]

Note that some compounds have only one component, while others have two or more compounds. Compounds with only one component are called **unary:**

> It is not the case that Fred is rich. [Component: "Fred is rich"]
> I believe that whales are fat. [Component: "Whales are fat"]

Those with two components are called **binary:**

> John is happy and Al is not. [Components: "John is happy," "Al is not happy"]
> Mary is happy or she isn't. [Components: "Mary is happy," "Mary is not happy"]

And of course compounds can have more than two components:

> Mary is happy, but Sue isn't and neither is Monique. [Components: "Mary is happy," "Sue is not happy," "Monique is not happy"]

Of special importance are five types of compound: negation, conjunction, disjunction, conditional, and biconditional.

A **negation** is a unary compound that expresses the denial of the component. For example,

> It is not true that *Luisa likes dogs.*
> It is not the case that *pigs can dance.*

A negation is false if the component denied is true; it is true if the component is false.

A **conjunction** is a binary compound that asserts of two components that they are both true:

> Fred is dead, and he looks it, too.
> Laura and Madonna both hate cheese.

A conjunction is false if even one of its components is false; it is true if and only if both components are true.

A **disjunction** is a binary compound that asserts that at least one of the components is true. If the disjunction also asserts that perhaps both of the components are true, we say that it is an **inclusive** disjunction. If the disjunction also asserts that not both of the components are true, we say that it is an **exclusive** disjunction. Examples of inclusive disjunctions include

> The student can satisfy the foreign language requirement by taking either French or German [or both].
> Terri might invite Mauricio or Boris to the party [or both].

Some examples of exclusive disjunctions follow:

> You may have either soup or salad with your dinner [but not both].
> Sue will go to either Penn State or the University of Illinois for grad school [but not both].

An inclusive disjunction is only false when both components are false; otherwise, it is true. An exclusive disjunction is also false when both components are false, but it is additionally false when both components are true (it "excludes" the possibility that both are true). A **conditional** statement states that if a first component is true, then a second one will be true as well. For example,

> If I win the lottery, I will buy you a new car.

A conditional does *not* assert that the first component, called the **antecedent,** is true or that the second one, called the **consequent,** is true but instead asserts the truth of the consequent *conditional on* the truth of the antecedent. In the example just given, I am not saying that I am going to win the lottery or that I'm going to buy you a new car. I'm only stating that *if* I win the lottery, I'll buy you the car. The key word is *if.*

Thus, a conditional is clearly true where the antecedent is true and the consequent is also true (I win the lottery and buy you a car); it is clearly false when the antecedent is true but the consequent is false (I win the lottery but do not buy the car). When the antecedent is false (that is, if I don't win the lottery) the conditional is still true.

Finally, a **biconditional** is a statement that says of two components that the first is true if and only if the second is; that is, they are either both true or both false together. For example,

> It will rain if and only if the barometer falls.
> You will succeed if and only if you work hard.

In ordinary contexts, we use a variety of synonyms to express the compounds discussed here. Negation is expressed by phrases such as "It is not true that . . ." and "It is not the case that . . . ." It is also expressed by words such as *not, lacks,* and *fails.* For example, the sentences

> John lacks success.

and

> John failed to achieve success.

both express the negation that John is not successful. Negation is often expressed by prefixes such as *un-* or *dis-* and suffixes such as *-less.* For example,

> He was ungrateful.

means he was not grateful. Similarly,

> She disbelieved his testimony.

means she did not believe his testimony.

English is rich in synonyms for conjunction. Figure 2.1 lists the most common ones.

The word *while* often expresses conjunction where the components are linked in time, as in

> Sol whistled while he shaved.

The words *although, even though, however,* and *but* usually express conjunction where the components involve contrast, as in

> Maria was rich but unpopular.
> Jean Luc was happy even though he was bald.

and	although
while	but
additionally	however
moreover	even though

Figure 2.1   *Words that express conjunction*

If *A*, then *C*. If *A*, *C*.	*A* is a sufficient condition for *C*.
A only if *C*. *C*, if *A*.	*C* is a necessary condition for *A*.

Figure 2.2 *Phrases that express the conditional*

The words *moreover* and *additionally* often express conjunction where the components are similar or additive, as in

Soren was morose; moreover, he was intensely shy.
Hilda was rich, and, in addition, she was popular.

There are fewer synonyms for disjunction—mainly *or* and *unless.*

I'll have either a burger or a burrito.
You will fail unless you study.

Regarding expressing conditionals, English is almost profligate. Figure 2.2 lists some of the most common phrases. *A* represents the antecedent; *C,* the consequent.

Notice that the word *if* always comes before the antecedent, while *only if* always comes before the consequent. In the phrase "is a sufficient condition for," the antecedent occurs at the beginning; whereas in "is a necessary condition for," the consequent occurs at the beginning.

Determining which component in a conditional is its antecedent and which is its consequent is very important to grasping its meaning. For instance, there is a great difference between the claim that if you were rich, you would eat regularly, and the claim that if you eat regularly, you are rich.

Finally, the biconditional is only expressed by a few phrases. "If and only if," "when and only when," and "is a necessary and sufficient condition for" are the most common. For example,

If and only if Joni works hard will she pass the class.
The bell rings when and only when someone presses the button out front.
Being friendly is a necessary and sufficient condition for being popular.

Exercise 2.2A

For each of the following compound statements, identify the simplest components and its type.

Example: Paula is both rich and famous.
Answer: The components are "Paula is rich" and "Paula is famous." This is a conjunction.

Example: Dweezil isn't both rich and famous.
Answer: The most simple components are "Dweezil is rich" and "Dweezil is famous."

This compound is a negation of a conjunction.

1. Luigi is not happy.
2. Mandy is either maladjusted or unfriendly.
3. If Yoshi is hungry, he will let us know.
4. Either you are alive or dead.
5. She will be happy if and only if she gets into law school.
6. If she gets angry, you'll see fireworks.
7. It is not the case that pigs can dance.
8. Quiller isn't either a spy or a thug.
9. It's not true that a pig is happy if and only if it reads Plato.
10. Sue is not happy if and only if she is not rich.
11. Bill is not angry, but is either lonely or unfriendly.
12. If Fred is dead and Wanda is not well, we should not invite them to dinner.
13. If the barometer is not broken, it will rain if and only if the barometer falls.
14. Either Fred or Ted will die if and only if the bomb detonates.
15. If Sue is not dead, then if she is not fooling she must be asleep.
16. Unless John is careful, he will not pass the test.
17. Sue is not rich, although she is not poor.
18. You will be happy if and only if you do work you enjoy.
19. Amy will leave when and only when the clerk refunds her money.
20. It is not true that you will win only if you cheat.

Exercise 2.2B

The following statements are from *Drawing on the Right Side of the Brain* by Betty Edwards (1989). For each, identify the simplest components and the form of the compound
(negation, conjunction, disjunction, conditional, biconditional). If it is a conditional, identify the antecedent and consequent.

1. These skills are not drawing skills.
2. Each of my students goes through this struggle, and so will you.
3. Later, one almost forgets about having learned to read, learned to drive, learned to draw.
4. In order to attain this smooth integration in drawing, all five component skills must
   be in place.
5. I'm happy to say that the fifth skill . . . is neither taught nor learned, but instead
   seems to emerge as a result of acquiring the other four skills.
6. The basic strategy for gaining access to R-mode, my term for the visual, perceptual
   mode of the brain, was stated but not emphasized in the original book.
7. In order to access the verbal, analytic L-mode, it is necessary to present the brain
   with a task appropriate to L-mode.
8. This ability is difficult, perhaps impossible to acquire unless one has learned to perceive the relationships of lights and shadows through drawing.
9. Handwriting, however, is a form of drawing and can likewise be improved.

10. In order to gain access to the subdominant visual, perceptual R-mode of the brain, it is necessary to present the brain with a job that the verbal analytic L-mode will turn down.

3   *Statement Forms: Particular and General*

Let us look more closely at simple statements. Compare these two sets of statements:

Set A	Set B
Fred is dead.	Someone is dead.
Sue is happy.	Most people are happy.
Yoshi is seated between Al and Juan.	Everybody is seated near Yoshi.
The election was held Tuesday.	Elections were held last year.

Notice that the statements in set A refer to particular things (persons, objects, events, or whatever), while the statements in set B refer to things in general (some, most, a few, all). Simple statements that refer to individuals we call **particular;** those that refer to groups of individuals we call **general.**

Of course, particular and general statements can be compounded together. For example, the statement

> Fred and Jean Luc are happy.

is a conjunction of two particular statements. The statement

> If all people were rich, then all people would be envied.

is a conditional with two general statements as components. And the statement

> While Luigi is rich, most people aren't.

is a conjunction of a particular statement with a general one.

Let us examine a bit more closely the structure of particular statements. Consider the following examples:

> Fred is rich.
> Maria is the sister of Luisa.
> Al is seated between Chi Chi and Jack.

These statements name one or more particular individuals and then attribute a property (such as "is rich") or a relationship ("is the sister of," "is seated between") to it or them. Particular statements involve **names** (particular individuals) and **predicates** (properties or relations among those individuals).

Now consider the following general statements:

> All frogs can dance.
> Some pigs are musical.
> Most donuts are full of fat.
> No dogs can dance.

Instead of attributing predicates to particular individuals, these statements use expressions such as "all," "most," "some," "a few," and "none" to talk in general about groups of unnamed individuals. These expressions are called **quantifiers.**

A common structure of many (but by no means all) general statements is

(quantifier) (subject) (copula) (predicate)

where the subject and predicate are properties of some kind, and the copula is a tense of the verb *to be*. Some examples:

All pigs are mammals.
Most pigs are friendly.
Many pigs are evil.
No pigs are beautiful.

We will examine such statements in detail in Chapter 10.

Exercise 2.3A

For each of the following simple statements, determine whether it is particular or general.

1. Hitler was evil.
2. Most frogs are green.
3. All frogs are evil.
4. Kermit the frog is green.
5. President Clinton was elected in 1992.
6. Somebody was elected in 1992.
7. People love to gossip.
8. Jodie loves to gossip.
9. Things are getting worse.
10. My life is getting worse.

Exercise 2.3B

For each of the compound statements listed here, state what type of compound it is (negation, disjunction, conjunction, conditional, or biconditional), and identify its simplest components as particular or general.

1. If Kermit is dead, so is the Cookie Monster.
2. If rats can't dance, they can't go to nightclubs.
3. If and only if Kermit can dance can he sing as well.
4. If Kermit is dead, so is everybody.
5. If Miss Piggy can sing, so can Kermit.
6. Miss Piggy is ugly, but nobody cares.
7. Neither Kermit nor the Cookie Monster can dance.
8. Everyone can sing, but nobody can dance.
9. Miss Piggy is ugly if and only if everybody is ugly.
10. Either rats or cats can sing.

Exercise 2.3C

For each of the following statements, (1) determine whether it is particular or general; then (2) if it is particular, identify the particular individuals and what is predicated of them; (3) if it is general, identify the quantifier.

1. Christopher Robin is happy.
2. Winnie the Pooh is yellow.
3. All boys like honey.
4. Most bears like honey.
5. Some bears are imaginary.
6. Christopher Robin and Tigger dislike honey.
7. Tigger can't dance.
8. Everybody likes Tigger.
9. Winnie the Pooh dances well.
10. A few people like Tigger.

+4 *Statement Content: Necessary versus Contingent*

In the preceding two sections, we focused on the form or structure of statements, namely as simple or compound, particular or general. In this and the following section, we want to focus on the content statements can have.

Let's begin by looking at "content" at the highest level of generality. Consider these statements:

1. All people desire wealth.
2. All people are people.

How would you determine the truth of statement 1? Presumably, by doing psychological research. In particular, you would look at people who *seem* to be uninterested in wealth and examine whether they are in fact uninterested. How would you determine the truth of statement 2? Here, no research is needed. You only need to understand the words in the sentence to see that the statement has to be true. Statements that cannot possibly be false we call **necessarily true** (or simply **necessary**). Statements that cannot possibly be true we call **necessarily false** (or simply **contradictory**). Statements that are neither necessarily true nor necessarily false we call **contingent.**[*]

Sometimes, statements can be seen to be necessary or contradictory at a glance:

---

[*]Strictly speaking, we ought to distinguish between formal tautologies and analytic truths. A **tautology** is a statement that remains true no matter what statements are substituted for its basic components. It is a statement that is necessarily true by its structure. An **analytic truth** is a statement that is true due to the meanings of the words involved. Necessary truths are often held to consist of just tautologies and analytic truths, but this distinction will not concern us.

> All dogs are dogs.
> If a person likes bagels, he likes bagels.
> A dog is not a dog.

Sometimes we have to think a moment about the meanings of the words involved. For example, in

> All bachelors are unmarried.

we have to notice that *bachelor* means "unmarried male of eligible age" to see the necessity. And suppose someone says:

> Only losers lose.

This statement may be necessary or not depending on what the speaker means by *loser.* If that term just means "the loser at the contest at hand," then the statement is necessary:

> Only the loser of this contest is the loser of this contest.

But if the term *loser* means a habitual failure, then the statement is contingent—indeed, contingently false:

> Only habitual failures in life lose.

Yet even habitual winners in life occasionally lose specific contests or games. Thus, the same sentence that may be necessary for one person may be contingent for another, if they assign different meanings to some of the terms involved.

The certainty of necessary statements comes at a price, however. Necessary statements are uninformative. It is because they say nothing about the world that they are not contingent on the world. To say "Either life exists on Mars or it doesn't" is to speak the truth but say nothing about Mars (or anything else). A statement is informative if it tells you something about the world, and if it does it runs the risk of being false.

A note of clarification is in order. Consider the claim "Chimeras are monsters." Let's suppose you don't know what the word *chimera* means. So you look it up in a dictionary and find that its primary meaning is "a monster of classical mythology." At that point you realize that the claim that chimeras are monsters is a necessary one. It is uninformative, although it *is* new to you, in that you had to learn the meaning of a term you hadn't met before.

We have just made two important points. First, necessity can be hard to spot (because you have to reflect on the meanings of the words involved). Second, whether a statement is necessary has important consequences in terms of how you investigate the claim being made (after all, why waste research money investigating a statement that is true by definition, hence uninformative?). These points show that being able to detect when a statement is necessary is a valuable skill. For example, consider this quote:

> Factor-analytic studies of instruments use to measure hypochondriasis . . . and
> clinical descriptions of the syndrome have identified the following set of behaviors
> that are typically associated with hypochondriasis: excessive concern with health
> and bodily functioning, exaggerated attention to an unrealistic interpretation of

physical signs or sensations, multiple bodily complaints, and belief or fear of hav-ing a serious illness. Descriptions of an individual as hypochondriacal usually are based on the presence of one or more of these behaviors. (Smith, Snyder, and Perkins, 1983)

It certainly appears that the research proved that hypochondriacs are excessively worried about their health—in other words, that people excessively worried about their health are excessively worried about their health. What a discovery!

Exercise 2.4

Determine whether each of the following statements is contingent or necessary.

1. People love pets.
2. People who don't love pets are insensitive.
3. People who don't love pets are non–pet lovers.
4. Assuming Fred is diffident, he will avoid people wherever possible.
5. Auto workers tend to vote Democratic in federal elections.

+5   *Statement Content: Factual versus Evaluative*

Consider the two sets of statements given here:

Set A	Set B
John weighs 158 pounds.	John is evil.
Tomatoes are nutritious.	Tomatoes are good.
People hate outsiders.	People should hate outsiders.
Gold is a heavy metal.	Gold is valuable.

Clearly there is a difference. Roughly put, the A statements are judgments of fact, or what we shall call **factual** (or "descriptive") statements. They aim to describe the world. (I say "aim," because some factual statements fail to describe the world because they are false: "The Earth is flat," for instance, is quite false, but it is still a factual claim.) On the other hand, the B statements aim to judge the value of something or things in some regard, to prescribe rather than describe. These we call judgments of value or prescriptive or **evaluative** statements.

Evaluative claims come in a variety of sorts. Perhaps the three most common are state-ments of moral obligation, moral worth, and nonmoral worth. **Statements of moral oblig-ation** are statements about what people ought to do, are morally obligated to do. (The terminology I am using here is from Frankena [1973]). There are particular statements of moral obligation:

Fred should volunteer to fight.
Sue should be nicer to her sister.
America should increase its foreign aid.

There are general statements of moral obligation:

People should not harm others.
All nations should promote peace.
Any teacher should try to avoid bias in grading.

Statements of moral worth are judgments about the moral desirability of people's character traits and motives. Again, there are particular statements of moral worth—

Fred is an evil man.
Sue's jealousy of her sister is disgusting.

—as well as general:

Hatred is a vice.
Charity is admirable.

Finally, **statements of nonmoral worth** are judgments about the desirability of objects or sensations. These can be particular—

Gold is valuable.
This candy is worth the money.

—or general:

Pleasure is desirable.
Wealth is desirable.

It is customary to distinguish between intrinsic and instrumental nonmoral worth. Something has **instrumental** (or extrinsic) worth if it is valuable as a tool to obtain something else that is desirable. Something has **intrinsic** (or inherent) worth if it is desirable in and of itself. For example, for most people, money has instrumental worth (in that it can buy things they want) but no intrinsic worth (they want money because of what it can buy, *not* because the printed paper has any inherent value). Dollars would not be desirable if they could not be traded for other things.

Statements of moral obligation, moral worth, and nonmoral worth are statements in the realm of morals. A fourth category of value statements are **statements of aesthetic value**— judgments about the artistic worth of literary, musical, or artistic works. For example,

Picasso was a great artist.
Concerto in F is a fine piece of music.
That movie was lousy.

Moving from evaluative claims to factual claims, two important groups of factual claims are those about the physical world (**physical claims**) and those about the mental world (**psychological statements**). Physical statements can be particular—

Lincoln died in 1865.
This cap is made of metal.
The Sun is 93 million miles from the Earth.

—or general:

All objects released in a vacuum near the surface of the Earth fall with accelera-
tion of 32 feet/second^2.
Politicians are often influential.
Wolves are pack animals.

Scientific laws ("laws of nature") are one type of general physical claim. Psychological statements can also be particular—

Fred has a toothache.
Sue loves her mom.
The designer of this bottle cap intended it to be childproof.

—as well as general:

Americans admire wealthy people.
People hate foreigners.

Basically, then, psychological statements are statements about the beliefs, goals, intentions, and feelings of individual persons or groups of people.

Be careful not to confound statements of value with psychological ones. It is one thing to say that, as a matter of fact, people hate strangers. That is a statement of psychological fact. It is another thing to say people *should* fear people. That is a moral judgment. Again, it is one thing to say a given novel is popular—that is a psychological claim about the preferences of the readers. It is quite another thing to claim that the novel in question is good—that is an aesthetic claim about its quality.

Determining whether someone is making a value judgment or a statement of psychological fact is usually easy, but not always. Suppose someone said, "Ethel Smertz is a renowned pianist." Is the person claiming merely that Ethel Smertz, as a matter of psychological fact, is admired generally? Or is the person claiming that Ethel Smertz is a fine pianist? It is unclear because words like *eminent, renowned, famous,* and *well respected* can be used to make your own aesthetic judgments as well as to report the aesthetic judgments of others.

Also, distinguishing between physical and psychological claims occasionally can be tricky. Consider:

Maria appeared frightened.

Is this meant as the psychological claim that she was frightened? Or is it merely a factual report about her overt physical behavior? Again, it can be unclear.

In distinguishing evaluative from factual claims, we do not commit ourselves to the controversial view that there is an unbridgeable gap between the two. We only want to be clear about the assertions we make.

Exercise 2.5

For each statement determine whether it is factual or evaluative. If factual, determine whether it is physical or psychological. If evaluative, determine whether it is a statement of moral obligation, moral worth, nonmoral worth, or aesthetic worth.

1. Fred is dead.
2. Fred is stupid.

3. Fred is evil.
4. Fred is handsome.
5. Fred should help his father.
6. Sue loves cheese.
7. Sue is a loner.
8. Sue suffered a brain injury several years ago.
9. Historically, Native Americans have been abused by the federal government.
10. Adolf Hitler was a monstrous dictator.
11. All matter is composed of atoms.
12. Sam Spade felt real pain when the fat man struck him.
13. People respect successful businessmen.
14. Courage is admirable.
15. All is fair in love and war.

InfoTrac College Edition

You can locate InfoTrac College Edition articles about this chapter by accessing the InfoTrac College Edition Web site (www.infotrac-college.com/wadsworth/). Using the InfoTrac College Edition subject guide, enter the search terms relevant to this chapter, and then read abstracts for relevant articles.

Chapter 3

Understanding Questions

---

1   *Questions and Sentences*

In Chapter 2 we discussed what statements are and how they may be categorized. In this chapter we will do the same with questions.

A **question,** roughly defined, is a request for information. In Section 2.1, we distinguished between *statements* (attempts to convey information) and *sentences.* We found that while we typically *use* a declarative sentence of English to *make* a statement, we can use many other sentences (declarative or not, English or not) to do the job or even use gestures and body language. Similarly, we should distinguish between *questions* and *sentences.* Usually, we *use* an interrogative English sentence to *put* a question. (An **interrogative sentence** is one that ends with a question mark.) For example, to ask how much you earn, I might use the sentence "How much do you make?" But, as before, we shouldn't confound questions with interrogative sentences. We can see why by considering a few points.

First, many different English interrogative sentences can put the same question. For example, the following interrogatives all put the question what time Godot will arrive:

> When will Godot arrive?
> When is Godot coming?
> What time is Godot due?
> Godot is due when?

Second, interrogatives from different languages can be used to ask the same question. For example,

> Where is my money?
> ¿Donde está mi dinero?

ask the same question.

Third, the same interrogative sentence can be used to put any number of different questions. For example, the interrogative sentence

> Am I really happy?

asks a different question for every person who utters it.

Fourth, we need not use an interrogative sentence to ask a question. For example, the declarative sentence

I guess a car like that costs a lot of money.

can be used as a polite way to ask somebody how much he paid for his car. (You might call this a "rhetorical statement.")

Finally, we can ask a question without using a sentence at all. For example, upon seeing you with a black eye, I might just raise my eyebrows, to ask (nonverbally) what happened.

Recognizing what question is being asked is as important as identifying what statement is being made. The idea is to put the question in the simplest interrogative possible, without losing essential points. This may involve simplifying verbosity or filling in omitted information. For example, the interrogative

Upon which date, and at which time, will the requisite payment be tendered in full?

puts the simple question

When will you pay?

And the cryptic interrogative

What's happening?

can ask the question

What is going on in your life?

The two basic aspects to any question are what it presupposes and what counts as a direct answer to it. A **direct answer** to a question is a statement that completely answers the question but gives no more information than is needed to answer the question completely. (The terminology and basic approach I am using here is from Belnap and Steel [1976]). Table 3.1 gives some examples of questions and their direct answers.

A **presupposition** of a question is any statement that has to be true if that question is to have any true answer. Presuppositions are important, because if the presupposition of a question is false, trying to answer the question may waste time.

TABLE 3.1 Examples of Questions and Their Direct Answers	
Questions	Some Direct Answers
Who is the president of the United States today?	Clinton is president today. Mickey Mouse is president today.
Do unicorns exist?	(Yes) Unicorns exist.
When did Lorraine say she would get here?	She said she would arrive at 1:00 P.M. She said she would arrive at 1:15 P.M.
What is an example of a sexy car?	A Corvette is an example of a sexy car. An Oldsmobile is an example of a sexy car.

TABLE 3.2 Examples of Questions and Their Presuppositions	
Questions	Some Presuppositions
Who is the president of the United States today?	The United States exists and has a president today.
Do unicorns exist?	No presuppositions.
When did Lorraine say she would get here?	Lorraine exists and Lorraine said she would get here.
What is an example of a sexy car?	There are sexy cars.

Consider the classic question "Have you stopped cheating on your wife?" Two direct answers are possible:

(Yes) I have stopped cheating on my wife.
(No) I have not stopped cheating on my wife.

Neither of these possible answer can be true unless I have a wife and have cheated on her in the past. We call questions that have false presuppositions **loaded.** Table 3.2 offers some examples of questions and their presuppositions.

Recognizing the possibility that one or more of the presuppositions of a question may be false (which means that the question has no true direct answer), we need to introduce the notion of a "corrective answer." A **corrective answer** to a question is an answer informing the questioner of a false presupposition. For example, one corrective answer to the question "Have you stopped cheating on your wife?" would be "I have never married." Another corrective answer would be "I have never cheated on my wife at all."

Exercise 3.1A

For each of the following, (1) put the question in the simplest interrogative you can; (2) state an obvious presupposition, if any; (3) give an example of a direct answer (make it complete); and (4) give an example of a corrective answer.

Example: How about those Dodgers? Aren't they fantastic?

1. Aren't the Dodgers a good team?
2. Presupposes the Dodgers are a team.
3. (Yes) The Dodgers are a good team.
4. The Dodgers were all killed this morning in a plane crash.

1. When, oh, when are you going to learn to dance?
2. What movie shall we see?
3. You remember Suzy—she walked with a limp because of the alligator incident. Where is she living now?
4. Have you stopped stealing cars?
5. Where is the best spot for us to open our lemonade stand?
6. Why are Americans so unhappy, Mr. Sociologist? Just answer that.

7. The killer must have hidden the gun somewhere in this house—but where, Watson, where?
8. Was it through stupidity or dishonesty that this administration has destroyed the independence of the Supreme Court?
9. What I am curious about is this: do any sea-dwelling mammals like cheeseburgers?
10. Dear Gas Company: Can I have instruction on how to light the pilot light in my furnace?
11. Mr. Jason, you have stalled long enough. When can we expect to see this bill paid?
12. Daddy, does Santa Claus really exist?
13. Do Martians exist?
14. When did Mom say the train would arrive?
15. Can you keep a secret?

Exercise 3.1B

Each of the following declarative sentences can be used to ask a question. Identify which question would be asked.

> Example: Perhaps you are tired at this point.
> Asks: Are you tired?

1. It seems to me you might know just why it is your sister wasn't in her room last night.
2. There has to be a reason you chose to study philosophy.
3. I guess we should decide what movie to see.
4. I suppose you know where we are going.
5. A house like this has to cost a lot!

2 *Types of Questions*

When we discussed statements in Chapter 2, we took time to classify statements in various ways—simple, compound, and so on. We want to do the same now with regard to questions.

We will first distinguish between simple and compound questions. **Simple questions** are those that do not contain other questions or statements as components, such as "How's your mother?" **Compound questions** are those that do contain at least one other question or statement as components, such as "How is your mother, and how is your father?" (Some textbooks call compound questions *complex questions.*)

To classify simple questions, we need to examine a bit more closely their structure. In our view, a simple question consists of two parts: a subject and a request. The **subject** of a question is the range of alternatives presented. The **request** indicates how many of the true alternatives are desired in the answer and how complete that list of true alternatives is. For example, the question "Do you own a car?" presents the alternatives

1. You own a car.
2. You do not own a car.

and requests the respondent to select the one that is true.

With this in mind, we can distinguish two basic types of simple questions. **Whether-questions** are those that present their subjects (their ranges of alternatives) explicitly and request the respondent to select from among them. For example,

1. Is Alfredo rich?
2. Which should Laura take: COBOL, FORTRAN, C+, or BASIC?

Question 1 presents the alternatives "Alfredo is rich" and "Alfredo is not rich." Question 2 presents the alternatives "Laura should take COBOL, "Laura should take FORTRAN," "Laura should take C+," and "Laura should take BASIC." Notice that the second question *uses* the word *which* to *ask* a whether-question. To reiterate what I said in the last section, you should not confound a question with the interrogative used to ask it.

Which-questions are questions that present their subjects by means of some description, and they request that the respondent select the things that fit the description. For example,

3. Which cars are expensive?
4. Who will come to the party?
5. What are Maria's office hours?

Question 3 presents the subject via the phrase "*X* is an expensive car," 4 by "*X* is a person and is coming to the party," and 5 by "*X* is one of Maria's office hours."

Two important types of which-question are why-questions and how-questions. A **why-question** is a request for explanation or proof. Requests for explanation ask the respondent to explain what is taken to be a fact:

What is the cause of the oversupply of Ph.D.'s?
Why do dogs bark?

Requests for proof ask the respondent to justify or back up what is taken to be disputable:

Why do you say Alex is unhappy?
What are your reasons for buying that stock?

Finally, **how-questions** are requests for the techniques for doing some task. These techniques may be stated as a set of verbal instructions:

How can I get to Oklahoma City?
How can we buy a new car?

But these techniques may be nonverbal physical skills:

How do you dance a fox trot?
How do you get this bottle cap off?

Notice that with why- and how-questions, the subject is a description, such as "*X* is a set of facts that explains . . ." or "*X* is a set of instructions for . . . ." While for other more ordinary which-questions the subjects characterize *things*, the subjects of why- and how-questions characterize facts or statements.

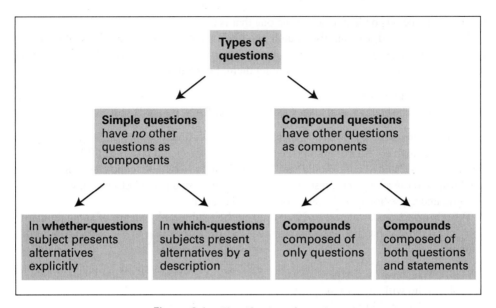

Figure 3.1   *Classification of questions*

So much for simple questions. **Compound questions** we define as questions that do contain (one or more) questions as components. Compound questions can be composed of only component questions, as in the following:

> Who is that masked man and what does he want?
> Where and when shall we get together again?

But compound questions also can be composed of questions and statements:

> If Lola wants to buy that car, where will she get the money?
> Jones probably will be renominated, but if he isn't, who else might the Democrats turn to?

Our classification of questions is summarized in Figure 3.1.

Exercise 3.2A

For each of the simple questions listed here, indicate the subject and the request, and then classify it as a which- or a whether-question.

1. Do you listen to jazz?
2. Do you believe in magic?
3. Which should I order: steak, chicken, or seafood?
4. When did the burglary occur?
5. Why did the bridge collapse yesterday?
6. How do you lower the roof on this car?

7. How many grams of fat does a rib-eye steak have?
8. What is the capital of British Columbia?
9. Who shot the sheriff?
10. Which do you want, the upper or the lower bunk?

Exercise 3.2B

For each of the following questions, indicate whether it is simple or compound.

1. Where and when will you decide to cash that check?
2. Who is minding the store?
3. If she does show up at the party, will you ask her to dance?
4. I hate Fred, that's true, and do you know why?
5. Who made you the boss?
6. When did you find time to learn how to dance?
7. What did the president know, and when did he know it?
8. How can I start this motorcycle?
9. How can we prove Fred is the murderer, and how can we get the police to take us seriously?
10. If you decide to go to the dance, who will you take?

3 *Responsive Answers*

In this section we look at the rules governing answers to questions. Actually, that's a bit too broad. To be more precise, we need to define two terms. We say a statement is a **responsive answer** to a given question if it has the appropriate logical form of a possible answer to that question. We say that a statement is a **correct answer** to a question if it is responsive *and* true (that is, a true responsive answer). What we want to do is formulate rules governing responsive answers to questions, for that is something we can determine logically. It typically takes empirical investigation to determine when an answer is empirically correct.

Four basic rules govern the responsiveness of answers. The first three rules govern simple questions and the fourth governs compound questions.

Rule 1: The answer to any simple question must be direct, corrective, or an admission that the answer is unknown. Given a pertinent question, the logical response is to answer it directly, to correct it—that is, to indicate which presuppositions of it are wrong—or to state clearly that you don't know. For example, to the question

Has Fred stopped his drug abuse?

the answers

Yes, he has.
No, he hasn't.

are responsive, because they are direct answers. The answer

Fred never abused drugs.

is responsive, because it corrects the original question by pointing out a false presupposition. The answer

> I don't know.

is also responsive. But the following answers are not responsive:

> Drug abuse is a growing problem.
> Fred's not the only one who abuses drugs.
> Take a hike, cupcake!

But rule 1 has to be spelled out further, because we haven't specified what counts as a "direct" answer to a question. The next two rules address that issue.

Rule 2: A direct answer to any simple whether-question is a selection from one of the alternatives presented in the subject. For example, the question

> Is it going to rain today?

presents the alternatives

> Yes (it will rain today).
> No (it will not rain today).

and one of those would be a direct answer. The following would thus not be direct answers:

> The probability of rain today is 60 percent.
> I love rain.
> Let's go to a movie.

Again, the question

> Where should we go: the mall, the movies, or the beach?

can only be directly answered by one of its three explicit alternatives:

> We should go to the mall.
> We should go to the movies.
> We should go to the beach.

Be clear: Rule 2 lays down the logical requirement for direct answers, rule 1 for responsive answers. Thus, the statement

> We shouldn't go anywhere.

is not a direct answer to

> Where should we go: to the mall, the movies, or the beach?

but it is a corrective answer, so it is responsive.

Recall from the last section that simple questions come in two forms: whether- and which-questions. Rule 2 applies to whether-questions. The next rule applies to which-questions.

Rule 3: A direct answer to a which-question is a selection of things that fit the description in the subject. For example, the question

> When will Godot arrive?

presents the range of alternatives by the description

> Godot will arrive at time *t*.

Hence, the following are all direct answers:

> Godot will arrive at 1:15 A.M.
> Godot will arrive in fifteen minutes.
> Godot will arrive at 4:30 P.M.

But the following would not be direct answers:

> Godot is dead.
> I don't give a damn when Godot will arrive.

Together, the first three rules govern answering simple questions. The last rule deals with compound questions.

Rule 4: A responsive answer to any compound question is a compound of responsive answers to all its component simple questions. For example, the compound question

> Who should we promote to sales manager, and what shall we pay him or her?

is a conjunction of two which-questions:

> Who should we promote to sales manager?

and

> What shall we pay the sales manager?

Thus, direct answers to the compound will be conjunctions of direct answers to the component questions, such as

> We should make Maureen sales manager and pay her $50,000 per year.

and corrective answers to the compound question will be corrections to one or more of the components, such as

> We should make Ted sales manager, but he works for free.
> We don't need a sales manager at all.

Let's finish this section by returning to a point we made at the outset: we can tell by looking at a question what a *responsive* answer would look like, but we need to look further to discover the *correct* answer. For instance, logic alone tells you that the question

> Does Santa Claus exist?

has no presuppositions, so no corrective answers, so can only be responsively answered by giving one of two direct answers:

> Yes (Santa Claus exists).
> No (Santa Claus does not exist).

or by saying "I don't know." But it takes research of some kind to determine which answer is in fact true.

Exercise 3.3

Give one example of a responsive answer and one of an unresponsive answer to each of the following questions.

1.   Are dogs carnivores?
2.   Are unicorns carnivores?
3.   When was Fred born, and what is his social security number?
4.   Which computer language should I take: BASIC, COBOL, or Ada?
5.   How long ago did *Homo sapiens* appear, and were there any competing species?
6.   Why don't cats swim?
7.   Why has the rate of drunk driving increased, and what can we do about it?
8.   How many angels can fit on the head of a pin?
9.   When did the American Civil War begin, and when did it end?
10.   How can we get our cat to dance?

4   *Fallacies of Questions*

In Chapter 1 we defined the term **fallacy** very broadly to mean a mistake in reasoning. A number of fallacies can occur when questions are asked and answers are given. I divide fallacies of questions into two broad groups: fallacies of **question framing** and fallacies of **answer formulation.**

Often, when a question is put, a fallacy is committed in the very framing of the question. This takes the form of asking a question with a false or debatable presupposition. We call questions with false or debatable presuppositions **loaded questions** (some textbooks call this fallacy "complex question"[*]). For example,

1.   Aren't you glad you use Romeo deodorant?
2.   Why is Congress so insensitive to the needs of the elderly?
3.   Are you still hot-tempered?
4.   Why do large objects fall more quickly than small ones do?
5.   Where do flying saucers come from?

Question 1 presupposes that I use deodorant, which is quite true, but it also presupposes that the brand I use is Romeo, which is false. Question 2 presupposes the highly dubitable claim that Congress is insensitive to the needs of the elderly. Question 3 presupposes the debatable claim that you are hot-tempered. Question 4 presupposes the false claim that large objects fall more quickly than small ones do. And question 5 presupposes the debatable claim that flying saucers exist.

---

[*]Let me be more precise. The term *complex question* means compound question, and the "fallacy of complex question" is said to occur when someone asks a compound question with a loaded question as one of the components. But asking a compound question is no more inherently fallacious than making a compound statement. The fallacy occurs in framing the loaded question.

The fallacy of loaded question is used often to introduce or establish a claim without having to argue for it. A common use of loaded question is in sales. For example:

> I can see you're impressed with this coffee maker. Will this be cash or charge?

The salesperson in this case is trying to avoid proving to the customer that the customer should buy the coffee maker by raising the issue of manner of payment. Another common use of loaded questions is to obtain damaging admissions in legal proceedings. For example, a police agent or prosecutor might ask a suspect

> What did you do with the stolen money?

hoping to trick the suspect into blurting out a confession.

More ominously, loaded questions by interrogators can influence eyewitness testimony. The eminent psychologist Elizabeth Loftus (1996: xii), who has studied memory and testimony, reports:

> For example, the way a question is phrased and the assumptions it makes have a subtle yet profound effect on the stored information. In one experiment we conducted witnesses were shown a movie of an automobile accident and afterward were questioned about it. One of the questions, the critical one, was phrased in two different ways to two different groups of witnesses. One group was asked, "How fast were the cars going when they smashed into each other?" The other group was asked, "How fast were the cars going when they hit each other?" A week later, all witnesses returned and were asked. "Did you see any broken glass in the accident?" In actuality, there had been no broken glass, but witnesses who were originally queried with the verb "smashed" were substantially more likely to erroneously report (that is, to remember) the presence of broken glass than were subjects originally queried with the verb "hit."
>
> This result raised obvious issues about the whole process of questioning witnesses, whether by the police prior to trial or by counsel during trial. In either case the questions asked may deposit information in memory that radically alters subsequent testimony.

We will examine testimony and memory in detail in Chapter 11.

Fallacies of answer formulation are just cases in which the respondent doesn't give a responsive answer to a pertinent question. As we saw in the last section, faced with a pertinent question, we respond to it by giving a corrective or direct answer or admitting that we don't know the answer. When a person does not give a responsive answer, we say that person is **ignoring the issue.** For example, if a person is asked

> Does Santa Claus exist?

and answers

> I hear that question a lot these days.

clearly he or she is ignoring the issue. The issue is whether Santa Claus exists, not whether the question is a common one.

In defining the concept of ignoring the issue, we need to be careful. We certainly don't want to say that any person is obligated to answer any question put to him or her, no matter how silly. That is why we specify that the question at hand be **pertinent**—that is, reasonably related to the general context of conversation. (Other terms for *pertinent* are *appropriate, reasonable, serious,* or *apt.*) For example, suppose we are enrolled in a beginning calculus class, and we are at the first class meeting. The professor has just gone over the syllabus and has asked the class whether they have any questions. Questions such as the following would clearly be pertinent:

> How many tests will we get, and what format will they be in?
> Do you collect the homework?
> What chapters will we cover?
> Do you grade on a curve?
> Do you give the benefit of the doubt in borderline cases?

Questions such as the following, however, would clearly be impertinent:

> What type of underwear do you like?
> Can you dance the tango?
> What cheese do you like on your burgers?

The fallacy of ignoring the issue is a very important one, and we will discuss it in detail in Chapter 8.

   Note that a loaded question is a fallacy committed by the questioner (the question *framer*), while ignoring the issue is a fallacy committed by the answerer (the question *respondent*). These fallacies can occur together. Consider this exchange:

> FRED: Have you stopped abusing drugs yet?
>
> TED: Maybe you should ask your mom that question!

Here, Fred has asked a loaded question. That is one fallacy. Ted does not correct the question or answer it directly; he ignores the issue. That is a second fallacy.

Exercise 3.4A

The following questions are loaded. Explain how.

1. Haven't you promised yourself a diamond long enough?
2. Attention, buyers: why is Southern Mortgage Company different?
3. Why do I know more than other people? Why, in general, am I so clever?
4. Why are musicians more illogical than the rest of us?
5. When did Americans give up their respect for achievement?

Exercise 3.4B

For each of the following questions, determine whether it is loaded.

1. Does the Tooth Fairy exist?
2. Have you decided to confess your crime?
3. Was it through stupidity or greed that this administration bungled the latest trade accord?

4. When were you born?
5. How many rats do you like on your pizza?

Exercise 3.4C

Imagine you are at a press conference being held by the president of the United States. Give five questions that would be pertinent in that context. Give five questions that would clearly be impertinent in that context.

InfoTrac College Edition

You can locate InfoTrac College Edition articles about this chapter by accessing the InfoTrac College Edition Web site (www.infotrac-college.com/wadsworth/). Using the InfoTrac College Edition subject guide, enter the search terms relevant to this chapter, and then read abstracts for relevant articles.

Chapter 4

Identifying Arguments

---

1 Premises and Conclusions

In the preceding two chapters, we have explored the first two major building blocks of critical thought, statements and questions. We are now in position to define the concept of an argument. An **argument** is a set of statements, all but one of which (called the *premises*) are taken as potential evidence for the remaining statement (called the *conclusion*). Arguments are thus structured sets of statements, with the premises listed above the conclusion. This is the common or standard format for arguments, so we will call it **standard form.** Also, we will put three dots before the conclusion to abbreviate *therefore.*

An argument as we define the term has at least one (and often more than one) premise. There are one-premise arguments:

1. Men are greedy.
   ∴ Any social system that requires altruism is doomed to failure.

There are two-premise arguments:

1. One should only negotiate from a position of strength.
2. America is weaker than Russia.
   ∴ America should not negotiate with Russia.

There are three-, four-, five-, even hundred-premise arguments. Consider the following:

1. Unemployment is high.
2. Inflation still rages.
3. The Russians are pushing us around.
4. Our relations with our allies have deteriorated.
5. The energy crisis is getting worse.
   ∴ The president is doing a bad job.

Note that by itself a statement is neither a premise nor a conclusion, any more than a person is by him- or herself a sibling or a cousin. Being a premise, like being a cousin, is being related in a certain way to something else. The same statement may be a premise in one argument and a conclusion in another. Thus, "Smith is good at foreign policy" is a conclusion in

1. Smith has improved relations with China.
2. Smith has strengthened our alliances.
3. Smith has helped Haiti become democratic.
4. Smith achieved some measure of peace in the Middle East.
∴   Smith is good at foreign policy.

Yet the same statement is a premise in

1. Smith is good at foreign policy.
2. Smith is good to little children.
3. Smith is good at domestic policy.
∴   Smith is a good president.

Put another way, the main feature of an argument is not so much what makes it up (statements) but how they are structured. Thus, the arguments

1. She is a real gambler.
∴   She will take the gamble of dating Fred.

and

1. She will take the gamble of dating Fred.
∴   She is a real gambler.

are quite different. In the first set, we take her being a gambler to be a known fact and then infer that she will try dating Fred. In the second, we take it as known that she will date Fred and infer from that fact that she must be a gambler.

Arguments are often presented singly. For example, a short letter to the editor of a newspaper may just present reasons to justify a single claim. However, arguments are more often found woven together, especially in longer writings such as essays, chapters in nonfiction books, and articles in professional journals. For example, a main argument with, say, four premises might be presented together with four "subsidiary" arguments, each directed at proving one of the premises of the main argument. We will devote all of this chapter to learning how to identify arguments, both taken singly and interwoven. In Chapter 5, we will learn more about the nature of arguments.

2 *Identifying Single Arguments*

Recognizing arguments we meet is a crucial skill in critical thinking. The skill of identifying arguments has three major components or subskills. First, faced with a passage, we must learn to figure out whether any arguments are in it at all. Second, suppose we know for a fact that the passage in front of us contains exactly one argument. We must learn how to identify it—that is, to determine what the premises are and what the conclusion is. We must learn to put the argument in standard form. Third, if the passage contains (as often happens) several arguments interwoven in complicated ways, we must learn to diagram such multiple arguments.

The second subtask is the central one: Knowing how to put single arguments in standard form is the key to both determining how many arguments are present (if any) and how they are interrelated. Accordingly, let us start with it. The first task will be addressed in the next section of this chapter, while the third will be discussed later in the chapter.

The basic problem of identifying single arguments—spotting premises and conclusions—is that the order, type, and number of sentences occurring in a passage usually bear little resemblance to the logical structure of the statements in the argument.

Consider first the order of occurrence. The sentence that expresses the conclusion may occur first in the passage:

> The Swiss must be hated. After all, they are a lucky people, and people hate lucky people.

On the other hand, the conclusion may occur somewhere in the middle, as in

> The resources of this planet are finite. So there must be a limit to population growth, since an infinite population would require infinite resources.

Here, the conclusion is that there must be a limit to population growth; the conclusion is flanked by two premises.

Consider next the type of sentences. Remember that in natural languages, sentence form and function do not always coincide. For example, rhetorical questions are not questions; they are statements. This can obscure the logic of the passage:

> Should we be unconcerned about the Chinese menace? No! They threaten to subvert stable governments, they are growing in military strength and they soon are going to be the biggest economy on Earth!

Note that there are no declarative sentences, only an interrogative and two exclamations. But there is an argument there:

1. The Chinese are soon going to be the biggest economy on Earth.
2. The Chinese subvert stable governments.
3. The Chinese are growing in military strength.
   _____
∴ The Chinese are a menace we should worry about.

To add to the difficulty, the number of sentences in the passage and the number of statements in the argument are almost never equal. For one thing, a statement may take two or more sentences for its expression, or it may be repeated by different sentences (recall that markedly different words can express the same thought). For example:

> Nope. I can't buy that. Not at all. I'm sorry, I just don't agree that those workers should be fired for striking. They didn't have a "no-strike" clause in their contract, nor is their strike a threat to national security. No threat at all.

In this passage, eliminating the repetition, we have the simple two-premise argument:

1. The workers' strike does not threaten national security.
2. The workers did not sign a "no-strike" contract.
   _____
∴ They should not be fired.

Another reason the number of sentences in the passage may not equal the number of statements in the argument is that the passage may contain material that is not actually a part of the argument in the strictest sense but that fills in the argument in various ways. These rhetorical "argument fillers" include such things as (1) comments that amplify or clarify some of the premises or the conclusion, (2) illustrations of premises or conclusions, (3) comments that provide the background or setting for the argument, (4) definitions of central terms in the statement of the argument, or (5) humorous remarks intended to capture the audience's attention. (We are ignoring for now the common situation in which the passage contains a central argument and other material that proves or backs up premises of that central argument. Such a passage really contains multiple arguments, a topic we will consider shortly.)

For an example of a passage containing argument fillers, consider this one:

> Bess James was sixty-seven when she ran her first race. Now she holds many marathon records. If Bess can run races, Mom, so can you, because you are only forty-three years old.

Probably the best way to put this argument in standard form is as follows:

1. You are younger than Bess James.
2. Bess James can run marathons.
∴ Probably, you can run marathons.

It is not generally easy to distinguish which material in the passage is strictly part of the argument and which amplifies or explains statements in it.

To sum up, a passage is a sequence of sentences and an argument is a set of statements, one of which is the conclusion, the others being the premises. There is no necessary match-up among order, type, and number of sentences in the passage and the structure of the argument.

How, then, can we identify premises and conclusions of arguments? It takes practice (which you will get in a moment), but a couple of rough guides are helpful.

First, English has certain indicator words that allow the observer to "decode" the argument contained in the passage. Certain words are **premise indicators,** in that they signal that the clause which follows probably expresses a premise. On the other hand, certain words are **conclusion indicators,** in that they signal that the clause which follows probably expresses the conclusion. Table 4.1 is a list of the most common indicator words.

Note that the rule discussed here is only rough, not absolute. Indicator words do not always signal an argument. For example, in

> Sue is so angry she could explode.

the word *so* does not indicate that any kind of inference is involved but rather is used to express the degree of Sue's anger. In the passage

> Sonny paid the man, then they left.

the word *then* merely indicates a temporal link between the two events: Sonny paying the man and the two of them leaving.

A second rough rule is this. Look to the context of the passage for any indications of "relative certitude." (By **context** we mean the passages surrounding the one in question

TABLE 4.1 Common Indicators	
Premise Indicators	Conclusion Indicators
for . . . since . . . because . . . due to . . . as . . . inasmuch as . . . otherwise . . . as indicated by . . . after all . . . for the reason that . . . considering that . . . in view of the fact that . . . as shown by . . . follows from . . . being as . . . being that . . . in the first place . . . seeing that . . . firstly/secondly . . . may be deduced from . . . may be concluded from . . . may be inferred from . . . may be derived from . . .	thus . . . therefore . . . so . . . hence . . . it follows that . . . ergo . . . accordingly . . . we may conclude that . . . which entails that . . . which means that . . . which leads to . . . as a result . . . which implies that . . . so it is obvious that . . . in this way one sees that . . . demonstrates that . . . bears out the point that . . . should lead you to believe that . . . showing that . . . allows us to infer that . . . which shows that . . . which proves that . . . you see that . . .

or—when dealing with part of a conversation—the rest of the conversation.) As a general rule, what the writer of the passage takes to be more certain is probably what he or she will offer as evidence. For example,

Suppose the following exchange takes place between two baseball fans in a Pittsburgh bar:

> SUE: Why do you say the Pirates should try to get Fernando from the Dodgers?
> BARBARA: Look, winning requires good pitching. We're weak there.

By the very context, we can assume that Barbara believes that

1. The Pirates do not have good pitchers.
2. Good pitchers are needed for a winning team.
3. It would be nice if the Pirates were a winning team.
4. Fernando is a good pitcher.

And her conclusion (the truth of which Sue had doubted):

> ∴ The Pirates should try to get Fernando from Los Angeles.

Considerations of context are an important feature of the handling of arguments. For now let us adopt the policy of stating premises and conclusions in such a way that nothing is left to context (that is, so that things are explicit rather than implicit).

Exercise 4.2A

Each of the following passages contains exactly one argument. Put each argument in standard form.

1. I think that tax indexing is the best cure for inflation. It would give Congress less of our money to waste, and it would create confidence in the money market.
2. The Padres won't win this year. After all, they have weak pitching. Also, their best hitter has been injured.
3. The unemployment rate for blacks is almost double what it is for whites. So any unemployment program should be aimed at blacks. After all, government programs should be aimed at the heart of the problem they are designed to address.
4. Unemployment is down. The stock market is up. I believe this shows that the recession is over. Why, even the budget deficit is shrinking.
5. Fernando is injured. Steve is injured. Ron is injured. And those are the best players on the team. And you say the team will win?
6. Why are you surprised that many jazz musicians have heart disease? They are constantly performing, they don't get much sleep, they drink and take drugs, and they eat high-cholesterol food in greasy dives.
7. Why not simply cut off all military aid to Central America? Didn't we learn in Vietnam that military aid leads to direct military involvement? And don't we want to avoid direct military involvement?
8. No, I don't think it would be a good idea for you to go to that rock concert! Don't the kids use drugs? And they drink like fish!
9. If you don't shut up, I'm going to smack your face! You don't want your face slapped, do you? Then shut up!
10. Treason is worse than murder, for the murderer only kills one person, while the traitor—if he succeeds—kills a whole nation.
11. Whoever preaches violence should be arrested. And whoever advocates universal suffrage is in fact preaching violence. So Ted should be in jail, because he advocates universal suffrage.
12. I was so happy to hear Professor Larch tell us that the bacteria he has developed to eat the oil in oil spills are harmless! I'm glad that I don't have to worry about them attacking the oil in fish or on human skin, or about them attacking oil-drilling platforms or surviving on the microscopic layer of oil on the ocean's surface! I'm so relieved!
13. No, I don't believe it. I can't believe it! I can't believe it! Are you really suggesting that we give Jason a job? Are you kidding? Don't you realize that he is a hopeless incompetent?
14. Left on his own, that kid would burn the house down, so we'd better take him with us, since I sure don't want to lose my house. Yes, we had better take the little brat with us.
15. The life expectancy of women is about five years greater than that for men. Since women live longer than men, any life insurance system that pegs premium rates to life spans will discriminate against women.

16. Laura has known Steve for a long time. Gosh, I think they were going together even in high school. And, you know, that wasn't exactly yesterday. Anyway, it is surprising that they've broken up, since relationships that have lasted for years tend to continue.

17. The patient led a sedentary life, was grossly overweight, and smoked. It's even reported that he smoked four packs a day and was known to have loved pizza. These are risk factors in heart disease. So his heart attack comes as no surprise, especially in view of his attempt to run twenty miles. What a foolish thing to do.

18. Don't get excited. Don't get so excited. If it was Mark who was in that car crash, the police would surely have notified us by now. Just relax, okay?

19. If America continues to neglect our educational system, it will cease to be a great power. If that happens, our enemies will destroy us. Do you want that to happen? Then we shouldn't continue this damned neglect!

20. If you come any closer, I'll shoot. So you should keep your distance, unless you love being shot!

Exercise 4.2B

The following passages contain exactly one argument. Put each in standard form.

1. Science is based on experiment, on a willingness to challenge old dogma, on an openness to see the universe as it really is. Accordingly, science sometimes requires courage—at the very least the courage to question the conventional wisdom.
   Carl Sagan, *Broca's Brain*

2. As positive proof that the earth is flat, Voliva cites statements from engineers that no allowance was made for curvature of the earth in building canals and railroads. In addition, the issue of the periodical includes a picture taken at Lake Winnebago in Oshkosh, Wisconsin. The opposite shore, 12 miles away, is clearly visible, "proving beyond any doubt that the surface of the lake is a plane, or a horizontal line."
   Daisie and Michael Radner, *Science and Unreason*

3. Although the studies differ in their approach, their results are consistent: Computer-assisted instruction works.
   First, it seems that CAI gives students the opportunity to practice what they've learned, and to get better at it. . . .
   Second, in some circumstances CAI may teach students better study habits.
   Trudy Bell, "My Computer, My Teacher," in *Personal Computing* (June 1983)

4. When an individual is sleeping and resting comfortably, the intervertebral discs reabsorb fluid and become plumper—to use a common expression—and the spine thus increases in length.
   A point, then, to remember is—if you are going to take a physical examination and you want to be at your tallest—appear for the examination in the morning.
   Charles Linart and August Blake, *How to Increase Your Height*

5. If you can get together a college degree—two years are OK, four are preferred—do so, even if you are a dozen years behind. You will be paid back lavishly in higher

earning potential, increased mobility, and more interesting jobs. It is a kind
of passport.

> Tom Jackson, *Guerrilla Tactics in the Job Market*

6. Kelli Stewart, Instructor of Dance for the Department Physical Education, has
requested that the Division consider the inclusion of courses in Dance as partial
fulfillment of the area of concentration requirement for the Associate of Arts in
Humanities and Creative and Performing Arts. The argument for this inclusion is
that Dance is a performing art and, at many universities, is housed in the fine or
performing arts area.

7. The crucial aspects of any possible future world which might develop from the present situation are now seen in terms of only two variable quantities: the growth of
world productivity as a whole, and the distribution of the fruits of that productivity
between the rich and poor countries. Each variable may go in either of two directions compared with the present situation: more or less growth, more or less equality between nations. So we are left with only four kinds of possible future world to
consider:
   a) High growth, high equality (a big cake fairly shared)
   b) High growth, low equality (a big cake hogged by the rich)
   c) Low growth, high equality (a small cake fairly shared)
   d) Low growth, low equality (a small cake hogged by the rich)

> John Gribbin, *Future Worlds*

8. Where before winning meant total victory without regard to one's adversary, we
know today that it's no longer appropriate for one person to walk away with all the
rewards and love and self-esteem. . . .

   The most vivid proof of this I have, perhaps, is the kind of people who are enlist-
ing in my seminars on negotiation. Increasingly, they are people who have found
that the win-it-all manner in which they had always functioned isn't working for
them any longer.

> Tessa Albert Warschaw, *Winning by Negotiation*

9. It came to me today, walking in the rain to get Helen a glass of orange juice, that
the world exists only in my consciousness (whether as a reality or as an illusion
the evening papers do not say, but my guess is reality). The only possible way the
world could be destroyed, it came to me, was through the destruction of my consciousness. This proves the superiority of the individual to any and all forms of
collectivism. I could enlarge on that, only I have what the French call "rheuma-
tism of the brain"—that is, the common cold.

> James Thurber, *Selected Letters,* edited by Helen Thurber and Edward Weeks

10. Inequality may even grow at first as poverty declines. To lift the incomes of the
poor, it will be necessary to increase the rates of investment, which in turn will tend
to enlarge the wealth, if not the consumption, of the rich. The poor, as they move
into the work force and acquire promotions, will raise their incomes by a greater
percentage than the rich; but the upper classes will gain by greater absolute
amounts, and the gap between the rich and the poor may grow.

> George Gilder, *Wealth and Poverty*

11. Enemy-making of men would ultimately subvert the whole dream of a women's
    culture based on mutuality and altruism. The very process of projecting the negative
    part of their own psychic potential onto males, and failing to own these themselves,
    would tend to make such women's groups fanatical caricatures of that which they
    hate. The dehumanization of the other ultimately dehumanizes oneself. One dupli-
    cates evil-making in the very effort to escape from it once and for all, by projecting
    it on the "alien" group.

    Rosemary Radford Reuther, *Sexism and God-Talk*

12. Many therapists would admit the possibility that some people have a subconscious
    cause for their agoraphobia and need psychoanalysis. I do not close my mind to this
    possibility, but it is interesting that over thirty years of practice and after curing
    many hundreds of agoraphobic people, it was not necessary for me to use psycho-
    analysis on any of my patients.

    Claire Weekes, *Agoraphobia*

13. Real winners—people who are self-actualizing and who respond authentically to
    life—do not need losers. Women winning does not mean that men must lose, any
    more than men winning should mean that women must lose. If women have more
    options, so too will men. More choices for women means more choices for men.
    For example, it has long been acceptable for a married woman to quit her job
    and stay home, explaining, "I'm tired of working. I'm going to relax and do
    something different for a while." Yet how many married men—no matter how
    tired or pressured—would be greeted with the same degree of acceptance if they
    announced, "I'm tired of working. I'm going to stay home with the family for a
    while?"

    Dorothy Jongeward and Dru Scott, *Women as Winners*

14. Without perceiving some sacredness in human identity, individuals are out of touch
    with the depth they might feel in themselves and respond to in others. Given such a
    sense, however, certain intrusions are felt as violations—a few even as desecrations.
    It is in order to guard against such encroachments that we recoil from those who
    would tap our telephones, read our letters, bug our rooms: no matter how little we
    have to hide, no matter how benevolent their intentions, we take such intrusions to
    be demeaning.

    Sissela Bok, *Secrets: On the Ethics of Concealment and Revelation*

15. We have become far too accommodating and tolerant for our own good. In the name
    of sympathetic understanding, we tolerate second-rate workmanship, second-rate
    habits of thought, and second-rate standards of personal conduct. We put up with
    bad manners and with many kinds of bad language, ranging from the common-place
    scatology that is now ubiquitous to elaborate academic evasion. We seldom bother
    to correct a mistake or to argue with opponents in the hopes of changing their
    minds. Instead we either shout them down or agree to disagree, saying that all
    of us have a right to our opinions.

    Christopher Lasch, *The Revolt of the Elites and the Betrayal of Democracy*

16. Fifty years ago there were 435 congressmen and 96 senators. Today there are 435
    congressmen and 100 senators. The number of legislators is fixed; the legislature's

workload has grown exponentially. So the legislature's work is increasingly done elsewhere, no matter what you read in your high-school civics text.

George F. Will, "More Government, Less Control," *Newsweek* (July 4, 1983)

17. Since biological determinism possesses such evident utility for groups in power, one
might be excused for suspecting that it also arises in a political context, despite the
denials quoted above. After all, if the status quo is an extension of nature, then any
major change, if possible at all, must inflict an enormous cost—psychological for
individuals, or economic for society—in forcing people into unnatural arrangements.
In his epochal book, "An American Dilemma" (1944), Swedish sociologist Gunner
Myrdal discussed the thrust of biological and medical arguments about human nature: "They have been associated in America, as in the rest of the world, with conservative and even reactionary ideologies. Under their long hegemony, there has
been a tendency to assume biological causation without question, and to accept
social explanations only under the duress of a siege of irresistible evidence. In
political questions, this tendency favored a do-nothing policy." Or, as Condorcet
said more succinctly a long time ago: They "make nature herself an accomplice
in the crime of political inequality."

Stephen Jay Gould, *The Mismeasure of Man*

18. After years of research and thousands of documents declassified with the aid of the
Freedom of Information Act, Eisenhower's shabby place in history was explained.
America's most popular hero was America's most covert President.

Blanche Wiesen Cook, *The Declassified Eisenhower*

19. As an academic and professional discipline, economics lives with a fundamental
internal contradiction: what is taught in conventional micro-economics is incompat-
ible with what is taught in macro-economics. In the former, every market is a price-
auction market that clears based on competitive bidding within a framework of
supply and demand. Accordingly, any market is always in equilibrium, having no
unsatisfied bidders, and every individual is a maximiser in his decisions to consume
and produce. Macro-economics, on the other hand, is basically the study of markets
that do not clear and are not in equilibrium. Such contradictions, of course, are
not peculiar to economics. Physics uses both particle theory and wave theory to
describe electromagnetic phenomena. But the contradictions in economics are
perhaps more severe than in other disciplines.

Lester Thurow, *Dangerous Currents*

20. The two skinny, illiterate kids behind the palm trees had obviously been given the
job of following us everywhere. We'd be walking down a street and suddenly Henry
would pivot around and snap their pictures, while they would break out in peals
of laughter. They hid behind bushes from us, waved through the leaves and flirted
with me.

We would walk in one side of the cathedral with appropriate dignity, then dash
out the side door and lose them.

It was all endlessly diverting, but it was a deadly defeating diversion. I understood
their tactics all too well: no one from the guerillas would dare to contact us so long as
the skinny ones were about. That was their final card in this strange game.

Georgie Anne Geyer, *Buying the Night Flight*

Exercise 4.2C

Find five arguments from newspapers, magazines, or books, and put them in standard form.

3 *Spotting Enthymemes*

In the preceding section, we discussed the identification of arguments. We noted that arguments are often stated with amplifying material and repetition that can make identifying the underlying argument tricky. Even more sticky is the fact that many, if not most, arguments are stated with premises or even conclusions left out. We say a passage presenting an argument is an **enthymeme** if part of that argument is unstated but taken for granted by the speaker.

Why do arguers often leave out statements when giving arguments? For three reasons. First, it is rhetorically effective to dwell on important points and not waste time on what our listeners believe obvious. For example, imagine a man who has borrowed money from a loan shark, facing two of the loan shark's enforcers:

> Look, pal. We don't like guys who don't pay on time. They wind up looking funny. Get the picture?

The argument stated explicitly in standard form:

1. If you don't pay on time you will be physically injured.
2. You don't want to be physically injured.
∴ You should pay on time.

The enforcers are dwelling on premise 1—the explicit threat. They don't bother to focus on premise 2— it's obvious to most people that physical injury is undesirable (pain hurts!). You might think that precisely because premise 2 is automatic, it is not worth spelling out. However, it *is* a crucial premise, and it is also not necessarily true—some people in fact enjoy having pain inflicted on them, namely masochists. And the enforcers didn't bother to state the conclusion, again because it is obvious in the context—why else would they be paying the hapless borrower a visit? To teach him how to dance?

The second reason premises or conclusions go unstated is that an arguer may want to avoid discussion of key claims because he or she cannot defend them. Put another way, sometimes we omit statements so as not to belabor the obvious, but sometimes we omit statements because we can't defend them. For example, consider this pitch given by a "Beamer" salesperson to a prospective customer:

> Look, compare this gorgeous Beamer to the Cadillac Eldorado, and you immediately see that the engineering of the Beamer is totally superior. In fact, the engineering here is on a par with the Mercedes, but the equivalent model Mercedes costs $10,000 more than this Beamer. Really, this Beamer is your only choice.

The salesperson's argument assumes implicitly that the BMW, the Cadillac Eldorado, and the Mercedes are the only luxury cars worth considering by the prospective buyer. But, of course, there are many other luxury cars out there (such as the Infinity, the Lexus, the Acura 3.5RL, and so on). The salesperson conveniently ignores these other cars in his pitch.

The third reason premises often go unstated is simply that the speaker or writer overlooks them. This is especially true when someone is arguing orally and just trying to get his or her point of view expressed in a brief period of time.

Because assessing arguments requires that the complete argument be present for examination, we need to identify all the premises unstated but implicit. In this we are guided by **the principle of charity:** try to fill in the unstated premises to make the most defensible possible argument, consistent with what the author intends, before you turn to criticize it. When we talk about making the argument "most defensible," we mean supplying missing premises (or conclusions) that are plausible, relevant, appropriately qualified, and nontrivial. Let's consider these in turn.

Plausibility

To begin with plausibility, when filling in a premise, we want to choose the one that is most likely to be factually correct. For example, suppose someone says

> Suzie lied to her father. So I think she's immoral.

One way to flesh out this argument is to view as (where we bracket the unstated premise):

1. Suzie lied to her father.
[2. Anybody who lies is immoral.]
∴ Suzie is immoral.

Now, is it not likely that someone would believe that *any* lying, no matter how trivial, is automatically immoral. After all, we all believe it's okay to tell lies sometimes—for example, if a wife is hiding from an abusive husband (or vice versa), and the abusing spouse asks you where the victim is hiding, and you know, you would naturally lie and say, "I don't know." So a better (that is, more charitable) interpretation would be as follows:

1. Suzie lied to her father about something important.
[2. Unless a greater harm is prevented by the act, lying about something is generally wrong.]
[3. Suzie did not lie to stop a greater harm from happening.]
∴ Suzie is immoral in this case.

This is a far more defensible argument.

Relevance

The second feature we look for when we try to fill in a missing premise is relevance; that is, the candidate premise should tie together the stated premises with the conclusion. For example, suppose someone says

> Mandy won't bite. After all, she's a golden retriever.

Now one candidate for the missing premise might be "Golden retrievers are fine hunting dogs," but that premise would be irrelevant—it doesn't connect being a golden retriever to having a nonbiting disposition. Much more relevant would be

1. Golden retrievers cannot bite.
2. Golden retrievers never bite.
3. Golden retrievers seldom bite.
4. Golden retrievers seldom bite unless provoked.

Of these, probably premise 4 is the most plausible.

Appropriate Qualification

The third factor we look for in choosing a candidate for a missing premise is that it is appropriately qualified, that it doesn't overstate or understate the matter. For example, suppose someone says

Bob's a wealthy entrepreneur. So he's probably a Republican.

The following candidate premises are clearly relevant and plausible:

1. Some wealthy entrepreneurs are Republican.
2. Most wealthy entrepreneurs are Republican.
3. The vast majority of wealthy entrepreneurs are Republican.

But of those candidates, only premise 2 seems to fit the strength of confidence with which the conclusion is stated. Premise 1 is too understated—if only some (but not most) wealthy entrepreneurs are Republican, the premises together would not support the claim that *probably* Bob is Republican. On the other hand, premise 3 is too overstated—if indeed the vast majority of wealthy entrepreneurs are Republican, then the speaker would express more confidence in the conclusion (by saying, for instance, "he's almost surely a Republican").

Nontriviality

Finally, when looking for the best candidate for stating an omitted premise, we want one that is nontrivial—that is, one that does not merely have the form "If <stated premise> then <stated conclusion>." For instance, suppose someone says

Mandy won't bite. After all, she's wagging her tail and not growling.

We could just add the premise

If Mandy is wagging her tail and not growling, she won't bite.

But more informative would be the nontrivial addition

Mandy is a dog, and dogs typically show aggressive signs such as growling (and not friendly signs, such as tail wagging) before biting.

To summarize the last two sections, when faced with a passage, we identify the argument by a series of stages.

Stage 1: Try to determine what bottom line the writer (speaker) is trying to get you to believe or do. Look for conclusion indicators.

Stage 2: Try to state the major pieces of evidence offered. Look for indicator words.

Stage 3: Ask whether the stated premises even remotely support the conclusion. If not, ask whether some key claims went unstated.

Stage 4: If claims have been left unstated, try to find the most charitable (that is, plausible, relevant, appropriately qualified, and nontrivial) premises to include, assuming you are not in a position simply to ask the arguer to clarify his or her position.

Exercise 4.3A

For each of the following enthymemes, choose the best (most relevant and plausible) missing premise.

1. All pigs can fly. So Porky can fly.
   a. Porky is lucky.
   b. Porky is a pig.
   c. All pigs can run.
   d. No pigs can run.
2. All pigs can fly. So all pigs can dance.
   a. All pigs can dance.
   b. Some pigs can fly and dance.
   c. All things that can fly can also dance.
   d. Most things that can fly can also dance.
3. Some people like cheese. So some people like wine.
   a. All people like cheese.
   b. If some people like cheese, then some people like wine.
   c. Any person who likes cheese likes wine.
   d. Some people who like cheese also like wine.
4. Most people can dance. So most people can move.
   a. Any person who can dance can move.
   b. If most people can dance, most people can move.
   c. Most people who can dance can move.
   d. Most people can move.
5. Sam likes meat. So Sam likes steak.
   a. If Sam likes meat, Sam likes steak.
   b. Most people who like meat like steak.
   c. Steak is a type of meat.
   d. Sam is not a vegetarian.

Exercise 4.3B

Redo the exercises in 4.2A, filling in all unstated premises or conclusions, if any.

Exercise 4.3C

Redo the exercises in 4.2B, filling in all unstated premises or conclusions, if any.

4   *Telling Arguments from Other Things*

We are now able to identify single arguments. We next want to address the fact that ordinary language contains a number of things that resemble arguments but in reality are not. These include positive assertions, repeated assertions, conditionals, announcements, rephrasals, examples, descriptions, and summaries.

Let's begin with positive assertion. **Positive assertion** is the emphatic assertion of a claim without any warrant. For example,

> My bill is the only bill worth supporting! It's the best.

Here, the person is not giving any reason to adopt the bill but merely asserts dogmatically ("positively") that it will.

Related to this is repeated assertion. **Repeated assertion** is the technique (used by propagandists especially) of cleverly repeating one's claim over and over until the listeners take it as proven fact. For example, Hitler and his gang repeated the lie that Jews were responsible for Germany's problems, and they repeated the canard so often, in so many different forms, that many people came to accept it as fact. Advertisers use a similar tactic with "spot ads," constantly repeating an ad such as "drink Ratz beer—it's the best!" until it is drummed into people's heads.

A third thing often confused with an argument is a type of statement called a conditional. A **conditional** is a compound statement in which the truth of one component is asserted as being conditional upon the truth of another. For example, "If President Jones gets the support of blue-collar voters, he will win" is a single statement. It is not an argument, because the statement "President Jones gets the support of blue-collar voters" is not claimed, nor is the statement "He will win." All that is claimed is that if such-and-such happens, then something else will; that is, one event will happen on condition that another happens first. No premise, no conclusion, no argument.

On the other hand, the sentence "Because Jones is getting the support of blue-collar voters, we can be certain that he will win" does express an argument. Two claims are made: that President Jones has the support of blue-collar voters and that he will indeed be elected. The argument here is probably an enthymeme:

1. President Jones has won the support of blue-collar voters.
2. He was already close to having the votes needed to win.
∴ He will win.

Also often confused with argument is explanation. An **explanation** is a direct answer to an explicit or implicit why question. Consider some examples:

QUESTION: Why did our team lose?

ANSWER: Our team lost because its best quarterback was not in the game.

QUESTION: Why can't we see black holes?

ANSWER: A black hole is a collapsed star with so much gravity that nothing can escape its surface. Because light can't escape, it appears black.

In both examples, the word *because* seems to indicate that an argument is being given, but that's not what is going on.* The person answering the question isn't trying to give evidence that the event being explained happened. Rather, the respondent is trying to give the reasons that it occurred. In other words, in an argument we offer evidence that something is true, whereas in an explanation we are trying to show a connection between truths. In the first example, we are not trying to give evidence that our team lost—we already know that—but we are explaining that fact by pointing out the fact that our team's best quarterback wasn't able to play and (we assume) that teams usually lose without their best quarterbacks.

Distinguishing explanation from argument is often a tricky matter (and, indeed, in many passages you find explanation and argument occurring together). No precise rules can be given, but a rough rule is this: "A because B" expresses an argument if the context of its occurrence indicates that A needs proof while B does not. On the other hand, if A is presented as at least as true as B, then "A because B" probably expresses an explanation. We can only judge, and judge according to context. Explanations are of great importance in critical thinking, and we will devote all of Chapter 15 to the topic of explanation.

Another thing often confused with arguments are announcements. An **announcement** is a statement about where some person or group stands on some issue.

> We, the members of the South State Republican Women's Club, have come out against the new tax law. Ours is a club of fifty-five members, and our decision was unanimous.

The writer is only announcing her club's opinion, not justifying it by laying out evidence for it.

Another thing often confused with argument is rephrasing. To **rephrase** a point is to restate it in other words. We often rephrase to make something clearer. The expressions *that is* and *i.e.* are usually used to signal to the listener that one is rephrasing a point, as in the following examples:

> Intraspecific aggression is rather rare; that is, animals rarely attack others of their own kind.
> But don't people really seek domination; i.e., don't they really want someone to tell them what to do?

Similar to rephrasing is exemplification. To **exemplify** a claim is to give an example or illustration of it to make it clearer. General statements especially call out for examples. But to cite an example of some general claim is not to prove that claim.

---

*Some philosophers contend that while explanations aren't arguments, they always (or at least typically) have the *form* or structure of arguments; that is, they can always be put in standard form. Other philosophers deny that view. We will take no position on the issue in this text.

> Kids do the darnedest things. For example, my little Flukey just set fire to her brother's hair.

(Notice that in the textbook you are reading a general claim or definition usually followed by one or more examples.)

Again, description should not be confused with argument. To **describe** is simply to give a set of propositions that characterize a situation. For example, the passage here describes Fred's financial situation:

> Fred is the owner of a large house in Los Angeles, and a small vacation home in Hawaii. He has a large savings account and a modest portfolio of stocks. He also has a retirement income from the company for which he used to work.

Compare this with an argument intended to prove Fred is not poor:

> Fred can hardly be considered poor. He owns houses, has a savings account, owns stocks, and has a steady income. Poor people don't own much or have good incomes, now, do they?

Finally, summaries should not be confused with arguments. A **summary** is a set of statements that highlight or repeat points made earlier in a passage. For example:

> We have seen the following: first, that Fred is rich; second, that he is dishonest; and finally, that he is probably a criminal.

Summaries of narration are not arguments, since they don't set forth some of the statements as evidence for another of the statements.

One last complication. Even where an argument is present, it can be unclear whether the author is giving that argument, reporting that argument and agreeing with it, or reporting that argument and disagreeing with it. Compare these three examples:

1. Pigs can't dance. Their legs are too short, and they aren't very coordinated.
2. I doubt that pigs can dance. The well-known pig expert Professor Porcine has pointed out in this regard that pigs are rather uncoordinated and their legs are altogether too short to dance properly.
3. Some have argued that pigs cannot dance. For instance, a certain Professor Porcine has claimed that pigs are uncoordinated and have legs too short for dancing.

In argument 1, the writer simply gives the argument. In argument 2, the writer reports and evidently agrees with an argument given by Professor Porcine. In argument 3, the writer reports Porcine's argument but uses phrases ("some . . . have argued," "a certain professor . . . has claimed") that seem to signal that the writer does not agree with the argument. (To determine better whether the writer accepts the argument she reports, we would need to look at the context of the passage.)

Exercise 4.4A

For each of the following passages, determine whether it contains any arguments, and—if it does—identify the premises and conclusions. If it does not, tell what kind of technique is being used.

1. I've heard this story a thousand times before. I don't care where you heard it or who told it to you. The whole story is a lie. Do you hear? A lie!
2. Dear Editor:
   Regarding Lou Salome's review of Wagner's latest play, *The Big Man,* I can only express my utter contempt. Such sycophantic twaddle. Is she kidding, or what?
3. Why can't he get a date? Because no girl is totally devoid of taste!
4. If he had brains, he'd be dangerous. But because we know he isn't dangerous, that tells us he has no brains.
5. Get away. I don't want you around. You hurt me, going out with that other guy. Because he had money. Big deal. So go date him. I don't care. Get lost. I don't want to be around people who hurt me.
6. Given the high cost of medical care, health insurance is a must. But that means we'll have to put that in our contract, because the company won't volunteer anything. Not a damn thing. It never does.
7. I think he got cancer because he worked with brake linings, because brake linings contain asbestos, and because studies have shown asbestos causes cancer.
8. My friends, you heard my client say on three occasions that she didn't murder her husband. I know she didn't do it. You should know that. She simply couldn't have done such a terrible thing.
9. I know you think otherwise, but Fred couldn't have been the one who stole the carpet, since Fred hates Persian carpets.
10. He was an autodidact; that is, he taught himself what he knows.

Exercise 4.4B

Some of the following passages contain single arguments, while the rest contain no arguments. For each passage, state whether it contains an argument, and if it does, put that argument in standard form.

1. Since the late 1960's America's economy has been slowly unraveling. The economic decline has been marked by growing unemployment, mounting business failures, and falling productivity. Since about the same time America's politics have been in chronic disarray. The political decline has been marked by the triumph of narrow interest groups, the demise of broad-based political parties, a succession of one-term presidents, and a series of tax revolts.

   These phenomena are related. Economics and politics are threads in the same social fabric. The way people work together to produce goods and services is intimately tied to the way they set and pursue public goals. This link is perhaps stronger today than at any time in America's past because we are moving into an era in which economic progress depends to an unprecedented degree upon collaboration in our workplaces and consensus in our politics.
   Robert Reich, *The New American Frontier*

2. American values have been transformed during the 1960's and 1970's, leaving us with a legacy of noble concerns. The society we have created is indeed more compassionate for those who are old, in trouble, or are yet unborn. We have become more cautious, perhaps more responsible. But these good deeds and intentions are

not without a price. We shall pay for them through slowth (slow growth). That price can be expressed not only monetarily but also in our feelings of well-being, emotions that we still measure in very concrete and individual ways. For us as individuals, slower growing material standards arising from these values will mean disappointment, a loss of confidence, and an eclipse of hope. The way rising living standards have become intertwined with our identities makes this an unavoidable consequence of any protracted economic slowdown.

    Martin Kupferman, *Slowth: The Looming Struggle of Living with Less*

3. Japanese still tend to think in terms of personal relationships and subjective circumstances in their business dealings. Thus an agreement between a Japanese and a foreign businessman should be reduced to its basic elements, and each point thoroughly discussed, to make sure each side understands and actually does agree to what the other side is saying.

    Boyne De Mente, *The Japanese Way of Doing Business*

4. Although the United States remains the largest single market for telecommunications equipment, with approximately $15 billion in sales in 1980, the non-U.S. market is now almost twice as large. Moreover, the non-U.S. market is growing more rapidly. Unless AT&T becomes a greater force in world exports, its global market share will steadily decline.

    Hunter Lewis, *The Real World War*

5. Most of the behavioral "traits" that sociobiologists try to explain may never have been subject to direct natural selection at all—and may therefore exhibit a flexibility that features crucial to survival can never display.

    Stephen Jay Gould, *The Mismeasure of Man*

6. Before starting this diet (or any diet) get your doctor's approval. And after you've begun, use your good sense in choosing the foods you eat. Protect your heart by watching your intake of saturated fats (dieting or not dieting, you should do that); protect your liver by including many protein-rich foods (eggs, cheese, fish and meat); protect your overall health by including foods rich in vitamins and minerals, by supplementing your diet with a multivitamin every day. Finally, bear in mind that if you remain on a low-carbohydrate diet more than two weeks, you should be sure to include limited—but daily—quantities of milk and citrus fruit.

    The New Carbohydrate Gram Counter

7. On the whole, concentration is a natural state which can easily be reproduced by simple methods. It is only supposed to be exceptional because people do not try and, in this, as in so many other things, starve within an inch of plenty. Those who do try have never been disappointed in the process but have sometimes experienced disappointment in themselves.

    Ernest Dimnet, *The Art of Thinking*

8. I never cease to be amazed at the public unawareness of elementary legal procedures and techniques, and of the widespread suspicion and hesitation about going to a lawyer. Because of this, I felt a real need existed for this book.

    Edward Siegal, *How to Avoid Lawyers*

9. There are so many books on writing as an art or as a craft that one naturally asks some questions about any new book. How is this book different from others? Is it for me? Will it help me to write more effectively and with more joy?

  Write and Publish differs from most books on writing because it does not deal exclusively with any one type of writing; rather it gives a writer an opportunity to take a guided tour of the wide writing field. Second, from the first chapter it encourages the writer to think, feel and believe for himself, and promotes writing as a natural form of communication growing out of what he has already discovered about himself.

  In my own writing and in years of teaching classes, conducting workshops and lecturing to writers' groups I have found that some advice is particularly helpful to both beginners and those who have already written for publication. This is the advice I have included in this book.

  Helen Hinkley Jones, *How to Write and Publish*

10. This book is an attempt to redress the balance, to begin to integrate the rational and intuitive approaches to knowing, and to consider the essential complementarity of these two modes of consciousness as they are manifest in science in general, in psychology in particular, and within each person psychologically and physiologically. A growing body of evidence demonstrates that each person has two major modes of consciousness available, one linear and rational, one arational and intuitive.

  Robert Ornstein, *The Psychology of Consciousness*

11. The purpose of Freud's lifelong struggle was to help us understand ourselves, so that we would no longer be propelled, by forces unknown to us, to live lives of discontent, or perhaps outright misery, and to make others miserable, very much to our own detriment. In examining the content of the unconscious, Freud called into question some deeply cherished beliefs, such as the unlimited perfectibility of man and his inherent goodness; he made us aware of our ambivalences and of our ingrained narcissism, with its origins in infantile self-centeredness, and he showed us its destructive nature. In his life and work, Freud truly heeded the admonition inscribed on the temple of Apollo at Delphi—"Know thyself"—and he wanted to help us do the same.

  Bruno Bettelheim, *Freud and Man's Soul*

12. I was on my own in Cambridge, but I was not left alone for long. One evening in November, when I was hunched over my desk and the mice were nibbling at the crumbs I had set out for them, our doorbell rang. Mrs. Roff allowed as how there were two young gentlemen come to see me. Two students in black gowns stood in my doorway. One had a bird-like head and manner; his name was James Klugman. The other had black, curly hair, high cheek bones, and dark, deep-set eyes. His entire body was taut; his whole being seemed to be concentrated upon his immediate purpose. His name was John Cornford.

  Michael Straight, *After Long Silence*

13. It should be apparent by now that this book will deal with certain physical disorders that are capable of mimicking emotional disturbances and mental disease. These sicknesses can start with tension, with vitamin deficiency or an imbalanced diet,

with a disturbance in body chemistry, with allergy, even with a virus infection. All
the symptoms overlap, even though the causes are so different, for the brain and the
nervous system have limited ways in which to express reaction to insult.

Carlton Fredericks and Herman Goodman, *Low Blood Sugar and You*

14. Stick to Your Subject. Beware of introducing irrelevant matters. They distract read-
    ers. In writing for any public whatever, use no words, phrases, or thoughts which
    turn the reader's attention from your main point, even for an instant. Every diver-
    sion, however slight, tends to make him lose interest in what you have to say.

    Walter Pitkin, *The Art of Useful Writing*

15. But enough of that. In my effort to tell you about the facts of educational life, I
    seem to be getting awfully moralistic. Let's pass on to something else—to the un-
    derlying question of why you should improve your reading.

    There is a simple answer to that question: You should improve your reading so
    that you can easily read *Silas Marner* by George Eliot.

    No, I am not joking. I am just drawing a logical inference from well-known,
    established facts. These are the facts:
    1. Educational experts agree that the highest purpose of reading is the study of
       literature.
    2. The most important works of literature are required reading in our schools.
    3. The book most widely required in our schools is *Silas Marner.*
    So, in essence, you learn to read so that you can read *Silas Marner.*

    Rudolf Flesch, *How to Make Sense*

16. More than twenty-five million people, ranging from employers to relatives and
    from friends to co-workers, are directly or indirectly involved in the problem [of
    alcoholism]. It affects three percent of our workers, and that costs industry at least
    three billion dollars yearly. This means that anything even remotely helpful to alco-
    holics is worthy of investigation.

    Carton Frederick and Herman Goodman, *Low Blood Sugar and You*

17. The Bible is the most-read book that has ever existed, and there are uncounted
    millions of people in the world who, even today, take it for granted that it is the
    inspired word of God; that it is literally true at every point; that there are no
    mistakes or contradictions except where these can be traced to errors in
    copying or in translation.

    There are undoubtedly many who do not realize that the Authorized Version (the
    "King James Bible"), the one with which English-speaking Protestants are most fa-
    miliar, is, in fact, a translation, and who therefore believe that every one of its words
    is inspired and infallible. Against these strong, unwavering, and undeviating beliefs,
    the slowly developing views of scientists have always had to fight.

    Biological evolution, for instance, is considered a fact of nature by almost all
    biologists. There may be and, indeed, are many arguments over the details of the
    mechanics of evolution, but none over the fact—just as we may not completely un-
    derstand the workings of an automobile engine and yet be certain that a car in good
    working order will move if we turn the key and step on the gas.

    There are millions of people, however, who are strongly and emotionally
    opposed to the notion of biological evolution, even though they know little or noth-

ing about the evidence and rationale behind it. It is enough for them that the Bible states thus-and-so. The argument ends there. Well, then, what does the Bible say, and what does science say? Where, if anywhere, do they agree? Where do they disagree? This is what this book is about.

> Isaac Asimov, *In the Beginning*

18. If we read on in *Mein Kampf* we find that Hitler gives us a description of a child's life in a lower-class family. He says:

> Among the five children there is a boy, let us say, of three . . . . When the parents fight almost daily, their brutality leaves nothing to the imagination; then the results of such visual education must slowly but inevitably become apparent to the little one. Those who are not familiar with such conditions can hardly imagine the results, especially when the mutual differences express themselves in the form of brutal attacks on the part of the father toward the mother, assaults due to drunkenness. The poor little boy, at the age of six, senses things which would make even a grown-up person shudder . . . . The other things the little fellow hears at home do not tend to further his respect for his surroundings.

In view of the fact that we know that there were five children in the Hitler home and that his father liked to spend his spare time in the village tavern where he sometimes drank so heavily that he had to be brought home by his wife or children, we begin to suspect that in this passage Hitler is, in all probability, describing conditions in his own home as a child.

> Walter C. Langer, *The Mind of Adolf Hitler*

19. Twenty years after arriving at Harvard as a graduate student, I returned as Professor of Psychology. I had spent five of those years as a postdoctoral fellow at Harvard and the rest on the faculties of the University of Minnesota and Indiana University. In Minnesota I had married Yvonne (Eve) Blue, and in 1938 our daughter Julie was born. Later that year *The Behavior of Organisms* was published. During the war I taught pigeons to guide putative missiles, and in the Guggenheim year that followed I worked on my book on verbal behavior, built the "baby-tender" for our second daughter, Deborah, and wrote *Walden Two*. An invitation to give the William James Lectures brought me back to Harvard, and while there I was asked to join the department. *Walden Two* was published a few months before I returned to Cambridge.

> B. F. Skinner, *A Matter of Consequences*

20. Individual Japanese industries are efficient, but not to the degree the world has been led to believe. Much of their advantage is based on unsavory practices. Japan has "borrowed" or copied foreign technology, or acquired it through joint-venture agreements which it has later disavowed. When this has failed they have resorted to bribery, industrial espionage and outright theft. Its industries often act in concert, as did the prewar Japanese cartels, the zaibatsu, targeting their competitors in other nations and dumping their products at a temporary loss in order to win larger and larger shares of the world's markets and eventually achieve monopoly positions. The Japanese educate their scientists and engineers in American and European universities; they then return home to use their new skills in a trade war against those

who educated them. Japan, it is now becoming clear, is winning the trade war because it refuses to play by the rules.

> Boye DeMente, *The Japanese Way of Doing Business*

Exercise 4.4C

Find five passages that look like argumentation is taking place but that do not contain arguments. Explain in each what is going on (that is, positive assertion, repeated assertion,
and so forth).

5 *The Uses of Arguments*

In ordinary life, arguments are used to do any number of things. Let us just briefly look at
a few common purposes of argument.

We very often use arguments to fix new beliefs—to determine what new things to believe (add to our worldview) by looking at what the evidence shows. We might for example, put forward the argument

   1.   Very few third-party candidates have even come close to winning the presidency.
   ∴   The third-party candidate will not win in this election.

with the intention of establishing the conclusion as true. Normally, a person will construct
an argument to convince an audience of a point by selecting premises agreeable to that audience. Or, again, the belief we are establishing may be a decision:

   1.   I need to buy a car.
   2.   This car has the best features for the least money.
   ∴   I will buy this car.

A second use of arguments is to persuade—that is, to cause people to act in desired
ways. Someone may well knowingly use an illogical argument to persuade someone else
to do or believe something. This situation should be distinguished from the case where
someone sincerely tries to prove a point but unknowingly uses an illogical argument. Logically good arguments can be used in morally bad ways, and logically bad arguments can
be used in morally good ways.

A third use of argument is to prove. In a proof, the arguer already believes the conclusion but wants to establish it as being certain.

A fourth use of argument is to justify behavior—that is, to give reasons for some action
one has taken. Suppose, for instance, that Nicole has chosen to major in computer science,
and someone asks her why (that is, asks her to justify her choice). She gives this argument:

   1.   Computer scientists earn very good wages and will continue to be in great
        demand for the indefinite future.
   2.   My goal is high pay and good job security.
   ∴   I chose computer science.

This would not be the best representation for two reasons. First, there is a difference between reasons and causes. Specifically, Nicole's reasons may not be the cause of her action—perhaps she impulsively chose computer science and only later thought up good reasons for it. Second, even if she had recognized that, given her goals, computer science was the best choice for her major, she still might have chosen otherwise. * For these reasons, we will get in the habit of representing action-justifying arguments as being of this form:

1. The person involved has goals 1, 2, 3 . . . .
2. Action A would best fulfill those goals.
∴ The person ought to do A.

A fifth use of argument is to show off. We all know someone who loves to argue to show how smart he or she is. The show-off will, for example, ask you how you voted in the last election. No matter what you say, the show-off will try to argue that your choice was all wrong.

A sixth use of argument is to provoke, to cause an emotional reaction in a listener. One spouse might pick a fight with another if that spouse feels ignored or neglected.

A seventh use of arguments is to amuse. We can offer an argument as a joke or as a sarcastic device. For example:

> Why are you so mad that somebody stole your Porsche? Surely your mother taught you to share your toys with others.

The nineteenth-century logician Charles Dodgson wrote children's books under the pen name "Lewis Carroll" that are full of fallacious arguments intended as jokes. Using arguments as jokes is derivative from their use to establish belief. Part of getting the joke is seeing how the argument is illogical—that is, how it would not be genuine proof of the conclusion. This point was well put by the famous nineteenth-century logician Richard Whately (1826: 202–203):

> [I]t may not be improper to mention the just and ingenious remark that, Jests are fallacies; i.e., Fallacies so palpable as to not be likely to deceive any one, but yet bearing just the resemblance of argument which is calculated to amuse by the contrast; in the same manner that a parody does, by the contrast of its levity with the serious production which it imitates. There is indeed something laughable even in fallacies which are intended for serious conviction, when they are thoroughly exposed. There are several different kinds of joke and raillery, which will be found to correspond with the different kinds of Fallacy: the pun (to take the simplest and most obvious case) is evidently, in most instances, a mock argument founded on a palpable equivocation of the middle Term: and the rest in like manner will be found to correspond to the respective fallacies, and to be imitations of serious argument.

---

*This last claim has been disputed; some have argued that if a person truly believes that a course of action is in that person's best interest, that person will do it. This whole issue falls under the heading of "the problem of free will" and is beyond the scope of this book.

It is probable indeed that all jests, sports or games, properly so called, will be founded, on examination, to be imitative of serious transactions; as of war, or commerce. But to enter fully into this subject would be unsuitable to the present occasion.

The eighth use of argument is to force the audience to examine their beliefs. For example, the seventeenth-century philosopher René Descartes begins his book *The Meditations* by asking how he knows he is awake (as opposed to asleep somewhere and dreaming). He does this not to convince himself or his audience that he is awake, nor is he trying to amuse or show off, and he certainly isn't trying to provoke the reader to get angry! Rather, he is trying to get the reader to examine how certain we are about even the most common-sense knowledge.

In ordinary critical thinking contexts, the first four uses of argument are the predominant ones.

Exercise 4.5

Each of the following passages contains an argument. Put the argument in standard form, and state the most likely purpose for which the argument is intended: (1) to fix belief, (2) to prove, (3) to persuade, (4) to justify behavior, (5) to show off, (6) to provoke, (7) to amuse, or (8) to get people to examine their beliefs.

1. Why should you vote for the Labor Party candidate? Well, just think about the poor working man, ripped off by the blood-sucking capitalists, tortured by the slave drivers, deceived by turn-coat officials, and ridiculed by intellectual parasites! Doesn't that poor working man deserve a voice?
2. I suggest that you don't buy a Ford. Mine never runs right.
3. You say Professor Smith is criticizing the tenure system? I wouldn't pay much attention to what he says—he was denied tenure last semester. Sour grapes, you know.
4. Some dog is happy. My dog is happy. So my dog is some dog!
5. So you voted for the Liberal Party, did you, Mr. Social Justice? Well, since you have such concern for the poor, why don't you start giving away your own money? You know, just to show the rest of us what compassion is all about?
6. REPORTER: Senator Jones, did you vote for the education bill because the teachers' unions promised to financially support your reelection campaign?
    SENATOR JONES: No way! No, it was the merits of the bill which swayed me. This bill will put more teachers in the classroom, and it will pump much-needed funds into teacher training. Moreover, this bill will expand the school lunch program to cover breakfast and dinner, too!
7. Professor Richard Sutch of the Economics Department of the University of California at Berkeley vigorously defends the mass class [that is, lower-division classes with enrollments of many hundreds of students], and in the process he reveals its importance in propping up the academic culture.
    "Because it packs students into large lecture courses as freshmen and sophomores," Sutch explained, "the University saves a great deal of money which is then used to offer an amazing diversity of upper-division and graduate level courses."
    Charles J. Sykes *Prof Scam! Professors and the Demise of Higher Education*

8. I think that we can all agree that you are a complete loser. After all, you're ugly, stupid, and you have a repulsive personality.

9. I know you find it hard to believe that Susie stole the money, but consider the facts. The money was in the room when she went in, nobody else was in the room while she was there, and when she left it was gone.

10. Why did I take that coat? Everybody takes things now and then. And I was cold. Also, I'm a philosopher, so I shouldn't have to worry about petty little conventions like paying for things.

6   *Interwoven Arguments*

In this section we will refine our abilities to represent in the fairest and most accurate way the logical structure of a given passage.

We must first distinguish between single support and linked support among premises. **Single support** is the support of a conclusion by a premise taken singly, as in the arguments given here:

> Fred is rich and famous; therefore, he is rich.
> All men are mortal, so if Kim is a man he is mortal.
> The square root of 2 is an irrational number; thus, there is at least one irrational number.

In contrast, **linked support** is the support of conclusion by two or more premises that work together. Consider this example:

> All frogs are green. Kermit is a frog. Therefore, Kermit is green.

Knowing only that all frogs are green does not automatically justify the inference that Kermit is green; after all, he might be an anteater. Again, knowing only that Kermit is a frog does justify the inference that he is green; after all, frogs might all be pink. Only taken together do those premises support that conclusion.

Two points must be understood about linked support. First, any number of premises can link together to support a conclusion, as the following examples should make clear.

> All people are mortal. All mortal beings are lonely. Therefore, all people are lonely.
> All people are mortal. All mortal beings are lonely. All lonely beings are frightened. Therefore, all people are frightened.
> All people are mortal. All mortal beings are lonely. All lonely beings are frightened. All frightened beings are anxious. Therefore, all people are anxious.

Clearly, we can generalize the preceding argument to any number of premises:

> All people are P_1.
> All P_1 beings are P_2 . . . .
> All P_n beings are P.
> Therefore, all people are P.

A second point to note is that many arguments in which a premise appears to singly support the conclusion are in fact enthymemes (that is, have premises omitted). For example,

>Zaphod has two heads. Therefore, Zaphod needs two hats.

seems to be a case of one premise singly supporting a conclusion. But, in fact, that argument omits the premise "Any being with two heads needs two hats," which is not altogether obvious (can't one big hat fit over two small heads?). Telling single from enthemematic linked support is not always easy, even after considerable thought. For instance, it is hotly debated whether Descartes's famous aphorism "I think, therefore I am" is in fact an argument with one premise or an enthymeme of some sort.

We can represent single support of a conclusion by the diagram and linked support of a conclusion by the diagram (where we use capital S_x to stand for arbitrary statements)

$$\frac{S_1}{\downarrow}$$

and linked support of a conclusion by the diagram

$$\frac{S_2 + S_3}{\downarrow}$$

We will call any group of mutually linked premises (including any one single-support premise) a **premise cluster.** All of the examples so far given in this section have been simple arguments, in which one premise cluster supports one conclusion. But we often encounter interwoven arguments, in which one or more premise clusters support one or more conclusions. Many patterns of interwoven argumentation are possible; however, four patterns are especially common and deserve special attention. Those four patterns are listed in Figure 4.1.

We shall consider each of the four patterns given in Figure 4.1 in turn. Consider first *diverging arguments,* which begin at the same premise cluster but draw out different and quite often complementary conclusions. For example,

>The American dollar is very strong in comparison with the European currencies. This means that European goods here will be real bargains, but it also means that our exports abroad will be at a competitive disadvantage.

We can see that this argument fits the pattern listed earlier by numbering the statements in it and then diagramming the argument.

>1 = The American dollar is strong in comparison with the European currencies.
>2 = European goods here will be a bargain.
>3 = American goods abroad will be at a competitive disadvantage.

The diagram is accordingly

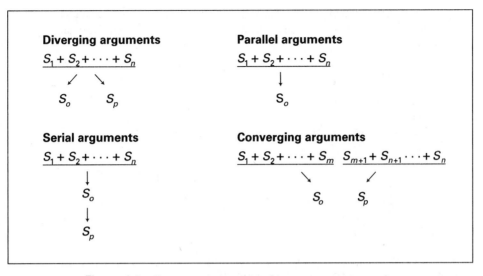

Figure 4.1   *Four common patterns of interwoven argumentation*

Sometimes arguments move alongside one another, in *parallel,* quite often to establish contrasting conclusions. A case in point is the following:

> While I'm going to bomb physics, I'm really going to do well in chemistry. My physics grades are F, D, and D–, whereas my chem grades are A, A+, and B+.

Here again, since it is easier to express in numbers than it is to express in whole sentences, we number the statements first:

1 = I'm going to do poorly in physics.
2 = I'm going to do well in chemistry.
3 = My physics grades were F, D, and D–.
4 = My chem grades were A, A+, and B+.

We then construct the diagram:

$$\frac{3}{\downarrow} \quad \frac{4}{\downarrow}$$
$$1 \qquad 2$$

The third common pattern of multiple or interwoven argumentation is *serial argumentation.* In serial argumentation, the conclusion of one argument becomes the premise cluster for another. Typically, serial arguments involve the successive unfolding of implications from some initial facts. For example,

Jazz is improvisational music. This tells us that jazz is better appreciated live than on record. But that in turn means that a true jazz lover should go out to jazz nightclubs.

Once again, we label the different statements and construct the appropriate diagram:

1 = Jazz is improvisational music.
2 = Jazz is better appreciated live than on record.
3 = Jazz lovers should go to jazz nightclubs.

$$\frac{1}{\downarrow}$$
$$\frac{2}{\downarrow}$$
$$3$$

Converging arguments involve the elaboration of two different lines of attack on the same ultimate conclusion. Again, an example will make this pattern clear:

Evidence for the existence of the Great Pumpkin comes from two quite different directions. First, there is the undeniable unanimity of the testimony of small children. When testimony is unanimous, it is very convincing. Second, fossils reveal pumpkin seeds the size of tennis shoes. The only way to account for such mammoth seeds is to postulate the existence of the Great Pumpkin.

We number the different statements and diagram:

1 = The Great Pumpkin exists.
2 = Small children are unanimous in their testimony about the Great Pumpkin.
3 = Unanimous testimony is especially convincing.
4 = Fossils reveal giant pumpkin seeds.
5 = Postulating the existence of the Great Pumpkin is the only way to explain those seeds.

$$\frac{2+3}{\searrow} \qquad \frac{4+5}{\swarrow}$$
$$1$$

These four basic patterns (divergent, parallel, serial, and convergent) of interwoven arguments can be combined in all manner of ways. Here are just a few of the many possibilities:

As we have seen a number of times before, any complex problem is easier to solve if it is broken down into simple parts. The following sequence of steps will help you diagram passages more easily.

> *Step 1:* Read through the passage, and number every different statement put in the simplest words. Eliminate redundancies, and also eliminate irrelevant or extraneous material. Try to fill in any unstated premises.
>
> *Step 2:* Go back to the passage, and focus your attention on the indicator words. Attempt a first pass at diagramming the passage.
>
> *Step 3:* Return again to the original passage, and double-check to verify that you have diagrammed the structure correctly. Remember to fill in all premises that were unstated. (Use the principle of charity.)

Let us work through several passages from Melvin Konner's (1982: 34) fine book *The Tangled Wing:*

> I would be amazed if the creature in question [that is, a direct primate ancestor of the human race of five million years ago] did not have, as part of its reproductive life, competition among males for access to females, occasionally erupting into violence; infants kept in contact with their mothers and nursed freely; and males that, after maturity, rarely attempted to mate with their own mothers. If it violated any of these generalizations, it would be the most freakish higher primate that ever lived in the Old World; so unusual, in fact, that I would not be inclined to believe that it existed.

Step 1: Number the essential statements.

> 1 = Our primate ancestors probably had competition among males for access to females.
> 2 = Our primate ancestors probably had infants in close contact with their mothers.
> 3 = Our primate ancestors probably had males that did not try to mate with their mothers.
> 4 = All Old World higher primates have competition among males for access to females.
> 5 = All Old World higher primate infants are kept in close contact with their mothers.
> 6 = All Old World higher primate males do not attempt to mate with their mothers.

Step 2: Construct a provisional diagram.

We seem to have simply three parallel arguments:

$$
\begin{array}{ccc}
\underline{4} & \underline{5} & \underline{6} \\
\downarrow & \downarrow & \downarrow \\
1 & 2 & 3
\end{array}
$$

Step 3: Recheck.

Have we not left out an unmentioned premise? It seems so: we need to add to our original list a statement to the effect that what is true of all known Old World higher primates would probably be true of any primate ancestor of ours:

> 7 = What is generally true of present Old World primates is likely to be true of any primate ancestor of ours.

We can then refine our earlier diagram:

$$\begin{array}{ccc} \dfrac{4+7}{\downarrow} & \dfrac{5+7}{\downarrow} & \dfrac{6+7}{\downarrow} \\ 1 & 2 & 3 \end{array}$$

(Note that the same premise links with each of the others.)

Exercise 4.6A

Diagram the following multiple arguments. These passages are constructed so as to have a minimum of extraneous material, but some passages contain enthymemes.

1. Surely everyone loves money. So I feel confident that Ed will respond to the money we have offered him and thus take the job.
2. People hate snitches. So it stands to reason that people hate Richard and fear him.
3. Franklin is a dog. Most dogs bark, so Franklin probably barks, so he will probably disturb the neighbors.
4. Andrea likes cheese. Thus, Andrea likes something. Thus somebody likes something.
5. Since everybody loves everybody, Sonja loves everybody. Since Sonja loves everybody, she loves John.
6. Rhonda just bought a Pomeranian, and Pomeranians bark like crazy. So Rhonda's dog will bark a lot, and since old man Crandall hates noise, he's going to hate Rhonda's dog.
7. Politicians are crooks, and Walter is a politician, so he's probably a crook. But, politicians are also sly, so he's sly. Face it—he's a sly crook.
8. Bill is a loner, and loners are distrusted. So we can expect that Bill will be distrusted. But people who are distrusted are disliked, so we can expect further that Bill will be disliked.
9. Unlike the American economy, the Japanese economy is diversified. So while the American economy can be expected to stagnate, the Japanese economy will probably move ahead.
10. People are basically greedy. So communism is bound to fail, since communism demands of people that they be unselfish. And so capitalism will win in the end.
11. Either Smythe or Tammy or the butler killed Lord Louse. Since Smythe was in Blythe, we can rule him out. And Tammy was in Miami, so she couldn't have been the killer. Since the butler hated Lord Louse, and since the other suspects (Smythe and Tammy) have been ruled out, the butler must have done it.

12. Food shortages in the Third World are increasing in frequency, and the high oil prices have taken their toll. The Third World is, therefore, in desperate economic straits; and so the Western nations must greatly increase their aid. After all, the communist nations are themselves nearly bankrupt, and hence can't afford to give away any more aid.

13. Since no third-party candidate has won the presidency in the last fifty years, it's obvious that either the Republican or the Democrat will win. But if either the Republican or Democrat win, then no third-party candidate will win in the immediate future, because when any party is in office, it tends to become entrenched.

14. The use of computers in education is to be welcomed. After all, computers are endlessly patient, they force the student to interact rather than just passively watch, and they remind students of video games. Since they are to be welcomed, we ought to be putting more computers into the schools. Also, we need to start training more teachers in computer science.

15. Since people fear crime, the number of police officers should be increased. Since any increase in government workers requires an increase in taxes, we ought to increase taxes. After all, police officers are government workers. Since we ought to increase taxes, we ought to make the tax system more fair. Let's face it, if the tax system is unfair, people will be unwilling to pay the increase.

16. Given the fact that many people will be crowding the beach this summer, we ought to open a hot dog stand there. Also, it really gets hot out there on the sand, and people get thirsty in the heat, so we should sell cold drinks. So we should open a hot dog stand that sells cold drinks.

17. Since people are basically dishonest, and since they are basically greedy, you can expect any legal system to be open to abuse. But given that, no society will ever be free from crime. Also, no society will be free from lawyers. Thus (since crimes mean criminals), every society will have lawyers and criminals.

18. Computers really do have the power of creative thought. We can conclude two things. First, computers will eventually be able to replace the really highly paid workers, such as doctors and lawyers. Moreover, we should no longer treat computers as mere inanimate objects.

19. We know that Fred was out of the country when the murder was committed. And we have just learned he passed a lie detector test. So he didn't commit the crime. That means he should be immediately released, and the police should start searching for a new suspect.

20. Dogs are pack animals, while cats aren't. So dogs are able to work together in hunting, while cats aren't. Furthermore, dogs are sociable, whereas cats aren't.

Exercise 4.6B: Challenge exercises

The following passages are from *The Starr Report: The Finding of Independent Counsel Kenneth Starr on President Clinton and the Lewinsky Affair* (Starr 1998). Each contains a multiple argument. Diagram each. (Original footnotes have been omitted.) These exercises are difficult.

1. In his civil deposition, the President stated that he had talked to Vernon Jordan only about Ms. Lewinsky's job. But as the testimony of Mr. Jordan reveals, and as the President as much as conceded in his subsequent grand jury appearance, the President did talk to Mr. Jordan about Ms. Lewinsky's involvement in the Jones case—including that she had been subpoenaed, that Mr. Jordan had helped her obtain a lawyer, and that she had signed an affidavit denying a sexual relationship with the President. Given their several communications in the weeks before the deposition, it is not credible that the President forgot the subject of their conversations during his civil deposition. His statements "seems like that's what Betty said" and "I didn't know that" were more than mere omissions, they were affirmative misstatements.

2. The President told the grand jury: "[D]id I hope [Ms. Lewinsky would] be able to get out of testifying on an affidavit? Absolutely. Did I want her to execute a false affidavit? No, I did not." The President did not explain how a full and truthful affidavit—for example, an affidavit admitting that they engaged in oral sex and that Vernon Jordan had been involved, at the President's request, in late 1997 and early 1998 in obtaining Ms. Lewinsky a job—would have helped her avoid a deposition.

3. One can draw inferences about the party's intent from circumstantial evidence. In this case, the President assisted Ms. Lewinsky in her job search in late 1997, at a time when she would have become a witness harmful to him in the Jones case were she to testify truthfully. The President did not act half-heartedly. His assistance led to the involvement of the Ambassador to the United Nations, one of the country's leading business figures (Mr. Perelman), and one of the country's leading attorneys (Vernon Jordan).

The question, therefore, is whether the President's efforts in obtaining a job for Ms. Lewinsky were to influence her testimony or simply to help an ex-intimate without concern for her testimony. Three key facts are essential in analyzing his actions: (i) the chronology of events, (ii) the fact that the President and Ms. Lewinsky both intended to lie under oath about the relationship, and (iii) the fact that it was critical for the President that Ms. Lewinsky lie under oath.

There is substantial and credible information that the President assisted Ms. Lewinsky in her job search motivated at least in part by his desire to keep her "on the team" in the Jones litigation.

4. The statements the President made to her on January 18 and again on January 20 or 21—that he was never alone with Ms. Lewinsky, that Ms. Currie could always see or hear them, and that he never touched Ms. Lewinsky—were false, but consistent with the testimony that the President provided under oath at his deposition. The President knew that the statements were false at the time he made them to Ms. Currie. The President's suggestion that he was trying to refresh his memory when talking to Ms. Currie conflicts with common sense: Ms. Currie's confirmation of false statements could not in any way remind the President of the facts. Thus, it is not plausible that he was trying to refresh his recollection.

The President's grand jury testimony reinforces that conclusion. He testified that in asking questions of Ms. Currie such as "We were never alone, right" and "Monica came on to me, and I never touched her, right," he intended a date restriction on the questions. But he did not articulate a date restriction in his conversations with Ms. Currie. Moreover, with respect to some aspects of this incident, the President was unable to devise any innocent explanation, testifying that he did not know why he had asked Ms. Currie some questions and admitting that he was "just trying to reconcile the two statements as best [he could]." On the other hand, if the most reasonable inference from the President's conduct is drawn—that he was attempting to enlist a witness to back up his false testimony from the day before—his behavior with Ms. Currie makes complete sense.

The content of the President's statements and the context in which those statements were made provide substantial and credible information that President Clinton sought improperly to influence Ms. Currie's testimony.

5. On January 21, 1998, the day the *Washington Post* first reported the Lewinsky matter, the President talked to his long-time advisor Dick Morris. With the President's approval, Mr. Morris commissioned a poll that evening. The results indicated that voters were willing to forgive the President for adultery but not for perjury or obstruction of justice. When the President telephoned him that evening, Mr. Morris explained that the President thus should not go public with a confession or explanation. According to Mr. Morris, the President replied, "well, we just have to win, then."

The next evening the President dissuaded Mr. Morris to "blast [] Monica Lewinsky 'out of the water.'" The President indicated that "there's some slight chance that she might not be cooperating with Starr and we don't want to alienate her."

The President himself spoke publicly about the matter several times in the initial days after the story broke. On January 26, the President was definitive: "I want to say one thing to the American people. I want you to listen to me. I'm going to say this again: I did not have sexual relations with that woman, Miss Lewinsky. I never told anybody to lie, not a single time. Never. These allegations are false."

The President's emphatic denial to the American people was false. And his statement was not an impromptu comment in the heat of a press conference. To the contrary, it was an intentional and calculated falsehood to deceive the Congress and the American people.

6. There also is substantial and credible information that President Clinton endeavored to obstruct justice by suggesting that Ms. Lewinsky file an affidavit to avoid her deposition, which would "lock in" her testimony under oath, and to attempt to avoid questions at his own deposition—all to impede the gathering of discoverable evidence in the *Jones v. Clinton* litigation.

During the course of their relationship, the President and Ms. Lewinsky also discussed and used cover stories to justify her presence in and around the Oval Office area. The evidence indicates—given Ms. Lewinsky's unambiguous testimony and the President's lack of memory as well as the fact that they both planned to lie under oath—that the President suggested the continued use of the cover stories even after Ms. Lewinsky was named as a potential witness in the Jones litigation. At no time did the President tell Ms. Lewinsky to abandon these stories and to tell the truth about her visits, nor did he ever indicate to her that she should tell the truth under oath about the relationship. While the President testified that he could not remember such conversations about the cover stories he had repeated the substance of the cover stories in his Jones depositions. The President's use of false cover stories in testimony under oath in his Jones deposition strongly corroborates Ms. Lewinsky's testimony that he suggested them to her on December 17 as a means of avoiding disclosure of the truth of their relationship.

Exercise 4.6C

Find and diagram five multiple arguments from newspapers, magazines, or books.

InfoTrac College Edition

You can locate InfoTrac College Edition articles about this chapter by accessing the InfoTrac College Edition Web site (www.infotrac-college.com/wadsworth/). Using the InfoTrac College Edition subject guide, enter the search terms relevant to this chapter, and then read abstracts for relevant articles.

Chapter 5

Types of Argument

---

1 *Two Types of Evidential Relations*

In the last chapter we defined the term *argument* much more narrowly than often is done. We said that an **argument** consists of a set of statements, of which one is the conclusion and the rest are the premises. We learned to identify arguments, both singly and in webs. But the main task of logic is to *evaluate* arguments—that is, to figure out which are good (and why) and which are bad (and why). How can this evaluation be done? What exactly are we looking for?

Consider this argument:

    1.   All frogs are street fighters.
    2.   All street fighters are devoted to nonviolence.
    ∴   All frogs are devoted to nonviolence.

Is this argument "good"?

In one sense it is not. From a factual point of view, this argument is ridiculous. Frogs can hardly be "street fighters," carrying knives and such. Similarly, a street fighter can hardly be considered a person devoted to nonviolence. But in another sense, the argument is good: the premises would establish the conclusion if they were in fact true.

As logicians we will be interested in the structure rather than the factual content of arguments. Given an argument, we look to see not whether the premises are in fact true, but instead whether they would, if true, support the conclusion. We want to know what sort of *evidential relation* (if any) holds between the premises and the conclusion of the given argument. **Logic** is the study not of the factual content of arguments but of the evidential relations between premises and conclusions of arguments.

But a question arises here. How many types of evidential relations are there? One? Two? Several? Infinitely many? The consensus among logicians is that there are just two types of evidential relations. Consider these two arguments:

    1.   All frogs are green.
    2.   There is a frog in my briefcase.
    ∴   The frog in my briefcase is green.

1. Almost all frogs are green.
2. There is a frog in my briefcase.
∴ The frog in my briefcase is green.

Are both these arguments "good"? Remember: the question here, again, is not whether the premises are true but rather whether those premises, if true, would support their respective conclusions.

You may have doubts about the second argument. Clearly the first argument is logically acceptable, but the second? Consider it for a moment. Granted you would not stake your life on the truth of the conclusion, even if you were convinced of the truth of the premises. Still, if you were betting money, you would choose to bet that the conclusion is true.

This distinction—between arguments whose conclusions follow absolutely from their premises and those whose conclusions follow only probabilistically from their premises—is what we mean to capture by the following two definitions. First, an argument is **deductively valid** if and only if it is impossible for all the premises to be true and the conclusion false. Second, an argument is **inductively strong** if and only if it is not impossible but it is unlikely that the conclusion would be false given that all the premises are true.

Since *logic* is the study of the evidential relations between premises and conclusions of arguments, and since there are exactly two such relations (*validity* and *strength*), it follows that there are two branches of logic: deductive logic and inductive logic. **Deductive logic** is the study (including analysis and assessment) of arguments from the point of view of validity. The deductive logician is concerned to figure out what validity is and how to detect it. **Inductive logic** is the study (again including analysis and assessment) of arguments from the point of view of inductive strength. The inductive logician is concerned with the notion of probability, what it is and how to measure it.

Of course, many if not most arguments are neither deductively valid nor inductively strong. That is, many if not most arguments are bad—the evidence in the premises does not support the conclusions absolutely or probabilistically. We earlier defined the term *fallacy* broadly as a mistake in reasoning. When we are referring to reasoning in an argument, we say that an argument is **fallacious** (that is, a **fallacy** in the narrow sense) if it is neither valid nor strong.

Several important points can be made regarding deductive validity and inductive strength. To begin with, truth and validity are different notions, although they are related. It is a mistake to say (as people often do) "so-and-so's argument is true" or "so-and-so's statement is valid."

To illustrate the point, consider these arguments:

Argument 1
1. All cats are mammals.
2. All mammals are animals.
∴ All cats are animals.

Argument 2
1. All cats are good poker players.
2. All good poker players are gamblers.
∴ All cats are gamblers.

Argument 3
1. All cats are fish.
2. All fish are huge.
∴ All cats are huge.

Argument 4
1. All cats are fish.
2. All fish are mammals.
∴ All cats are mammals.

Note that each of these four arguments is valid: Of each it is correct to say that if the premises were true, then the conclusion would have to be true also. Indeed, they all share the same structure.

1. All *A* are *B*.
2. All *B* are *C*.
∴ All *A* are *C*.

But the **truth values** (that is, whether the statements are T or F) of the statements in each vary. In the first argument, both the premises are true, and so is the conclusion. In the second argument, the first premise is false but the second is true, while the conclusion is clearly false. In the third argument, both the premises and the conclusion are false. In the fourth argument, whereas the premises are false, the conclusion is surely true.

Thus, our first point is that an argument can be valid without consisting of true statements. In that important sense, the notions of "truth" (which applies to statements, not arguments) and "validity" (which applies to arguments, not statements) are different. But they are related: by the definition of validity, every combination of truth values is possible in a valid argument except the premises being all true and the conclusion false.

Put another way, the fact that an argument is valid does not guarantee that the conclusion is true. Validity only guarantees that one will not be taken from all true premises to false conclusions. Thus, we prefer our arguments to be more than just valid: we want them to be *sound*. An argument is **sound** if and only if it is valid and in fact has true premises.

The second point is that there is no correlation between the nature of the evidential relation and the degree of generality of the statements in any given argument.

Sometimes people speak of inductive and deductive "reasoning." They mean by "inductive reasoning" something that allegedly goes on in the empirical sciences and by "deductive reasoning" something that supposedly goes on in mathematical work. They hold that inductive reasoning is reasoning from particular statements to general statements. Thus, the paradigm of inductive reasoning is generalization, as in this example:

1. Frog 1 is green.
2. Frog 2 is green.
   .
   .
   .
n. Frog *n* is green.
∴ All frogs are green.

They also hold that deductive reasoning is reasoning from general rules to particular statements. The following example is typical:

1. All frogs are green.
2. Fred is a frog.
∴ Fred is green.

In this example, the first premise, at least, is "general." Unfortunately, this neat account is wrong. For one thing, it confuses the questions about *logic* (the study of evidential relations between statements) with questions about *scientific method* (the study about how scientists should do their work). But even from the point of view of logic, the traditional account is mistaken. It is mistaken because there is no connection between the nature of the evidential relation between statements and their generality or particularity, as the examples in Table 5.1 show:

Logic studies evidential relations, and these are of two types having nothing to do with the degree of generality of the statements involved.

One last point. Notice that inductive strength is a matter of degree. The premises can make a conclusion very probable, somewhat probable, or only barely probable. Validity is an all-or-nothing relation—an argument either is or is not valid. But the premises of an argument may offer inductive evidence ranging from near zero to near certain. For example, imagine you are sitting on a jury in a case in which a guy named Jason is accused of murdering a convenience store clerk. The prosecutors present their first piece of evidence: on the night of the shooting, police were called about a shooting at the store, and when they arrived, they found Jason standing over the clerk's body, holding a smoking gun. That is *some* evidence Jason shot the clerk. Next, the prosecutors put an expert witness on the witness stand who testifies that the clerk was killed by a bullet fired from that gun and that the gun is registered to Jason. That is *more* evidence. Next, the prosecutors produce twelve customers who were in the store when the crime occurred, and on the stand these witnesses all swear under oath that they saw Jason do it. That is even more and very compelling evidence. Finally, suppose that the prosecutors show you a videotape for the store's security camera showing what sure looks like Jason shooting what sure looks like the

TABLE 5.1   Examples of Valid and Strong Arguments

Valid Arguments	Strong Arguments
Deductively valid particular to particular: 1. Fred is rich and ugly. ∴ Fred is rich.	Inductively strong particular to particular: 1. The man stood over the corpse with a bloody knife. ∴ The man may have killed the victim.

Deductively valid particular to general:
1. Lois has only two children, Sue and Mary.
    Both Sue and Mary are girls.
∴ All Lois's children are girls.
	Inductively strong particular to general:
	1. Frog 1 is green.
	    .
	    .
	    .
	n. Frog *n* is green.
	∴ All frogs are green.

Deductively valid general to particular: 1. All frogs are green. ∴ If Fred is a frog, then he is green.	Inductively strong general to particular: 1. Almost all frogs are green. ∴ If Fred is a frog, then he is green.
Deductively valid general to general: 1. All rats are rodents. 2. All rodents are animals. ∴ All rats are animals.	Inductively strong general to general: 1. Mammals and marsupials occupy similar ecological niches. ∴ There are species of each that are morphologically similar.

Figure 5.1 *The scale of evidential strength*

clerk. The evidence would now be very convincing. With each new piece of evidence, the argument gets stronger. (More precisely, each additional premise creates a new argument, inductively stronger than the one before.)

Note that the final argument, while highly inductively strong, is not valid. It is possible for all those pieces of evidence to be true while the conclusion is false. Imagine that on the night of the murder, Jason was doped and hypnotized. An actor, made up to resemble Jason exactly, actually killed the clerk (using Jason's gun). This is what is taped. Then Jason is led in to stand over the body. And the eyewitnesses were all bribed to go along with the frame-up. This scenario is, of course, ridiculously implausible, but it is conceivable. Hence, the argument is not valid. Figure 5.1 summarizes this point.

Exercise 5.1

Each of the following arguments is already in standard form, and none are enthymemes. Relying on logical intuition, determine of each whether it is valid, strong, or neither valid nor strong.

1. 1. All mice love cheese.
    ∴ All mice love crackers.
2. 1. All mice love cheese.
    2. Anything that loves cheese loves wine.
    ∴ All mice love wine.
3. 1. Almost all mice love cheese.
    2. Anything that loves cheese loves crackers.
    ∴ Almost all mice love crackers.
4. 1. If Nicole were a money-grubber, she wouldn't be dating Gary.
    2. Nicole is dating Gary.
    ∴ Nicole is not a money-grubber.
5. 1. Kelli and Nicole are sisters.
    ∴ Kelli and Nicole are nice to one another.
6. 1. If Juan were lonely, he'd call Nicole.
    2. He called Nicole.
    ∴ Juan is lonely.
7. 1. Either Kelli or Nick stole the book.
    2. Kelli didn't steal it.
    ∴ Nick stole it.
8. 1. We randomly pulled five hundred strips of paper out of the bucketful of two thousand strips of paper, and 95 percent of them were green.
    ∴ The next slip of paper will be green.

9. 1. All of the slips of paper drawn were green.
    ∴ The first was green.
10. 1. I have rolled these dice twelve times, and number 7 has come up each time.
    2. The dice are not loaded.
    ∴ The next roll will probably not come up as number 7.

2   *Deductive Argument Forms*

The number of valid deductive argument patterns is infinite. But certain patterns are commonly met. In this section we will review briefly a number of valid forms, leaving it to Chapters 9 and 10 to investigate these forms more closely.

Let us start with a group of arguments that turn on the sentence connectives *or, not, and, if-then,* and *if and only if.* In this discussion we will let capital letters represent arbitrary statements.

Disjunction

To begin with disjunction, one common valid argument is **disjunctive syllogism.** This pattern is

    1. A or B
    2. Not A
    ∴ B

Suppose, for example, that you know that either Eileen or Rachel took the car, and you discover subsequently that Eileen did not take it. It would follow that Rachel did.

Don't confound disjunctive syllogism, which is valid, with the fallacy of **affirming a disjunct:**

    1. A or B
    2. A
    ∴ Not B

where the *or* in premise 1 is the inclusive *or.* This argument is invalid, because inclusive disjunction allows that both alternatives might be true.

Conjunction

Let's turn next to a couple of arguments involving conjunction. The first is **simplification.**

    1. A and B
    ∴ A

For instance, if you know that Yoshi is both rich and popular, it follows that he is rich. Another such form is **conjunction:**

1. *A*
2. *B*

∴ *A* and *B*

If Yoshi is rich, and you also discover he is happy, then you can infer that he is both rich and happy.

Conditionals

Recall that in Chapter 4 we noted that the most important compound is the conditional: if *A,* then *B.* Quite a few basic, common argument forms involve the conditional. A very central such form is **modus ponens,** or **affirming the antecedent:**

1. If *A,* then *B.*
2. *A*

∴ *B*

For example, suppose it is true that if I win the lottery, I will buy a Porsche. Suppose I subsequently win the lottery. You can conclude that I will buy a Porsche.

Don't confound modus ponens, which is valid, with the fallacy of **affirming the consequent:**

1. If *A,* then *B.*
2. *B*

∴ *A*

Although at first glance they look alike, affirming the consequent is invalid. Consider an example: Suppose you know that if Luis were rich, he would own at least one suit. Suppose you discover that he does in fact own at least one suit. Can you conclude he's rich? Not at all—even people who are not rich can buy suits!

Another valid argument form involving conditionals is **hypothetical syllogism:**

1. If *A,* then *B.*
2. If *B,* then *C.*

∴ If *A,* then *C.*

Suppose that if Hillary lies, she'll appear dishonest, and that if she appears dishonest, people will distrust her. Doesn't it follow that if Hillary lies people will distrust her?

A third valid argument form involving the conditional is **modus tollens,** or **denying the consequent:**

1. If *A,* then *B.*
2. *B* is not true.

∴ *A* is not true.

Suppose you know that if I were alive, I would have a pulse. Suppose you find out that I don't have a pulse. You can deduce that I am not alive.

Again, don't confound modus tollens, which is valid, with the fallacy of **denying the antecedent:**

1.　If *A*, then *B*.
2.　*A* is not true.
∴　*B* is not true.

To see that denying the antecedent is invalid, consider the following case. It is certainly true that if you sit on an exploding hydrogen bomb, you will die. But now suppose you do not sit on an exploding hydrogen bomb or stand anywhere near it. Does it follow that you will *not* die? Hardly. All people die of something, though not necessarily from hydrogen bombs!

Biconditionals

Finally, we might look at a couple of valid argument forms involving the biconditional:

1.　*A* if and only if *B*.
∴　*A* and *B* are both true or false.

1.　*A* if and only if *B*.
∴　If *A*, then *B*; and if *B*, then *A*.

Both these forms merely express the notion of biconditionals.

Class Arguments

Let us turn now to a second group of arguments, class arguments. *Class arguments* are those whose validity turns on statements about classes or groups of things. For example, the statement

Fred is dead.

can be restated as the class statement

Fred is a member of the class of dead things.

Similarly, the statement

Some people like cheese.

can be restated as

Some members of the class of people are members of the class of cheese lovers.

Using class statements, we can state any number of valid class argument forms. For example, there are valid one-premise arguments (called *immediate inferences*), such as

1.　1.　All *X* are *Y*.
　　　∴　No *X* are not *Y*.
2.　1.　Some *X* are *Y*.
　　　∴　Not all *X* are not *Y*.

3. 1. No *X* are *Y.*
    ∴ All *X* are not *Y.*

We can also state valid two-premise arguments, such as

4. 1. All *X* are *Y.*
    2. All *Y* are *Z.*
    ∴ All *X* are *Z.*
5. 1. Some *X* are *Y.*
    2. All *Y* are *Z.*
    ∴ Some *X* are *Z.*
6. 1. All *X* are *Y.*
    2. No *Y* are *Z.*
    ∴ No *X* are *Z.*

We will examine class logic in detail in Chapter 10.

Exercise 5.2A

Identify each of the following arguments as disjunctive syllogisms (DS), simplification (Simp), conjunction (Conj), modus ponens (MP), hypothetical syllogism (HS), or modus tollens (MT).

1. If Sue is happy, so is Al. Sue is happy. So Al must be.
2. Either Sherri or Monique stole the enchiladas. But Sherrie didn't do it, so it must have been Monique.
3. Fred is sneaky and vile. So he's sneaky.
4. If America neglects its educational system, it will cease to be a great power. If America ceases to be a great power, its enemies will destroy it. So if America neglects its educational system, its enemies will destroy it.
5. Lori is a liar. She's also a thief. So she's a liar and a thief.
6. If Sam liked Fords, he'd own one. But he doesn't own a Ford, so he must not like them.
7. Either both Sue and Maria will go to the dance, or both Maureen and Eileen will. But since not both Sue and Maria are going, both Maureen and Eileen will go.
8. If both America and Japan get into a trade war, the world will face economic ruin. If the world faces economic ruin, real war will inevitably occur. So, if both America and Japan get into a trade war, real war will follow.
9. John's going to college, so is Myra. So they're both going.
10. If John and Sue are involved, there is evil brewing. So evil *is* brewing, because they're involved.

Exercise 5.2B

For each of the following class arguments, identify which of the six valid class argument forms discussed earlier (the three one-premise arguments, and the three two-premise arguments) it illustrates.

1. No people are friendly, so all people are unfriendly.
2. Some people like cheese; thus, not all people are cheese haters.
3. Every dog is evil, so no dogs are not evil.
4. All cats have fur, so it follows that no cats lack fur.
5. All cats are mammals, and all mammals are animals, so all cats are animals.
6. No mammals are animals, yet all dogs are mammals. Therefore, no dogs are animals.
7. All men are criminals, and some criminals are men, so some criminals must be evil.
8. All cats must be nice. After all, all cats are mammals, and all mammals are nice.
9. Some men are pigs, so some men must be ugly, since all pigs are ugly.
10. No cats must be nice, for no animals are nice, and all cats are animals.

3   *Inductive Argument Forms*

Let us review now a few of the most common inductively strong argument forms. Since inductive reasoning is the most common reasoning in areas other than mathematics and mathematical science, we would do well to focus on induction. This section is merely an introductory survey; Chapters 11 through 15 explore these patterns in greater detail.

To begin with, there is **inductive generalization:**

> 1. x percent of observed A's are B.
> ∴ x percent of all A's are B.

Here, x is any number between 1 and 100. For example,

> 1. 98 percent of observed frogs are green.
> ∴   98 percent of all frogs are green.

To introduce terminology that will be useful later, the cases we observe are called the **sample,** and the whole group is called the **population.** Such reasoning must be qualified or subject to restrictions to be strong, and we will explore them more in Chapter 12.

If inductive generalization is reasoning from sample to population, inductive instantiation is reasoning from population to sample. **Inductive instantiation** has the following form:

> 1. x percent of A's are B.
> ∴   This/these A is B.

where x is between 51 and 99. For instance,

> 1. 90 percent of college students like pizza.
> ∴   Susie, a college student, probably likes pizza.

Notice that if $x = 100$, we no longer have inductive instantiation but deductive (specifically, universal) instantiation:

1. 100 percent (that is, all) college students like pizza.
∴ Susie (a college student) likes pizza.

Notice also that if x is less than 51 percent, the inference is no longer inductively strong: if only 28 percent of college students like pizza, then (absent other knowledge) it is not even probable Susie likes pizza.

A third common inductive argument is analogy. An *analogical argument* involves inferring something about your present situation by comparing it to similar situations in the past. Specifically, an **argument from analogy** has the form

1. A is like $B_1, B_2, \ldots, B_n$.
2. $B_1, B_2, \ldots, B_n$ all have property P.
∴ A has P.

For example, suppose I am shopping for a new car, and I am looking at a Toyota on a car lot. If I owned several Toyotas in the past similar to this one (same models, same condition when purchased, same engine size, and so forth) and they all lasted past a hundred thousand miles, then I might reasonably infer that this one will too. Again, certain restrictions must be placed on this reasoning if it is to be strong. We will explore restrictions in detail in Chapter 13.

If inductive generalization is reasoning from sample to population and inductive instantiation is reasoning from population to sample, we can view analogy as reasoning from sample to sample. We can view analogy as a kind of hybrid of inductive generalizations and inductive instantiation. On the basis of what we've observed in the past, we generalize to a group as a whole. Then, we apply this general statement—we instantiate—to the case in front of us. In an argument form:

1. Most A's I've observed have been B.
∴ Most A's are B. [inductive generalization]
∴ This A will be B. [inductive instantiation]

We have framed the three central forms of inductive inference in terms of general and particular statements. Inductive generalization we viewed as moving from particular to general, inductive instantiation as moving from general to particular, and analogy as moving from particular to particular. This, however, is not entirely accurate. We can have arguments of all three sorts that involve only general statements. For example, the argument

1. Pigs love cheese.
2. Dogs love cheese.
3. Cats love cheese.
∴ Most mammals love cheese.

is clearly an inductive generalization, even though the statements in it are all general. Again, the argument

1. Most mammalian species have fun.
∴ Probably, cats have fun.

is clearly an inductive instantiation, even though the statements in it are all general. Finally, the argument

1. Cats like cheese.
2. Cats are like dogs.
∴ Probably dogs like cheese.

is clearly an argument from analogy, even though the statements in it are all general.

So, we need to refine our analysis a bit. Reconsider the following argument:

1. Pigs love cheese.
2. Dogs love cheese.
3. Cats love cheese.
∴ Most mammals love cheese.

While it consists of general statements, the premises are less general in that they refer to subgroups of the more general group referred to in the conclusion. Let us call the more general group the **population** and either the individual who is a member of the population, or the group that is a subgroup of that population, the **sample.** Being more careful, then, we can say that inductive generalization is reasoning from sample to population, inductive instantiation is reasoning from population to sample, while analogy is reasoning from sample to sample.

Another form of inductive argument is **testimony,** which is accepting a conclusion on the basis of what people report observing. As an argument form:

1. People (*A, B, C, . . .*) report observing that *p* is true.
∴ *p* is probably true.

Once again, we must restrict such reasoning greatly if it is to be inductively strong. We talk about observation and testimony in Chapter 11.

Another important type of inductive argumentation is *causal inference,* or reasoning about cause and effect. There are a number of causal argument forms, which we will discuss in Chapter 14.

One last form of inductive argument should be mentioned here. Suppose a parent of a four-year-old child hears a noise in the kitchen. The parent rushes over and sees the following: The kid is red-faced, standing in front of a cookie jar lying in pieces on the floor. A stepladder is in front of the refrigerator, on top of which the cookie jar formerly rested. Now, what would explain the situation? The parent might think that space aliens landed in the kitchen and went for the cookies. But a simpler explanation suggests itself: The kid went for the cookies. Besides explaining the observed facts, the explanation is also consistent with the known behavior of small kids. The parent is reasoning in a fashion called **inference to the best explanation,** or the "IBE" for short:

1. Certain facts $F_1, \ldots, F_n$ are known to be true.
2. The best explanation for $F_1, \ldots, F_n$ is E.
∴ E is probably true.

As with the other forms of inductive reasoning we have examined, the IBE must be restricted and qualified for it to be strong. This we discuss in Chapter 15.

Exercise 5.3

Identify the following arguments as inductive generalizations, inductive instantiations, arguments from analogy, or inferences to the best explanations.

1. Most people like movies. After all, I do.
2. Tigers are like cats. Tigers are hunters. So cats probably are.
3. The milk is spilt, and there are cookie crumbs all over the place. My best guess is that our daughter got into the refrigerator last night.
4. Most people are basically friendly. So this guy will be friendly, even though I just hit his car.
5. Seventy-two percent of the people surveyed in our sample favored going to war. So most people favor war.
6. People are like dogs. Dogs are greedy. So probably people are.
7. This bacteria culture dish shows mold in one corner, and the bacteria colonies around that mold are dead. The best explanation for that is that the mold gives off a bacteria-killing substance.
8. Ninety-eight percent of all men like football. So probably my neighbor Mr. Smith will like today's football game.
9. Most cats eat meat. Most dogs eat meat. Most people eat meat. So most mammals eat meat.
10. Almost all dogs fear bears. So probably my dog Mandy is afraid of bears.

InfoTrac College Edition

You can locate InfoTrac College Edition articles about this chapter by accessing the InfoTrac College Edition Web site (www.infotrac-college.com/wadsworth/). Using the InfoTrac College Edition subject guide, enter the search terms relevant to this chapter, and then read abstracts for relevant articles.

Part Two

Chapter 6

The Goals of Critical Thinking: Clarity, Relevance, Consistency, Justification, and Explanatory Power

Pitfalls of Language

---

1 Pitfalls of Language

In this chapter we discuss a number of features of language and the fallacies that can arise from them. Since fallacies can result from the misuse of language, the critical thinker must pay attention to the words used in any argument and the manner in which they are used.

The features of language we will discuss are verbosity and jargon, vagueness, loaded language, overstatement and understatement, ambiguity, synonymy, and figurative language. (In the next chapter we will discuss tools for combating problems of language.) The point I want to emphasize is that these features of language are *not* inherently bad—in fact, these features are generally useful. They facilitate learning and forceful communication. But what is by nature good can be used in bad ways, as we shall see.

2 Verbosity and Jargon

A very important skill in critical thinking is the ability to state propositions clearly—that is, to express them by clear and simple declarative sentences. The first two obstacles to this are verbosity and jargon.

We say that a sentence is **verbose** if it is needlessly wordy. For example, the thought expressed by the long sentence

> Buttressed by ample potable spirits that cost a king's ransom, the delectable comestibles served constituted an ineffably delightful repast.

is more simply put by

> The food was excellent and served with a lot of fine wine.

Jargon is technical terminology or vocabulary. Technical terminology can be very useful, because it allows technical thoughts to be expressed accurately and succinctly. But jargon can also serve to obscure thought, because people often put a lot of needlessly technical terms in their sentences to make the thoughts expressed appear more profound or more worthy of credence. In the prior example, words such as *comestible* (which simply means "food") and *repast* (simply "meal") make the description of the dinner look very learned. Another example (from Wheeler 1983: 1):

> A number of studies have indicated that the psychic and economic returns available in an occupation, the psychic and economic costs required to prepare for an occupation, and the labor market conditions affecting the availability of jobs in an occupation are considered by individuals making occupational choices.

This long sentence simply says that when a person chooses a job, he or she considers the various costs and benefits of the jobs available, along with the chances of getting them. This is hardly a surprising claim!

Or consider this stunning insight:

> Speakers generate utterances to satisfy cognitive, affective, or aesthetic urges, selecting specific lexical combinations from a personal lexicon determined by the context of the interaction.[*]

The amazing discovery here is that people speak to inform or move other people, and they choose their words appropriately!

The eminent philosopher Sir Karl Popper (1994: 70–71) has commented on the growing trend to jargon-laden writing in the academic world:

> Many years ago I used to warn my students against the widespread idea that one goes to college in order to learn how to talk and write "impressively" and incomprehensibly. At the time many students came to college with this ridiculous aim in mind, especially in Germany. And most of those students who, during their university studies, enter into an intellectual climate that accepts this kind of valuation—coming, perhaps, under the influence of teachers who in their turn had been reared in a similar climate—are lost. They unconsciously learn and accept that highly obscure and difficult language is the intellectual value *par excellence*. There is little hope that they will even understand that they are mistaken, or that they will ever realize that there are other standards and values—values such as truth, the search for truth, the approximation to truth through the critical elimination of error, and clarity. Nor will they find out that the standard of 'impressive' obscurity actually clashes with the standards of truth and rational criticism. For these latter values depend on clarity. One cannot tell truth from falsity, one cannot tell good ideas from trite ones, and one cannot evaluate ideas critically—unless they are presented with sufficient clarity. But to those brought up in the implicit admiration of brilliance and "impressive" opaqueness, all this (and all I have said here) would be *at best,* "impressive" talk: they do not know any other values.
>
> Thus arose the cult of incomprehensibility, of "impressive" and high-sounding language. This was intensified by the (for laymen) impenetrable and impressive

---

[*]From "Analyzing Utterances as the Observational Unit," *Human Communication Research* (Winter 1985).

formalism of mathematics. I suggest that in some of the more ambitious social sciences and philosophies . . . , the traditional game, which has largely become the unconscious and unquestioned standard, is to state the utmost trivialities in high-sounding language.

Many books on writing explain how to simplify your prose. Two I like are *On Writing Well,* by William Zinsser (1980), and *The Art of Plain Talk,* by Rudolf Flesch (1946).

Exercise 6.2

For each of the following sentences, reexpress the statement made by using a shorter declarative sentence. Try not to lose any important information in rephrasing, and assume that each sentence is meant sincerely, not employed as sarcasm or irony.

1. Members of an avian species of identical plumage congregate.
2. It is fruitless to become lachrymose over precipitately departed lacteal fluid.
3. It is fruitless to attempt to indoctrinate a superannuated canine with innovative maneuvers.
4. A plethora of individuals with experience in culinary techniques vitiates the potable concoction produced by steeping certain comestibles.
5. In answer to your question, sir, I don't believe that we can say very precisely or even with normal precision whether or not the man died before midnight.
6. The overriding interest of the KGB, the primary mission it has, is to ensure that every Russian man, woman and child, at home and abroad, complies with the desires of the ruling Soviet oligarchy.
7. While I certainly support your right to express critical remarks regarding my artistic ability, I find that I must respectfully disagree.
8. It is surely of tremendous benefit to the state that each person should enjoy liberty, perfectly unlimited, of expressing his or her (or—in this age of artificial intelligence—its) own sentiments on any issue of concern.
9. [From an insurance form.] In consideration of the acceptance of this note by the Company as an extension of credit to the Insured, the Insured hereby agrees that all installment payments must be received by the Company at its office as above designated on or before the due dates as above specified and any payment transmitted by mail or paid to an agent of the Company, or transmitted or paid in any other matter, shall constitute payment according to the terms of the note only if, as and when actually received by the Company at its said office within the time specified.
10. During the past fifteen years, an increasing amount of evidence has accumulated indicating that parents play an important role in stimulating the acquisition of intellectual skills in their children. . . . Environmental stimulation of intellectual development by parents may be particularly important in the preschool years when children are acquiring basic intellectual competencies that can assist in the mastery of academic tasks in school. . . .

    John R. Bergan, Albert J. Neumann II, and Cheryl L. Kapp, "Effects of Parent Training on Parent Instruction and Child Learning of Intellectual Skills," *Journal of School Psychology* 21 (1983): 31–39

11.   These results reveal that the lonelier an adolescent, the more likely he or she was to be anxious, depressed, show an external locus of control, have high levels of public self consciousness and social anxiety, and exhibit low levels of happiness and life-satisfaction. In addition, loneliness was associated with a reluctance to take social risks.

> "Loneliness at Adolescence," *Journal of Youth and Adolescents* 12, no. 2 (1983)

12.   Extensive empirical research findings indicate that children exhibit more observed stress behaviors during participation in less developmentally appropriate learning activities than did children participating in more developmentally appropriate activities.

13.   Ah, make the most of what we yet may spend,
      Before we too into the Dust descend;
      Dust into Dust, and under Dust, to lie,
      Sans Wine, sans Song, sans Singer and—sans End!

> *The Rubaiyat of Omar Khayam*

14.   A plausible research orientation of those who wish to study the meaning of social phenomena is to conduct investigations amongst individuals who are directly experiencing such phenomena. Yet a difficulty, or limitation, of this approach is that personal descriptions of experience are obviously confined to the order of things of which individuals are readily aware. Taken-for-granted, or "latent" meanings cannot be easily expressed because they are locked into patterns of feeling and behavior in an unquestioned, tacit form.

> Stephen Fineman, "Work Meanings, Non-Work, and the Taken-for-Granted," *Journal of Management Studies* 2 (1983)

3   *Vagueness*

A word is **vague** if it lacks a precise meaning—that is, if its application has blurred boundaries. Consider the notion of being rich. It's clear that having an income of $5,000,000 a year qualifies you as rich; it's also clear that having an income of $5,000 a year does not qualify you as rich. But, so the cliché goes, where do you draw the line? Does $50,000 a year make you rich? Most adjectives that deal with matters of degree ("rich," "happy," "ugly") allow borderline cases. The test of vagueness for an adjective is whether you can ask, "How x?" "Rich" is vague because we can always ask, "How rich?" Yet, as the philosopher Ludwig Wittgenstein (1889–1951) pointed out, even common nouns can be open to borderline problems. His example was the word *game*. Poker, chess, and tennis are clearly games. But how about Russian roulette? Bullfighting? Dog racing?

We should distinguish vagueness from three other features of language with which it can be confused. A word or phrase is **unspecific** if its reference is unstated. For example, the sentence "Some women are U.S. citizens" does not specify which women are being talked about. A word or phrase is **ambiguous** if it has more than one meaning. For example, in the sentence "Fred went to court," we can mean that Fred went to a courtroom (say, if he is defendant in a trial), or we can mean (in a less common meaning of *court*) that Fred went to woo some lady.

Finally, a word or phrase is **referentially unclear** (also called *referentially opaque*) if the reader/listener cannot determine to whom the word or phrase applies. For example, in the sentence "That guy is a jerk!" (uttered in a room full of men), it would be unclear to whom the speaker was referring (unless the speaker gestured to the man referred to). We will discuss ambiguity and referential opacity later in this chapter. For now, it is enough for you to see the difference between vagueness and those other concepts.

Consider "Bob Josephsonski, Social Security number 569-74-5555, standing right in the northwest corner of this room, is tall." There is nothing unspecific about that sentence, or ambiguous, or referentially unclear. But the word *tall* is certainly vague.

Many, if not most, words are vague to some degree. As Williamson (1994: 2) puts it, "The limits of vagueness are themselves vague." But this need not be so frightening. Vagueness allows language to grow in the face of new conditions. The very vagueness of the word *rich,* for example, enables it to continue to be meaningful in times of inflation (where the real value of currency diminishes at a rapid rate).

However, when a key term in an argument is so vague that its application cannot be figured out by the participants, when vagueness impedes a discussion, the participants have to resort to defining terms more precisely. For instance, a discussion about whether "the rich" are paying their fair share of taxes will likely be a waste of time unless the participants get a precise idea of what income level is to be counted as being "rich."

As we shall see with ambiguity as well, a word can *be* vague without being *used* vaguely. The same feature (vagueness, ambiguity) can help or hinder a dialogue depending on use and context.

Consider an example. *A* argues in favor of allowing political refugees to be granted citizenship without having to wait the normal period of time. *B* replies, "Look, where are you going to draw the line? After all, anybody trying to leave his country can be considered a political refugee, since bad economic conditions are the result of inept government. But we don't have room for all the poor people of this world!" What *B* has done is exploit the vagueness of the phrase "political refugee" to change the issue. We say that *B* is committing the "slippery slope" fallacy—a fallacy we will discuss further in Chapter 8.

The best reply *A* could make would be to point out to *B* that even though there are borderline cases, that does not mean there are not extremely clear nonborderline cases. Clearly, a person who has opposed a government and is fleeing from that government is a political refugee, while somebody who is looking for a better job is not a political refugee. Whether such economic refugees should be granted asylum is irrelevant to *A*'s point. Borderline cases may exist (such as small business owners leaving a country just taken over by Marxists), but that does not make *A*'s claim so hopelessly vague that *B* cannot address it.

Exercise 6.3

1. Explain how the following words are vague.
   a. intelligent
   b. wealthy
   c. happy
   d. strong
   e. large
2. Find a vague word or phrase from a newspaper or magazine article. Cut out the article, and turn it in with an explanation of whether the vagueness interferes with the communication.
3. Devise three excessively vague sentences. Explain in what way they are vague.

4 *Loaded Language*

A word or phrase is **loaded** if it has theoretical and/or emotional connotations. A word can be loaded in the sense of being theoretically loaded or emotionally loaded or both. As examples, consider the words *bourgeois* and *proletarian*. Both are loaded with Marxist economic theory (which posits those economic classes) and emotion (*proletarian* being laden with positive and *bourgeois* with negative emotional connotation). Of course, terms can be theoretically loaded without being emotionally loaded (*electron, ionic bond*) or emotionally loaded without being theoretically loaded (*dirty rat, punk*).

It is again worth emphasizing that loading is an extremely pervasive feature of language. Very likely, most words are loaded with overtones. That, per se, is not bad. It is how the loaded word is used that makes it good or bad. If a theoretically loaded term is used in a situation in which the theory at hand is not under question, that is okay. If an emotionally loaded term is used in a context (a conversation, say) in which expressing emotion is the central purpose, that is fine. But if the language is loaded to persuade without proving, that can be bad. Such a situation (in which loaded language is used to slant evidence) is often called **biased description.**

The nature of biased description is best conveyed by Bertrand Russell's "conjugation of an irregular verb": "I am firm, you are stubborn, he is a pig-headed fool." The same trait (holding fast to one's beliefs) is described favorably or unfavorably by using loaded terms. Biased description is the stock in trade of the "yellow journalist" and the propagandist. For instance, an incident (a riot by some of the workers at a factory) might be described this way by a leftist journalist:

> Yesterday, the oppressed proletarians at Smith Clock Works rose up in indignation. The fascistic agents of the capitalists battled the heroic workers for hours.

Yet the same incident could be described this way by a rightist:

> Yesterday, union goons and shiftless malcontents tried to destroy private property at the Smith Clock Works. Brave public guardians tried for hours to restore law and order.

All we can safely conclude from reading such slanted accounts is that some violence occurred yesterday at Smith Clock Works. A more neutral description might be as follows:

> A riot occurred yesterday at Smith Clock Works, apparently caused by labor discontent. The police fought the rioters for several hours.

Biased description may be impossible to avoid completely. Loading is, like vagueness, a matter of degree. But differences in degree can amount to differences of kind that are important. Clearly, the following sort of description (given by a writer trying to argue that the National Science Foundation should not have funded a certain project) is so biased, so loaded, that the argument is worthless.

> Now our government's really gone loco with your tax dollars—blowing $6,710 to study how religion influences life in a small Spanish town! The nitwit-run National Science Foundation (NSF) has awarded money to a U.S. university student who plans to go to the province of Huelva in Spain for his incredibly useless study.

The student got the grant after convincing NSF's bozos that it's important to examine the influence of religion on the politics and economics of Huelva. An NSF official insists the project is a "well-thought-out proposal which will help us understand meaning and power in complex societies." But its meaning for U.S. taxpayers is already clear—they're getting shafted for more bucks, declares Rep. Bill Chappell (D-Fla.). "I doubt whether the NSF should be spending $6,710 on such a personal academic project," he said.

When a person uses language highly loaded with overtones that he has no right to employ in the discussion at hand, we say he or she is committing the **fallacy of loaded language.**

Loaded language has been shown to influence memory and testimony. For example, in an experiment discussed by the psychologist Elizabeth Loftus (1996: 77–78), subjects viewed a film of a traffic accident. Some of them were asked, "About how fast were the cars going when they smashed into each other?" The others were asked, "About how fast were the cars going when they hit each other?" The group asked the question with the loaded term *smashed* estimated the speeds higher than the other group. A week later, the group asked the question with the loaded term tended to recall seeing shattered glass at the accident more often than the other group. In fact, no shattered glass was at the scene, but of course there likely would be if the cars had been traveling at high speeds. It seems clear that the choice of the word influenced memories and testimony.

Two points bear repeating. First, vagueness and loading are matters of degree, but it does not follow that the amount of degree is unimportant. For example, the difference between wealth and poverty is one of degree, but few would hold it to be unimportant. Second, something can be vague or loaded without being used to commit a fallacy. For example, in a context where the theory is not under question, theoretically loaded descriptions may well be appropriate.

Exercise 6.4A

1. Think up three "conjugations of irregular verbs" similar to Russell's.
2. In the following passage, substitute for the emotion-laden terms words with the same literal meaning that do not have emotional overtones.

Ah, make the most of
what we yet may spend,
Before we too into the
Dust descend;
Dust into Dust, and
under Dust, to lie,
Sans Wine, sans Song,
sans Singer and—sans End!

   The Rubaiyat of Omar Khayam

Exercise 6.4B

Each of the following passages contains loaded language. Indicate the words that are loaded.

1. Fuzz-brained bureaucrats are actually spending $32,744 of your hard-earned tax money on safari for a study of child rearing in Africa.

   The ridiculous grant was awarded to a researcher from New England University by the National Institute of Mental Health. Here's the gobbledy-gook explanation of the study's aim, as it was listed on the grant request: "The theoretical treatise on the cultural context of child development will serve as a force for the decentralization of current psychological approaches to development as well as an investigation of anthropological and psychological theories."

2. Savage cuts—The federal appropriation for public broadcasting has already been drastically cut for the fiscal years 1982 through 1985, and now further savage cuts are proposed for this period. This is compounded by the targeting of cuts in the funds for agencies that traditionally support public broadcasting programming.

   It would seem that a concerted effort is under way to deprive the American people of anything that remotely resembles cultural intelligence.

   People who think that the public deserves more than the insulting rubbish put out by the commercial networks should notify their congressional representatives of the fact. The alternative is all wasteland.

3. Science is attacked these days from both the left and the right. The disputes described here represent a reaction from a highly conservative population; but interest in local control, increased participation, objection to the dominance of scientific values and the role of expertise will be familiar to people located anywhere along the spectrum of political ideologies. The textbook disputes provide a means of exploring the relationships between science and its public, and of examining how the growing criticism of science can bear on public policy.

   Dorothy Melkin, *The Creation Controversy*

4. As Americans, we don't worry much about terror. Not the way people do in the Middle East or Northern Ireland, where it has been an instrument of government policy for decades. In the United States, we have seen relatively little organized violence for political ends. But terror is not really about violence. It's about fear, and the climate of intimidation, repression and chaos such fear creates.

   In the eighties, America has given birth to a new form of terror, a campaign of fear and intimidation aimed at the hearts of millions. It is in two great American arenas—religion and politics—that this new terror has raised its head. In the past few years, a small group of preachers and political strategists have begun to use religion and all that Americans hold sacred to seize power across a broad spectrum of our lives. They are exploiting this cherished and protected institution—our love of country—in a concerted effort to transform our culture into one altogether different from the one we have known. It is an adventurous thrust: with cross and flag to pierce the heart of Americans without bloodshed. And it is already well under way.

   Flo Conway, and Jim Siegelman, *Holy Terror*

5. This is nuts! Your tax dollars help foreigners compete with U.S. farmers!

   While American peanut farmers are battling to survive a crop surplus and low prices, lunatic bureaucrats are squandering nearly $10 million of your tax money to help foreigners compete with them.

Peanut-brains at the Federal Agency for International Development (AID) are shelling out $9.85 million in an insane scheme to aid peanut growers in Senegal, Trinidad, Cameroon, Nigeria, Sudan, Thailand, and the Philippines.

6. We have concluded from studying lonely people that some of these reactions are much more helpful than others. Solitary television viewing—the most common diversion—seems to be almost as destructive as solitary drinking or pill taking, for example. Other, more active forms of solitude, such as reading and letter or journal writing, contribute to personal strength, self-awareness, and creativity. Establishing intimate ties with others is even more helpful. Since loneliness reflects a need for intimacy, friendship, or community, remedies that don't include these provisions won't work.

   Carin Rubenstein and Phillip Shaver, *In Search of Intimacy*

7. I have just been visually assaulted for a second time today by Channel 11.

   The latest of these insults, aired in the name of the Humane Society, showed, in slow motion, parts of certain rodeo events where bovine creatures were wrestled to the ground by their horns, or were thrown by means of a lasso. Both scenes focused on the twisting of the animals' necks in these events. The PSA then went on to bluntly question the "humanity" of the people partaking in the rodeo.

   This position, when taken to its logical end, calls for the elimination of the "beastly" humans (and conversely, the worship of the "divine" cows).

   Are we in India? Should we all become Hindus?

   Perhaps the Humane Society should also condemn any dog owner—as every dog born will strain any chain beyond belief. And all who eat chicken must surely be savages, having wrung their necks as the cowboys do to the poor "divine" cows.

   Personally, I am appalled at this blatant attempt to denigrate America and the sport that was derived from the success of her pioneers in their battle to subdue the wilderness.

8. I was asked by the Medical Committee for Human Rights, to speak on sex. All right, I really will.

   The oppression of women by men is the source of all the corrupt values throughout the world. Between men and women, we brag about domination, surrender, inequality, conquest, trickery, exploitation. Men have robbed women of their lives.

   A human being is not born from the womb; it must create itself. It must be free, self-generative. A human being must feel that it can grow in a world where injustice, inequity, hatred, sadism are not directed at it. No person can grow into a life within these conditions; it is enough of a miracle to survive as a functioning organism.

   Now let's talk about function. Women have been murdered by their so-called function of childbearing exactly as the black people were murdered by their function of color. The truth is that childbearing isn't the function of women. The function of childbearing is the function of men oppressing women.

   It is the function of men to oppress. It is the function of men to exploit. It is the function of men to lie, and to betray, and to humiliate, to crush, to ignore, and the final insult: It is the function of men to tell women that man's iniquities are woman's function!

I'm telling it to you as straight as I can. Marriage and the family are as corrupt institutions as slavery ever was. They must be abolished as slavery was. By definition they necessarily oppress and exploit their subject groups. If women were free, free to grow as people, free to be self-creative, free to go where they like, free to be where they like, free to choose their lives, there would be no such institutions as marriage or family. If slaves had had those freedoms, there wouldn't have been slavery.

Ti-Grace Atkinson, *Amazon Odyssey*

9.   When definitions are attempted of such concepts as Freedom or Duty, they usually consist of other abstract terms that need defining. The more careful and elaborate the definition, the harder it is for the arguing parties to remember and observe it. In the end, human agreement depends on good speech ways, that is, on controlling one's language by visualizing—and not switching—the same concrete embodiments of the concepts being tossed about in discussion.

For it is easy to think and talk without the image of anything at all present to the mind; words—the bare familiar sounds ending in *-tion* or *-ity* or *-ness*—will keep thought moving and make the thinker feel rational though he literally does not know what he is talking about. If the user of concepts—which is to say everybody—habitually fails to think of persons, things, events as they happen in the world of particulars, steady abstraction will land him in sheer nonsense or dangerous folly. For abstractions form a ladder which takes the climber into the clouds where diagnostic differences disappear.

Jacques Barzun, *A Stroll with William James*

10.   Feather-brained bureaucrats are wasting a staggering $130,000 of your hard-earned tax money to study the mating habits of song sparrows.

The outrageous $130,000 grant by the National Science Foundation was awarded to a researcher at a New York university.

He'll tiptoe through field and forest spending your money to explore "influences of a mate and territory on the fine temporal adjustment of reproductive functions in the sparrow."

Rep. Ron Paul (R-Tex.) charges, "It's incredible that our fine-feathered friends at the NSF would find this unbelievable way to squander our hard-earned tax money.

"It's unthinkable to spend $130,000 to find whether the presence of a mate, territory, nest sites, nesting materials and sufficient supply of food for feeding young affects the mating of the song sparrow.

"With many taxpayers worrying how to provide food to feed their young, wasting $130,000 of their money is not birdseed."

11.   "You are dictatorial." My dear sirs, just as you say. That is just what we are. All the experiences for the Chinese people, effect a people's democratic dictatorship. This means that the reactionaries must be deprived of the right to voice their opinions; only the people have that right.

Who are the people? At the present stage in China, they are the working class, the peasantry, the petty bourgeoisie, and the national bourgeoisie.

Under the leadership of the working class and the Communist Party these classes unite to create their own state and elect their own government so as to enforce their dictatorship over the henchmen of imperialism—the landlord class and bureaucratic capitalist class, as well as the reactionary clique of the Kuomintang, which represents these classes, and their accomplices. The people's government will suppress such individuals. It will only tolerate them if they prove tractable in speech or action. If they are intractable, they will be instantly curbed and punished. Within the ranks of the people, the democratic system is carried out by giving freedom of speech, assembly, and association. The right to vote is given only to the people, not to the reactionaries.

These two aspects, democracy for the people and dictatorship for the reactionaries, when combined, constitute the people's democratic dictatorship.

Mao Zedong, *On People's Democratic Dictatorship*

12. Individuals form classes according to the similarity of their interests, they form syndicates according to differentiated economic activities within these interests; but they form first, and above all, the State, which is not to be thought of numerically as the sum-total of individuals forming the majority of a nation. And consequently, Fascism is opposed to Democracy, which equates the nation to the majority; nevertheless it is the purest form of democracy if the nation is conceived, as it should be, qualitatively and not quantitatively, as the most powerful idea (most powerful because most moral, most coherent, most true) which acts within the nation as the conscience and the will of a few, even of One, which ideal tends to become active within the conscience and the will of all—that is to say, of all those who rightly constitute a nation by reason of nature, history or race, and have set out upon the same line of development and spiritual formation as one conscience and one sole will. Not a race, nor a geographically determined region, but as a community historically perpetuating itself, a multitude unified by a single idea, which is the will to existence and to power; consciousness of itself, personality.

This higher personality is truly the nation in so far as it is the State. It is not the nation that generates the State, as according to the old naturalistic concept which served as the basis of the political theories of the national States of the nineteenth century. Rather the nation is created by the State, which gives to the people, conscious of its own moral unity, a will and therefore an effective existence. The right of a nation to independence derives not from a literary and ideal consciousness of its own being, still less from a more or less unconscious and inert acceptance of a *de facto* situation, but from an active consciousness, from a political will in action and ready to demonstrate its own rights: that is to say, from a state already coming into being. The State, in fact, as the universal ethical will, is the creator of right.

Benito Mussolini, *The Doctrine of Fascism*

13. The bourgeoisie, wherever it has got the upper hand, has put an end to all feudal patriarchal, idyllic relations. It has pitilessly torn asunder the motley feudal ties that bound man to his "natural superiors," and has left no other bond between man and man than naked self-interest, than callous "cash payment." It has drowned the most heavenly ecstasies of religious fervor, of chivalrous enthusiasm, of philistine sentimentalism, in the icy water of egotistical calculation. It has resolved personal worth into exchange value, and in place of the numberless indefeasible chartered freedoms, has set up that single, unconscionable freedom—Free Trade. In one word, for exploitation, veiled by shameless, direct, brutal exploitation

The bourgeoisie has stripped of its halo every occupation hitherto honored and looked up to with reverent awe. It has converted the physician, the lawyer, the priest, the poet, the man of science, into its paid wage-laborers.

The bourgeoisie has torn away from the family its sentimental veil, and has reduced the family relation to a mere money relation.

Karl Marx and Friedrich Engels, *The Communist Manifesto*

5   *Understatement and Overstatement*

Understatement

To **understate** a claim is to use words that diminish the content or force of the claim. (The rhetorical term for understatement is **meiosis** or **litotes.**) For example, the claim "No pigs can fly" may be understated as "Almost no pigs can fly." We need to clarify first the ways claims can be understated and then the uses to which understatement is put.

One of the most common ways to understate a claim is to insert a detensifier. A **detensifier** is an adverb of degree used to tone down (that is, to diminish the power of) a predicate. The predicate in a sentence is the word or words that express what is affirmed or denied of the subject. For example, the word *nearly* is a common detensifier, and accordingly it can be used to understate claims:

1a. I am exhausted.	1b. I am nearly exhausted.
2a. He is finished.	2b. He is nearly finished.

English is rich in detensifiers, the most common of which are listed in Figure 6.1. (Detensifiers are often derogatorily called "weasel words," since, as we shall see, they are often used to weasel out of a rhetorical corner into which one has painted himself.)

Detensification is only one method of understatement. Qualification is another. Consider the following sequence of claims:

1. I will tell the truth.
2. I will tell you the truth.
3. I will tell you the truth about this matter.
4. I will tell you the truth about this matter today.

Notice that the claims get weaker: claim 1 commits the speaker only to telling the truth *to the listener;* claim 3 commits the speaker only to telling the truth to the listener *about the area under discussion;* claim 4 further qualifies the promise to apply only to *the day of the discussion.* A **qualifier** is a phrase that limits the application of the predicate.

So far we have been dealing with *unmodalized assertions*—that is, statements that do not contain modalities. A **modality** is a word that expresses the degree of confidence the speaker has in a given claim. The following modal words indicate that no doubts are had about the claim: *be sure, surely; be obvious, obviously; be evident, evidently; be certain, certainly; be clear, clearly; must, has to.* The following modal words indicate confidence but some doubt: *think, suppose, believe, probably, presumably, supposedly, should.* The

sort of (coll.)	pretty much
rather	in many/some/most respects
relatively	slightly
kind of (coll.)	somewhat
typically	a fair amount
more or less	a little
quite	partially
enough	mainly
to some extent	in part
moderately	mildly
a bit	scarcely
barely	almost
technically	virtually
basically	nearly/very nearly
essentially	practically

Figure 6.1   *Common English detensifiers*

following modal words indicate less confidence, more doubt: *guess, conjecture; seem; can, could; may, maybe, might; possibly; perhaps; conceivably.*

Modalized assertions are open to a fourth understatement—namely, where the modality is weakened, as in these examples:

1a.   I am sure that he is a thief.
1b.   I believe that he is a thief.
1c.   I suspect that he is a thief.

2a.   It is obviously a plane.
2b.   It is presumably a plane.
2c.   It is conceivably a plane.

3a.   The rabbit must have gone down this hole.
3b.   The rabbit probably went down this hole.
3c.   The rabbit might have gone down this hole.

As a special case of such assertions, unmodalized statements can be understated by adding modalities, typically parenthetically, as in the following examples:

1a.   The president is honest.
1b.   The president is, I believe, honest.

2a.   Pigs cannot dance.
2b.   Pigs, to the best of my knowledge, cannot dance.

The point is that when a speaker asserts a statement without a modality (for example, "Pigs cannot dance"), the listener assumes that the speaker has no particular doubts about the statement being made. To add a modality parenthetically is a way to signal doubt; hence, to understate.

These three devices for understatement (the use of detensifiers, the use of qualifiers, and the substitution of a weaker for stronger modality, including the addition of a modality) are not mutually exclusive. They can be used together, as in these cases:

1a. The president is honest.
1b. The president is probably honest about this matter.

2a. Hitler was evil.
2b. In my opinion, Hitler was not good.

3a. Fred is dead.
3b. Fred, I suspect, may be rather dead.

(In 1b, we inserted a detensifier and a qualifier. In 2b, we inserted a modality. In 3b, we used a parenthetical and a detensifier.)

Understatement has many uses. Quite often we understate to make a joke.

> *Scene:* Michelle and Tracy are watching Zach, a three-year-old boy, trying to pour milk. Zach spills the milk all over the kitchen.
> MICHELLE: Zach is not exactly the most coordinated kid I have ever seen.

> *Scene:* Two police officers watch a thoroughly inebriated man grope his way out of a bar.
> FIRST OFFICER: I could be wrong, but I really do suspect that that man may not be entirely sober.

People understate for other reasons as well. Sometimes we wish to be courteous—for example, "I'm not sure you are entirely correct in what you say" is a very polite way of calling somebody wrong. Sometimes we understate to avoid an argument. Another use of understatement is **innuendo.** An innuendo is a negative suggestion made by disguised or veiled comments about someone. For example, if someone said to you, "Oh, how nice! I see that you're sober today!" you would rightly be angry with them, because while what they say is narrowly true, it suggests that you are drunk or stoned a good deal of the time. Again, imagine that someone picked up a framed picture of your loved one and said, "Oh! Nice picture frame!" The insulting innuendo here is that while the picture frame is pretty, your loved one isn't! Innuendo often takes the form of (as the cliché goes) "damning with faint praise."

But we can commit a fallacy by understatement. **Hedging** is the fallacy committed when an arguer changes his claim by understating it during the course of an argument. Typically, the fallacy of hedging occurs when one participant tries to weaken his or her claim (so it is easier to defend) without the other participant noticing. For example,

> A: Why do you say that the poor don't need assistance?

> B: It just seems to me pretty clear that a lot of them could hold jobs if they really wanted to.

Overstatement

The converse of understatement is overstatement. To **overstate** a claim is to use words that increase the content or force of the claim. (The rhetorical term for overstatement is

absolutely	totally
positively	without exception
always	exactly
in all respects	precisely

Figure 6.2   *Common English intensifiers*

hyperbole.) For example, the claim "Most people are friendly" can be overstated as "All people are friendly." As with understatement, overstatement can occur in three basic ways.

First, a claim can be overstated by leaving out a detensifier. For example, the claim

I was somewhat disappointed with her performance.

would be overstated if we left out the detensifier:

I was disappointed with her performance.

Similar to omitting a detensifier is inserting an intensifier. Some intensifiers are given in Figure 6.2. Thus, the claim

I was disappointed with her performance.

would be intensified by adding an intensifier:

I was totally disappointed by her performance.

and the claim

Human beings are two-legged animals.

can be overstated by adding an intensifier:

Human beings are without exception two-legged animals.

A second way claims can be overstated is by omitting a qualifier. For instance, the statement

She was good at writing of this sort.

would be intensified if we left off the qualifier "of this sort."

Third, we can overstate a claim by substituting a stronger modality for a weaker one. For example:

Fred is probably wealthy.

would be overstated by saying

Fred is certainly wealthy.

These three methods of overstatement (dropping detensifiers/adding intensifiers, dropping qualifiers, and substituting a stronger for a weaker modality) can occur together. For example:

I believe that most people are trustworthy.
Overstated: I am certain that all people are trustworthy.

As with understatement, overstatement has many uses. But what is most important for us now is to see how it can be used to commit fallacies. In particular, a person in a dialogue may distort the other person's point of view by overstating it, so as to make it easier to attack. As we will see in Chapter 8, this sort of move is called "setting up a strawman," and is a way of ignoring the issue. In fact, strawman is the converse of hedging. In strawman, an arguer tries to overstate the opponent's position to make it harder for the opponent to defend. In hedging, an arguer tries to understate his or her own position so as to make it easier to defend.

Exercise 6.5A

Understate each of the following claims.

1. Dogs certainly bark.
2. I am positive that pizza tastes good.
3. Certainly, cats can climb trees.
4. Clearly, not everyone can dance.
5. People obviously go where the work is.
6. Clearly, Darwin devised modern evolutionary theory.
7. Beavers surely are smart animals.
8. Clearly, education is useful.
9. I am sure that photographs can lie.
10. It is a fact that people hate the truth.

Exercise 6.5B

Overstate each of the following claims.

1. I think dogs usually bark from time to time.
2. I suspect that pizza probably tastes good to many people.
3. Probably, some kinds of cats can climb trees.
4. It is likely that a few patriots are not really good people.
5. It is plausible to suggest that some animals can be less than friendly by nature.

6   *Ambiguity*

Another pervasive feature of language is ambiguity. A word or phrase is **ambiguous** (or *equivocal*) if and only if it has more then one meaning. For example, the word *code* is ambiguous: it means both a "system of laws" and "a system of symbols used to transmit messages."

There are two basic sorts of ambiguity: lexical and grammatical. **Lexical ambiguity** is ambiguity arising from multiple meanings assigned to a word in a sentence. **Grammatical ambiguity** is ambiguity resulting from the bad grammatical structure of a sentence. Let's discuss these in turn.

Lexical ambiguity of a phrase or sentence arises from the ambiguity of one or more words in it. Many, perhaps most, words are ambiguous. This is necessary because of the sheer size of the vocabulary of any natural language. To take the example of English, Jonathan Green (1996: 15) points out:

> The English language has been estimated at four million words, a figure based on adding together the largest current corpus to a variety of marginal vocabularies— slang, jargon, dialect—plus various neologisms yet to enter the dictionary and similar fringe terminology. But how accurate is this?
>
> There are, for instance, more than six million registered chemical compounds, and research throws up new additions every day. Medical terms, perhaps 200,000, would bulk the list even further. America's largest unabridged dictionary, *Webster's Third New International,* which takes its starting point as 1755 holds c. 450,000 words; the second edition of the *OED* [*Oxford English Dictionary*] . . . runs to approximately 475,000.

As it is, no English speaker has a command of more than a fraction of the vocabulary. If we had to have a separate word for every meaning, the vocabulary would become even more unwieldy.

The ambiguity of words is of two kinds. Words have connotational meaning and referential meaning, or (more commonly), sense and reference. The **sense** of a word is the concepts we define it to express; the **reference** of a word is the object or thing it talks about. For example, the phrase

> The president of the U.S.A. in June 1994

connotes a person who is president of the United States during the month indicated, but, in fact, it *refers to* (picks out, denotes) Bill Clinton. And just as words can have multiple senses, they can have multiple referents as well. The phrase

> the bald man

can refer to any number of men. We call such a phrase **referentially unclear.** Quite often, referential unclarity occurs because of the use of a pronoun. For example, in

> Sam told Irv that his sister was smart.

we don't know whether *his* refers to Sam or Irv.

So much for lexical ambiguity. Grammatical ambiguity we said is ambiguity arising from bad grammatical construction. A sentence that is ambiguous due to bad grammatical construction we call **amphibolous,** or an **amphiboly.** For instance,

> The tuna are biting off Washington Coast.

This can mean that off the coast of Washington the tuna are biting (fishermen's baited hooks) or that the fish are biting the coastline. Additional examples:

> I was thrown from my car as it left the road. I was later found in a ditch by some
>   stray cows.
> In my attempt to kill a fly, I drove into a telephone pole.

Note that any sentence containing an ambiguous word can have double meanings. But what makes a sentence an amphiboly is that the double meanings arise either because the object of the key term is not clear or because there is some other grammatical problem. If a sentence is an amphiboly, on either reading, the meaning of the individual words doesn't change. In the earlier example, under the two readings the word *biting* has the same meaning. What is unclear is what it is the tuna are biting. On the other hand, the sentence

> Police discover crack in Australia.

although ambiguous is not an amphiboly, because in the two obvious readings, *crack* means either crack cocaine or a physical crack in the landscape.

The most amusing amphibolies occur when unwary editors let poorly worded headlines slip by. Here are a few actual examples:

> Death Prompts Coach to Quit
> Paramedics Help Dog Bite Victim
> Firefighters Threaten to Sue If Killed on Job
> Cause of AIDS Found—Scientists
> Buildings Sway from San Francisco to LA

The comedian Jay Leno (1992) has published a book with similar examples.

Despite its pervasiveness, ambiguity is not normally a problem, because the context in which an ambiguous sentence is written or uttered usually indicates the intended meaning. For instance, the sentence

> Let's cut the turkey.

is ambiguous because it employs an ambiguous word, *turkey,* which can mean a type of bird eaten at Thanksgiving or a fool. If that sentence is uttered at the table at Thanksgiving dinner, it would be obvious to the listeners that the speaker intended the first meaning. If uttered by a gang member to the rest of his gang (in the presence of a member of a rival gang, the "turkey"), the second meaning would be intended. Yet another meaning would be intended if the sentence were uttered by a baseball manager in a clubhouse meeting. Again, the sentence employing the referentially unclear term *this—*

> This is a great car.

—would normally be uttered in the presence of a car, and so the listener would know to what car the speaker was referring. (But if the speaker and listener were standing between two cars, the reference would be unclear.)

Thus, ambiguity is like vagueness and loading in that it is a common feature of words that is not usually troublesome. A word can *be* ambiguous but not *used* ambiguously.

However, sometimes fallacies can arise from ambiguity. We will consider four fallacies of ambiguity: equivocation, accent, composition, and division.

Equivocation

Let's begin with equivocation. **Equivocation** has two forms. First, it occurs when a person uses an ambiguous word, phrase, or sentence one way in one premise of his argument, and a different way in another premise or the conclusion. We say that person is "equivocating."* Equivocation is invalid because it is possible for the premises to be true while the conclusion is false.

As an example of equivocation, consider this case. A person once came to my door representing a religion that believes in sending its members door-to-door in search of converts. One of his arguments was that while his religion was completely poor, the Catholic Church was wealthy. (He used this claim to support another claim to the effect that members of his faith were more devout.) His argument went as follows:

1. The Catholic church owns many churches.
2. Religion *X* does not own any churches.
3. Owning churches makes a religion wealthy.
∴ Religion *X* is less wealthy than the Catholic church.

Whatever other defects his argument had, it certainly involved equivocation, because upon questioning, it turned out that religion *X* does own property, but they do not call their houses of worship "churches." The point is that the word *church* is ambiguous. It can mean "mainstream Christian house of worship," and in *that* sense non-Christians such as Buddhists, Jews, and Moslems don't go to church. Or it can mean simply "any house of worship," in which case non-Christians *do* go to church although they may call it other things (for example, temple, synagogue, or mosque).

The second form of equivocation occurs when someone deliberately uses an ambiguous sentence to mislead the reader or listener. I can think of two common situations in which this occurs.

First, some unscrupulous newspapers will put amphibolous headlines above trivial, uninteresting stories that make those stories seem more interesting. All this, of course, is to trick the reader into buying the paper!

MY HUSBAND USED TO PUSH ME IN A BABY CARRRIAGE

In this example, one buys the paper, expecting to read a disgusting story about some new kind of sexual perversion, but the story merely says that when she was a baby, her husband—then seven years old—had to push her baby carriage.

NUN WALKS HUNDREDS OF MILES TO LOSE WEIGHT

This story merely says that this nun walks a few blocks every day, which adds up over the years to hundreds of miles.

BAD HABIT KILLS TEEN

The story with this headline goes on to explain that a teenage smoker hung himself after being sent to a correctional youth center where smoking is banned.

A second area in which one encounters intentionally misleading amphibolies is in fortune-telling and prognostication. Fortune-tellers will often try to use sentences that can be

---

*The term *equivocate* has another common meaning. A person equivocates in this second sense when he or she refuses to take a stand on an issue.

interpreted a number of ways so their predictions will always come true. For example, King Croesus is alleged to have asked an oracle whether he (the king) should attack a neighboring king, Cyrus. The oracle replied, "When Croesus shall o'er Halys River go, he will a mighty kingdom overthrow." Croesus decided to attack and was defeated. When he later expressed some disappointment with the oracle's powers, the oracle pointed out that the prediction did come true—for in going to war against Cyrus, Croesus had destroyed his own kingdom! Another more contemporary example is astrological forecasts. Michael Friedlander (1995: 91) makes this point in his entertaining book *At the Fringes of Science:*

> Predictions are usually phrased in such vague terms that there is great elasticity in interpreting a horoscope, something for everyone to identify with. Commercial astrologers seem to have been generally unwilling to undertake research and produce systematic measures of their effectiveness—or have not done so to the satisfaction of scientists. Skeptics, curious bystanders, and a number of astronomers have, however, investigated the astrological claims. Without exception, when critically examined, astrology has struck out, its predictions at best no more accurate than random guesses. Where successes have been claimed, there is sufficient flexibility in the forecasts that firm believers can always find a way of wriggling out of the corner. Michel Gauquelin, a French psychologist who became intrigued by astrology, carried out some simple tests with fascinating results.
>
> Responding to an advertisement by a commercial astrologer, he submitted birth data for ten notorious criminals without identifying them as such. The resulting horoscopes were benign, giving no glimpse of the true character of those murderers. He then himself advertised that he would supply free horoscopes. To the many people who sent in requests, he provided copies of the horoscope of a murderer. Most of Gauquelin's respondents claimed to see their own personalities described in the horoscope. There have been other tests of this sort, and the results show how prone we are to self-deception. Again, Gauquelin undertook perhaps the most extensive statistical examination of horoscopes. Puzzled by the survival of astrology over so many hundreds of years if it truly had no content, no predictive power, he analyzed the horoscopes of many thousands of people. He could find no relationship between their lives and the positions of the planets in the various astrological signs or houses at the times of their birth.

Accent

The fallacy of accent, like the fallacy of equivocation, involves change of meaning. But whereas in equivocation the word or phrase is already ambiguous as it stands, the fallacy of **accent** is the fallacy of changing the meaning of an unambiguous sentence, either by (orally or typographically) stressing part of it or else by omitting words. As examples of the first, consider Figure 6.3.

The second way to commit the fallacy of accent is by omitting words. This is usually signaled by three periods, called *ellipses*. Thus, an advertiser might change this sentence from a government report

> Very few tests have been done on the additive ABBA, but those that have been done indicate that while there is no great risk in its use, there is some hazard.

XYZ Corporation
P.O. Box 1234
Jones, Texas 56789

October 11, 2001

This check is valid only toward the purchase of
one set of stainless steel cookware.

Dollars	Cts
** 200	00

VOID AFTER November 11, 2001

REGISTERED $200 and 00 cts

Pay
to the
order of

GARY JASON
678 ELM ST.
SAN DIEGO, CA

George Smith

Figure 6.3(a)

METRO BANK

No. 02345

2/25/01

REQUEST CERTIFICATE

Fill in any amount from $4,000 to $20,000

AMOUNT

Gary Jason
P.O. Box 789.
Generic, CA

VOID AFTER May 15, 2001
OXL 72

Please complete the form attached to this
voucher and mail in the enclosed prepaid
envelope.

James Rick
Authorized Signature

Figure 6.3(b)

to

> . . . tests have been done on the additive ABBA . . . [that] indicate . . . that there is
> no great risk in its use . . . .

which changes the meaning of the original into something more favorable to ABBA.

Composition and Division

The next two fallacies of ambiguity are composition and division. These are converses of
each other, and each comes in two varieties. We begin with **composition.** The first form of
this fallacy is arguing that what is true of the parts of a thing must be true of the whole. It

Figure 6.3(c)

is clearly ridiculous to argue that since each part of a grandfather clock is light, the whole clock must be light. Equally illogical would be to argue that since Fred can run the half-mile in two minutes, he can run a mile in four minutes.

The second form of the fallacy of composition can be defined only after we introduce some technical terms. By **general term** we mean a word that refers to a group of things—people, nails, slugs, chairs. Any general term is inherently ambiguous, in that it can refer to the group as a collective whole, or it can refer to the members of the group as individuals. The **collective use** of a general term is the use of it to refer to the group as a whole; the **distributive use** of a general term is the use of that term to talk about the members of the group as individuals.

This ambiguity is brought out by the old school riddle: Why do white sheep eat more than black ones? Because there are more of them! The point of the riddle is that as individuals all sheep eat about the same, but (since most sheep are white) white sheep collectively eat more.

We can now define the second form of composition. It is the fallacy of using a general term distributively in the premises and collectively in the conclusion. For example,

1. All people die at some time.
∴ There will come a time when all people are dead.

1. Assistant professors earn less than full professors.
∴ Assistant professors take up a smaller percentage of the college budget than do full professors.

There are similarly two forms of **division.** The first form is the fallacy of arguing that what is true of the whole must be true of the parts. It would be silly to conclude that a dorm room must be large because the whole dorm is or that a given division of a corporation must be doing well since the corporation as a whole is.

The second form of the fallacy of division involves using a general term collectively in the premises and distributively in the conclusion. For example,

> Prostitutes have been practicing their profession since biblical times. How can they keep going so long? [They have been practicing their profession since biblical times *collectively,* not as individuals.]
>
> Philosophy professors average $50,000 per year; so if I become a philosophy professor, I will earn that much.
>
> Panda bears are nearly extinct, so this panda must be nearly dead. [Note that *average* and *extinct* indicate that a collective whole is being referred to.]

Exercise 6.6A

The following words are ambiguous. Give the different meanings of each.

1. dumb	6. punch
2. loaf	7. kick
3. sound	8. sick
4. carp	9. unctuous
5. dough	10. action

Exercise 6.6B

The following sentences are ambiguous. For each one, (1) give the two possible readings, and (2) determine whether the ambiguity is lexical (due to ambiguity of the meanings of words) or grammatical (due to amphibolous structure).

1. The ladies of the church have cast off garments of every kind, and they can be seen in the church basement as of Friday afternoon.
2. I had been driving my car for forty years when I fell asleep at the wheel and had an accident.
3. I was on my way to the doctor's office with rear-end trouble when my universal joint gave way, causing me to have an accident.
4. The ship was christened by Mrs. Clinton. The lines of her bottom were admired by the enthusiastic crowd.
5. Under the New Deal, many men got jobs, and women also.
6. MOTORIST WOUNDED BY SNIPER ON FREEWAY
7. He chased the woman in his car.

8.   She likes shopping more than her husband.
9.   Germans drink millions of gallons of beer every year.
10. Suzie plays the piano by ear.

Exercise 6.6C

The following passages contain fallacies of ambiguities. Identify and explain each.

1.   *Headline:* FORGET THE SMALL CAR MYTH—BIG CARS SAVE MORE GAS
     Story: Americans are getting far better gas mileage these days—not because
     they're driving smaller cars but because almost all cars are more fuel-efficient, says
     a government economist. American-made automobiles—no matter what their size—
     are built to get more miles to the gallon. In fact, the overall fuel economy of all new
     cars has risen by more than 75 percent since 1973, said Dr. Philip Patterson of the
     Department of Energy.

2.

> Main Sweepstakes Center
> 188 S. Bogus Dr., Bovine, CA 99999
>
> October 9, 2001
>
> This CREDIT VOUCHER is valid only toward the
> purchase of merchandise offered by Main Sweepstakes
> Center with an advertised price of over $250.00. This
> offer is subjectto the terms of the enclosed order form.
>
> ONLY ONE CERTIFICATE PER ITEM
>
> **VOID AFTER**   October 20, 2001   Dollars/Cts
>
> *THE SUM 200 Dols 00 Cts*   200.00
>
> To the order of   Mr. GARY JASON
>
> DEPT. OF PHILOSOPHY
> WASHBURN UNIV   Series A31   No. 3039 18
> TOPEKA, KANSAS 66621

3.   (This passage is taken from Lewis Carroll's children's book, *Alice in Wonderland.*)
     "Who did you pass on the road?" the King went on, holding his hand out to the
     messenger for some hay.
          "Nobody," said the messenger.
          "Quite right," said the King; "this young lady saw him too. So of course Nobody
     walks slower than you."
4.   The way I figure it is this. If the ingredients are harmless, the whole mixture is
     harmless also.
5.   *Headline:* REDS GO TO WAR
     Story: Candy addicts are seeing red. Manufacturers took the red M&M's
     off the market in 1976 in the midst of a red-dye cancer scare. Now the 35-member
     Society for the Restoration and Preservation of Red M&M's wants them back.
     Founder, Paul Hethmon, 19, of Knoxville, Tennessee, said the society is
     petitioning President Reagan and the M&M–Mars company to get their
     favorite snack back.

6. FRED: My gosh, Sue, you look scared!
   SUE: I am. I just looked at the life insurance tables, and my life expectancy is only ten years. I don't want to die that soon.

7. Each person's happiness is a good to that person, and the general happiness, therefore, a good to everybody.

8.

ARKE'S USED CARS
** BONUS CHECK **

NO. 4891

March 16, 2001

Pay___*The Sum 512 Dols 00 Cts*___   **DOLLARS**___$512.00___

Pay to the order of   Mr. GARY JASON
240 W Palizada
San Clemente CA 92672

** This is a coupon to be used only for the purchase of a car.

9. Should we not assume that just as the eye, the hand, the foot, and in general each part of the body clearly has its own proper function, so man, too, has some function over and above the function of his parts?

10. It is predicted that the cost-of-living index will rise again next month. Consequently you can expect to pay more for butter and eggs next month.

11. (*Note:* The following should be taken as humorously as it was intended.)
    AUSTIN, Texas (UPI)—His rhetoric is indisputable and his record is spotless. Face it, Nobody's perfect.

    The Nobody for President campaign charmed a crowd of 500 at the University of Texas Monday, offering an alternative to the somebodies on the presidential ballot.

    Working for the crowd for Nobody in particular was a character called Wavy Gravy, Hugh Romney of the Hog Farm commune in the San Francisco Bay area. Gravy is Nobody's chief aid, a position he calls Nobody's Fool.

    "Who was president before George Washington?" Gravy, dressed in a clown suit, asked the crowd.

    "Nobody!" responded the crowd.

    "Who honored the treaties with the Indians?"

    "Nobody?"

    "Who do you want to run your life?"

    "Nobody!"

    The address was so stirring—it was obvious Nobody cares—that one man stepped forward and said, "I've never voted for anybody, but this year I'm going to vote for Nobody."

Curtis Spangler, Nobody's campaign manager, went onto explain Nobody knows how to dispose of nuclear waste, Nobody has brought peace, Nobody fed the hungry and the destitute, and Nobody keeps all his campaign promises.

In fact, Spangler argues, Nobody actually won in 1976, although Jimmy Carter was permitted to take office. Spangler says only 40 percent of eligible Americans voted, leaving 60 percent voting for Nobody.

12. If the parts of the universe are not accidental, how can the whole universe be considered as the result of chance?

Therefore, the existence of the universe is not due to chance.

13.

FREE ALCOHOL

24-hr. Counseling Line

3-minute recorded message
explains how to help
someone drinking too
much alcohol.

14. He must be a bad doctor, because he is certainly a bad person.

15.

THIS BOTTLE OF BEER COST $50 MILLION

Why have we spent $50 million to develop Pal's Old Time Lager?

Because we've always believed in making every effort to produce the best tasting bottle of beer. So we took a long, hard look at how a beer is made.

Most beers are heat-pasteurized. And that can affect a beers's taste.

But Pal's Old Time Lager isn't heat-pasteurized. It's cold filtered.

We spent a lot of time and effort to develop the cold-filtered process.

It's an exclusive method that doesn't alter the rich, smooth, pure taste of beer.

Cold-filtered Pal's Old Time Lager. What our $50 million buys you is a beer that's as real as it gets.

16. All phenomena in the universe are saturated with moral values. And, therefore, we can come to assert that the universe for the Chinese is a moral universe.

Thome H. Fang, *The Chinese View of Life*

17.

Free Mystery Water

Enshrined in Its Own Crystalline Reliquary

Mystery Water
Box 1511 San Clemente, CA 92672

Please send me the Mystery Water encased in its Crystalline Reliquary. Even though this miracle keepsake can bring me countless thousands of dollars of good luck in lotteries and bingo alone, it's mine absolutely Free. I'm not obligated to buy a thing now or ever, and I will not be askedfor any donation.

Although there is no charge for Mystery Water, we must ask that you enclose five dollars ($5)to cover the cost of postage and handling.

18. Uncommon events happen every day. But whatever happens every day is common. Therefore, uncommon events are common events.

19. David Morehouse became the first UCLA undergraduate president to be recalled Wednesday when election results revealed that 73.9 percent of 3,827 students voted to remove him from office.

20. Those who love honey can follow the advice of Thelma McElhinney of Moberly, Missouri, who will receive $5.00 for her ingenuity.

    She stretches a 40-ounce jar of honey by mixing it with a pint of light corn syrup—which is less expensive than honey.

21. Every human group is born, grows, declines, and dies, as it must if it is an aggregation of individual living beings.

22. If you can't lick them, join them.

23. Show me a good loser and I'll show you a loser.

7 *Synonomy*

Synonyms are words with identical or nearly identical meanings. Just as a dictionary lists the various meanings of words, a thesaurus lists synonyms. One particular type of synonym can create problems with the clear expression of ideas: euphemism. A **euphemism** is a phrase that is a gentler or more appealing way of expressing a concept. For example, "passed away" is a softer term for dying than to say "died" or (even worse) "croaked." Euphemisms are, if you will, phrases with positive connotations. I give you a few more examples in Table 6.1.

For a good (and amusing) survey of euphemisms and the ways people devise euphemisms, I highly recommend *The Wordsworth Book of Euphemisms,* by Judith Neaman and Carole Silver (1995). Neaman and Silver list two main motives for using euphemisms: fear (for example, we talk about "The big C" instead of mentioning the dread disease cancer) and the

TABLE 6.1 Euphemisms and Their Equivalents

Euphemism	More Blunt Phrase
Made love to	Had sexual intercourse with
Was deferential toward	Sucked up to
Ethnic cleansing	Genocide
Rocky mountain oyster	Bull testicle
Bosom	Breast
Expropriate	Steal
Liberate (often)	Steal
Perspiration	Sweat

desire to avoid offending others (such as when we talk about "special people" when we mean the mentally retarded) (13–14).

Euphemism has its role to play: softening language to avoid hurt feelings. But when it is used to disguise the truth or avoid having to justify questionable policies or positions, it impedes critical thinking. For example, the Pentagon called the invasion of Grenada a "pre-dawn vertical insertion," which blurred the reality of what was happening.

Exercise 6.7

The following words are euphemisms. Give less flattering terms.

1. Substance abuser
2. Chronically unemployed person who is unmotivated
3. Financially insolvent
4. Sexual deviant
5. Ethically challenged

8   *Figurative Language*

The last pitfall of language we want to consider is figurative language. A **figure of speech** (or **trope**) is a word or words used in a nonliteral way to increase the emotional or rhetorical effect of the sentence. **Figurative language** is just language utilizing figures of speech. While ancient rhetoricians defined about 250 figures of speech, we will examine only a few.

One figure of speech is *hypostatization,* or *reification.* Suppose you said to a friend, "Suzie has really lost her looks." And suppose your friend replied, "Yes, she has. Perhaps we had better help her look for them!" You would conclude that your friend is either joking or stupid. Suzie can lose her keys, her car, her watch, and it would make sense for her to search for them. But if she lost her temper, composure, or looks, it would not make sense for her to search for them. One's temper or looks are not concrete objects but, rather, abstractions. These abstractions are not separable from an underlying object or objects. You can't separate a person's temper, looks, or build from him or her. When a person treats an abstraction as if it were a concrete object, we say he or she has committed the fallacy of **hypostatization** (from the Greek word *hypostatos,* which means "having an existence in a substance only") or **reification** (that is, making an abstraction into a real object).

Now, it might seem that hypostatization is only the basis for silly puns, as when Lewis Carroll (in *Alice in Wonderland*) describes a Cheshire cat as disappearing except for its smile. Or it might seem that it is only the basis for grandiose philosophizing, as when someone talks about the nature of Beauty and Truth, as if they were objects to be located and described. But there is an ominous use of hypostatization. Some thinkers have talked about the State, the Aryan Race, and the Proletariat as if these were real entities whose interests are separate from and superior to the interests of actual human beings, with disastrous political consequences. For example, a political theorist might argue that since the State is greater than the particular citizens of a given time, the interests of the State should be represented by a Great Leader rather than elected representatives. Such a course of thought often leads to fascism.

Somewhat similar to hypostatization is personification. To hypostatize is to treat an abstraction as if it were a concrete object. To **personify** is to treat a nonhuman object as if it were human. To talk about plants having rights or computers having minds is to personify. Usually, personification is merely a useful literary device—as when we speak of the angry sea or the patient earthworm. But personification can lead to some debatable political views, as when one argues that since trees have rights, people can't own them or cut them down. There can be all manner of good arguments against cutting down trees (that deforestation endangers the ecosystem, that it makes a beautiful environment ugly, or the like), but arguments based on personification are silly.

Hypostatization and personification can occur together. For example, the statement

> Nature will only reveal her secrets to those who speak mathematics.

both reifies nature and treats it as a woman with an inordinate fondness for mathematics.

Another pitfall of language is irony. **Irony** is the use of words with literal meaning the opposite of what is really meant. For example, you might sarcastically say to someone, "My, but you look lovely today!" and really mean "You look unattractive today." Irony can allow us to express our thoughts more forcefully, but it can confuse listeners who may not know when we are being ironic.

Another figure of speech is metaphor. A **metaphor** is a case in which a word or phrase meaning one kind of thing is applied to another kind of thing for the purpose of suggesting a likeness between the two. A metaphor is thus an implicit analogy. For example, in "Fred vomited forth words of hate," we are saying vividly that Fred spoke hatefully and suggesting that uttering such hatred is like throwing up. Metaphor is probably the most common and important literary device, and it is a common way words acquire new meanings. For example, the leg of a table was once a figurative use of the word *leg* but is now literal.

Related to metaphors are similes. A **simile** is a stated comparison between different things, using the explicit word *like* or *as*. Similes are explicit analogies.

One last figure of speech we will mention is metonymy. A **metonym** is the use of a word or phrase to stand for something to which it has an important relation, such as effect to cause, or part to whole.[*] For example, we speak of a rancher owning thousands of heads of cattle, but we literally mean that he or she owns thousands of cattle (not just the heads!).

Exercise 6.8A

Give an example of hypostatization.

Exercise 6.8B

Give an example of personification.

---

[*]Some texts refer to the use of a term that means the part of a thing to stand for the whole as **synecdoche.**

Exercise 6.8C

Express the following statements ironically.

1.   You are unfriendly.
2.   This food tastes bad.
3.   Your car is dirty.
4.   Fred sings poorly.
5.   Sue hates fish.

Exercise 6.8D

Express the following metaphors literally.

1.   My love is my life.
2.   Fred, the dirty dog, ran for his life.
3.   We walked under a broiler sky.
4.   Her kisses were wine to his lips.
5.   His words cut deep into her heart.
6.   The tornado sliced through town.
7.   The fog crept in on little cat's feet.
8.   After eating cake and ice cream, the children were bouncing off the walls.
9.   The night was deathly quiet.
10.   Her boyfriend was a millstone around her neck.

InfoTrac College Edition

You can locate InfoTrac College Edition articles about this chapter by accessing the InfoTrac College Edition Web site (www.infotrac-college.com/wadsworth/). Using the InfoTrac College Edition subject guide, enter the search terms relevant to this chapter, and then read abstracts for relevant articles.

Chapter 7

Definition and Classification

---

1   *Two Tools for Organizing Thought and Clarifying Language*

We saw in Chapter 6 that certain features of language (such as vagueness and ambiguity) can obscure ideas and lead to fallacious reasoning. In general, then, critical thought requires that we use words carefully, organize what we encounter in the world intelligently, and make sure that our concepts are well thought out. The tools for achieving these goals are definition and taxonomy. Roughly stated, **definition** is the assignment of meanings to *words,* whereas **taxonomy** is the classification of *objects.* In this chapter we will explore these tools.

    One point should be made at the outset. Medieval scholars distinguished two sorts of definition: real and nominal. **Real definition** is the definition of a thing or object, by which was meant the description of the most important attributes of that thing, whereas **nominal definition** is the definition of a word. However, modern usage confines definition to just the definition of words; that is, definition is just nominal definition. What was called "real definition" is included in what we call classification. To **classify** objects is to group them into categories depending on various properties or characteristics of those objects. From the modern view, then, while we don't "define" objects (we only define words), we do analyze the properties of objects and label them accordingly. We will begin by considering definition, and then we will discuss classification.

2   *Types of Definition*

The word *definition* refers to an activity, something we do with language. Stated most generally, to define a word is to give its meaning. Before we look more closely at how definition can be done, we ought to reflect for a moment on just why it is that we define words at all. What are the purposes of definition?

    At the most general level, there are two basic purposes for defining a term: to report existing meaning or to suggest new meaning. Let us examine these in turn.

Reportive Definitions

A **reportive definition** is a definition that attempts to report how people use a given word. (Reportive definitions are also called *dictionary definitions* and *lexical definitions*.)

Reportive definitions are empirical claims, factual statements about actual usage, and as such they are either true or false. For instance,

> *elephant* (def.): A very large Asian or African mammal with a long, flexible trunk and long tusks

is a true report of the meaning of the word *elephant;* the statement

> *elephant* (def.): A left-handed person who dances in small-town ballet performances

is false.

Note that word usage changes and that various groups give special meanings to many words. The people who compile dictionaries (lexicographers) will often try to be more specific in their reportive definitions by qualifying them with words such as *archaic* (meaning that the word is no longer used that way) or *colloquial* or *slang* (meaning that the word is used that way only by certain people). But it is still true that reportive definitions are intended to capture actual usage.

It is important to realize that the idea that words should be compiled and defined in a book took centuries to develop, and the results (dictionaries available for everybody to use) have been very beneficial. For a good survey of the history of dictionaries and the people who make them, I suggest Jonathan Green's (1996) *Chasing the Sun: Dictionary Makers and the Dictionaries They Made.*

Suggestive Definitions

A **suggestive definition** is one that suggests (that is, proposes) that a given term be used in a certain way. Suggestive definitions come in several varieties. A **coining definition** (also called a **stipulative definition**) is the assignment of meaning to a new word or term (a *neologism*). For instance, a mathematician might coin the word *poset* by saying,

> Let *poset* = (def.) a set P together with a partial ordering of the elements in it.

Since scientists and other scholars quite often invent neologisms, coining definitions is not uncommon. There are good reasons for introducing new terminology. For one thing, a judicious use of new words can increase the readability of the writing, by shortening many of the sentences involved. Thus, we express $2 \times 2 \times 2 \times 2 \times 2 \times 2 \times 2 \times 2 \times 2 \times 2$ more economically as 2^{10}. In mathematics one often sees chains of coining definitions.

Besides increasing readability through economy of expression, coining new words serves another purpose: it can allow the scientist to substitute a less emotionally charged term in a given context. So it is that a psychologist may prefer to use "exceptional child" instead of "gifted" or "retarded."

A **precising definition** is a definition that seeks to reduce the vagueness of a term— that is, to make the definiens more precise. For a precising definition to succeed in clarifying a term, it must agree with the existing application of the term in the *clear* cases, before it goes on to assign new meaning in the unclear borderline cases. Precising definitions are met often in the law. For example, the concept of a "truck" for regulatory purposes came to include vans and sport utility vehicles.

The earlier example brings up an important point. The suggestive extension beyond the clear cases should not be purely arbitrary or subjective. In the case of legal reasoning, past precedent and other analogies are used by jurists to justify their rulings. Even where such precedent is lacking, considerations about social goals and social realities are brought in.

A third variety of suggestive definition is reformative definition. A **reformative definition** is one in which the proposer seeks to establish a new meaning for a term already in general use. The two forms of reformative definition are theoretical definition and persuasive definition. In **theoretical definition,** a scientist seeks to define a term (such as *elementary particle, force, learning, compound*) in a way that brings its meaning more into line with current theoretical understanding. In such a definition, the scientist is reforming the meaning of a term by suggesting new meaning based on those features that the scientist's theory indicates are the most important. For example, a scientist might define *momentum* as being the product of mass times velocity. This definition is not intended to capture what people ordinarily mean by that term but instead to attach those characteristics that are most useful in explaining and predicting the behavior of physical objects.

A second form of reformative definition is persuasive definition. A **persuasive definition** is one that aims to influence attitudes. For instance, a Marxist critical of Cuba might define *Cuban socialism* as state capitalism. Such a Marxist would be trying to influence other Marxists, trying to create in them negative feelings about Cuba by classing it with capitalist countries (countries of which any Marxist can be presumed to disapprove). Naturally, by influencing attitudes, the speaker hopes to influence action as well.

Persuasive definitions are inherently open to sophistical abuse, because they can allow very substantive moral, scientific, or political programs to be advanced by semantic legerdemain rather than by the force of evidence. Our focus being on the use of evidence to improve our worldviews, we will accordingly not dwell here on persuasive definitions, although we will speak more of them in Chapter 18. Figure 7.1 summarizes our discussion so far.

Exercise 7.2

Find an example of each of the five types of explanation discussed: reportive, coining, precising, theoretical, and persuasive.

3   *Sense and Reference*

In Chapter 6 we briefly touched on a distinction between two types of meaning. Let us readdress that distinction and elaborate on it. A word can have two meanings: sense and reference. The **sense** of a word is the set of qualities or attributes that the word connotes. For example, the sense of the word *philosopher* is one who loves wisdom. Other terms for sense are *intension, intensional meaning,* and *connotation.* The **reference** of a word is the

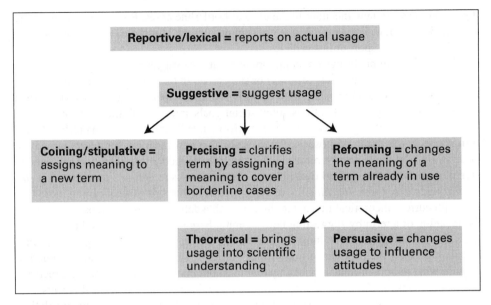

Figure 7.1   *Types of definition*

object or objects to which it correctly applies. For example, the reference of the phrase "First President of the U.S.A." is George Washington. Other terms for reference are *extension, extensional meaning,* and *denotation.*[*]

Whereas some words and phrases have both sense and reference, some lack one or the other. Proper names, for example, would appear to have reference but no sense—George Washington" has denotational meaning but not connotational meaning.[†] And many words have sense but no reference. For example, the word *unicorn* has connotational meaning (that is, a four-legged mammal with a single tusk in its forehead) but no denotational meaning.

When terms have sense and reference, the sense determines the reference. That is, the sense serves as a criterion for determining to which things the term correctly applies. The properties that form the connotational meaning of the word *horse,* for example, enable us to tell which animals are picked out by *horse.*

We can often arrange words in terms of increasing or decreasing sense and increasing or decreasing reference. For example, the terms *college student, student, female college student,* and *person* can be ordered thus:

> *Increasing sense:* person, student, college student, female college student
> *Decreasing sense:* female college student, college student, student, person

---

[*]Please note that the terms *connotation* and *denotation* are used in a different way in the study of grammar. In that context, the denotation of a word is its literal or strict meaning, while the connotation of a word is the nuances or side meanings.

[†]Some philosophers argue that proper names *do* have sense. They view a name such as "John Smith" as a shorthand word for a description such as "the guy who lives next door" or as the causal chain of events from the time the name is first given. We will not take a position on the issue.

> *Increasing reference:* female college student, college student, student, person
> *Decreasing reference:* person, student, college student, female college student

Notice that in this example, as sense increases, the reference decreases and vice versa. But this isn't always so. Consider:

> griffon; happy griffon; yellow, happy griffon; yellow, mellow, happy griffon

The series has increasing sense but the same reference (nothing, because griffons do not exist).

Of course, not all groups of words can be put in order of increasing sense; for example,

> pig, dog, pickle, frog

cannot be so ordered, because none of the senses include any of the others.

Exercise 7.3A

Put the following terms in order of increasing sense, and determine whether the reference increases, stays the same, or decreases.

1. Women over the age of twenty-one, women, women over the age of twenty-one who have attended college, women over the age of twenty-one who have graduated college
2. Green dogs who have been to the moon, dogs who have been to the moon, dogs, green dogs who have been to college and been to the moon
3. Pizzas with olives; pizzas; pizzas with olives, pepperoni, green peppers, and onions; pizzas with olives and pepperoni
4. Educated pink unicorns that love pizza, pink unicorns, pink unicorns that love pizza, unicorns
5. Bored logic students; bored students; students; fidgeting, bored logic students

Exercise 7.3B

Put the following terms in order of increasing sense, or explain why they cannot be so ordered.

1. People, frightened people, men, young men
2. Frightened young men, men, young men, people
3. Friendly horses, horses, shy horses, friendly young horses
4. Unicorns, dragons, yellow dragons, mythical beasts
5. Animals, pine trees, living things, things

4   *Methods of Definition*

Earlier we discussed the basic types of definition (reportive and suggestive) and the purposes for them. We need now to look at the actual methods used to carry out definition. We will look at these techniques or methods of definition first for denotative definition, then connotative definition.

Denotative definition, definition of the reference of a term, involves picking out the object to which the term applies. This can be done two ways. In **ostensive definition** a term's reference is indicated by pointing to it. For example, if someone asks, "What's a kiwi fruit?" in the supermarket, we can define the term ostensively by dragging the person over to the kiwi fruit and pointing. We can also point by using words. For example, if asked, "What's an umpire?" at a football game, we could answer, "One of those guys in the striped shirts."

A second way we can denotatively define a term is by enumeration. **Enumerative** definition is defining a term's reference by naming the things in it. For example, we might denotatively define the term *Cycladic Island* as meaning the Greek islands of Delos, Paros, Naxos, Tinos, Mykonos, and Samos.

Denotative definition is inherently limited. If the extension of a term is empty (*centaur, solid-gold mountain*), we obviously can't point (physically or verbally) to any referents. The same problem arises with nonobservable things like dreams or numbers. Worse yet, when we point, we are relying on context to indicate to which feature of the objects we are referring. To point to a rabbit (in response to a child's query "What is a rabbit?") is at the same time to point to a part of a rabbit, to a period in a rabbit's life, to an area of space, and so on.

The upshot is that defining a term by enumerating some of its extension is at best of limited effectiveness. More effective is *connotative definition,* or definition of sense. Connotative definition can be done in a variety of ways. Two common methods are explicit definition and analogical definition. Analogical definition we will discuss later (Section 6); for now we will discuss explicit definitions.

Explicit definition is probably the most common method or technique of definition. An **explicit definition** of a term A is a direct equation of the meaning of A with the meaning of word or phrase B. Explicit definitions are expressible using a declarative sentence of the form

A is defined as "B," or, more compactly: A = (def.) B.

or

A means that "B."

We will use that format in what follows. A will be called the **definiendum** (that which is defined); B will be called the **definiens** (that which does the defining). We view definition as being the assignment of a concept (given by the definiens) to a word (the definiendum).

Explicit definition is thus the direct equation of meaning between the definiens and the definiendum. One variety of explicit definition—a rather uncommon variety—is **synonymic definition,** whereby we give the meaning of one word by giving another word. For example,

Loquacious means "talkative."
Affluent means "wealthy."
Moron means "idiot."

A more useful form of explicit definition is **operational definition,** wherein one specifies the meaning of a term by giving the operational criteria that must be met for that term to apply. For example, *liter* = (def.) a unit of liquid capacity equal to the volume of one kilogram of distilled water at 4°C.

A third form of explicit definition very common and useful is definition by genus and difference,[*] a technique that derives from Aristotle.

Some classes of objects can be subdivided into subclasses. When these subclasses don't have any members in common, we can call them **species** of the overarching class, which we can call the **genus.** (The terms here are not being used as the reader may have learned them in biology.) Thus, for example, the genus "polygon" includes the species "pentagon," "rectangle," "triangle," and so on.

The relation between genus and species is relative. Therefore, the class of rectangles is a species of polygons, but it is also a genus that includes squares as a species.

The characteristics that the members of a species share but that are not shared by members in the other species of that genus are called the **specific difference.** So, for example, the specific difference of triangles (in contrast with other polygons) is that all and only triangles have three sides.

We have surveyed briefly only some of the many types of definition. For a much fuller discussion, I recommend Richard Robinson's (1954) masterful treatment of the topic entitled *Definition*.

Exercise 7.4

1. Define the phrase "my immediate family" enumeratively.
2. Define the word *physician* synonymously.
3. Define the phrase *the textbook for this course* ostensively.
4. Define the word *mammal* by genus and difference.
5. Define the word *voracious* synonymously.
6. Define the term *Baltic countries* enumeratively.
7. Define the phrase *driving under the influence of alcohol* operationally.
8. Define the word *thesaurus* by genus and difference.
9. Define the word *shotgun* by genus and difference.
10. Define the word *proboscus* synonymously.
11. Define the word *sky* ostensively.
12. Define the phrase *traffic court* by genus and difference.
13. Define the phrase *pea coat* by genus and difference.
14. Define the word *despicable* synonymously.
15. Define the phrase *American dollar* by genus and difference.

5   *Rules for Explicit Definitions*

Explicit definitions are by far the most common definitions. All explicit definitions should conform to certain commonsense rules.

---

[*]Called in Latin *per genus et differentiam* and in various books *definition by division* or *analytical definition*.

Rule 1: A definition should state the important properties of what is being defined. In
traditional terms, this is called framing a definition by indicating *essential* rather than
accidental properties of what is defined. For instance, the ancient Greek Diogenes, upon
hearing that some philosophers of Plato's Academy had defined *man* as "a featherless
biped," plucked a live chicken and presented it to them. The point he made so cruelly was
that their definition focused on accidental rather than essential features of human beings.

Rule 2: The definition should not be circular. A definition should not contain in the
definiens either the definiendum or a synonym of it. Thus, the definition

> *sun* = (def.) star that shines by day

is no good, because *day* is itself defined in terms of the sun's shining.

Rule 3: A definition should be put in positive rather than negative terms. Saying what a
thing is *not* usually does not separate it sufficiently from other things. For example, the
definition of *dog* as "an animal that is not a cat" does not distinguish *dog* from *frog*. We
cannot always avoid negative definitions because some terms are intrinsically negative in
that they refer to the *lack* of some property. For example, *bald* means "lacking hair." And
words beginning with a negative prefix such as *in-* (as in *insincere*) usually require a negative definition.

***Rule 4: The definition should not include figurative, vague, emotionally toned, or am-
biguous language.*** Using such language may load a term with unintended meanings. For
example, the definition of *businessman* as "a brutal parasite who exploits the poor" would
be a poor definition because it is highly biased and also figurative.

***Rule 5: The definition of a term should not be too broad; that is, it should specify only
the things to which the definition applies.*** A definition is too broad if it makes the term
cover more than intended. For example, the definition of *whale* as "a large aquatic animal" is too broad, because that definition would include sea lions, among others.

***Rule 6: The definition of a term should not be too narrow; that is, it should specify all
the things to which the definition applies.***
A definition is too narrow if it makes the term cover less than intended. For example, the
definition of *whale* as "a black and white mammal of the biological order Cetacea" would
be too narrow, because while some whales are black and white (such as killer whales), not
all of them are.

Note that a definition can be both too narrow and too broad at the same time. For example, the definition of *whale* as "a black and white animal" is too broad in that it includes some things that are not whales (such as penguins) and excludes some things that
are whales (gray ones, for instance).

Exercise 7.5

For each of the following definitions, determine whether it meets all six rules listed earlier. If it violates any rules, explain how.

1. *terrorist* = (def.) a person who engages in acts of aggression
2. *terrorist* = (def.) a man or woman who engages in terrorism
3. *cook* = (def.) a man who works in the kitchen
4. *cook* = (def.) a woman who works in a restaurant
5. *cook* = (def.) a person who makes raw ingredients stand up and demand to be eaten
6. *cook* = (def.) a person who works in a restaurant and is not a waiter or waitress
7. *mountain* = (def.) a big pile of dirt
8. *win* = (def.) to not lose
9. *beauty* = (def.) a phony property that lies solely in the eyes of the observer
10. *bogus* = (def.) fake
11. *antagonistic* = (def.) not friendly
12. *antagonistic* = (def.) filled with hatred
13. *omelet* = (def.) a dish made from eggs and other ingredients
14. *girlfriend* = (def.) a gift from heaven, a joy to behold, and a complete soul-mate
15. *draft dodger* = (def.) a person who did not serve in the military

+6   *Analogical Definition*

In this section we will discuss another common method of definition, analogical definition.

An *analogy* is a comparison of two (or more) things. We can state any analogy in the following form:

$$A \text{ is like } B_1, B_2, \ldots, B_n.$$

Analogies can be used for a number of different purposes, which we will explore in detail in Chapter 13. For now, we want to focus on the use of analogies to define.

For instance, we might define *wolf* as "an animal like a dog but larger." Often, an analogical definition defines a word by setting up a proportion of meaning: "*a* is to *b* as *c* is to *d*." We can define *wolf* in this manner: "*wolf* is to *dog* as *tiger* is to *cat*." We often see such definitions put as proportional equations:

$$a : b :: c : d$$

Such an equation asserts that the relation between the two terms on the left-hand side of the :: sign is the same as the relation between the terms on the right-hand side. A wolf is an animal that is of the same genus as the dog but bigger. A tiger is an animal that is of the same genus as the house cat but bigger.

Students taking standardized exams often are called on to recognize or complete analogical definitions. We should note at the outset that doing well on standardized tests involves being able to "play against the clock"—that is, to know when to skip a problem, when to work a problem only partway to eliminate some possible answers (and then guess from among the rest), when to figure that an answer must be a trick, and so on. I recommend in this regard *The Princeton Review: Cracking the GRE* by Adam Robinson and John Katzman (1993; see Chapter 4 in particular). What I want to focus on is the strategy for reasoning out the correct answer without considering the time factor. In such a situation we can distinguish two cases: (1) the case in which you know the meanings of all the words in the problem and (2) the case in which some of the words are unfamiliar to you. Of course, in the case in which you don't know the meanings of some words used in the problem, you have to resort to strategies for guessing. As before, books such as *Cracking the GRE* can give you those.

Let us consider the first situation (in which you know the meanings of all words). The essence of the problem is this: Given an initial pair of words, which we will call the *stem* (the term is used by ETS, the company that devises the GRE and other tests), choose the pair from the list of choices that most closely captures the semantic linkage in the stem. For example,

dislike : hate ::

a. fire : oven   d. admire : idolize
b. dog : cat   e. hate : injure
c. water : ice

The stem is "dislike : hate," read "dislike is to hate as . . . ." Now, what is the relationship between dislike and hate? Clearly, it is one of degree: hatred is intense dislike. And of the choices, clearly (d) is the closest match—idolization is an intense form of admiration.

Now, be clear on two points, which we will put as rules.

Rule 1: The relationship we are looking for must be semantically based. For example, in the stem

bus : car

one relationship we can point to is that, in some places in our society, people who ride the bus tend to be less wealthy than those who own a car. But this is a purely factual distinction that is true only in some areas. In terms of meaning, on the other hand, a bus is a large vehicle, while a car is not. Remember, we are talking about analogical definition problems, so we are looking at the meanings of the terms rather than what factually characterizes them.

Rule 2: The relationship we are looking for should be clear and strong rather than minor or weak. For example, in the stem

doctor : hospital

the relationship "both have to do with medicine" is semantically based but weak. The relationship "doctors work in hospitals" is clearer and stronger.

The strong semantic relationships that you need to look for are generally of the following sorts:

1. degree (warm : hot)
2. cause and effect (hurt : pain)
3. category and example (dog : poodle)
4. part and whole (wheel : wagon)
5. antonyms or opposites (up : down)
6. "to be is to have" (rich : money)
7. "to be is not to have" (poor : money)

8.   agent and action (police officer : arrest)
9.   synonymy (kitten : infant cat)
10.   goal or purpose of (win : play)
11.   type or case of (cat : mammal)

The best way to proceed is *first* to formulate a sentence that captures a strong specific semantic relationship in the stem and *then* check every choice to see whether that relationship applies. If you achieve a match, great, although you should be sure to keep going to see whether there is a closer match later in the choices. If you don't find a match, formulate another sentence that captures another strong specific semantic relationship, and repeat the process. The following examples should be of help.

Example: Select the term that, if substituted for *x*, is correctly defined analogically.

mechanic : car :: *x* : human body

a. officer   c. doctor
b. repairman   d. dog

Answer: The best strategy to follow in solving analogical definition problems is to find the most obvious relation that holds between the terms on the left-hand side of the equality sign, and then substitute each of the possible answers for *x* to see whether the same relation holds between the terms on the right-hand side. If none of the answers fits well, go back to the left-hand side and try to find another relation that holds between the terms and repeat the process again. In our example, *mechanic* is related to *car* in the obvious sense that mechanics fix cars. Substitute *officer* for *x*, and we do not have the same relation: officers do not fix bodies. Try *repairman*. Repairmen *do* repair, but not human bodies. Doctors *do* fix bodies, so perhaps the answer is (c). Plug in the last possibility, just to make sure—do dogs fix human bodies? Far from it!

Example: Select the term that, if substituted for *x*, is correctly defined analogically.

scalpel : surgeon :: *x* : electronics technician

a. car   c. knife
b. dog   d. oscilloscope

Begin by asking what relations hold between a scalpel and a surgeon. Well, a scalpel is a knife that a surgeon uses. *Car* and *dog* bear no particular relation to electronics technicians, so our interest focuses on (c), *knife*. Certainly, electronics technicians do occasionally use knives, but no more than do truck drivers or ballet dancers. An oscilloscope is not any kind of knife. So the relation of being a commonly used knife is not what is being utilized in the analogical definition.

Now work backward. An oscilloscope is a tool, a tool used by electronics technicians. Go back to the original pair:

scalpel : surgeon

Sure enough, a scalpel is a tool that *specifically* surgeons use. Thus, (d) is the most adequate answer.

In this example, had we immediately quit when we found a plausible answer (*knife*), we would have overlooked a more adequate answer (d). On any exam containing analogical definition problems, you are well advised to examine all the possible answers.

One last note: The problems we have been discussing here are analogical definition problems such as those on the GRE, SAT, and LSAT. If you are called on to take the Miller Analogy Test (the MAT), the strategies you have just learned won't necessarily apply, because Miller analogies are based on *factual* knowledge rather than *semantic* knowledge.

Exercise 7.6A

For each of the following stems, identify the semantic relationship that holds between the terms.

1. happy : sad
2. teacher : ignorance
3. cat : animal
4. stomach : digestion
5. criminal : crime

6. bomb : damage
7. chapter : book
8. greedy : money
9. fuel : coal
10. transistor : radio

Exercise 7.6B

For each of the following stems, either formulate a strong semantic relationship that holds between the terms or explain why no such relationship exists.

1. apple : orange
2. cat : pet
3. hide : deception
4. frog : meal
5. tortuous : curves

6. sanctuary : protection
7. trip : punish
8. herd : cattle
9. lethargic : energetic
10. apostate : religion

Exercise 7.6C

For each of the following, choose the pair that most closely matches the relationship expressed in the stem.

1. dog : mammal ::
   a. bus : vehicle
   b. cow : desert
   c. hunger : thirst
   d. cat : shelter
   e. cow : barnyard
2. illicit : legal ::
   a. anger : hatred
   b. crime : punishment
   c. attack : wound
   d. rich : money
   e. dead : alive

3. stone : sculptor ::
   a. brick : house
   b. words : poet
   c. bust : portrait
   d. scalpel : surgeon
   e. mine : ore
4. aviary : bird ::
   a. sanatorium : nurses
   b. gallery : paintings
   c. library : books
   d. penitentiary : inmates
   e. dictionary : words

5. ramification : branches ::
    a. speculation : factions
    b. forestation : grass
    c. theorizing : rumors
    d. replication : duplicates
    e. animation : characters

Exercise 7.6D

For each of the following, choose the word that is best analogically defined by the proportion equation.

1. house : apartment :: x : bus
    a. truck
    b. car
    c. towel
    d. flashlight
2. cat : dog :: x : cat
    a. pig
    b. car
    c. mouse
    d. cheese
3. cowardice : soldier :: x : scholar
    a. friendliness
    b. patience
    c. hostility
    d. ignorance
4. dark : light :: x : happy
    a. fearful
    b. sad
    c. eager
    d. lonely
5. profligacy : poverty :: x : obesity
    a. hostility
    b. overeating
    c. ignorance
    d. slyness
6. fast : slow :: x : short
    a. tall
    b. blonde
    c. terrific
    d. quick
7. wrench : mechanic :: x : writer
    a. pen
    b. park
    c. book
    d. cab
8. actor : play :: x : novel
    a. writer
    b. artist
    c. character
    d. book
9. general : army :: x : corporation
    a. soldier
    b. sailor
    c. president
    d. friend
10. tiger : mammal :: x : bird
    a. rifle
    b. dog
    c. cat
    d. eagle

7   *Classification*

We often need to group things—that is, divide a collection of things into subgroups. We might divide the students in a class into study groups, or divide sales leads to give to salespeople, or divide eggs to put in cartons—the examples are endless. Grouping objects, like defining words or clarifying concepts, is a useful aid to critical thinking.

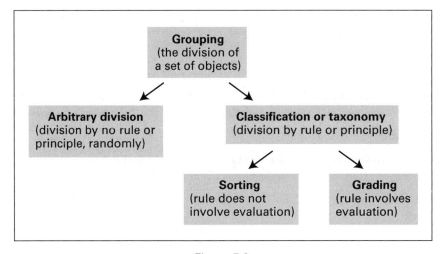

Figure 7.2

We can group objects by arbitrary division, as, for example, when we randomly package assorted balloons twenty to a pack. But we often group objects according to some principle or rule, as when we group students by their ages or grade averages. When we group objects nonarbitrarily—that is, divide them by some rule—we are **classifying** them. The science of classification is called **taxonomy.**

Classification is essential in life—otherwise, everything we encounter would be unique, and the world would be very hard to understand indeed. Not only is taxonomy important in ordinary life, but it is also indispensable in science. For example, the eighteenth-century biologist Carolus Linnaeus' taxonomy of plants and animals was a tremendous intellectual achievement.

Classification, then, is division according to some rule. Obviously, the rule we adopt will depend on the purpose we have in mind. For instance, we could classify eggs in any number of ways, but in fact egg producers classify eggs by size because the public has shown it will pay more for bigger eggs. If the public had shown, say, that it would pay for more dense eggs than for less dense eggs, the egg producers would certainly classify eggs by density. Your goal determines your classification scheme (that is, your classification rules).

We can distinguish further between two types of classification: sorting and grading. **Sorting** means classification without evaluation. For example, we might sort students by the first initial of their last names. **Grading** means classification with evaluation. For example, we might grade students by their performances on a particular examination. Figure 7.2 summarizes what we have defined so far. (This terminology is from Purtill 1972: Chapter 2.)

Any good classification scheme (that is, classification method or rule) should meet four requirements:

Requirement 1: The classification should be exhaustive, meaning that every member of the group to be divided gets placed in one of the subgroups by the rule chosen. For example, consider the two classification schemes for grouping pigs according to weight given in Table 7.1. Clearly, scheme A is not exhaustive, since some pigs would be unclas-

TABLE 7.1 Size Classification Schemes I

Scheme A	Scheme B
0–100 lbs. = tiny	0–100 lbs. = tiny
120–200 lbs. = small	100–200 lbs. = small
220–300 lbs. = average	200–300 lbs. = average
320 & above = large	300 & above = large

TABLE 7.2   Size Classification Schemes II

Scheme B	Scheme C
0–100 lbs. = tiny	Less than or equal to 100 lbs. = tiny
100–200 lbs. = small	More than 100 lbs. but less than or equal to 200 lbs. = small
200–300 lbs. = average	More than 200 lbs. but less than or equal to 300 lbs. = average
300 & above = large	More than 300 lbs. = large

sified by it—for instance, a pig weighing 110 pounds. By contrast, scheme B *is* exhaustive—no matter how much a pig weighs, it will fall into one class or another.

One way to make an unexhaustive classification exhaustive is to add a catch-all "miscellaneous" category. But care should be taken that the miscellaneous (or "other") category doesn't become bigger than the others. A political scientist who categorized voters as either "Republican" or "other" would produce research inherently flawed.

Requirement 2: The classification should be exclusive, meaning that the scheme should place no member into more than one subgroup. Again, consider two classification schemes for grouping pigs according to weight, given in Table 7.2. Scheme B is not exclusive since, for example, a pig weighing exactly 100 pounds would be classified both as tiny and as small. Scheme C, however, is exclusive. No matter what a pig weighs, it fits into only one class. By the way, scheme C is also exhaustive, but not all exclusive schemes are exhaustive.

Requirement 3: The classification principle should be clear, meaning it should be clear how to apply the rule to the members of the group to be divided. A rule such as "Classify all reasonably plump pigs as large" is so vague that we would not know to which pigs it applied.

Requirement 4: The classification should be adequate, meaning that it should divide the group along the lines intended. (This requirement is a factual rather than logical one.)

A classification scheme should capture those cases that are intuitively clear. For example, a classification scheme that included seals in the category of whales would be inadequate from the biological point of view, as would be a scheme that excluded killer whales from the category of whales. Of course, what counts as adequate depends on what we are trying to accomplish. If we, say, had a scheme that placed seals and whales together as ocean-dwelling animals protected from hunting, it would be adequate for our purpose (ecological protection) even if not for the purposes of the professional biologist.

The process of classification involves several dangers. First, you should avoid forcing things into a classification scheme. It is okay to have a scheme that categorizes job applicants by personality traits (such as introverted, extroverted, creative, detail oriented, and so forth), but it is not okay to make the scheme so rigid that people are forced into labels that don't take into account subtle differences or individual characteristics.

Second, you should not overclassify—that is, classify things that don't need to be classified or create more categories than are needed. For example, trying to devise a category scheme to classify your friends is a waste of time. Why categorize them at all? You're their friend, not their teacher, therapist, or jailer! As an example of the second sort of overclassification, consider a neurotic professor assigning grades such as A– – – – –. You want to say to such a person that the standard grading scale is okay—we don't need to expand it to the fifth degree!

On the other hand, people can underclassify things as well. Saying that everybody has one goal in life, to get rich, does not distinguish real differences among people and their goals. Or grouping others as either friend or foe again leaves out important cases, such as people who don't know you, people who like you to a small degree, people who dislike you but have no desire to cause you harm, and so on. This sort of situation we call the fallacy of **false dilemma,** which we will discuss later.

Exercise 7.7A

For each grouping described here, determine whether it amounts to arbitrary grouping, sorting, or grading. Explain your answer, indicating the group divided and how the division is done.

> Example: Determining those who will attend the concert by handing out the tickets to people as they walk up to the ticket window, until all the tickets are gone
> Answer: This is arbitrary grouping of potential concertgoers into those who get to attend the concert and those who don't, on the basis of random appearance ("first come, first served").

1. Determining what price to assign to Christmas trees, based on their heights
2. Dividing up people at an airport between those who use the bathroom and those who don't
3. Selecting a group of people by choosing the first twenty you see
4. Determining who is a candidate to receive a transplant organ by looking at the patients' ages and overall physical conditions
5. Selecting a sample of people to interview in a political poll by looking at their voter registration

Exercise 7.7B

For each of the following classification schemes, determine whether it satisfies the four criteria given earlier. If not, state which criterion or criteria are not met and why.

1. Classification of ages:
   0–12 years = child
   13–18 years = adolescent
   19–29 years = young adult
   30–49 years = middle-aged adult
   50–85 years = old-aged

2. Classification of ages:
   0–12 years = child
   12 years, 1 day and up = old person

3. Classification of Christmas trees:
   0–4 feet = small
   4–6 feet = medium
   6–8 feet = large
   8 feet and above = oversized

4. Classification of Christmas trees:
   less than or equal to 4 feet = small
   over 4 feet but less than or equal to 6 feet = medium
   over 6 feet but less than or equal to 8 feet = large
   over 8 feet = oversized

5. Classification of gifts:
   inexpensive but tasteful = nice
   moderately expensive = really nice
   expensive = just super
   grotesquely expensive = fabulous

InfoTrac College Edition

You can locate InfoTrac College Edition articles about this chapter by accessing the InfoTrac College Edition Web site (www.infotrac-college.com/wadsworth/). Using the InfoTrac College Edition subject guide, enter the search terms relevant to this chapter, and then read abstracts for relevant articles.

Chapter 8

Topical Relevance

---

1   *Relevance and Questions*

Beginning with this chapter, and continuing on through our discussion of deductive logic (Chapters 9 and 10) as well as inductive logic (Chapters 11 through 15) and beyond, we will need to be aware of the concept of relevance. It would therefore be useful to define the concept here and discuss it in general terms.

Relevance is an **erotetic** concept—that is, a concept tied to the notion of a question and its possible answers. Since what follows thus depends on the material covered in Chapter 3, you might want to review that chapter before proceeding further. We say that a statement is **directly relevant** to a question if it is a responsive answer to that question. Recall from Chapter 3 that a responsive answer is either a corrective or a direct answer to a question, or a statement that the respondent doesn't know the answer (an "admission of ignorance"). Consider the following question:

> Can dogs dance?

Directly relevant statements include these:

1. Dogs no longer exist. (corrective answer)
2. Dogs are fictional creatures. (corrective answer)
3. Yes, dogs can dance. (direct answer)
4. No, dogs cannot dance. (direct answer)
5. I have no idea. (admission of ignorance)

We say that a statement is **indirectly relevant** to a question if it is evidence for (that is, if its truth makes more likely) some responsive answer. For the question

> Can dogs dance?

indirectly relevant statements would be

5. Fifi, my friend's dog, dances well.
6. A weird virus has just killed all dogs.
7. Dogs' legs are too short and stiff to allow them to make proper dance steps.

Statement 5 is indirectly relevant because it is evidence for answer 3; statement 6 is indirectly relevant because it is evidence for answer 1; statement 7 is indirectly relevant because it is evidence for answer 4.

A statement is **relevant** to a question if it is either directly or indirectly relevant. For the prior question, here are a few irrelevant replies:

8. Dogs make great pets.
9. Oh, shut up.
10. Cats can't dance.
11. Who wants to know?

Statement 8 is irrelevant because, unless there is some connection between being a good pet and being a good dancer, it doesn't help prove any responsive answer. Statement 9 is irrelevant because it doesn't correct the question by showing one of the presuppositions is false or admit ignorance about the answer. Statement 10 is irrelevant, unless there is some connection between cats being able to dance and dogs being able to dance. Also irrelevant is statement 11, because it answers a question with another question and so doesn't first correct, admit ignorance about, or answer directly the original question.

In this chapter we will discuss fallacies of relevance—that is, cases in which a person irrelevantly replies to a question. We will divide these into three groups: fallacies of refusing to answer, fallacies of emotional appeals, and ignoring the issue.

Exercise 8.1

For each of the following questions, (1) give a corrective answer, (2) give a direct answer, and (3) give an irrelevant answer.

1. Do you own that car?
2. When did the American Civil War end?
3. Where is Bosnia located?
4. Why do dogs run in packs?
5. Which subject are you majoring in?
6. Where did you go to college?
7. How often do you jog?
8. Do ghosts really exist?
9. Who is governor today?
10. Why do dogs occasionally eat grass?

2   *Fallacies of Refusing to Answer*

Recall again from Chapter 3 that we distinguished between pertinent and impertinent questions. *Pertinent questions* are ones that are appropriately, legitimately, reasonably related to the conversational context. A rule of rational conversation is that people ought to address pertinent questions. Alas, people often refuse to do this. When they do, we say they commit a *fallacy of refusing to answer.*

People refuse to answer a pertinent question in two common ways. First a person can tell the questioner simply to shut up—that is, to not respond at all. Second, a person can answer a question by asking a counterquestion. We call these nonresponsive fallacies *pooh-poohing* and *shifting the burden of proof,* respectively.

The fallacy of **pooh-poohing** occurs when someone dismisses a pertinent question or legitimate request for proof rather than gives a responsive answer or evidence for a responsive answer. In pooh-poohing, a person treats a pertinent question as impertinent. Sometimes this dismissal is outright. For example:

> STUDENT: Dean, we are hereby presenting you with our list of grievances.
>
> DEAN: Being told what you don't like about the university is about as interesting to me as being told that you don't like strawberries.
>
> REPORTER: Mr. President, did you have an affair with that young White House intern?
>
> PRESIDENT: That's an absurd and salacious charge! I won't dignify it by an answer.

A more subtle way to pooh-pooh a point is to agree with it in general, but then to disagree with the specific case at hand.

> BUSINESSMAN: Our automobile industry needs protection from the Japanese.
>
> REPORTER: But doesn't that conflict with the whole idea of free trade?
>
> BUSINESSMAN: Now look, young lady, nobody is more in favor of free trade than I am. But I repeat, our automakers need protection.

Politicians often pooh-pooh embarrassing objections to their proposals in this way. Christopher Matthews (1988) explores the use of pooh-poohing as a political tactic in his insightful book *Hardball: How Politics Is Played Told by One Who Knows the Game* (see especially Chapter 9, "Always Concede on Principle"). He explains the tactic thus (151–152):

> The conventional view is that politicians like to argue and that they like to win arguments. Actually, they often have other priorities. The smart ones focus less on the principle than on the objective, the tangible result at issue. When sitting down to deal, they always separate the principle at stake from the actual stakes.
>
> Then, with the air thick with melodrama, they concede on the principle—and rake in the chips.

The fallacy of **shifting the burden of proof** occurs when one answers a question by raising a question. (It is not fallacious to raise a counterquestion *after* the question at hand has been answered). For example,

> A: Midwesterners are really uncreative.
>
> B: Why do you say such a thing?
>
> A: Well, can you name one creative midwesterner?
>
> B: Uh, no. . . .
>
> A: Well, then.

One variety of shifting the burden of proof deserves special mention. **Appeal to igno-rance**[*] is the fallacy of arguing that something must be true because nobody can prove it false or, alternatively, that something must be false because nobody can prove it true. Such arguments involve the illogical notion that one can view the lack of evidence about a proposition as being positive evidence for it or against it. But lack of evidence is lack of evidence, and supports no conclusion. An example of an appeal to ignorance:

Styrofoam cups must be safe; after all, no studies have implicated them in cancer.

This argument is fallacious because it is possible that no studies have been done on those cups or that what studies have been done have not focused on cancer (as opposed to other diseases).

Here are a few examples of arguing from ignorance, given by Richard Robinson (1971):

1. You believe in immortality?—I have not sufficient data not to believe in it.
2. To say that punishment does not always cause psychic damage is to evade the issue, for we do not know what reaction the punishment will cause in later years.
3. Although this hypothesis leads to a somewhat improbable conclusion, there is no reason for rejecting the possibility that it comes more or less near to the re-ality which is so hard to reconstruct.

In statement 1, the arguer concludes that he ought to believe in immortality because he does not have the data to refute it. In statement 2, the arguer concludes that punishment is always harmful, because we have no evidence that it does not cause later harm. In state-ment 3, the arguer concludes that the hypothesis is plausible, because we have no reason to reject it as impossible.

You should see clearly why appeal to ignorance is fallacious. When we are ignorant of the truth of proposition *p,* we ought not to conclude that not-*p* is true. Instead, we ought to ask whether the balance of evidence favors *p* or not-*p*.

Two seeming "exceptions" regarding appeals to ignorance are often mentioned. First, if the FBI, say, investigates a person who has applied for a security clearance and finds no evidence that he is a political extremist, is it not right for them to conclude he is not a po-litical extremist? Second, in a court of law, if no evidence is presented that proves the de-fendant guilty, is not the jury obligated to return a verdict of "not guilty"? Neither of those cases is an exception; that is, in neither case is it correct to say that the argument form

1. There is no evidence regarding statement *S*.
∴ *S* is true (or false).

is held to be logically acceptable. In the FBI case, the FBI is not arguing

1. There is no evidence that so-and-so is a political extremist.
∴ So-and-so is not a political extremist.

---

[*]Called in Latin *argumentum ad ignorantium.* It is wise to learn the Latin names of the fallacies because those labels are still widely used

Instead, it is arguing

1. If so-and-so were a political extremist, he would probably belong to organization *X* or *Y* or *Z*.
2. So-and-so does not belong to *X* or *Y* or *Z*.
∴ So-and-so is probably not a political extremist.

Again, in a court of law, from the lack of evidence proving the defendant is guilty, the jury does not conclude she is "innocent" (that is, that she positively did not commit the crime, but only that she is "not guilty" in the narrowly legal sense that her conviction is not justified by the evidence presented).

3   *Fallacies of Emotional Appeal*

The next group of fallacies are irrelevant emotional appeals of various sorts, including appeals to hatred, fear, pity, and our sense of belonging.

Arguing against the Person

The first of these fallacies is **arguing against the person** (*argumentum ad hominem*), which is the fallacy of criticizing a person who puts forward a proposal or claim rather than giving evidence to refute his point of view logically. Arguing against the person is illogical even if the attack is factually correct. It is illogical because good people can be wrong in what they say, and even bad people can be correct in what they say, so to figure out whether a statement is correct one has to look at it, not the person who originated it.

We can distinguish several varieties of personal attacks. One variety is the **abusive form,** in which the person's character is attacked. Dismissing a person's claim on the basis of her being a "fascist," or "pinko," or "nut," or "creep," or "thief," or any other (alleged) defect in her character is to commit the abusive form of this fallacy. Consider this example:

> Dear Editor:
>
> Regarding Fred Boar's claim (see his letter to this paper May 13) that the 55 mph speed limit doesn't save lives, I have this to say: Boar, you are the stupidest jerk I have ever run across. I would expect more smarts from a clump of fungus!

Logically speaking, one decides whether the 55-mile-per-hour limit saves lives by looking at the statistics concerning accident rates (among other things). Fred Boar's character is irrelevant to the issue.

The second form of personal attack is the **circumstantial** variety. Here, one does not so much attack the other person's character but rather accuses him of being biased. Again, whether the accusation is correct does not matter, because even biased people can be right. Some examples of this fallacy:

HILLARY CLINTON: My husband, President Clinton, has been under continuous investigation by Special Prosecutor Kenneth Starr! But Kenneth Starr is a highly partisan Republican, so I think all of his investigations are suspect!

Mrs. Clinton hasn't proven that Starr's work is flawed; she has only accused him of being a partisan.

Or consider this reply by someone who was accused of severe mismanagement:

Leonard J. Hansen, *Senior World's* founder, publisher and editor, says that while he has recently experienced "severe cash problems," a reorganization has cut over-head and put the newspaper on the road to good health. Hansen dismisses the allegations as being from "a couple of disgruntled former employees who are going around trying to assassinate me."

Has he proven those charges false merely by accusing those who made them of being prejudiced against him?

The third form of this fallacy is **tu quoque** ("you also"), in which a person's point of view is dismissed because of (alleged) hypocrisy. But, once again, even hypocrites can be right. It is illogical to dismiss your father's warning about the use of drugs merely because he drinks. Even if he is a hypocrite, his warnings may be right.

Consider this example of *tu quoque,* which took place during a debate between then California governor Jerry Brown and then San Diego mayor Pete Wilson. Brown asked Wilson to explain a $70,000 loan the mayor had gotten that allowed him to invest in a tax shelter and escape federal income taxes in 1980. Wilson responded that it was

the ultimate in brass even for Jerry Brown to come up with a comment on taxes. . . . Over the last three years, sir, I have paid more taxes than you. So if I have not paid a fair share of taxes, neither have you, brother.

The fourth variety of attacking the person is poisoning the well. To **poison the well** is to accuse the speaker of being a liar before he has a chance to speak—in effect, poisoning the minds of the listeners to what the speaker has to say. The tactic is to imply that the speaker is not to be trusted or believed. For example:

Friends, over the next few weeks you are going to hear a lot of stories about my husband, the president. Keep in mind that all of these tall-tales are generated by a vast right-wing conspiracy of liars.

One need not use words to commit the fallacy under discussion. Caricature involves using pictures or cartoons to attack one's opponent. Unfortunately, this technique is commonly employed by photojournalists and political cartoonists.

An especially frightening technique of photographic manipulation for attacking opponents flourished under the sociopathic Soviet dictator, Joseph Stalin. Stalin, over his brutal reign, killed tens of millions of people, including political enemies (real or imagined). When he disposed of a prominent rival, he would often have that rival's pictures erased from official photographs (Figure 8.1). David King has written a fascinating book that explores this technique: *The Commissar Vanishes: The Falsification of Photographs and Art in Stalin's Russia* (Metropolitan Books, 1997).

Another variety of personal attack deserves mention. Often, an idea (or theory, or practice, or proposal) will be attacked on the basis of its origins (its "genesis"), but the people

Figure 8.1(a)   *In 1925, Stalin posed with nine party members attending
the Fourteenth Party Conference. This group shot would become a classic
example of Stalinist photographic manipulation.*

who originated it are not named. We call this a **genetic fallacy.** For example, such a fallacy would be committed by someone who argued against the idea of a four-day work
week by saying it was a "communist" idea.

Do not confuse the genetic fallacy with guilt by association. **Guilt by association** is
the discrediting of a person by pointing to the group to which that individual belongs or
the friends or associates she has. The following is a case of guilt by association:

> Senator Jason has advocated this civil rights bill. But how dubious the bill is will
> become clear to you when I point out Jason's associates: Bill Steepwell, a well-
> known radical; Ted Wylong, a member of the Wallaby Communist Cell; and Sharon
> Blank, a left-wing activist.

In the genetic fallacy, an idea is attacked on the basis of the group that originated it. In
guilt by association, an idea is criticized on the basis of the person who advocates it, but
that person's character is attacked on the basis of the group to which he belongs. The effectiveness of guilt by association is explained by the psychologist Robert B. Cialdini
(1993: 190):

Figure 8.1(b) *Fourteen years after the original photograph was taken, this retouched and rearranged version was published in a biography of Stalin. More than half of those pictured in the original photograph have vanished.*

Our instruction in how the negative association works seems to have been primarily undertaken by the mothers of our society. Remember how they were always warning us against playing with the bad kids down the street? Remember how they said it didn't matter if we did nothing bad ourselves because, in the eyes of the neighborhood, we would be "known by the company we kept." Our mothers were teaching us about guilt by association. They were giving us a lesson in the negative side of the principle of association. And they were right. People do assume that we have the same personality traits as our friends.

When is it relevant to look at the character and background of a proponent of a point of view? That is, when is it not a fallacy to criticize the source? Two situations: when a person is testifying and when the issue at hand is the speaker's character or behavior. Let's examine each.

Quite often, a person will ask you to accept a point based on his testimony, his say-so. He is acting as a witness. In such a situation, it is obviously relevant and logical to look at the witness's credibility, character, qualifications, biases, and motives. (We will devote a separate chapter—Chapter 11—to assessing testimony.) But there is a great difference between *testifying* and proposing, theorizing, arguing, suggesting, speculating, and so on. In the latter activities, the proposals are the issue, and their truth or falsity has nothing to do with the veracity of the speaker.

The second area in which a person's background and character are relevant is when the character or behavior of the person is in fact the issue. For example, if we are trying to decide who to vote for, the candidates' past record, character, and biases are generally very relevant.

The following examples should help you see the difference between relevant and irrelevant (that is, fallacious) criticisms of a person.

Case 1
1. President Jason says he will lower taxes if reelected.
2. But Jason has promised to lower taxes many times in the past, and never delivered.

∴ Jason probably won't keep his promise.

Case 1 is not a fallacy, because the question at hand is whether Jason will act in a certain way, and his past behavior is relevant to that.

Case 2
1. President Jason advocates lower taxes as a way to create more economic growth.
2. President Jason is a liar, a drunken bum, and a filthy womanizer.

∴ We should not lower taxes.

Case 2 is an illogical argument, because the question at hand is whether lower taxes would cause economic expansion, and Jason's character or behavior is irrelevant to that issue.

Case 3
1. President Jason has had numerous affairs and recently cheated on his wife by having an affair right in the Oval Office with a White House intern.
2. Jason has numerous other character flaws, such as cowardice, dishonesty, and recklessness.

∴ We should not vote for Jason for reelection.

Case 3 is tougher, because it depends on how you view the presidency. If you view the president merely as another bureaucrat, whose performance in office is all that matters to his or her retention, the argument is fallacious because under that view, character doesn't matter in a president. On the other hand, if you view the president as a head of state (as a living representative of the country), if you view the president as a role model for the youth of the country, or if you view the presidency as an honor only to be bestowed on the most worthy, then of course the character of any candidate is of tremendous relevance.

One last note about arguing against the person: equally illogical is to argue *for* the person. An argument such as

> Freda is so kind. She is against President Jones, so I guess we should be, too.

is as fallacious as any argument against the person. Freda's kindness, smartness, integrity, or other good qualities tell us nothing about her stand on President Jones. Again, we are not talking here about cases of testimony: if Freda is a political scientist, her testimony regarding, say, Jones's Supreme Court appointments may be worth credence. Groarke, Tindale, and Fisher (1997: 270) call this "*Pro Homine*" reasoning. They cite the case of Col. Oliver North's testimony before Congress, which was investigating allegations that the Reagan administration had illegally sold arms to Iran. North, who was a major player in the affair, was called to testify before a committee looking into the situation. He appeared in his dress uniform, with full medals displayed. His patriotic demeanor made his testimony much more believable to the viewers. This fact was not lost on the congressmen, one of whom started wearing his own old uniform!

Appeal to Fear

The next fallacy is **appeal to fear,** called in Latin *argumentum ad baculum,* which means an argument directed to the "rod." (*Rod* here has the meaning of a stick for beating someone—as in "spare the rod and spoil the child.") A person can commit this fallacy in two ways. She can directly threaten to use force, as in these examples:

> "Politicians who do not deal with the Equal Rights Amendment in the Virginia legislature are playing a dangerous game if they plan to stay there." Those were the words of Barbara Lomax, one of the Virginia State Coordinators for LERN (Labor for Equal Rights Now), speaking at a massive pro-ERA demonstration in Richmond on January 22, as ERA lobbyists shifted their tactics from cool persuasion to outright threats.

From a punk rocker:

> Your rag says we're all rich kids spoiled with all kinds of money from our parents. *Esquire* says we're children from broken homes, left on our own for years by alcoholic and drug-addicted parents.
>   The hell with you. We live where we live and we do what we want. And if any of you tourists got anything to say, come down to the beach and we will make you wish you never came to California.

Sometimes the threat is not physical:

> Associated Students President Henry DeMarco walked out of yesterday's council meeting and threatened to resign after two business council representatives accused him of withholding important information from AS Council.

A more subtle method of appealing to fear is to use "scare tactics"—wildly implausible claims about what will happen if such-and-such is or is not done. For example, "If this proposition passes, the schools will be closed down within two weeks!"; "If this man gets elected, there won't be a free America after the election!" Consider the following ad (taken from Walton 1992: 230–271):

MICE CAN CARRY TICKS THAT CARRY DISEASE. EVEN DEAD MICE

When you pick up a trap, wherever it's been set, you may be picking up more than a dead mouse. There may also be disease-carrying ticks. And fleas. And mites. These parasites can carry serious diseases such as Rocky Mountain Spotted Fever, Colorado Tick Fever, Tularemia, Typhus.

Recently, you may have read about Lyme-disease ticks carried by the white-footed field mouse. People bitten by the Lyme-disease tick can suffer temporary paralysis of the facial nerves, pain in the joints and even severe neurological problems similar to multiple sclerosis.

So if you're a homeowner, be careful in your garage or in any barns or outbuildings you may have. While the mouse that carries Lyme-disease ticks has not been shown to enter homes, the ordinary mice found indoors can carry ticks that also may be threatening.

Why use traps?

With d-CON bait product, you never go near a mouse.

If you have mice in your home, you'll feel more secure using d-CON bait products instead of traps. All you do is set out the bait. Mice eat it, then leave and go off to die, without you ever having to touch them. Without you ever having to go near them. Or the ticks they can carry.

The ad is accompanied by a very large picture of a tick, magnified seven times.

Notice that the focus of the ad is on the dread consequences of Lyme disease, spread by infected ticks carried by field mice. But in passing, the ad itself admits that "the mouse that carries Lyme-disease ticks has not been shown to enter homes." So there is no relevance of the fear of Lyme disease to the product being sold.

A really nasty example of an appeal to fear is the letter that a friend of mine received (see Figure 8.2). She opened the letter, and, not noticing the ambiguous phrase "legal advertisement," assumed that the police were after her!

Once again, to fully understand the nature of the fallacy of appeal to fear, we need to be clear on the question at hand to understand whether a given response is relevant or irrelevant. Consider:

1. If you don't give me your wallet, I will shoot you.
2. You don't want to be shot.
   ∴   You should give me your wallet.

Note that the conclusion to this argument is ambiguous. Is the question here whether it is prudent for you to hand over your wallet? Then, yes, the ability of the mugger to inflict pain or bodily harm is clearly relevant. The argument would be an instance of an **argument from consequences:**

1. Act A has consequences C_A.
2. Consequences C_A are desirable/undesirable.
   ∴   Act A should/should not be done.

But if the question is whether the mugger deserves your wallet or is entitled to it, then his ability to inflict pain or bodily harm is irrelevant.

DUEY, CHEATUM & HOWE
Attorneys at Law

Chui Duey, AAL   Tele: 800-XXX-XXXX
Grabum Cheatum, AAL   Fax: 800-XXX-XXXX
Bogus Howe, AAL

May 13, 1998

LEGAL ADVERTISEMENT

Cynthia M. Meyer
5210 Melmac
Bovine, CA 92604

RE: FREE CONSULTATION

Dear Ms. Meyer:

Nobody is perfect, and sometimes that creates seemingly serious legal problems. It is my understanding that you find yourself facing criminal charges, and I strongly recommend that you seek out the advice of an experienced criminal defense attorney, in order to assure yourself that you are doing everything within your power to minimize the impact. This office handles a wide variety of criminal matters, and I am offering you a FREE CONSULTATION, at which time we can discuss the following:

1. The court procedures and penalties;
2. How to begin to prepare your personal defense and/or mitigate penalties;
3. What I can do for you at a fair and competitive cost; and
4. Any other concerns you may have regarding this type of violation or any other legal questions that you might have.

As your attorney, I will personally handle your case. I will explain all your legal defenses and take all steps necessary to obtain either a dismissal of all unwarranted charges or a mitigation of your penalties. Furthermore, in most cases if you retain an attorney you will not have to appear in court.

The sooner you call me at 800-XXX-XXXX, the sooner I will be able to advise you as to the likely consequences of the charges against you, and possible defenses to them, and hopefully alleviate your fears and concerns regarding your case.

Sincerely,

Chui Duey, AAL

Figure 8.2

Again consider:

1. If we cut funding for schools by 5 percent, the schools will have to close their doors!
2. This will lead to young kids running loose, which in turn will result in many of them being run over by cars.
3. That is an undesirable situation.
∴ We should not cut schools 5 percent.

Here, the focus of the fear is that children will be crushed under the wheels of cars, but since a 5 percent cut in funding is not going to cause that to happen, the focus of the appeal is irrelevant to the real issue.

Appeal to Pity

A third type of emotional appeal is appeal to pity. Quite often a person will try to persuade her listeners do what she wants by appealing to their sense of pity, by "pulling at their heartstrings"—that is, to persuade them she will try to make them feel sorry for some person or situation. This is called **appeal to pity** (*argumentum ad misericordiam*). Perhaps the best way to represent an appeal to pity is one having the following form:

1. People *A, B, C* believe statement *S.*
2. *A, B, C* . . . deserve pity because of their circumstances.
∴ So *S* is true.

This form is clearly fallacious.

Quite often appeals to pity picture small children or cute furry animals. This is especially true of many charitable appeals. (Figures 8.3 and 8.4 illustrate the practice.) The point is not that if you are logical you are without sympathy for your fellow beings. The point is that it is not a sufficient reason to donate to a particular charity that you want to help small children and cute animals; you should demand genuine evidence that the money you donate will be put to good use.

In case you think I'm being unduly harsh in my view, consider this article by Lisa Anderson (1998), a reporter for the *Chicago Tribune*. Under the heading "Deception Plays Big Role in Kid Charities," the article reads in part as follows:

> In Mali, a major children's charity accepted thousands of dollars from donors to sponsor children who were dead.
>
> In Africa, a charity worker fabricated letters to a donor on behalf of a child who had been dead for nearly four years.
>
> In Haiti, a charity denied malaria medicine to a sponsored child, explaining that it does not provide free care or medicine lest it promote "dependency."
>
> Americans are most familiar with child sponsorship through nightly TV fund-raising appeals that promise miraculous results for a donation of less than a dollar a day.
>
> Potential donors are told they can transform the life of a desperately poor child from one ravaged by disease and despair to one filled with health and hope merely by becoming sponsors.

I PRAY ..

SOMEONE
PLEASE

HELP US

TODAY

Feline And Canine Friends, Inc. would like to

**HELP SAVE MORE HOMELESS ANIMALS FROM
STARVATION, INJURY AND UNCERTAIN EXISTENCE**

BUT THEY NEED YOUR HELP – TO HELP US!
DO YOU KNOW THAT ONE OF **YOUR** TAX DEDUCTIBLE DOLLARS WILL HELP:

- SAVE ONE OF MY PALS . . . BY FINDING A COZY HOME.
- PROVIDE MEDICAL CARE FOR US WHEN WE'RE SICK.
- SERVE A NOURISHING DINNER TO A HOMELESS PUPPY.
- ALTER US . . . TO PREVENT MORE HOMELESS ONES.
- PROVIDE **HUMANE** EUTHANASIA . . . WHEN NO HOMES ARE FOUND.

PLEASE! WON'T YOU HELP US – TODAY?

CONTRIBUTE A DOLLAR – JUST ONE DOLLAR
THAT'S ALL IT TAKES TO HELP.
ISN'T THE LOVE WE GIVE YOU WORTH SUCH A SMALL SACRIFICE?
Mail Your Tax Deductible Contribution Today, or
Visit us at the Animal Adoption Center.

I wish you could see us – we know you would help . . .

Figure 8.3

But a year-long *Chicago Tribune* inquiry into four of the leading child-sponsorship organizations—Save the Children Federation Inc., Childreach, Children International and the Christian Children's Fund—found this promise of an affordable miracle to be achingly hollow.

Sponsored youngsters often received few or no benefits and in the worst cases children had been dead for years while unwitting donors continued to sponsor them.

Little Tina Hunts for Bottles and Cans!

Poor little Tina has to scavenge for bottles and cans to sell for what little she can get, because her parents are gone. All she needs is a helping hand. Won't you be that helping hand?

> For only $25 per month, you can provide Tina
> with three decent meals a day,
> PLUS all the clothes she needs to stay warm.

PLEASE send your donations to:
HELP THE KIDS, Inc.
P.O. Box 33344
Mohego, CA 92665

Figure 8.4

The *Tribune* found that the notion of individual child sponsorship exists primarily as a marketing myth. Costly, time-consuming and hampered by the logistical difficulties posed by some of the poorest and most remote places on Earth, child sponsorship succeeds far better as a marketing vehicle than it does as a vehicle for providing benefits to the children whose faces sustain it.

Child-sponsorship agencies vigorously defend their approach maintaining that their donors clearly understand that the money does not go to benefit individual children, but to the broader community in which the children live.

> "They know it is going for things like schools and water and clinics and village health workers," said Charles MacCormack, president of Save the Children Federation Inc. He argues that SCF's emphasis on individual children in television commercials, such as those featuring former actress Sally Struthers, is necessary. "An awful lot of people who sign on to a personal human being will not sign on to a well."

The article goes on to say that reporters for the *Tribune* sponsored a dozen children through the four charities listed in this excerpt for about a year. All received photos and letters "from" the children. But then the reporters flew directly to the villages in which the children lived, to see whether the sponsorship money did indeed change the children's lives. They found that while indeed the charities were doing good works in health care, education, and sanitation, the actual lives of the specific children involved were not affected. In a number of cases, the children being sponsored had died a considerable time earlier.

The charities defend their practices by pointing to the fact that the money collected putatively for individual children is pooled and then used for good works to benefit large numbers of people, children included. (See the comment by Charles MacCormack in the passage cited here.) Now, let's assume that claim is true—a big assumption, given that none of the reporters examined the books of the charities to see what percentage of their revenue actually did go for constructing schools, hospitals, and sewers. Still, the ads and the practices involved are clearly deceptive, and subsequent to the appearance of the exposé, the charities involved tightened their procedures and issued reprimands to staff for failing to report promptly the deaths of the children involved to the appropriate sponsors. More to the present point, notice that the ads involve irrelevant appeals to pity, since the sorrowful child pictured in the ad *by admission of the charity itself* is not the person who will benefit from your contribution.

You might think that the cautions here only apply to smaller, less well-known charities. But even the largest, most respectable charities have their problems. Two economists who studied the very largest health charities, James T. Bennett and Thomas J. DiLorenzo (1994: x–xi), wrote:

> Typically an organization considered "charitable" is viewed almost as a sacred cow largely immune from careful scrutiny by researchers, the media and the public.
> With their well-funded public-relations, the larger charities have been able to create an atmosphere in which questioning the activities, expenditures, and objectives of a charity is interpreted as an attack on charitable activities themselves, if not on the poor, the sick, or other recipients of charity. This is an absurd notion—implying, for example that the national uproar over the United Way of America was the result of a grand conspiracy against those in need of United Way's assistance—but it nevertheless prevails. Such a mind-set serves only those who would abuse and misuse charity.
> As we delved into the financial and annual reports of some of the major health charities in the course of our research, we were shocked by what we found: Health charities plead for money for programs to aid those in need while at the same time holding millions of dollars in cash, stocks, bonds, real estate and automobiles.

They claim to be volunteer organizations but, in many cases, salaries, fringe benefits, and payroll taxes account for half or more of their expenditures. Many implicitly allude to helping disease victims while admitting that they do absolutely nothing in terms of direct assistance. Instead, tens of millions of dollars are spent annually to educate high-income health professionals about disease while the poor are largely ignored. Most of the lifestyle advice given through "public education" programs is so simplistic that it's worthless or, worse, misleading and incorrect. . . .

All two often, there is a chasm between fund-raising rhetoric and the reality of health-charity programs. A case can be made that the primary beneficiaries of these organizations are their executives and staffs and members of the medical establishment, not disease victims, their families, or the general public.

As with appeal to fear, we have to be careful to see what is being "argued." Consider appeals to pity by defense lawyers. For example, here is the summation to the jury that the eminent defense attorney Samuel Leibowitz offered in defense of a man accused of killing his own son (Reynolds 1950: 176–177):

In his summation, Leibowitz made a frankly emotional appeal, and when overcome by his own emotion, he stopped, "the sobbing of the women spectators was the only sound in the courtroom," said the *New York Post.* "You talk about tragedy. You talk about purgatory. If that child had only been born blind or crippled or deaf and dumb—or even an invalid confined to a life in a wheel chair—the blow would not have been so terrible. But this child was just a lump of flesh.

"This mother would have taken her eyes out." Leibowitz declared. "She would have cut her arms off. This man would have cut his heart out—if that child could have taken just one step, could have said one word. This man's mind was worn down bit by bit. It was like a drop of water," he said. "Drop by drop, wearing down the stone. Hour after hour, week after week, and year after year, every moment—awake or asleep. Human flesh could not stand it! His mind could not stand it!" Before reviewing the actual killing, when Greenfield chloroformed his son, Leibowitz said, "Suppose you were walking along the street and saw a dog lying helpless in the gutter, his body torn by pain, after being run over by the wheel of an automobile—just a poor, yellow mongrel dog, lying there in agony? You would say, 'I wish some policeman would come along and put that poor thing out of its misery.' So Greenfield saw his boy in agony that day, as he had seen him so many times before. The boy couldn't tell him where he was being hurt. Then something dragged him to the closet, where he had kept the chloroform hidden for two months. He took it out. He put it on a handkerchief and placed it on his son's face. And life went out of that lump of flesh. No more torture at the hands of doctors. No more suffering for this poor woman." Here he pointed to Mrs. Greenfield. "If what he did was the moral thing to do, you can't find him guilty. How much more suffering does Greenfield deserve?"

Indeed, the jury found the defendant Greenfield not guilty. Taken as arguments that the defendant did not commit the crime, such appeals are logically irrelevant. But taken as attempts to remind the judge or jury that they ought to be merciful, that mercy is a virtue, such appeals need not be fallacious. Again, determining fallacy from legitimate reasoning requires clarity about the question at hand.

Appeal to the Crowd

The next fallacy to be discussed is **appeal to the crowd** (*argumentum ad populum*). To appeal to the crowd is to use the emotion of belonging or desire to belong instead of evidence to get a point accepted. This involves appealing to your audience's feeling of group loyalty. Such appeals come in many varieties. These include bandwagon arguments, appeals to tradition, mob appeals, and appeals to sex.

In a **bandwagon argument** the arguer asserts that because most people believe some proposition P, P must be true. In standard form, we can represent it as follows:

1. Most people believe P.
∴ P must be true

This conclusion is clearly illogical. Or we can represent this sort of argument as an enthymeme:

1. Most people believe P.
2. Whatever most people believe is true.
∴ P is true.

But the problem then becomes premise 2, since the majority of people often believe false things.

Illogical as it is, the bandwagon argument is common. For example, one car company argues in its commercials that its cars must be the best because they sell more than any other model.

We often see the bandwagon argument take the form of saying that you should believe or do something because "the winners" or "the leaders" or "the smart people" do so. Figure 8.5 illustrates this.

As we will see in the next chapter, to cite the testimony of experts to back your claim can be logically acceptable. But simply saying "The people in the know buy this product" does not constitute a reasonable citation of expert testimony.

Another form of appealing to the crowd is **appealing to tradition.** In appealing to tradition, someone argues that something is good or true because it has traditionally been believed or done. But because something has been widely believed in the past is no more evidence of its truth than that is widely believed now.

A more subtle (even sneaky) method of *ad populum* persuasion is to appeal to feelings of patriotism, ethnic or racial pride, religious clannishness, or hometown sentiment. We call this tactic of demagogues and advertisers **mob appeal,** also called **grandstand appeal.** Chevrolet advertises its cars by appeal to patriotism: "What does America love? Baseball, hot dogs, apple pie, and Chevrolet." (As if only a traitor would buy a Porsche!) Dodges are often pictured in ads in front of "hometown America"

Figure 8.5

scenes, such as family picnics and homecoming celebrations. Brands of TVs are advertised with the TV screens showing pictures of the Lincoln Memorial, the Statue of Liberty, and other national symbols.

One other form of appealing to the crowd is worth mentioning, which for lack of a better name I call **appeal to sex.** In this fallacy, allusions to sex replace rational evidence. This is not unheard of in advertising. For example, in Figure 8.6, an attractive model in a

Figure 8.6

bikini is used to pitch a vacation resort, and in Figure 8.7, a pretty young woman is featured in an ad for used engines. The use of attractive models is pervasive in advertising. Why? Again, I will quote the psychologist Robert Cialdini (1993: 191):

> Did you ever wonder what all those good-looking models are doing standing around in the automobile ads? What the advertiser hopes they are doing is lending their positive traits—beauty and desirability—to the cars. The advertiser is betting that we will respond to the attractive models merely associated with it.
>
> And they are right. In one study, men who saw a new-car ad that included a seductive young woman model rated the *car* as faster, more appealing, more expensive-looking, and better designed than did men who viewed the same ad without the model. Yet when asked later, the men refused to believe that the presence of the young woman had influenced their judgments.

When are appeals to popular sentiment relevant? Again, it depends on the question at hand. Consider some cases:

Figure 8.7

Case 1

1. Most people in this town say Ed's Restaurant is a great place to eat.
∴   Ed's Restaurant is probably a great place to eat.

This argument is reasonable, because the populace is being cited as actual witness to the truth of the claim about the quality of food at Ed's. The testimony of witnesses is reasonable, relevant evidence in this case.

Case 2

1. Most people in this town believe the fish from the local lake are contaminated by toxins.

∴ Probably the fish are contaminated by toxins.

This is a fallacious argument, because there is no evidence given that the majority of people in this town have professional competence to judge toxin levels in fish. (It would be different if we are told that this town is inhabited mainly by marine biologists!)

Case 3

1. This ad says that these beautiful people will date me if I send them money.

∴ Probably, I will be escorted by one of these beautiful people if I send them money.

This argument is not fallacious, because the issue at hand is precisely the "renting" of the people pictured in the ad. The beautiful model used to advertise an "escort" service *is* a relevant appeal since it is precisely her appearance or behavior that is the issue.

Case 4

1. This ad shows beautiful models using vitamin *x*.

∴ Probably, I should take vitamin *x*.

This argument is fallacious because even assuming that it is true that the beautiful models use *x,* no evidence is presented that those models are medical doctors who are in a position to testify professionally that it is precisely vitamin x that made them or kept them beautiful.

Case 5

1. The majority of Californians voted for Smith for governor.

∴ Probably, Smith should be permitted to become governor.

This argument is reasonable because, unless Smith has just committed a crime or is ineligible for some other reason, the preference of the majority regarding their rulers is what determines who takes office in a democracy.

Case 6

1. The majority of Californians voted for Smith for governor.

∴ Probably Smith is the best person for the job.

This argument is fallacious, because there is no evidence given that the majority of Californians have some special professional expertise in judging the fitness of candidates.

A more puzzling case is this one, suggested by Douglas Walton (1992: 87–88):

1. The majority of voters in Senator Smith's state favor capital punishment.

∴ Smith should vote for capital punishment.

This argument is reasonable, but not necessarily compelling. In a democracy, representatives should work to institute the wishes of the people governed. But there is a difference between a *direct* democracy, in which the people directly institute laws, and a *representative* democracy, in which the people elect leaders who are expected to use personal judgment in doing legislative work. The need to represent her constituents is one relevant reason for Smith to favor or oppose something, but there are other considerations as well, such as personal conviction.

So let us refine our statement of the fallacy of appealing to the crowd. An argument of the form

> 1. Most people (or most elite people, or most people of some preferred ethnic group, or most sexy people) believe *p*.
> ∴ *p* is probably true.

is a fallacy, unless the people cited are either credible witnesses to the truth of *p,* or else the truth of *p* is related to the behavior or choices of those people. Otherwise, the opinion of the crowd is irrelevant.

In sum, arguing against the person, appeal to fear, appeal to pity, and appeal to the crowd all involve substituting emotional manipulation for rational evidence. The first involves appealing to our hatred of or distrust for certain groups. Appeal to fear involves making us fearful. Appeal to pity usually involves appealing to our sympathy for certain groups (underdogs, little children, animals), of which we are not (and do not desire to be) members. Appeal to the crowd involves appealing to our desire to belong to a group (the rest of the people, or "the winners," or "the beautiful people") or else our feeling of loyalty to a group to which we do belong (nation, family, race, religion, hometown, and so on).

We have examined appeals to hate, crowd, and pity. These are the most common such appeals, I suspect because they are such common emotions. But there are as many appeals to emotion as there are emotions. For example, envy, pride, and love are also common emotions. And we can construct irrelevant (hence fallacious) appeals based on them.

Case 1: Appeal to Envy
> 1. Rich people live disgustingly well, with big homes, fast cars, and lots of food.
> ∴ We should increase taxes on the rich.

In argument 1, no relevant evidence is given that we should increase taxes on the rich— not that it would help society, not that it is just, but simply because it would hurt people who (it is urged) live better than we do.

Case 2: Appeal to Pride
> 1. If we build an expensive new football stadium, our city will feel a burst of civic pride.
> ∴ We should build the stadium.

Again, no relevant evidence is given, evidence showing that the stadium will, say, pay back the startup costs and provide jobs for the citizens.

Case 3: Appeal to Love
> 1. You love me very much.
> ∴ You should buy me this car.

Once again, no relevant evidence is given, for example, that such a gift is justified because the person loved helped earn the money to buy the car.

But these appeals can be classed as special cases of the broader categories discussed earlier. Appeal to envy is a kind of appeal to hate, and appeals to pride and love are kinds of appeals to the crowd.

Exercise 8.3

Each of the following passages contains one or more of the fallacies discussed in the last two main sections: pooh-poohing, shifting the burden of proof, arguing against the person, appeal to fear, appeal to pity, and appeal to the crowd. State what is wrong with the passage in specific terms (do not just repeat the argument, but criticize it), then pick a label that best identifies it. The best heuristic rule to follow is to compare the problem on which you are working to the examples given in the book, and the closest match will determine which label to choose. Do not just look at the definitions of the labels—look at the cases to which they were applied.

Example: The American Bar Association thinks it would be dandy if Uncle Sam would foot the bills for interested citizens who want to be heard in regulatory proceedings but lack the wherewithal for that representation. Part of the reimbursable expenses, of course, would be legal fees—a little point which makes the ABA proposal sound considerably less noble and altruistic. In fact, it makes it look like a full-employment scheme for lawyers.

Response: The author doesn't address the merits of the ABA proposal but instead accuses the ABA of being biased. Attacking the person.

1. Dr. Jason, well-known astronomer, recently criticized Von Daniken, the man who theorizes that the Earth was visited by extraterrestrials in the past. It is difficult to chronicle all of Von Daniken's illiteracy, Jason said. "The claim that the Maya Indians [of Central America] knew the Moon's orbit to the fourth decimal place is meaningless." Jason also pointed out that Von Daniken wrote his second book, *Gods from Outer Space,* while in a Swiss prison on a conviction for "embezzlement, fraud, and forgery." Jason noted that during the trial, a psychiatrist had found that Von Daniken has "a tendency to lie."

2. Because of your recent diatribe against the San Diego medical community and the president of the San Diego County Medical Society, I direct you to cancel my subscription to *San Diego Magazine* effective immediately. I demand a complete refund of my subscription fee paid.

   Your attack was unfair and one-sided. At the very least, you should provide the San Diego County Medical Society, and/or its president, "equal time" and space in your next issue for a rebuttal, to present their side of the controversy.

   If the intended article is published, and if an apology is made for the harangue in this month's issue, I will be happy to continue as a subscriber of your magazine, and I will urge my colleagues, friends, and relatives to do the same. If you proceed to publish and make no apology, my actions will be to the contrary.

3. Bubba Smith's allegation that the 1969 Super Bowl was fixed was called "ludicrous" yesterday by National Football League Commissioner Pete Rozelle.

"I don't feel it merits even a comment. We shouldn't have to justify those things," Rozelle said.

4. Do you miss your mother? You don't ever have to miss her again. You don't ever have to miss any important telephone calls again.

   Superfone can automatically answer your phone and take messages when you're not home.

5. We call him Trixie. This puppy was painted with shoe polish and thrown from a third floor window. He's alive, paralyzed in the back. He wants to live as you can see by the hope in his eyes. We will see that he does, regardless of the cost. We will help Trixie as we do thousands of unwanted, mistreated, and abandoned animals. Will you help us? We know who threw him out of the window, but the witnesses are afraid to testify. Your gift is tax-deductible.

6. Lack of vitamins can cause you a slow, horribly painful death! Don't take chances. Take a vitamin pill.

7. Dodge—America's driving machine!

8. To Lester Jones, on your article about Jim Morrison: I don't rightly care for you or your damn opinions. You put the man down through the whole article and at the end tried to say you like him. Can't you make up your mind?

   At least Morrison had his own style about everything he did. Maybe you're just jealous 'cause you couldn't make it past being a plain old hippie. It takes a lot of guts to be different and not a plastic person who does only what other people want him to do. If anyone's a bozo, you are.

   I read your opinion of Morrison so you can read my opinion of you!

9. Mayor Pete Wilson of San Diego thinks California ought to have a law requiring "the gubernatorial candidates of the two major political parties to square off in debates."

   "Were such a requirement to exist," Wilson said, "I'm confident that TV stations throughout the state would be inclined to broadcast them in prime time."

   We suppose Wilson's suggestion ought to be taken seriously, even if it does involve him in a conflict of interest. He is a prospective Republican candidate for governor next year, and he also has a reputation as a rough, tough debater.

10. A Million English Women Can't Be Wrong. For over 40 years, the natural ingredient of YEAST has been ending the skin problem blues of English lasses. Blackheads, grease-filled pores, and other acne causing impurities are drawn out by the natural action of deep-cleansing agents fortified with yeast.

11. Phillip Smith's defense of Rose Bird ("Letters," September 17) is what one might expect from a resident of Beverly Hills. It simply reeks of that parlor liberal elitism that emanates from our local Mount Olympus and whistles down the nearby canyons like so much hot air.

12. Mayor Fred Turkle was outraged that critics have criticized his park program. He said in reply to them, "I challenge you to provide documentation that shows some other program is better than mine!"

13. Ilie Nastasc, asked whether he ever has second thoughts about his behavior on the court: "No. Why should I? The crowd doesn't have second thoughts for me. And when I lose, they're happy afterward."

14. Do you want people to be offended by your presence? Do you want children to run away when you walk by? No? Then you need Tuffstuff Deodorant Spray.

15. The beautiful people have discovered Magic Cream. The legendary lifestyle you live year round starts with Magic Cream. The ultimate in a radiant complexion can be yours. Enjoy the look of confidence and contentment that comes from looking and feeling your best.

16. Editor:

I can't believe that you wrote the opinion about Golden West [College's] care of their landscape. First of all, their budget is probably the same as ours. They choose to spend their budget hiring and training quality personnel. Isn't that what efficiency is all about, doing a good job? Since when is that worth criticism? Do you think that their landscape grew suddenly during a fiscal crisis? The care of our landscape has been an embarrassment for years. Your opinions should have asked why don't we get the same "bang for the buck."

It is crazy for you to write an editorial about the efficient use of money and personnel and ignore the business-as-usual attitude at Orange Coast College. Why can't we have the same standard of excellence that Golden West maintains? Or are you insisting that we bring them down to our level?

Sandra Smith
Orange Coast College Student

Editor's note: Ms. Smith, seeing as how you are so enraptured by the pretty landscapes of Golden West, might we suggest you consider attending class there?

17. The following notice was prominently displayed on an envelope containing an ad for perfume.

This Is an Important Notification
Regarding Your Zip Code

Official Notice: Contact us at once regarding checks being delivered to your zip code.
Warning: This Zip Code notification may not be legally delivered by anyone
except U.S. Government employees.

Attention Postmaster

Postal customer shown below is the only person eligible to receive this mailing.
From: Auditing Department
Box 22341
Washington, DC 11821

---

18. An ad:

Cancer
You don't have to be next! 118 page
guide to avoid, detect and combat
cancer. $3.50. Fred Smith Books,
117 E. Nowhere Dr., Camden, CA 92673

---

19.   An ad for St. Gary's Indian School:

> Dear Special Friend:
>
> Rosie, a young Indian mother was crying as she shared her story. Her four-month-old baby was sleeping peacefully in her arms. Randy, her three-year-old son, watched his mother; tears came to his eyes and he cried with her.
>
> "I am ashamed and embarrassed," she said between sobs. "I never had to ask for help, but we are desperate and have nowhere else to go. Frank has been out of work for more than a year, and we are two months behind in our house payments; we have no heat and now they are going to turn off our electricity. What are we going to do?

20.   Dear Editor:

I have this to say to those who oppose abortion rights.

The following is a direct quote form the *People's Almanac,* No. 3, page 31, copyrighted and trademarked by David Wallechinsky and Irving Wallace, 1981. It is self-explanatory: "Anti-abortionists have often accused the other side of having Hitlerian philosophy. Hitler was *against* abortion, not in support of it. As he wrote in *Mein Kampf,* 'I'll put an end to the idea that a woman's body belongs to her. Nazi ideals demand that the practice of abortion shall be exterminated with a strong hand.' (Hitler sentenced Aryan women who had abortions to hard labor after the first offence, to *death* after the second.)"

We all know how "pro-life" Hitler was. I hope the pro-lifers realize whose side they're on.

21.   Dear Editor:

It is discouraging to pick up your magazine and read articles that promote drugs, alcohol, and partying. Surfing and surfers have lived out with a bad reputation for long enough.

We are trying to change that. Your magazine plays a major role in influencing our young surfers. Please, if you care about them and not just making a buck, let's start using some discretion about the articles and photos you print. We will all benefit from. Your decisions on this will determine whether or not I continue to buy, read and support your magazine.

Billy Blaze
Huntington Beach

22.   Millions are following "Dear Tony," the newsletter published by world famous psychic Tony D'Angelo. Tony is America's most popular psychic consultant. Subscribe now!!

23.   OFFICIALS SAY THEIR TRIPS ARE JUSTIFIED.

Seventy-five of the top-ranking employees at the Immigration and Naturalization Office in Laguna Niguel made 1,000 trips from January 1990 to April 1992. Here are six of the Employees: . . .
    Name: Jill Blaze
    Title: Regional Chief immigration inspector

Travel bill: $21,329

Blaze was the top spender of the 75 employees. She said her expenses were high because she has a staff of only two and needs to travel a lot.

In October 1991, she went to Bangkok, Thailand, where the INS has an office. Blaze said she taught INS inspectors about the Immigration Act of 1990 as part of a nationwide training program. "I'm not going to try to give excuses. I don't think I need to. I don't see any abuses."

24. QUESTION asked of a high-ranking Israeli official: We read, see and hear a lot about the Palestinian uprising here. If you were defense minister . . .
     ANSWER: I'm not.

25. Aren't you glad you use Dial. Don't you wish everybody did?

26. Kelly Segraves, who brought suit in California to have the teaching of "creation science" included in the school curriculum on behalf of his son, has written many textbooks, heavy in creationism, which are published and printed by the organization he heads. The adoption of textbooks by school systems can involve tremendous profits for the publishers and significant royalties for the authors. Before we become swayed by the silver tongues of some of these "Moral" Majority, "born again" spokesmen who want to tell us how to live, what to read and what to teach in our schools, a check on their incomes and investments might be in order.

> Jim Hawk, "Evolution Argument Ignores Natural Science Goals," *Kaleidoscope,* August 2, 1983, p. 5

27. In his January 7 letter, Judge Bruce Mcm. Wright cites as historical fact the story that Thomas Jefferson had a slave mistress, Sally Hemmings, and had children by her. It is simply ridiculous that this patent lie should still be seen in print. Its origin is almost as old as our Republic.

On July 14, 1798, the Federalist Congress passed the Sedition Act, which made publishing anything false or scandalous against the Government a crime. In May of 1800, James T. Callender, a Scottish immigrant and pamphleteer, went on trial in Richmond for violation of that act.

Callender was a pathetic creature, an alcoholic and hypochondriac, who never seemed able to extricate himself from debt. Jefferson had befriended him a few years earlier and had advanced him funds to enable him to continue his writing. At his trial, Callender was convicted and sentenced to nine months in prison and fined $200.

When Jefferson became President in 1801, he pardoned Callender. Since Callender had already completed his prison term the effect of this was to refund his fine and clear his name. When Callender received his money three months later, he had grown bitter against Jefferson and his party for the delay and the time he had spent in prison. He decide to chastise the President and succeeded beyond even his expectations.

In September 1802 in *The Richmond Recorder,* he published the story of Sally Hemmings, the slave mistress of the President. Callender cited no support for the story, saying merely that it was "well known." He subsequently changed elements of the story repeatedly to bring them into line with the facts of Jefferson's life. Several times he changed the version of how the affair began, and the number of children supposedly produced by it. To those who knew Jefferson's high moral standards and devotion to his dead wife's memory, the story was laughable.

I find it incredible that a story that all reputable historians, led by Jefferson's able biographer Dumas Malone, have discredited for years, should still find its way into print. Without the strictest accuracy, history is worthless.

Author's note: In 1998, DNA tests done on descendants of Hemmings and Jefferson proved to fairly high probability that Jefferson did indeed father children by Hemmings.

28. Every criminal, every gambler, every thug, every libertine, every girl ruiner, every home wrecker, every wife beater, every dope peddler, every moonshiner, every crooked politician, every pagan Papist priest, every shyster lawyer, every K. of C. [Knight of Columbus, member of a Roman Catholic lay organization], every white slaver, every brothel madam, every Rome controlled newspaper, every black spider—is fighting the Klan. Think it over.
Which side are you on?

>   From a Ku Klux Klan circular

29. House Speaker Thomas P. O'Neill, Jr., today characterized President Reagan's State of the Union address as little more than "clever rhetoric" from a "kindly old man."

    The Massachusetts Democrat in his sharpest attack on the president since Reagan's landslide victory last November, repeatedly called Reagan an "old man" in a news conference on Capitol Hill.

    He said Democrats have been easy on Reagan because "we didn't want to hurt a kindly old man that America loves on his 74th birthday, an old man who has captured the nation's imagination . . . this kindly old gentleman, this kindly old man."

>   Associated Press, February 7, 1985

30. According to R. Grunberger, author of *A Social History of the Third Reich,* the Nazi publishers used to send the following notice to German readers who let their subscriptions lapse: "Our paper certainly deserves the support of every German. We shall continue to forward copies of it to you, and hope that you will not want to expose yourself to unfortunate consequences in the case of cancellation."

4   *Fallacies of Ignoring the Issue*

We have looked at several ways a pertinent question can be evaded: by telling the questioner to shut up (pooh-poohing), by countering with another question (shifting the burden of proof), and by playing on irrelevant emotions (attacking the person and appeals to pity, fear, and the crowd).

The next fallacy of relevance is perhaps the most pervasive of all. Quite often, faced with an issue he cannot logically address, a person will ignore the issue at hand and instead talk about something else. We call this **ignoring the issue** (*ignoratorio elenchi,* which means "ignorance of the question at hand"). This fallacy is also called *irrelevant conclusion,* in that whatever evidence is given supports only a conclusion irrelevant to the discussion at hand. As you might imagine, politicians often commit this fallacy: rather than admit they do not know the answer to a question they will talk on and on about matters they can address. This looks better than trying to brush the matter aside (pooh-poohing) or pushing emotional buttons (appeals to emotion). It does not matter whether the irrelevant evidence is indeed good enough to establish the irrelevant conclusion—the point is the question at hand has been ignored. The only way to represent such a fallacy as an argument form would be

$$\frac{P \text{ is true.}}{\therefore \quad Q \text{ is true.}}$$

which is not very helpful. It is better to view this fallacy as breaking a rule implicit in rational dialogue: if a question is pertinent, answer it instead of changing it.

Varieties of this fallacy are often considered fallacies in their own right. They include glittering generalities, caviling, diversion, red herring, strawman, slippery slope, and apples and oranges. We will discuss in turn each variety of ignoring the issue.

Glittering Generalities

We begin with **glittering generalities.** It is expected of people that they try to propose solutions to the problems they face. But these proposals need to be supported by reasons. When a person supports her proposal by speaking in generalities (such as how terrible the problem is) rather than specifics (such as why this particular proposal will solve the problem and solve it in the best way), she ignores the issue. Politicians commit this fallacy with depressing regularity. Ask a senator to justify his bill on unemployment, and he will very likely give you only glittering generalities about how terrible it is to be unemployed, how it hurts the family and saps a person's self-esteem, and so on. All true, but all irrelevant to the real issue: why vote for this bill? (What makes the generalities "glittering" is their obvious truth and compassionate nature.)

Caviling

The converse fallacy of glittering generalities is **nit-picking** (also called **caviling**), which is the fallacy of focusing on petty details to ignore the larger issue at hand. For example, it would be caviling to nit-pick that, whereas your opponent claims an unemployment rate of 10.3 percent, it is "really only 10.25 percent." In so doing, you are failing to come to grips with his claim that the unemployment rate is too high.

Diversion

Another form of ignoring the issue is **diversion,** which is to change the subject by joking. Two recent presidents stand out for their exceptional ability to evade embarrassing or tough issues by joking: John Kennedy and Ronald Reagan. Wit is an admirable quality, but not if it is used to evade one's responsibility to justify his beliefs. An example of diversion (from Copi and Cohen 1998: 179):

> The story is told about Wendell Phillips, the abolitionist, who one day found himself on the same train with a group of Southern clergymen on their way to a conference.
>
> When the Southerners learned of Phillips' presence, they decided to have some fun at his expense. One of them approached and said, "Are you Wendell Phillips?"

"Yes, sir," came the reply.

"Are you the great abolitionist?"

"I am not great, but I am an abolitionist."

"Are you not the one who makes speeches in Boston and New York against slavery?"

"Yes, I am."

"Why don't you go to Kentucky and make speeches there?"

Phillips looked at his questioner for a moment and then said, "Are you a clergyman?"

"Yes, I am," replied the other.

"Are you trying to save souls from Hell?"

"Yes."

"Well—why don't you go there?"

In this example, *ad hominem* attacks are going on by both Phillips and the clergyman, but there is also diversion: Phillips jokes his way out of the issue—namely, why he does not give antislavery speeches in the South.

We saw earlier that an argument can be given as a joke. But that is not what happens in diversion. In diversion, a joke is used to evade the responsibility for rational argument, to avoid the burden of proof. Indeed, we might have called ignoring the issue "avoiding the burden of proof," in contrast to our earlier fallacy of shifting the burden of proof.

Red Herring

The third way to ignore the issue is to **raise a red herring issue.** That is, faced with a difficult issue on which he is not prepared to give logical evidence, a person will often cloud the waters by raising controversial issues superficially like the one at hand, but essentially different. As an example, while a feminist was speaking on a talk show in favor of the Equal Rights Amendment (ERA), the question was put to her whether the ERA would require the drafting of women into combat in times of war. The feminist responded by asserting that the draft was immoral, that in a world run by women politicians there would be no war, that wars are due to capitalism, and that women already serve in the armed forces and deserve equal pay. All interesting issues—a pity they were utterly irrelevant to the issue at hand!

Strawman

A fourth variety of ignoring the issue is **strawman,** which is the distortion of another person's position. (The name arises from the metaphor of setting up a straw man, a dummy, and vainly trying to prove your prowess by knocking it down.) A person can distort her opponent's position by oversimplifying it (leaving out important qualifications and details) or by extending it to situations to which it was never meant to apply. For example,

> CANDIDATE: My opponent wants to increase the number of day care centers. But do we really want the government to take over child rearing? I say: let the parents raise the kids!

Here is a letter opposing California State Senator Bob Wilson's anger at the use of the tax-payers' money to support unusual forms of art:

> So State Sen. Bob Wilson doesn't like Paul Fericano's poetry. Or he doesn't under-stand it. And he can't relate to any of a list of California Arts Council special pro-jects. That's unfortunate, but does Wilson really think that lack of appreciation entitles him to decide what a legitimate expression of artistic effort is, and what it is not? I suspect that not even the most jaded art critic would undertake that sort of pretension. One can say, quite honestly, that one likes or does not like this or that. And one can give reasons. But art should not have to shoulder the burden of a pub-lic official's approval merely to exist. Perhaps most of the projects on Wilson's list are, in fact, pointless to all but their creators. So what. No one has a God-given right to decide, in advance, what should or shouldn't be created. I suggest that Bob Wilson have an extended conversation with William Wilson, the *L.A. Times* distin-guished art critic. Better yet, he should enroll in an art appreciation class. And he should stop taking himself so seriously—no one else does.

Wilson did not say that those artists should be forbidden to create whatever they wanted, only that the taxpayers' money should not be spent to support it!

Politicians often set up strawmen. During the Carter-Ford campaign of 1976, Carter said that he would not automatically kick Italy out of NATO if the people there voted in a communist government. During one of their debates, this strawman exchange occurred:

> FORD: Mr. Carter has indicated that he would look with sympathy to a communist government in NATO. I think that would destroy the integrity and the strength of NATO, and I am totally opposed to it.
>
> CARTER: Now Mr. Ford, unfortunately, just made a statement that isn't true. I have never advocated a communist government for Italy, that would obviously be a ridiculous thing to do for anyone who wanted to be president of this country.

Slippery Slope

A fifth way to ignore the issue is by slippery slope. A fallacy of **irrelevant slippery slope** occurs when the arguer changes the issue to some other irrelevant issue by degrees. That is, faced with some issue, the arguer says, "But if we agree to A, then why not A_1? Or A_2? Or A_3? But A_3 is obviously absurd!" and the conclusion is drawn that the original issue or claim A is false too. What allows this fallacy to appear plausible is that the claims A_1, A_2, A_3, and so on, differ by degree only. Consider this example:

> Dear Editor:
>
> The PTA has asked the television networks if they [the PTA] can have the power to stop programs with a lot of violence in them from being aired. I am outraged by the PTA's request. If the PTA is allowed to determine what shows I can watch, maybe they can next determine what I can eat, when I should sleep, and what I read. I sup-pose they'll be burning books next!

Notice that the writer has shifted away from the real issue ("Should the PTA be allowed to decide whether a TV program has too much violence to be aired?") to a much easier one to refute ("Should the PTA be allowed to burn books?")

Another example:

> Some have suggested lowering the voting age to eighteen. But if we lower it to eighteen, why not seventeen? Or sixteen? Or fifteen? Or fourteen? But can you imagine the way fourteen-year-olds would vote? My God, some rock star would be elected president!

Here again, the real issue ("Should we lower the voting age to eighteen?") has been ignored. We, the listeners, have been carried down a slippery slope to an entirely different issue.

Recall our discussion of vagueness in Chapter 6. People often exploit vagueness to commit slippery slope fallacies.

One caution here. As Walton (1992b) points out in his exhaustive treatment of slippery slope arguments, not all slippery slope arguments are fallacies. Many slippery slope arguments are causal in nature. A **causal slippery slope** argument is a negative argument from consequences with a key causal premise:

1. If A_1 occurs, then it will cause A_2, which in turn will cause A_3, which in turn will cause $A_4, \ldots$, ultimately causing A_n.
2. But A_n has negative consequences.
∴ We should not do A_1.

The term *cause* here is defined broadly. We can have in mind physical cause, as in

1. If you smoke marijuana, it will cause you to desire harder drugs, and then still harder drugs, until you will become a heroin addict.
2. The life of a heroin addict is hideous.
∴ You should not smoke marijuana.

But the term *cause* can mean socially cause or socially give rise to, as in

1. If we allow mercy killing, society will become coarsened, and will eventually allow killing people who are deemed "inferior."
2. That would be a gross violation of human rights.
∴ We should not allow mercy killing.

Also, the term *cause* can mean legally cause or be a legal precedent for, as in

1. If we allow government to prohibit pornography, that will become legal precedent for prohibiting controversial literature, which in turn will be legal precedent for prohibiting radical political speech.
2. But the control of radical political speech would be dangerous to our freedom.
∴ We should not allow government to prohibit pornography.

Notice that the crucial relevant premise in a causal slippery slope argument is that causal linkage between the different things along the slope. When this linkage is asserted, the argument is not logically bad (that is, fallacious), although it may be factually bad—as the examples given earlier illustrate. An irrelevant slippery slope fallacy occurs when a person mentions several other issues but does not assert (explicitly or implicitly) a causal link.

Apples and Oranges

A sixth form of ignoring the issue is **apples and oranges.** In this form of the fallacy, the speaker lumps issue *A* in with another issue *B* and then proceeds to defend *B* instead of the real issue *A*. For example, proponents of welfare programs will often lump together Aid to Families with Dependent Children (AFDC—the program that gives money to women with children whose fathers refuse to support [now called TANF]) with programs to support people with disabilities, and they then defend both programs by focusing their remarks on the second. Another example:

> Still, criticism persists that much of what the NSF does fails to meet any reasonable definition of spending priorities. Its defenders say scientific advancement and improved technology depend upon the foundation's continued growth. Last March, when Rep. John Ashbrook (R-Ohio) offered an amendment to cut $14 million from the foundation's biological, behavioral, and social science research, some warned that he could be denying money that might lead to breakthroughs in medical research.
>
> "How many people here would vote for $100,000 to study the growth of viruses in monkey kidney cells?" asked Rep. Tom Harkin (D-Iowa). While that foundation-funded research had no immediate payoff, Harkin said, Dr. Jonas Salk a few years later used the study in his own research and came up with a polio vaccine.
>
> But Harkin and Ashbrook, it seemed, were talking about apples and oranges. Ashbrook was not attacking medical research. Instead, he was criticizing studies that he argued were indefensible and simply wasted tax dollars. Like the $83,839 the foundation gave to the American Bar Association to study the social structure of the legal profession.

Ashbrook attacked social science funding; Harkin responded by exploiting the fact that the same agency that funds social science also funds medical science, to defend social science funding by defending the irrelevant issue of medical funding.

It might be helpful to consider an imaginary case to see the difference between the varieties of ignoring the issue. Suppose Jones and Smith are arguing about lowering the drinking age, and Jones has expressed the view that the drinking age should be lowered to eighteen. If Smith replied, "I'm against that. Substance abuse is a terrible problem facing our country today. Families are being destroyed because of drugs and alcohol!" he would be ignoring the issue by speaking in generalities. If Smith replied, "Jones, you're always pushing the booze! Didn't I see you last night laying out on the street with a bottle of wine in a paper bag?" he would be joking (diversion). If Smith replied, "If we're going to talk about lowering the drinking age, why not mention the fact that eighteen-year-olds face the draft—isn't it about time we freed them from that archaic, militaristic system?" he would be raising a red herring. If Smith replied, "Jones, pushing kids at eighteen to get into booze, cocaine, and other narcotics is an obscene outrage!" he would be setting up a strawman. If Smith replied, "Well, if we're going to lower it to eighteen, why not seventeen? Or sixteen? Or fifteen? Or fourteen? But the thought of fourteen-year-olds drinking makes me sick," he would be giving a slippery slope argument.

Ignoring the issue is extremely common in political contexts. In Chapter 18 we will explore the point further.

Exercise 8.4A

Each of the following passages contains at least one fallacy of ignoring the issue. For each, state what the specific issue is and what the writer talks about instead.

1. Wally Schirra, an international publicity spokesman for *Realty World,* was asked what an astronaut was doing in real estate. He replied, "Who's seen more real estate, anyway?"

2. Boston's pitcher Bill Lee was asked why baseball doesn't go to a three-ball walk to speed up the game. Lee: "Why don't they go to three balls and two strikes? Or just eliminate the pitchers and put the ball on a batting tee? Soon you could have all the managers sit down in Florida with presto boards and they could conduct the season electronically."

3. QUESTION: Are there any dangers in experimenting with gene transplants on humans?
   ANSWER: Experimentation on human patients is done all the time. There are always experiments on human beings—patients with diseases. How else would we learn how to control diseases? Don't you think we experiment on patients with leukemia or cancer? Most patients, or a great number of patients, with leukemia or cancer here are treated with experimental protocols. It is the very basis of medical research. If you're going to do medical research it has to be on humans.

4. After long speaking out against federal bail-outs of troubled industries, Reagan indicated last week he might support federal aid as a last resort to help rejuvenate the nation's steel industry. And he has indicated he might back price supports for farmers.

   But ask Reagan and he denies emphatically that he's changed any of his positions—or even shifted closer toward the middle ground—to win favor with organized labor or other voting blocks.

   At a plane-side news conference in Birmingham, Ala., several days ago, Reagan bristled at the suggestion.

   "Look, I've been on the mashed potato circuit so long. I was on radio so many years with those five-day-a-week commentaries. I had a twice-a-week newspaper column that was in more than 100 newspapers. How could I have changed my position? I'm still where I was these last 20 years."

5. Legislators say that raising the drinking age will save lives. Using this logic, they should not stop at nineteen or twenty-one years. Why not raise it to thirty and save more lives, or outlaw drinking altogether?

6. QUESTION: What would you do as president to counter Soviet-backed subversion in the Caribbean?
   ANSWER: There, I think, is one area where this administration has been woefully lacking. There's no question but that the Caribbean is being made—by way of Cuba, the Soviets' proxy—into a Red lake. It is so vital to us with regard to the sea-lanes: We forget that the overwhelming majority of minerals essential to our industry are imported and come in by ship and that the Caribbean intersects a great many of those sea lanes. There is also the Communist move into Central America. While we look at the far stretches of the world, we're long overdue for the United States to really make an effort to align ourselves with the other countries in the Americas.

When I announced my candidacy, I proposed that we develop a North American accord—Canada, the United States, and Mexico. It shouldn't be done by Big Brother trying to impose something: let's go to them and ask what their ideas are.

7. How can we afford to sell our world famous soft contacts at this price? $139. The question is can you afford not to buy them at this price?

8. Proposition 5 [a proposal to restrict smoking in restaurants] is chipping away at people's rights. The government has its hand in too many things already. First it's smoking, then they'll be telling us how many children we can have, or what kind of car we can drive, or the type of food we should eat. Today it's smoking, tomorrow it's something else. Vote No on Prop 5.

9. Dear Editor: Roger Smith is right when he wrote to protest letting that kid go—you know, the ten-year-old kid who was caught writing graffiti. Smith is right when he says graffiti invades our privacy, but that is the least of it. A strap-hanger's logic tells him that if a ten-year-old can get away with writing on a subway train, an eleven-year-old can kick out windows, a twelve-year-old can snatch purses, and a thirteen-year-old can commit murder and get away with it.

10. QUESTION: Mr. President, how certain are you that the economy is going to begin to turn around by the end of spring?
    ANSWER: Well, I'm not going to pick any particular month or anything and then find myself having to be held to that. . . . I'm going to tell you that I believe, in these months ahead and the coming year, I think we're going to see the recession bottomed out and we're going to see interest rates begin to fall.

11. QUESTION: Just where would you slash the federal budget if you were sitting in the Oval Office today?
    ANSWER: Everyone seems to think that the only way to cut government is to eliminate programs. Of course, there are unnecessary programs. My experience in California as governor showed me that some programs do not benefit the people. But—more importantly—virtually everything run by government has an overhead higher than that of the private sector. I found that our greatest savings in California—and they were tremendous—resulted from the elimination of waste and fraud and abuse rather than elimination of programs.

    I think it's significant that in the federal department that used to be HEW—now the Department of Health and Human Services—they recently eliminated waste, fraud and abuse. They eliminated it by having a meeting of all the department heads in which Secretary Patricia Harris made a rule that henceforth they would no longer use the words fraud, waste, and abuse. Those words won't appear any more; officials will refer now to mismanagement.

12. QUESTION: How do you get interest rates down?
    ANSWER: The problem is monetary policy. The literal problem today in the United States is that there's an enormous run on the dollar, and that run is picking up steam. You can see it in the development of money market funds, dollar accounts, gold accounts, etc. How much does it cost you today to hold a hundred dollar bill in your back pocket for a year? It will cost you 15 to 20 percent, 15 to 20 dollars. People don't hold money to go bankrupt. People hold money to augment their wealth, not to reduce it.

    Unless people have the belief that the thing called a dollar is going to be worth about the same in the future as it is now, they're going to drop dollars, and you can see the numbers very clearly in the velocity of money. The velocity of money since 1965 has gone up, what, 70 percent?

13. From an antievolutionary theory pamphlet:

Evolution is the faith seldom doubted as the way to a natural good life that will come to man. It says we are growing up from low animals. It says that we are becoming better man-like animals by stretching our bodies and expanding our minds. It says we are getting higher and higher.

It would be nice to be able to believe some of the things evolution is saying about us. That people are becoming nicer, smarter and better adapted to our environment. But it takes blind faith to believe that humanity is evolving. We have to be blind not to see: That instead of adapting to our environment we are ruining it. Instead of behaving wisely and lovingly toward our fellow man we are behaving beastly and we aren't very nice.

People with their eyes closed might see evolution going up but people with their eyes opened see devolution going down. God made us to be like him, Genesis 1:26 (you can't be much better than that). We didn't evolve. We decided we wanted our way, not his, Romans 3:23.

Scientists who said they wanted to give us a better mankind did it by giving us better bombs, biological warfare and atomic pollution. . . . That's what we call Devil-ution.

14. If absolute accident prevention were the reason for having a speed limit of 55, then I am sure that those imposing the limit would have dropped the limit to 45. But that would not do a complete job of preventing accidents.

Would 30 mph do the job—or 10 mph? I doubt it, from my own experience. In the past ten years, each of the two auto accidents I've been involved with concerned one auto stopped and moving cars traveling at less than 10 mph.

15. As the war in the Persian Gulf began to appear unavoidable in the late fall of 1990, Michael Moore gave a speech at the Law School of the University of Michigan condemning any American military action against the Iraqi regime of Saddam Hussein: "The day that Bush and so-called UN forces invade, this campus has got to be shut down. People have to take a significant stand. It's going to have to be stopped." A student asked him what he thought America should do in the light of the probability that Saddam Hussein had or was acquiring nuclear weapons. Moore replied: "What should we do about Israel? They have the bomb. Does Hussein have the bomb? What if he did? It keeps eyes off the depression we're heading toward or we're already in. It keeps the focus off the Palestinian cause. It does a lot of things to prevent the pickle Bush was almost finding himself in."

The Michigan Daily, November 29, 1990

Exercise 8.4B: Review exercises

Each of the following passages contains at least one of the fallacies discussed in this chapter: pooh-poohing, shifting the burden of proof, arguing against the person, appeal to fear, appeal to pity, appeal to the crowd, and ignoring the issue. First, state in specific terms what is wrong with the argument; only then find a label that describes it. Several labels may correctly apply; if so, select the best one.

1. It is one of the most unique works of original jewelry ever created. It contains at least nine magnets. For their size they are unbelievably powerful. In fact, since it was first introduced in Japan just two short years ago, over three million people have purchased it, worn it, and valued its effects. Currently more than 100,000 necklaces per month are being sold, and it would not be stretching a point to say that it is the most popular necklace in all of history. Its appeal is universal. It is worn by men and women, young and old. As more and more people experience the powers of this mysterious necklace, word has begun to spread around the world. Articles about its vast popular acceptance have appeared in leading American newspapers.

2. Give the gift America's been giving since 1842! Whitman's sampler.

3. Will you open up your heart to lovable little Jamie? More than 100,000 special children in America have never felt the love, warmth, and security of a permanent family. Their parents gave them up for adoption. But they haven't been adopted because they are very special children with mental, physical, or emotional problems. Here is another touching story of a special child who needs a home and a family full of love. Send money right away.

4. America's true colors come through on GE. The rich green of Miss Liberty. The bright red of a football jersey. The vibrant yellow of a harvest moon. These are America's true colors—colors that come through vivid and lifelike on GE TV. GE color TV: It brings America's true colors into your life. We bring good things to life.

5. I object to Ted Smith's record review of George Harrison's *Somewhere in England.* Actually, it wasn't a review at all; it was more like a senseless putdown. His comments on the record were as twisted as his own mind with his stupid insults of a truly great artist and musician. With this guy doing this sort of weirdness, it's not doing the magazine any good. He wasn't the right person for the article and, yes, it upsets me and I'm sure plenty of others also, seeing how you put him in there and printed all that trash. You ought to be responsible enough to let someone who knows what he is doing write a new article. This is the real truth.

6. Thanks, America. We're celebrating our 100th birthday and you've made us your favorite soap.

7. The attempt by Seymour Minot ("Letters," October 17) to tie the demands for corporal punishment to this year's desegregation efforts smacks of the type of intellectual flabbiness and dishonesty that I have grown to expect from psychology professors.

8. INTERVIEWER: At Baylor University, Fundamentalists burned records by the Beatles, Rolling Stones, Bee Gees, Eagles. . . . Do you support this kind of activity?
   FALWELL: We have never done that.
   INTERVIEWER: I asked if you supported it.

9. There will be no Christmas for "Red." Red has become our symbol in the fight to stop suffering and cruelty. This poor Irish Setter could barely stand when our investigators reached him. Our vets tried to save him, but we were too late. Red's owner just let him starve to death. We were alerted to this tragedy by a neighbor. This winter and its cold will bring us more strays, more abandoned, starving and sick animals. We cannot help them all, but we try to help as many as we can. We're doing our best, but we cannot continue without your help. A dollar goes a long

way with us. This Christmas more than any before, we need your help in trying to eliminate some of the suffering. Please! The animals need your help.

10. How to stop feeling guilty about worldwide poverty—Every caring person knows there is a great deal of poverty in the world. Just the mention of places like Uganda, Thailand, India, and Guatemala brings to mind heartbreaking pictures we've all seen.

     And here we are, a people with so much material wealth. But what can one person do that will make any difference? You can do the single most important and loving thing of all: you can change one child's life for the better. That's the whole purpose of our fund.

11. Why do I know more than other people? Why, in general, am I so clever?

12. You Americans criticize our country for so-called human rights violations. But what moral right do you have to act as preachers of freedom and democracy, given your own history of racial and social problems?

13. Interior Secretary James G. Watt's appearance on NBC's *Meet the Press* (February 21) leads me to the following observations:

     Watt's appearance was a sorry spectacle of deceit as he attempted to demean the reporters with his transparent answers to the searching questions on his former positions and policy statements on wilderness areas, environmental pollution, and national parks. It made one wonder about his professed commitment to Christ and God. To hear a man utter such calculated misstatements and lies on the Sabbath leads a person to believe he is a devil's disciple, rather than a lover of the Lord.

14. REPORTER: Why does O.J. Simpson carry the ball so often?
    COACH MACKAY: Why not? It isn't very heavy!

15. Blap's beer—America's brew!

16. Enlarge your bosom three full cup sizes in only seven days! What is the secret of larger breasts? The lush, big, round, firm bosoms that get all the love, admiration, and attention of men everywhere! The only permanently easy and safe answer is a "New" active energizer enlarger "Big Bosom Pill" called Aero-plus 3! Developed after 20 years of extensive scientific and medical research and a quarter century of interplanetary and computer experience by a famous lab. If we helped put a man on the moon, we surely can put a big beautiful bosom on a deserving lady. Know the pleasure and fulfillment of going from an A to a D cup. Only $20.00 complete.

17. The first step is registration of handguns, the second step is total ban on handguns, the third step is registration of rifles and shotguns, and the final step is total gun control—confiscation of all guns, just as in Nazi Germany.

     We who oppose gun control will do all in our power to see that our Second Amendment and other constitutional rights are not violated.

18. Maybe it's time for you to do what over one million French women have done for years. Rely on the famous French Suave Beauty Treatment for your body. Its sole purpose is to make your derrière, upper arms, and legs look more beautiful. The Suave Beauty Treatment for your body.

19. "It would be dumb to think we made the wrong choice by starting the season with Haden at quarterback," Rams coach Malavasi said Tuesday at his weekly breakfast

with the media. "Anybody who thinks that is stupid and doesn't know football. I wouldn't waste time discussing it if someone brought it up."

20. I find it necessary as one who does not wallow in Donald Smith's pompous world of pseudointellectualism to answer his absurd article, "Roll over, Beethoven! The Disco Beat is Bach."

   Smith must not be aware that it takes real people who understand and love the classics to appreciated the "Hooked on Classics" record. Obviously, he is also insensitive to talent and the innovative ability to make money for a worthy cause.

   Perhaps Smith can use his enormous ego, limited insights, and questionable knowledge to implement a program as successful as "Hooked on Classics" to save our San Diego Symphony instead of wasting his time criticizing a gutsy and talented individual like Louis Clarke.

21. Under the ERA, its foe Phyllis Schlafly contended, women would be drafted and sent into combat, separate lavatories for men and women would vanish from the public scene, homosexual marriages would be legalized, and legal protection for divorced women would be undermined.

   "Every argument made by Phyllis Schlafly is wrong, and I can answer them," says Elizabeth Griffith, former vice chairman of the National Women's Political Caucus. "But you have to be very specific and very technical, and it takes a longer time to answer a charge than to make one."

22. Ratzo Cigarettes—the cigarette winners smoke.

23. The patronizing tone of your February 5 editorial makes it clear just where your self-righteous mentality lives: in the dreary world of uncreative sameness. To assert that student fees should not be used to pay for art is indicative of your ill-informed small-mindedness. This is exactly the way student fees should be spent.

24. QUESTION: Should we develop solar power?
   ANSWER: The problem lies in converting sunshine into usable, affordable energy to heat and light our homes and operate our appliances. At today's rates, if we tried to convert all our oil, gas, and nuclear power systems to solar, it would cost hundreds of billions of dollars.

25. Omoro—The only one you need! Millions of people have counted on Omoro for their vitamins and mineral protection. Omoro is the only one you need. With thirty-one vitamins, minerals, and other important nutrients, it's the multivitamin that looks out for your well-being. Try this exclusive master formula and get the healthful vitamin and mineral insurance you deserve.

26. Don't take chances! Take a vitamin supplement!

27. Great American Car Sale!! Uncle Sam says "lower interest rates mean low payments!"

28. We should dramatically increase defense spending. I know that those who oppose this idea live under the delusion that our country doesn't need to defend itself anymore, but they're totally wrong.

29. Socialized medicine is a must. Anybody who doubts that is a fool who thinks that private HMOs will take care of poor people for free.

30. I'm thoroughly disgusted with all the slobbering going on about the cut in school lunches! Will someone please explain to me why the taxpayers should be providing

food for children? Where are their parents? Don't parents accept any responsibility for their offspring at all?

Why don't we go all the way and just let the government take over altogether, just as they do in the communist countries? I've come to the conclusion that what the people in this country really want is communism. Why else are our citizens always clamoring for the government to provide them with food, clothing, and shelter? Oh, for the good old days when individuals took responsibility for their own actions instead of whining away at the government's doorstep.

InfoTrac College Edition

You can locate InfoTrac College Edition articles about this chapter by accessing the InfoTrac College Edition Web site (www.infotrac-college.com/wadsworth/). Using the InfoTrac College Edition subject guide, enter the search terms relevant to this chapter, and then read abstracts for relevant articles.

Chapter 9

Truth-Functional Logic

---

1   *Basic Concepts of Deductive Logic*

Deductive logic is a tool of great importance to philosophy, mathematics, computer science, and other subjects as well. In this chapter we will take a brief look at deductive logic as a tool to aid critical thinking. We will focus now on the logic of compounds; in Chapter 10 we will look at the logic of class statements.

Deductive logic studies a group of important concepts: consistency, entailment and validity, equivalence, contradiction, and necessary truth. In the following sections, we will develop tools for exploring those concepts in detail. For now, we merely want to define and briefly characterize these deductive concepts. We will start with the notion of consistency, as it is central to critical thinking, and all the other deductive concepts can be defined in terms of it.

We say that a set of statements (or group of beliefs) is **consistent** if and only if it is possible for all of the statements in the set to be true at the same time. A set of statements is **inconsistent** if and only if the statements in the set cannot all be true at the same time. For example, the following three claims cannot all be true:

1. Monique eats cheese.
2. If Monique eats cheese, she is evil.
3. Monique is not evil.

Note that to say a set of statements is consistent is not to say that the statements in it are all in fact true or even that *any* of them are true. It is only to say that they *could* all be true at the same time. For example, the statements

1. No dogs exist.
2. No cats exist.
3. No people exist.

are perfectly consistent—we can easily imagine a universe without dogs, cats, and people—but are all, in fact, false.

We next turn to the extremely important concept of validity, which we met earlier in Chapter 5, and the related notion of entailment. The concepts of validity and entailment apply to sets of statements. We say that a statement or statements $A_1, A_2, \ldots, A_n$ (jointly) **entail** (or "imply") a statement B if and only if it is impossible for $A_1, \ldots, A_n$ to all be T and B to be F. Validity we defined in Chapter 5, Section 1. An argument is **valid** if and only if it is impossible for the premises all to be T and the conclusion F. Validity and entailment are interdefinable: in a valid argument, the premises jointly entail the conclusion; and if a set of statements $A_1, \ldots, A_n$ jointly entail another statement B, the argument consisting of $A_1, \ldots, A_n$ as premises and B as a conclusion is valid.

Logical equivalence, or more simply "equivalence," is a concept that applies to *pairs* of statements. Two statements are **equivalent** if and only if they both convey the same information about the world—that is, if they are both true or false in tandem in every conceivable situation. For example, the statements

1. All dogs are animals.
2. No dogs are nonanimals.

are equivalent.

Related to the notion of equivalence are the notions of contradictions, contraries, and subcontraries. Each of these concepts also applies to pairs of statements. We say two statements are **contradictory** if and only if they have opposite truth values in every conceivable situation. For example,

1. Fred Smith is president.
2. It is not the case that Fred Smith is a president.

are contradictories (assuming we are talking about the same person, time, and presidency!). If statement 1 is T, statement 2 must be F, and vice versa.

We say that two statements are **contraries** if and only if they cannot both be T, although they can possibly both be F. For example, the statements

1. Sue is happy.
2. Sue is sad.

are contraries: Sue cannot be both happy and sad at the same time, although she could be neither—say, if she were unconscious or just in a neutral state of mind. Don't confound contradictories with contraries: the contradictory of statement 1 would be

3. It is not the case that Sue is happy.

which is a different and broader statement than 2.

We say two statements A and B are **subcontraries** if and only if A and B cannot both be F, although they can possibly both be T. For example, the statements (about Kim Jones, some person):

1. Kim Jones is male.
2. Kim Jones is female.

can both be T (if Kim is a hermaphrodite) but cannot both be F (Kim is a person, not a robot).

We next turn to necessity and contingency, which are concepts that apply to single statements. Necessary truth we defined in Chapter 2, Section 4. A statement is **necessarily true** if and only if it is not possible for it to be F. A statement is **necessarily false** if and only if it is not possible for it to be T. A statement is **contingent** if and only if it is neither necessarily true nor necessarily false.

Matters stand as follows: There are a group of deductive notions, with the concept of consistency at the center of them. These concepts are easy enough to define, but we want a tool to analyze them. For example, how can we determine whether a given set of statements is consistent or inconsistent? We can rely on intuition—but that is very unreliable. Consider the following set of statements:

1. If John shows up at the party, Mary will leave.
2. John is *not* showing up.
3. Mary will leave anyway.

Statements 1 through 3 may intuitively look inconsistent, but in fact they are consistent. Intuition needs help. The method we are about to develop applies to compounds only, but in that realm it is quite useful. It is called **the truth table method.** This method has two stages, the first in which we symbolize the statements, the second in which we do calculations of compound statements. We will learn the calculation skills first, and then the symbolization skills second.

2 *Truth Table Calculations*

The method of truth tables utilizes the compounds we introduced in Section 2 of Chapter 2. Let us briefly review those, introducing some handy symbols as we do.

Recall that we defined a statement as "simple" if it had no other statements as parts or components. For example, the statement

Pat is ugly.

is simple. By contrast, a statement is "compound" if it does contain one or more statements as components. Unary compounds have one component—for example,

I believe that whales are fat.

Binary compounds have two components, such as

Pat is happy, but Al is not.

In addition, of course, there are compounds of more than two components.

Now, there is a special group of compounds that we call **truth-functional compounds** (or more simply *truth functions*). A truth-functional compound is one whose overall truth value is solely a function of (that is, is totally determined by) the truth values of its components. To grasp this definition, compare two statements:

1. It is not the case that Denver is in Colorado.
2. John Smith believes that Denver is in Colorado.

In statement 1, if we know that the component "Denver is in Colorado" is false, we automatically know that the whole statement is true. But in statement 2, even if we know that Denver is not in Colorado, we can't tell whether the whole statement is true unless we also interrogate John Smith after injecting him with truth serum!

TABLE 9.1 Negation	
A	*–A*
T	F
F	T

TABLE 9.2 Conjunction		
A	*B*	*A & B*
T	T	T
T	F	F
F	T	F
F	F	F

We will focus on five truth-functional compounds: negation, conjunction, disjunction, the conditional, and the biconditional. A **negation** is a unary compound that expresses the denial of the component. We will use a dash to express negation:

It is not the case that Fred is dead.

will be expressed as:

–(Fred is dead).

A negation is false if the component denied is true; it is true if the component is false. Table 9.1 summarizes this, where *A* is any arbitrary statement.

A **conjunction** is a binary compound that asserts of two components that they are both true. We will express conjunction by an ampersand (&). Thus,

John is happy and Sue is happy.

will be expressed as

(John is happy) & (Sue is happy).

A conjunction is false if even one of its components is false; it is true if and only if both components are true. Table 9.2 summarizes this.

A **disjunction** is a binary compound that asserts at least one of the components is true. If the disjunction also asserts that perhaps both of the components are true, we say that it is an **inclusive** disjunction. We will represent inclusive discussion by a wedge (∨). Thus,

Either John or Sue is coming to the party.

will be expressed as

(John is coming to the party) ∨ (Sue is coming to the party).

TABLE 9.3 Inclusive Disjunction		
A	*B*	*A* ∨ *B*
T	T	T
T	F	T
F	T	T
F	F	F

TABLE 9.4 Conditional		
A	*B*	*A* → *B*
T	T	T
T	F	F
F	T	T
F	F	T

If the disjunction asserts that not both of the components are true, we say that it is an **exclusive** disjunction. We will worry about exclusive disjunctions in the next section. For now, we will focus on inclusive disjunction (see Table 9.3).

A **conditional** statement is a binary statement that asserts that if the first component is true, then the second one will be true as well. We will express the conditional with an arrow (→). Thus, the conditional

> If I win the lottery, I will buy you a new car.

will be expressed as

> (I win the lottery) → (I buy you a new car).

A conditional does *not* assert that the first component, called the **antecedent,** is true or that the second one, called the **consequent,** is true but instead asserts the truth of the consequent *conditional upon the truth of the antecedent.* In the example here, I am not saying that I am going to win the lottery or that I'm going to buy you a new car. I'm only promising that *if* I win the lottery, I'll buy you the car. The key word is *if.*

Thus, a conditional is clearly true where the antecedent is true and the consequent is also true (I win the lottery and buy you a car); it is clearly false when the antecedent is true but the consequent is false (I win the lottery but do not buy the car). When the antecedent is false, the conditional is true (if I don't win the lottery, my promise is not broken). Table 9.4 summarizes this point.

Finally, a **biconditional** is a binary compound that says of two components that the first is true if and only if the second is—that is, they are either both true or both false together. We will express the biconditional as a double-arrow (↔). Thus, the biconditional

> It will rain if and only if the barometer falls.

will be expressed as

(It will rain) ↔ (the barometer falls).

Table 9.5 summarizes this idea.

We can use these tables to calculate the truth value of any truth-functional compounds given the truth values of its components. To do that, we use a simple crossing-out method. We begin by writing underneath each simple component statement its truth value. (In what follows, we will simply arbitrarily assign the truth values. Later when we do truth tables for arguments, we will see that the component letters get specific values assigned in a given context.) We then calculate connective by connective, crossing out truth values as we go. We are done when each letter and connective has a truth value underneath it, and all are crossed out but one. The one that remains is the overall value. Some examples will make that clear. In what follows, we will assume that *A, B,* and *C* are T, while *X, Y,* and *Z* are F. (The letters *A, B, C, X, Y,* and *Z* are just arbitrarily chosen symbols representing statements.)

Example 1: Determine the truth value of the compound

$-A \leftrightarrow B$

Step 1: Write directly underneath each letter the assigned truth value.

$- A \leftrightarrow B$
TT

Step 2: Do the dash calculation first.

$- A \leftrightarrow B$
F T̸   T

Step 3: Do the double-arrow calculation next.

$- A \leftrightarrow B$
F̸T̸ F T̸

We are done, since every letter and connective has a truth value underneath, and they are all crossed out but one. That remaining value is the final answer.

Reviewing example 1, we should note two things. First, these calculations will be much easier for you if you spend a little time memorizing the simple tables for the dash, wedge,

TABLE 9.5 Biconditional		
A	*B*	$A \leftrightarrow B$
T	T	T
T	F	F
F	T	F
F	F	T

ampersand, arrow, and double arrow. Second, we're adopting the convention that if there are no parentheses indicating otherwise, a dash applies to the nearest letter.

Example 2: Find the truth value of the compound

–(A ↔ B)

Step 1: Write underneath each letter the truth value assigned to it.

–(A ↔ B)
  T   T

Step 2: Since the parentheses show that the dash applies to the whole biconditional, we must work the double arrow first.

–(A ↔ B)
  T T T

Step 3: Apply the dash.

–(A ↔ B)
F T T T

Let's try a longer example.

Example 3: Determine the truth value of

–(A ∨ X) → (B & Z)

Step 1: Assign the truth values.

–(A ∨ X) → (B & Z)
  T   F   T   F

Step 2: Do the smallest calculations first; that is, work what is inside the parentheses.

–(A ∨ X) → (B & Z)
  T T F   T F F

Step 3: Apply the dash.

–(A ∨ X) → (B & Z)
F T T F   T   T F F

Step 4: Now do the arrow calculation.

–(A ∨ X) → (B & Z)
F T T F   T   T F F

Under the arrow we see the final answer.

One last example. In some cases, we need to have parentheses within parentheses. In such cases, we will use brackets and braces to make it easier to read.

Example 4: What is the truth value of

$$-\{[X \rightarrow (A \vee B)] \rightarrow -A\}$$

Step 1: Assign the values.

$-\{[X \rightarrow (A \vee B)] \rightarrow -A\}$
F T T T

Step 2: Work the smallest calculations.

$-\{[X \rightarrow (A \vee B)] \rightarrow -A\}$
F ~~T~~T~~T~~ F~~T~~

Step 3: Work what is in the brackets.

$-\{[X \rightarrow (A \vee B)] \rightarrow -A\}$
~~F~~ T ~~T~~~~T~~T F~~T~~

Step 4: Now work what is inside the braces.

$-\{[X \rightarrow (A \vee B)] \rightarrow -A\}$
~~F~~ ~~T~~ ~~T~~~~T~~~~T~~ F ~~F~~~~T~~

Step 5: Finally, apply the dash.

$-\{[X \rightarrow (A \vee B)] \rightarrow -A\}$
T ~~F~~ ~~T~~ ~~T~~~~T~~~~T~~ ~~F~~~~F~~~~T~~

This very simple skill of calculating the truth values of compounds given the truth values of the components is crucial to what follows. Take some time to practice it.

Exercise 9.2

In the following, assume that *A, B,* and *C* are all T, while *X, Y,* and *Z* are all F. Calculate the truth value of each compound using the crossing-out method. *Note:* Before doing truth table calculations, you are strongly urged to memorize the five basic tables.

1. $A \rightarrow -B$
2. $C \leftrightarrow X$
3. $-(X \vee -Y)$
4. $--(X \rightarrow -A)$
5. $(A \rightarrow B) \rightarrow -X$
6. $-[(A \rightarrow X) \leftrightarrow X]$
7. $X \leftrightarrow -(A \,\&\, -A)$
8. $A \rightarrow (-B \vee C)$
9. $-A \leftrightarrow (-B \vee C)$
10. $-A \leftrightarrow (A \rightarrow C)$
11. $-(A \leftrightarrow B) \,\&\, -(X \leftrightarrow Y)$
12. $-[-A \,\&\, -(B \leftrightarrow -X)]$
13. $-[(A \leftrightarrow B) \leftrightarrow (X \leftrightarrow Z)]$
14. $-(A \leftrightarrow B) \leftrightarrow -(X \leftrightarrow Z)$
15. $-[-(A \rightarrow Z) \rightarrow (B \leftrightarrow Z)]$
16. $[-A \rightarrow (Z \leftrightarrow X)] \leftrightarrow [-X \rightarrow (A \,\&\, B)]$
17. $[-A \vee -(B \,\&\, C)] \leftrightarrow -(X \vee A)$
18. $-[-A \leftrightarrow (-B \leftrightarrow -X)] \vee Z$
19. $-[(-A \leftrightarrow (-B \leftrightarrow -X)) \vee Z]$
20. $-\{-[A \rightarrow (Z \vee B)] \,\&\, -[Z \leftrightarrow (B \vee X)]\}$

3 *Symbolization*

In the first section we indicated that the tool we are developing to investigate various logical concepts requires two skills: the skill of truth-functional calculation and the skill of symbolization. In the last section we learned the calculation skill. Let us now turn to the symbolization skill.

By "symbolize" we mean replacing English words by simpler, clearer symbols—in particular, capital letters and the five connectives introduced in section 2. Let me indicate a few general tips, then a general procedure for symbolization.

Tip 1: Represent simple statements by capital letters. You are free to pick any letters, but you have to be consistent: the same letter can't be used to represent different statements.

Tip 2: Learn the synonyms that express negation. Negation is expressed by phrases such as "it is not true that" and "it is not the case that." It is also expressed by words such as *not, lacks,* and *fails.* For example, the sentence

John lacks success.

can be rendered as

$-J$

where *J* obviously represents "John is successful."

Negation is also often expressed by prefixes such as *un-* or *dis-* and suffixes such as *-less.* For example,

He was ungrateful.

can be rendered as

$-G$

where *G* represents "He was grateful."

Tip 3: Learn the synonyms that express conjunction. The most common ones are given in Figure 9.1.

and	although
while	but
additionally	however
moreover	even though

Figure 9.1 *Words that express conjunction*

The word *while* often expresses conjunction where the components are linked in time, as in

   Sol whistled while he shaved.

which can be symbolized

   W & S

where *W* symbolizes "Sol whistled" and *S* symbolizes "Sol shaved." The words *although, even though, however,* and *but* usually express conjunction where the components involve contrast, as in

   Maria was rich but unpopular.

which can be symbolized

   R & –P

The words *moreover* and *additionally* often express conjunction where the components are similar or additive, as in

   Soren was morose; moreover, he was intensely shy.

which can be symbolized

   M & S

where *M* represents "Soren was morose" and *S* represents "Soren was shy."

Tip 4: Learn the synonyms for expressing disjunction. There are not many of them—mainly *or* and *unless*. For example,

   You will fail unless you study.

can be symbolized

   –P ∨ S

where *P* represents "You will pass" and *S* represents "You study."

Tip 5: Learn the synonyms for the conditional, which is expressed in a large number of ways. Figure 9.2 lists the most common phrases that express the conditional (where *A* is the antecedent; *C*, the consequent).

If *A*, then *C*.
If *A*, *C*.
A is a sufficient condition for *C*.

A only if *C*.
C, if *A*.
C is a necessary condition for *A*.

Figure 9.2   *Words that express the conditional*

Notice that the word *if* always comes before the antecedent, while the term *only if* always comes before the consequent. In the phrase "is a sufficient condition for," the antecedent occurs at the beginning, whereas in "is a necessary condition for" the consequent occurs at the beginning. For example, the statement

If Sue becomes a computer programmer, she will earn a lot of money.

can be symbolized

$$C \to L$$

where C represents "Sue becomes a computer programmer" and L represents "Sue will earn a lot of money."

Determining which component in a conditional is its antecedent and which is its consequent is very important to grasping its meaning. For instance, there is a great difference between the claim that if you were rich, you would eat regularly, and the claim that if you eat regularly, you are rich.

Tip 6: *Learn the synonyms for the biconditional.* The biconditional is expressed by only a few phrases: "if and only if," "when and only when," and "is a necessary and sufficient condition for" are the most common. For example,

Joni will pass the class if and only if she studies hard.

can be symbolized

$$P \leftrightarrow W$$

where P represents "Joni will pass the class" and W represents "Joni works hard."

The final tip regards the symbolization of the word *or.* Recall that there are two kinds of disjunction, inclusive and exclusive. Inclusive disjunction, such as

You can satisfy the science requirement by taking biology or physics.

expresses the idea that one or the other of two statements is true or possibly both. Exclusive disjunction—for example,

You may have soup or salad with your main course [but not both].

—expresses the idea that one or the other of two statements is true, but not both.

Tip 7: *Always symbolize the inclusive-or with the wedge.* Symbolize the exclusive-or phrase

A or B (but not both)

as

$$(A \lor B) \, \& \, {-}(A \, \& \, B)$$

Tip 8: *Symbolize the phrase "neither A nor B" as "–A & –B."* With these tips in mind, we can symbolize compounds by a step-by-step process. The steps in this process are:

Step 1: Read the sentence once, looking for the simplest statements.

Step 2: Pick capital letters to represent those statements.

Step 3: Symbolize a component, bracketing the letters and connectives.

Step 4: Repeat step 3 until all components are symbolized.

Example: Symbolize

John is not happy, yet he won't change.

Answer: Read the statement carefully. It is a compound with the simplest components "John is happy" and "John will change." (Remember: Negations are *compounds*.) Let us abbreviate "John is happy" by H and "John will change" by C. Then "John is not happy" becomes $-H$, and "John won't change," $-C$. Finally,

$(-H)$ yet $(-C)$

becomes

$(-H)$ & $(-C)$

when we remember that *yet* expresses conjunction. Parentheses serve to clear up ambiguity. We will adopt the convention that dashes apply to the nearest letter unless brackets indicate otherwise. In the prior expression, then, we can drop the parentheses:

$-H$ & $-C$

Example: Symbolize

Sue will not be happy if she has to major in philosophy.

Answer: The simplest components here are "Sue will be happy" and "Sue majors in philosophy." Represent the former by H and the latter by P. We then have

$-H$, if P

Finally, we get

$P \rightarrow -H$

Exercise 9.3

Symbolize the following compounds, using the letters given here:

A = Al likes sports.
B = Boris likes politics.
C = Charmaine likes music.
D = Doris likes math.

1. Al doesn't like sports.
2. Doris likes math, and Boris likes politics.
3. Charmaine likes music; however, Doris doesn't like math.
4. If Boris likes politics, Doris likes math.
5. If both Boris likes politics and Doris likes math, then Al likes sports.
6. Al doesn't like sports; but if he did, Doris would like math.
7. Al dislikes sports if and only if Boris dislikes politics.

8. If Charmaine dislikes music, then both Doris likes math and Al likes sports.
9. Either Al dislikes sports, or both Charmaine likes music and Doris likes math.
10. If either Al dislikes sports or Charmaine dislikes music, then both Doris dislikes math and Boris dislikes politics.
11. Al likes sports, unless Boris doesn't like politics.
12. Charmaine doesn't like music and Doris dislikes math, if Boris likes politics.
13. Doris doesn't like math only if Charmaine likes music—unless, of course, Al likes sports.
14. Al will like sports when and only when both Boris likes politics and Doris doesn't like math.
15. Either Al likes sports, or Boris doesn't like politics, but not both.

4   *Truth Table Testing for Consistency*

Suppose we have a set of statements we wish to test for consistency:

1. $-A$
2. $A \rightarrow B$
3. $-B$

We are asking whether it is possible for statements 1 through 3 to be true at the same time. Now, the relevant cases are determined by the basic components A and B. Since each statement is either T or F, we have four basic cases, given in Table 9.6. We put these four cases as rows in a truth table. We refer to these as rows 1 through 4, numbered top down, as in Table 9.7. In what follows, however, we will not explicitly put in the numbers.

TABLE 9.6

A	B
T	T
T	F
F	T
F	F

TABLE 9.7

Rows	A	B
1	T	T
2	T	F
3	F	T
4	F	F

After listing the basic components and the cases (the possible combinations of truth values), we list the statements to be checked for consistency, giving us Table 9.8. We then use the crossing-out method to calculate the value of each compound in each case. This is done in Table 9.9.

Let us introduce the notion of paths. A **T path** is a row in which all the statements under examination work out to be T. An **F path** is a row in which all the statements under examination work out to be F. An **M path** (for "mixed path") is a row in which one or more of the statements under examination work out to be T but also one or more work out to be F. Let us complete the table by identifying the paths (Table 9.10).

We are now in a position to answer the question whether the statements in the set {–A; A → B; –B} are consistent. The statements are consistent (by definition) if and only if they can all be T simultaneously. We can put this as a rule:

The statements are consistent if and only if there is at least one T path. The statements are inconsistent if and only if there are no T paths. Since in this example there is a T path, the set is consistent.

TABLE 9.8

A	B	–A	A → B	–B
T	T			
T	F			
F	T			
F	F			

TABLE 9.9

A	B	–A	A → B	–B
T	T	F T̶	T̶ T T̶	F T̶
T	F	F T̶	T̶ F F̶	T F̶
F	T	T F̶	F̶ T T̶	F T̶
F	F	T F̶	F̶ T F̶	T F̶

TABLE 9.10

A	B	–A	A → B	–B	Path
T	T	F T̶	T̶ T T	F T	M
T	F	F T̶	T̶ F F̶	T F̶	M
F	T	T F̶	F̶ T T	F T̶	M
F	F	T F̶	F̶ T F̶	T F̶	T

Let us try another example. Is the set of statements

1. $A \rightarrow -B$
2. $A \mathbin{\&} B$

consistent? Again, construct a table, fill in the calculations, and identify the rows as T paths, M paths, or F paths (Table 9.11). Notice that none of the paths is a T path, so we can conclude that the set of statements is inconsistent.

In the two examples we just worked, the statements in the set were composed of only two letters. What about sets of statements composed of more than two letters? If you think about it, if the statements in a set are built up out of, say, n letters, there will be 2^n rows in the table. Why? Because for each letter, there are two possibilities (T or F), so you have two times itself n times (that is, 2^n) possible combinations of truth values. Consider the following case:

Is the following set of statements consistent?

1. $M \rightarrow L$
2. $L \rightarrow Z$
3. $Z \mathbin{\&} -M$

Here, we have three letters, so we can expect $2^3 = 8$ rows. Table 9.12 shows that the set is consistent. Notice the shortcut: We stopped calculating when we found a T path.

TABLE 9.11

A	B	$A \rightarrow -B$	$A \mathbin{\&} B$	Path
T	T	T F F T	T T T	M
T	F	T T T F	T F F	M
F	T	F T F T	F F T	M
F	F	F T T F	F F F	M

TABLE 9.12

M	L	Z	$M \rightarrow L$	$L \rightarrow Z$	$Z \mathbin{\&} -M$	Path
T	T	T	T T T	T T T	T F F T	M
T	T	F	T T T	T F F	F F F T	M
T	F	T	T F F	F T T	T F F T	M
T	F	F	T F F	F T F	F F F T	M
F	T	T	F T T	T T T	T T T F	T
F	T	F				
F	F	T				
F	F	F				

An easy way to generate all the possible cases is to first figure out how many rows the table will have (2 to the nth power for n letters). Then under the first letter, write half the number of T's, followed by half F's. Next, under the second letter, alternate blocks of T's and F's in groups of half the previous number, and so on. Thus, the list of possibilities for a set of statements built up out of five letters (say, *A, B, C, D,* and *E*) will have $2^5 = 32$ rows, and the possibilities can be listed as in Table 9.13.

The examples given consisted of sets of already symbolized statements. To test sets of statements in English, just symbolize them first, then apply the method.

TABLE 9.13

A	*B*	*C*	*D*	*E*
16 T's	8 T's	4 T's	2 T's	T
				F
			2 F's	T
				F
		4 F's	2 T's	T
				F
			2 F's	T
				F
	8 F's	4 T's	2 T's	T
				F
			2 F's	T
				F
		4 F's	2 T's	T
				F
			2 F's	T
				F
16 F's	8 T's	4 T's	2 T's	T
				F
			2 F's	T
				F
		4 F's	2 T's	T
				F
			2 F's	T
				F
	8 F's	4 T's	2 T's	T
				F
			2 F's	T
				F
		4 F's	2 T's	T
				F
			2 F's	T
				F

For example, is the following set of statements consistent?

1. Sue is happy.
2. Moe is happy.
3. Sue is happy if and only if Moe isn't.

Step 1: Symbolize the statements. In this case, choosing the obvious letters.
    1. *S*
    2. *M*
    3. *S* ↔ –*M*

Step 2: Construct the table (see Table 9.14).

Step 3: Evaluate the result. Here, we see that there is no T path. That is, it is not possible for statements 1 to 3 to all be true together; hence, they are mutually inconsistent.

Exercise 9.4A

For each of the following sets of symbolized statements, determine by means of truth tables whether they are consistent or inconsistent.

1. {*A; –A*}
2. {*A* ↔ *B; –B; –A*}
3. {*A* ∨ *B; A* → *B*}
4. {*H* & *Z; Z* ↔ *H; –H*}
5. {*–A* ∨ *–B; B; B* → *A*}

6. {*A* & *B; B* ↔ *C; –A; C*}
7. {*A* ∨ *Z; –Z* & *–B; A* → *B*}
8. {*M* & *N; N* → *R; R* ↔ *M*}
9. {*L* ↔ *T; L* ∨ *T; –M* → *T; –L*}
10. {*H* → *B; –B; –B* → *R; –R*}

Exercise 9.4B

For each of the following sets of statements expressed in English, first symbolize them, and then determine by means of truth tables whether they are consistent or inconsistent.

1. a. Fred is happy.
    b. Fred is rich.
    c. If Fred is happy, he is rich.
2. a. Sue is mellow.
    b. Sue is mellow or angry.
    c. Sue isn't angry.

TABLE 9.14					
S	*M*	*S*	*M*	*S* ↔ –*M*	Path
T	T	T	T	↑ F ↑↑	M
T	F	T	F	↑ T ↑↑	M
F	T	F	T	↑ T ↑↑	M
F	F	F	F	↑ F ↑↑	M

3. a. Either Sue is mellow or angry.
    b. Sue isn't mellow.
    c. Sue isn't angry.
4. a. Fred is happy if and only if he is rich.
    b. Fred isn't happy, but he is rich.
5. a. Both Sue and Fred are happy.
    b. Sue is rich.
    c. Fred is happy if and only if Sue is not rich.
6. a. Fred is crazy, but Sue is crazy if and only if Ted is crazy.
    b. Ted is crazy, unless neither Fred nor Sue are.
7. a. If Al is happy, so is Meg.
    b. If Meg is happy, so is Rachel.
    c. If Rachel is happy, so is Al.
8. a. Betty is friendly, but Maureen isn't.
    b. If and only if Betty is rich is she friendly.
    c. Betty is rich if and only if Maureen is friendly.
9. a. Betty, Al, Sue, and Ted are evil.
    b. If Betty is evil, Ted isn't.
10. a. If people like cheese, they like crackers.
    b. People don't like crackers.
    c. If people like cheese, they like wine.
    d. If people don't like cheese, they like wine.

5   *Truth Table Testing of Implication and Validity*

Entailment is easy to check by the truth table method. If we want to know whether statement *A* entails statement *B*, we are really asking if denying *B* is consistent with asserting *A*. We can discover this in turn by constructing a consistency table and seeing whether there are any T paths.

Let's walk through an example. We want to know whether

   1. Luisa is rich and happy.

entails

   2. Luisa is happy.

We can answer the question by determining whether statement 1 can be T while statement 2 is F. To discover this, just symbolize them and construct a consistency table (Table 9.15) with statement 1 and the *denial* of statement 2: There are no T paths, so –*H* is inconsistent with *R* & *H*; hence, *R* & *H* entails *H*.

We can generalize this rule:

A set of statements A$_1$, . . . , A$_n$ *jointly entails a statement* **B** *if and only if the consistency table for {*A$_1$, . . . , A$_n$, –**B***} has no T paths.*

Example: Determine whether the statements

1. Fred likes cars.
2. Fred doesn't like trains.

together entail

3. Fred likes cars if and only if he likes trains.

Answer: Symbolize statements 1 through 3, and set up the consistency table (Table 9.16) for statement 1, statement 2, and the *negation* of statement 3. Since there is at least one T path, denying statement 3 is consistent with asserting statements 1 and 2, so statements 1 and 2 do not entail statement 3.

Moving to validity, we say an argument is valid if and only if it is impossible for premises to be true and the conclusion false. Put another way, an argument

$$1. \quad P_1$$
$$\cdot$$
$$\cdot$$
$$\cdot$$
$$\underline{n. \quad P_n}$$
$$\therefore \quad C$$

is valid if the denial of the conclusion, $-C$, is inconsistent with the truth of the premises $P_1, \ldots, P_n$. And we already know how to construct tables to check for consistency. So:

TABLE 9.15

R	H	R & H	-H	Path
T	T	⊤T ⊤	F⊤	M
T	F	⊤F ⊦	T	M
F	T	⊦F ⊤	F⊤	M
F	F	⊦F ⊦	T⊦	M

TABLE 9.16

C	T	C	-T	$-(C \leftrightarrow T)$	Path
T	T	T	F⊤	F ⊤ ⊤ ⊤	M
T	F	T	T⊦	T ⊤ ⊦ ⊦	T
F	T	F	F⊤	T ⊦ ⊦ ⊤	M
F	F	F	T⊦	F ⊦ ⊤ ⊦	M

An argument

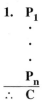

1. P₁
        .
        .
        .
       Pₙ
  ∴ **C**

is valid if and only if the consistency table for {P₁, . . . , Pₙ, −C} has no T paths.
   Consider an example. Is the argument

   1. $A \vee B$
   2. $-A$
   ∴ B

valid or invalid? Negate the conclusion and set up a consistency table (Table 9.17):
   Since there is no T path, denying the conclusion is inconsistent with asserting the premises, and thus the argument is valid. Let's consider another example:

   1. $A \rightarrow B$
   2. $B \,\&\, C$
   ∴ A

Again, this argument is valid if and only if the denial of the conclusion is inconsistent with the premises. Construct the table (Table 9.18). Row 5 is a T path; thus you can deny the conclusion consistent with asserting the premises, and thus the argument is invalid.
   Let's consider another example, this time where there is some translation involved. We want to know whether the following argument is valid:

   If Alfred is rich, then either Bill or Charlene are rich also. But while Alfred is rich,
      Charlene isn't. Therefore, Bill is rich.

First, we symbolize:

   1. $A \rightarrow (B \vee C)$
   2. $A \,\&\, -C$
   ∴ B

Next, we construct the table (Table 9.19). Table 9.19 shows that the original argument is valid.

TABLE 9.17

A	B	A ∨ B	−A	−B	Path
T	T	ⱦT ⱦ	Fⱦ	ⱦⱦ	M
T	F	ⱦT Ȧ	Fⱦ	TȦ	M
F	T	ȦT ⱦ	TȦ	Fⱦ	M
F	F	ȦF Ȧ	TȦ	TȦ	M

TABLE 9.18

A	B	C	A → B	B & C	–A	Path
T	T	T	T T T	T T T	F T	M
T	T	F	T T T	T F F	F T	M
F	F	T	T F F	F F T	F T	F
T	F	F	T F F	F F F	F T	F
F	T	T	F T T	T T T	T F	T
F	T	F	F T T	T F F	T F	M
F	F	T	F T F	F F T	T F	M
F	F	F	F T F	F F F	T F	M

TABLE 9.19

A	B	C	A → (B ∨ C)	A & –C	–B	Path
T	T	T	T T T T T	T F F T	F T	M
T	T	F	T T T T F	T T T F	F T	M
T	F	T	T T F T T	T F F T	T F	M
T	F	F	T F F F F	T T T F	T F	M
F	T	T	F T T T T	F F F T	F T	M
F	T	F	F T T T F	F F T F	F T	M
F	F	T	F T F T T	F F F T	T F	M
F	F	F	F T F F F	F F T F	T F	M

Besides checking given arguments for validity, we can use consistency tables to draw relevant inferences. For example, suppose we know that if Fred were rich, he would own a Porsche. Suppose we further investigate and find out that he does *not* in fact own a Porsche. What can we conclude regarding his wealth?

Let us first symbolize. The first premise is clearly

$$R \rightarrow P$$

The second:

$$-P$$

We are asked to draw a conclusion about whether Fred is wealthy. Let us symbolize this as

$$?R$$

where the question mark indicates that we don't know whether we should infer R or $-R$.

Now set up the consistency table (Table 9.20). Rows 1 through 3 cannot be T paths, since not all the premises are T. If we are to have a valid argument, $?R$ must be F in that row; that is, $?R$ must be F when R is F. So $-R$ is what follows from the premises.

Another example: What follows from

$$A \to (B \to C)$$
$$A \,\&\, -C$$

relevant to B? Set up the consistency table (Table 9.21). Only row 4 is a possible T path. We can block it if $?B$ is F in that row, which means that $-B$ is what follows from those premises.

Exercise 9.5A

Use truth tables to determine the following:

1. Do $\{A; B\}$ entail $A \,\&\, B$?
2. Do $\{A; A \to B\}$ entail $-A$?
3. Do $\{A \,\&\, B; -B\}$ entail Z?
4. Do $\{A \,\&\, -B; A\}$ entail Z?
5. Do $\{A \to B; B \to C\}$ entail $A \to C$?

TABLE 9.20

R	P	$R \to P$	$-P$	$?R$	Path
T	T	T T T	F T		M
T	F	T F F	T F		M
F	T	F T T	F T		M
F	F	F T F	T F		?

TABLE 9.21

A	B	C	$A \to (B \to C)$	$A \,\&\, -C$	$?B$	Path
T	T	T	T T T T T	T F F T		M
T	T	F	T F T F F	T T T F		M
T	F	T	T T F T T	T F F T		M
T	F	F	T T F T F	T T T F		?
F	T	T	F T T T T	F F F T		M
F	T	F	F T T F F	F F T F		M
F	F	F	F T F T T	F F F T		M
F	F	F	F T F T F	F F T F		M

Exercise 9.5B

For each of the following arguments, determine by constructing a consistency table whether it is valid or invalid.

1.   1. $A \rightarrow B$
     2. A
     ___
     $\therefore B$

2.   1. $A \vee B$
     2. $-B$
     ___
     $\therefore -A$

3.   1. $A \vee B$
     2. $B \vee -A$
     ___
     $\therefore B$

4.   1. $A \rightarrow (B \& C)$
     ___
     $\therefore A \rightarrow C$

5.   1. $M \rightarrow I$
     2. $I \rightarrow Q$
     3. $Q \rightarrow Q$
     ___
     $\therefore -M \vee Q$

6.   1. $-M \vee (T \& B)$
     2. $-M \leftrightarrow T$
     ___
     $\therefore T$

7.   1. $A \leftrightarrow (B \leftrightarrow C)$
     2. $A \& B$
     ___
     $\therefore C$

8.   1. $-A \leftrightarrow (B \rightarrow C)$
     2. $-A \& B$
     ___
     $\therefore -B$

9.   1. $-A \leftrightarrow (-B \vee -C)$
     2. $-C \vee -A$
     3. $A \& C$
     ___
     $\therefore -B$

10. 1. $-[A \vee (B \vee D)]$
     2. $-B \rightarrow -A$
     ___
     $\therefore -B$

Exercise 9.5C

For each of the following arguments, first symbolize it, and then construct a consistency table to determine whether it is valid.

1.   Either Mary or Sue will go to the party. Sue isn't going, so Mary will.
2.   If Sam goes into computer science, he will become rich. But he isn't going into computer science. So he won't become rich.
3.   Sue will be happy if and only if she goes into computer science. She is going into computer science. So she will be happy.
4.   Sue and Sam are both rich. But Al is not rich. So either Al or Sue is rich.
5.   If Sam goes to the market, he will either buy milk or butter. But he is not going to buy butter. So if Sam goes to the market, he will buy milk.
6.   Either Smith or Jones will win the election. But if Jones wins the election, we will go to war. Therefore, either Smith will win, or we will go to war.
7.   Alan is going to major in physics. Sue is going to major in math. So if Mary drops out, Alan will major in physics, and Sue will major in math.
8.   If Sue goes to the party, so will Al. If Al goes to the party, so will Wynona. So if Sue goes to the party, so will Wynona.
9.   If Sue goes to the party, so will Al. If Al goes to the party, so will Wynona. So if Wynona goes to the party, so will Sue.
10. If Sue goes to the party, so will Al. If Al goes to the party, then so will Wynona. So either Sue or Wynona will go to the party.

Exercise 9.5D

Use consistency tables to determine the following:

1.   What follows from $\{A \leftrightarrow B; -B\}$ relevant to A?
2.   What follows from $\{A \vee B; -A\}$ relevant to B?
3.   What follows from $\{A \rightarrow B; B \rightarrow C\}$ relevant to $-A \vee C$?
4.   What follows from $\{(A \& C) \rightarrow B; C \& A\}$ relevant to B?
5.   What follows from $[-A \vee -B; Z \rightarrow A; Z\}$ relevant to B?

+6   *Truth Table Testing for Other Deductive Concepts*

We have defined four terms that describe the logical relations between pairs of statements: logical equivalence, contradictories, contraries, and subcontraries. We need to extend our truth table method to test for those relations.

Let's start with equivalence. We said that two statements A and B are equivalent if and only if they cannot possibly differ in truth value—that is, if $\{A, -B\}$ and $\{-A, B\}$ are inconsistent. In a table, this means that the rows either have two T's or two F's, never a mixture. So: ***Two statements are equivalent if and only if their consistency table has no M paths.*** Let's work a couple of examples.

First are the statements

1. $A \rightarrow B$
2. $-B \rightarrow -A$

equivalent? Construct the table (9.22). The table shows no M paths, so the statements are equivalent.

Second, are the statements

1. $A \rightarrow (B \rightarrow C)$
2. $(A \rightarrow B) \rightarrow C$

equivalent? Construct the table (9.23). Row 6 is an M path, so the two statements can differ in truth value; hence, they are not equivalent.

TABLE 9.22

A	B	$A \rightarrow B$	$-B \rightarrow -A$	Path
T	T	T T T	F T T F T	T
T	F	T F F	T F F F T	F
F	T	F T T	F T T T F	T
F	F	F T F	T F T T F	T

Consider next contradictories. We said that two statements are contradictory if they must always differ in truth value. The truth table test for this is simply as follows: *Two statements* **A** *and* **B** *are contradictory if and only if the consistency table for* **A** *and* **B** *shows nothing but M paths.* For example, are the statements

    1. $-A \vee -B$
    2. $A \mathbin{\&} B$

contradictory? Construct the table (9.24). As the table shows, the statements are contradictory.

How about contraries? Well, two statements *A* and *B* are contraries if and only if they cannot both be T but can both be F. (That second clause is important: contradictories cannot both be T but cannot also both be F.) The table test is accordingly as follows: *Two statements* **A** *and* **B** *are contraries if and only if the consistency table for* **A** *and* **B** *has no T paths and at least one F path.* For example, are the following statements contraries?

    1. $A \mathbin{\&} B$
    2. $A \mathbin{\&} -B$

Construct the table (9.25). Sure enough, there are no T paths but at least one F path, so they are contraries.

TABLE 9.23

A	B	C	A → (B → C)	(A → B) → C	Path
T	T	T	T T T T	T T T T T	T
T	T	F	T F T	T T T F	F
T	F	T	T T	T T T	T
T	F	F	T T	T T T	T
F	T	T	T T T	T T T T	T
F	T	F	T T	T T F	M
F	F	T			
F	F	F			

TABLE 9.24

A	B	−A ∨ −B	A & B	Path
T	T	F	T T	M
T	F	T	T F	M
F	T	T	F	M
F	F	T	F	M

Finally, there are subcontraries. We said that two statements *A* and *B* are subcontraries if they cannot both be F but can both be T. The truth table test for this is as follows: ***Two statements* A *and* B *are subcontraries if and only if the consistency table for* A *and* B *has no F paths but at least one T path.*** For example, are the statements

1. $A \rightarrow B$
2. $A \rightarrow -B$

subcontraries? Construct the table (9.26). Sure enough, they are subcontraries.

You should be aware that the categories of equivalents, contradictories, contraries, and subcontraries are mutually exclusive but are *not* jointly exhaustive. That is, a pair of statements can be neither equivalents, nor contradictories, nor contraries, nor subcontraries. For example, the statements

1. $A \& B$
2. $A \vee C$

are neither equivalents, nor contradictories, nor contraries, nor subcontraries, as you can prove if you construct the appropriate truth table.

Having defined the method of truth tables for determining consistency of beliefs, we can use it to test for necessary truth, necessary falsehood, and contingency. Consider an easy example. The statement "Either Jones is now president or he isn't" is clearly necessarily true. If we symbolize it, we get

$J \vee -J$

Now set up a table (9.27) with the basic components on one side and the statement to be tested on the other.

TABLE 9.25

A	B	A & B	A & –B	Path
T	T	T T T	T F F T	M
T	F	T F F	T T T F	M
F	T	F F T	F F F T	F
F	F	F F F	F F T F	F

TABLE 9.26

A	B	A → B	A → –B	Path
T	T	T T T	T F F T	M
T	F	T F F	T T T F	M
F	T	F T T	F T F T	T
F	F	F T F	F T T F	T

Finally, in Table 9.28 we do the calculations in each row. Sure enough, every row is a T path; hence, the statement is indeed a tautology (that is, necessarily true by its logical structure).

We can generalize this approach: *A statement is a tautology if and only if its truth table has only T paths. A statement is a self-contradiction if and only if its truth table has only F paths. And a statement is contingent if and only if its table has at least one T path and at least one F path.* For example, consider

Juan likes cheese, and if Juan makes his mind up, he makes his mind up.

Picking the obvious letters, we can symbolize this as

$C \,\&\, (M \to M)$

Set up the table (9.29). We see that the compound is true in some cases and false in some. So it is contingent.

Finally, consider "Al is happy, and Barry is happy but Al isn't." Symbolically:

$A \,\&\, (B \,\&\, {-}A)$

Set up the table and carry out the calculations (9.30). Since the table has nothing but F paths (that is, is F in every case), we can conclude that it is a self-contradiction.

Again, the tables can get bigger (if there are more basic letters), but the insight is the same. For example, is

$[(A \,\&\, B) \to C] \leftrightarrow [A \to (B \to C)]$

TABLE 9.27

J	J ∨ –J	Path
T		
F		

TABLE 9.28

J	J ∨ –J	Path
T	⊤T F⊤	T
F	F⊤ ⊤F	T

TABLE 9.29

C	M	C & (M → M)	Path
T	T	⊤T ⊤⊤⊤	T
T	F	⊤T F⊤F	T
F	T	F⊤ ⊤⊤⊤	F
F	F	F⊤ F⊤F	F

a tautology, self-contradiction, or contingent? Construct the tedious table (9.31) All paths are T paths; hence, the statement is a tautology.

Exercise 9.6A

For each of the following symbolized statements, determine by consistency tables whether they are equivalents, contradictories, subcontraries, or none of those.

1. $\{A \to C; A \& -C\}$
2. $\{B \& Q; Q \leftrightarrow B\}$
3. $\{H \vee -T; -T \vee H\}$
4. $\{Q \leftrightarrow R; -Q \leftrightarrow -R\}$
5. $\{A \to (B \vee -B); (-B \vee -B) \leftrightarrow A\}$
6. $\{(A \& B) \& C; A \& (B \& C)\}$
7. $\{-[A \vee (B \vee C)]; [(B \vee A) \vee C]\}$
8. $\{-A \vee C; -B \& A\}$
9. $\{-A \& B; A \& -C\}$
10. $\{-A \leftrightarrow (B \vee C); A \leftrightarrow (B \vee -C)\}$

Exercise 9.6B

For the following pairs of statements, first symbolize them, and then determine by consistency tables whether they are equivalents, contradictories, contraries, subcontraries, or none of those.

TABLE 9.30

A	B	A & (B & −A)	Path
T	T	⊤F ⊤⊤⊤⊤	F
T	F	⊤F ⊤⊤⊤⊤	F
F	T	⊤F ⊤⊤⊤⊤	F
F	F	⊤F ⊤⊤⊤⊤	F

TABLE 9.31

A	B	C	[(A & B) → C] ↔ [A → (B → C)]	Path
T	T	T	⊤⊤⊤ ⊤⊤ T ⊤⊤ ⊤⊤ ⊤	T
T	T	F	⊤⊤⊤ ⊤⊤ T ⊤⊤ ⊤⊤ ⊤	T
T	F	T	T⊤⊤ ⊤⊤ T ⊤⊤ ⊤⊤ ⊤	T
T	F	F	⊤⊤⊤ T⊤ T ⊤⊤ ⊤⊤ ⊤	T
F	T	T	⊤⊤⊤ ⊤⊤ T ⊤⊤ ⊤⊤ ⊤	T
F	T	F	⊤⊤⊤ ⊤⊤ T ⊤T ⊤⊤ ⊤	T
F	F	T	⊤⊤⊤ ⊤⊤ T ⊤T ⊤⊤ ⊤	T
F	F	F	⊤⊤⊤ ⊤⊤ T ⊤⊤ ⊤⊤ ⊤	T

1. a. If Maria likes soup, she likes soup.
   b. Maria does not like soup.
2. a. Bob and Jill are Democrats.
   b. Bob is a Democrat, but Jill isn't.
3. a. Fred is dead if and only if he isn't moving.
   b. Fred is dead and moving.
4. a. Sue is happy but crazy.
   b. If Sue is crazy, she is happy.
5. a. If Bob and Carol are rich, so is Ted.
   b. Neither Bob nor Ted is rich.
6. a. Al is happy, but Sue isn't.
   b. Al isn't happy, or Sue and Fred are happy.
7. a. Al is happy if and only if Sue isn't.
   b. Sue is happy, and yet Fred isn't.
8. a. Neither Al nor Fred is alive.
   b. Either Al, Fred, or Sue is dead.
9. a. If Al is happy, so are Sue and Fred.
   b. If neither Sue nor Fred are happy, Al isn't.
10. a. Al, Sue, and Mona are evil.
    b. Al and Mona are not evil, or else Sue is.

Exercise 9.6C

For each of the following symbolized statements, determine by means of a truth table whether it is necessarily true, necessarily false, or contingent.

1. $A \vee B$
2. $A \rightarrow -A$
3. $(A \& B) \& (A \& -B)$
4. $(A \& B) \rightarrow -A$
5. $(A \& B) \rightarrow A$
6. $(A \& B) \rightarrow (B \& A)$
7. $(A \vee B) \rightarrow (B \vee A)$
8. $(A \rightarrow B) \rightarrow [(B \& A) \vee -(B \& A)]$
9. $(A \leftrightarrow B) \rightarrow [(B \& A) \vee (-B \& -A)]$
10. $A \rightarrow [A \rightarrow ((A \vee B) \vee C)]$

Exercise 9.6D

For each of the following sentences, first symbolize it, and then determine by means of a truth table whether it is necessarily true, necessarily false, or contingent.

1. Either Fred can fight, or he can't.
2. Fred can fight, but he can't.
3. Sue is rich and pretty.
4. If Marvin is rich, then he's rich.
5. Sue is rich, but Fred can fight or he can't.
6. Unless Fred can't dance, Sue can or Al can.
7. Sue can't fight, and neither Sue nor Terri can fight.
8. Fred is sane if and only if he is not insane, but neither Al nor Louise are sane.
9. If Moe is frisky, then he's both frisky and sly.
10. Fred is happy and rich if and only if it is not true that he is neither.

7   *Summary*

In this chapter we have looked at a number of deductive concepts, explaining them in terms of deductive concepts and in terms of two underlying concepts: consistency and inconsistency. We also developed a simple method—truth tables—to check for these various qualities. Table 9.32 summarizes the discussion.

TABLE 9.32

Term	Definition	Put in Terms of Consistency	Concepts Truth Table Test
$A_1, \ldots, A_n$ consistent	$A_1, \ldots, A_n$ can all be T		At least one T path in the table for $\{A_1, \ldots, A_n\}$
$A_1, \ldots, A_n$ inconsistent	$A_1, \ldots, A_n$ cannot all be T		No T paths in the table for $\{A_1, \ldots, A_n\}$
$A_1, A_2, \ldots, A_n$ entail/imply B	It is impossible for $A_1, \ldots, A_n$ to be T and B F	$\{A_1, \ldots, A_n, -B\}$ is inconsistent	No T paths in the table for $\{A_1, \ldots, A_n, -B\}$
A_1 · · · A_n ———— $\therefore B$ is valid	It is impossible for $A_1, \ldots, A_n$ to be all T and B F	$\{A_1, \ldots, A_n, -B\}$ is inconsistent	No T paths in the table for $\{A_1, \ldots, A_n, -B\}$
A, B equivalent	A and B cannot possibly differ in truth value	$\{A, -B\}$ and $\{-A, B\}$ inconsistent	No M paths in the table for $\{A, B\}$
A, B contradictories	A and B have opposite truth values	$\{A, B\}$ and $\{-A, -B\}$ inconsistent	All M paths in the table for $\{A, B\}$
A, B contraries	A and B cannot both be T but can both be F	$\{A, B\}$ inconsistent $\{-A, -B\}$ consistent	No T paths, but one or more F paths in the table for $\{A, B\}$
A, B subcontraries	A and B cannot both be F but can both be T	$\{A, B\}$ consistent $\{-A, -B\}$ inconsistent	No F paths, but one or more T paths in table for $\{A, B\}$
A is a tautology	A can't possibly be F	$\{-A\}$ is inconsistent	Only T paths in the table for A
A is self-contradictory	A can't possibly be T	$\{A\}$ is inconsistent	Only F paths in the table for A
A is contingent	A can be T and can be F	$\{A\}$ and $\{-A\}$ are both consistent	At least one T path and at least one F path in the table for A

InfoTrac College Edition

You can locate InfoTrac College Edition articles about this chapter by accessing the InfoTrac College Edition Web site (www.infotrac-college.com/wadsworth/). Using the InfoTrac College Edition subject guide, enter the search terms relevant to this chapter, and then read abstracts for relevant articles.

Chapter 10

Class Logic

---

1   *A Closer Look at Statements*

In Chapter 9, we defined the key deductive concepts of consistency, implication/validity, equivalence, and necessity. We developed a rough but handy tool, truth tables, to investigate those concepts. But truth tables only investigate the logic of truth functionally compound statements. This is just the first step in the development of deductive logic. To see why we need more powerful analytical tools, consider the following argument:

    1.   All clowns are evil.
    2.   Bozo is a clown.
    ∴   Bozo is evil.

This argument is clearly valid. But if we symbolize this using the approach in the last chapter, we get

    1. C
    2. B
    ∴ E

which is obviously invalid (construct a table and prove it invalid).

The point here is that the validity of many arguments turns on other features of the statements involved besides truth functional connectives. We need to increase our ability to analyze the internal structure of simple statements.

The first step along this path is to look at statements involving **classes**—that is, groups of things. Such statements are very common. Consider the following simple statements:

    Fred is evil.
    Sue is happy.
    Mona hates cheese.

Such statements can be viewed as claims that a particular individual is a member of some class: Fred is a member of the class of evil things; Sue is member of the class of happy things; Mona is a member of the class of cheese-hating things.

We can represent such statements using circles and squares in a manner first explored by the mathematicians Leonhardt Euler and James Venn. We call these diagrams Venn diagrams. We will represent classes by labeled circles, within a box that represents the **universal set**—the set of everything. For example, we can represent the class of pigs as Figure 10.1. Notice we label the circle representing the class with a capital letter, and then indicate what that letter represents of to the left of the box.

P = pigs

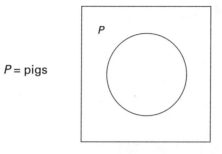

Figure 10.1

We represent individuals in Venn diagrams by selecting lowercase letters. We represent the claim that a given individual is a member of a class by putting the chosen lowercase letter inside the circle. For example, "Porky is a pig" is represented by the Venn diagram in Figure 10.2.

P = pigs

p = Porky

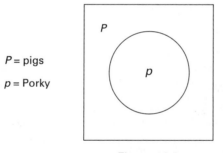

Figure 10.2

The claim that a given individual is not a member of a class is then represented by placing the letter outside the circle. Thus, "Donald is not a pig" is represented by Figure 10.3.

P = pigs

d = Donald

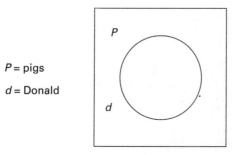

Figure 10.3

We can now represent many particular statements by Venn diagrams. But what about general statements? We can render them diagrammatically by using a check mark to represent the claim that a class has one or more members in it (that is, is not empty) and shading to represent that a class or part of a class is empty. For instance, the claim that there are pigs ("Pigs exist.") is represented by Figure 10.4. The claim that there are no pigs is represented by Figure 10.5.

P = pigs

√ = some

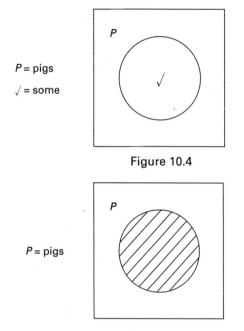

Figure 10.4

P = pigs

Figure 10.5

Think of the check mark as a generic name—it represents that some individual of a contain type exists, but we don't know its particular name (or names, if more than one such individual exists). Table 10.1 summarizes what we have done so far.

We can use Venn diagrams to express many claims. For example,

Sue is friendly.

becomes (Figure 10.6)

F = friendly things

s = Sue

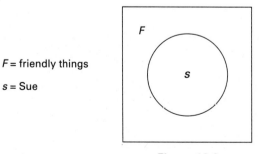

Figure 10.6

TABLE 10.1			
Proposition	Venn Representation	Proposition	Venn Representation
Individual *x* is *C*.	*C* ... *x*	Individual *x* is not *C*.	*C* ... *x*
Something is *C*.	*C* ... ✓	Something is not *C*.	*C* ... ✓
Nothing is *C*.	*C* (shaded circle)	Everything is *C*.	*C* (shaded outside circle)

Juan is not kind.

becomes

Juan is not a member of the class of kind things.

becomes (Figure 10.7)

K = kind things

j = Juan

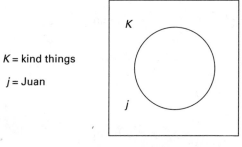

Figure 10.7

Everything is expensive these days.

becomes

There is nothing that is not a member of the class of things are expensive these days.

becomes (Figure 10.8)

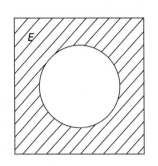

E = things that are
       expensive these days

Figure 10.8

Exercise 10.1

Represent the following propositions by one-circle Venn diagrams.

1. Maria is happy.
2. Luisa is not happy.
3. Moe is in love.
4. Everything is ugly.
5. Something is ugly.

6. Nothing is ugly.
7. Lola is pretty.
8. Lola is not pretty.
9. Nothing stays put.
10. Something stays put.

2   *Statements Involving Two Classes*

We can increase the power of Venn diagrams to represent propositions if we move to two circles, representing two classes. Consider first statements involving specific individuals. For example, we can represent

    Porky is a happy pig.

by overlapping two circles, one representing the class of happy things, and the other the class of pigs (Figure 10.9).

P = pigs

H = happy things

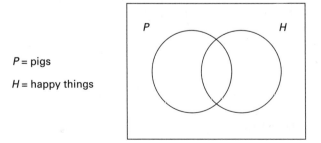

Figure 10.9

The area of overlap represents the set of happy pigs, so we can now represent the original statement by placing a *p* for "Porky" in the area of overlap between the two circles (Figure 10.10).

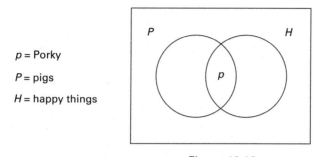

p = Porky

P = pigs

H = happy things

Figure 10.10

Let's try another example of a two-class statement about a specific individual. Consider:

Susie is neither rich nor happy.

Again, set up a diagram with overlapping circles representing the relevant classes (Figure 10.11).

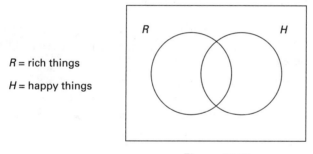

R = rich things

H = happy things

Figure 10.11

The area outside both circles represents the things that are not rich and not happy things. Thus, we can represent the original statement (using *s* for "Susie") as in Figure 10.12.

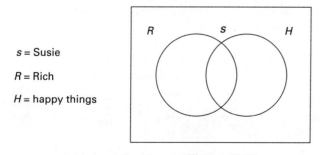

s = Susie

R = Rich

H = happy things

Figure 10.12

Before proceeding, you would do well to review the areas of a two-circle Venn diagram. This is given in Figure 10.13.

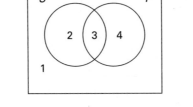

Region 1 = things that are neither *S* nor *P*
Region 2 = things that are *S* but not *P*
Region 3 = things that are both *S* and *P*
Region 4 = things that are *P* but not *S*

Figure 10.13

So far we have only looked at two class statements involving specific (that is, named) individuals. But there is a far larger important type of two-class statements called categorical statements: a **categorical statement** is one of the form

[Quantifier] [Subject class] [Copula] [Predicate class]

where by *quantifier* we mean "all" or "some" and by *copula* we mean either "is" or "are." We can delineate four basic forms of categorical statement: **A, I, E,** and **O.** The first statement form is termed *universal affirmative,* or **A** statements:

A*SP* = All *S* are *P*.

where *S* is the *subject* class and *P* is the *predicate* class. For example,

All pigs are fat.
All people are lonely.
All movie stars are vain.

(Note that by using a predicate such as *fat* that we are using it as a set-defining property.)
The second type of categorical statement is called *particular affirmative,* or an **I** statement. An **I** statement is any statement of the form

I*SP* = Some *S* is *P*.

For example,

Some men are happy.
Some dogs are friendly.
Some mushrooms are poisonous.

The third statement form is termed "universal negative," or **E** statement:

E*SP* = No *S* are *P*.

For example,

>   No cats are loyal.
>   No frogs are shy.
>   No house is safe.

Fourth, we distinguish "particular negative," or **O** statements.

>   **O**SP = Some *S* is not *P.*

For example,

>   Some fish is not fresh.
>   Some people are not friendly.
>   Some cats are not evil.

We can represent each of the forms by a Venn diagram. Figure 10.14 gives the diagrams.

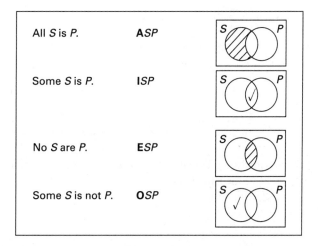

Figure 10.14

A huge number of English sentences express categorical statements without having an obvious (overt) **A, E, I,** or **O** structure.

A few tips may help you symbolize accurately.

Hint 1: Watch out for inverted word order. Sentences such as "Men are all sex maniacs" are rhetorically effective but logically deceiving. The sentence is best paraphrased as "All men are sex maniacs" and translated accordingly **A**MS.

Hint 2: Watch out for omitted quantifiers. Some sentences omit the quantifiers altogether. "Cats are sly" usually means "All cats are sly," which is **A**CS. On the other hand, the sentence "Children are present" means "There are children present," which is **I**CP ("Some children are present").

Hint 3: Watch out for omitted copulas. Sentences in ordinary language often omit the copula (some tense of the verb *to be*), as, for example,

> All people want money.

This can be paraphrased:

> All people are money wanters.

which is **A***PM*.

***Hint 4: Remember that English has many quantifiers besides* all *and* some.** Figure 10.15 lists the common ones.

Please note that something may get lost in the translation, as, for instance, in viewing

> Almost all dogs are friendly.

as

> Some dogs are friendly.

We can formulate a step-by-step method of translation, in this case, of putting statements expressed in ordinary language into normal form.

> [Quantifier] [Subject class term] [Copula *is* or *are*] [Predicate class term]

Step 1: Figure out what the subject is.
Step 2: If the verb is not *are* or *is,* substitute for it a synonymous phrase involving
    are or *is.*
Step 3: Determine what the predicate is—that is, what class is claimed to contain
    all, some, or none of the subject class.
Step 4: Determine the quantifier.

Let's work through a few examples.

Example: Some people are kind.

is explicitly an **I***SP* statement and can be expressed by Figure 10.16.

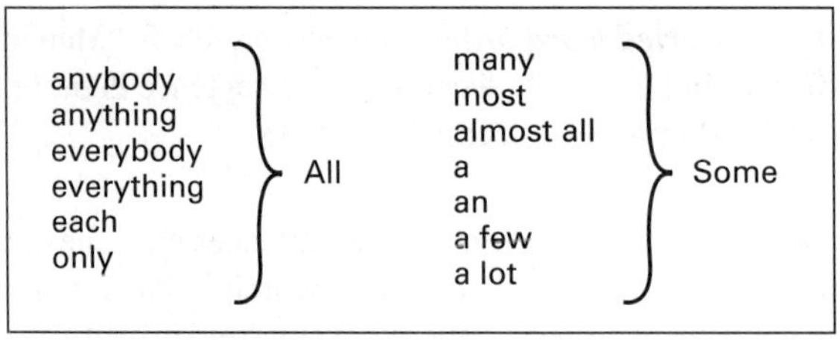

Figure 10.15

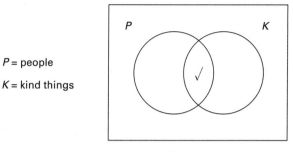

P = people

K = kind things

Figure 10.16

Example: Nobody doesn't like Sara Lee.

Here we have to work to express it in categorical form:

Every person is a Sara Lee liker.

which can be expressed by Figure 10.17.

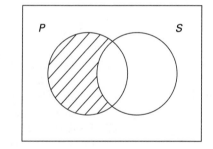

P = people

S = Sara Lee liker

Figure 10.17

Exercise 10.2A

The following statements are in an explicit categorical statement form. For each, symbolize it as one of the categorical statement forms (**A, I, E,** and **O**); then draw a Venn diagram to represent it.

Example: All cats are mammals

is

    A*CM*

and its diagram is (Figure 10.18)

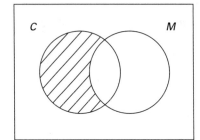

Figure 10.18

1. All mammals are cats.
2. All cats are brown.
3. No cats are brown.
4. Some cats are brown.
5. Some cats are not mammals.

6. Some mammals are not brown.
7. No brown things are cats.
8. No mammals are cats.
9. Some cats aren't brown.
10. All brown things are cats.

Exercise 10.2B

Restate these statements as an explicit categorical statement form, and then construct a Venn diagram for each one.

1. All people hate cheese.
2. All dogs bark.
3. Some dogs don't like cheese.
4. No birds fly backward.
5. All birds live underground.
6. People are strange.
7. Cats can't dance.
8. All that glitters isn't gold.
9. Women are all kind.
10. Police are nearby.

11. Almost all burglars are clever.
12. A few burglars are clever.
13. Only politicians love elections.
14. A lot of politicians love elections.
15. People hate losers.
16. Each cat is unique.
17. There are happy bachelors.
18. Dogs aren't selective.
19. Dogs aren't around.
20. Many dogs are happy.

3   *Venn Testing for Consistency*

In Chapter 9 we learned that a group of statements are (mutually) inconsistent if and only if they cannot all be true. And we learned to check for consistency in sets of truth functionally compound statements by truth tables. We can also check for consistency of class statements, using our new tool—Venn diagrams. The basic rule is this: ***A set of class statements is consistent if and only if their diagrams of the statements in the set are all compatible.***

Some examples will make this clear. First, suppose we want to know whether the statements

1.   Mandy is a dog.
2.   All dogs are friendly.
3.   Mandy is unfriendly.

are consistent. Begin by setting up a Venn diagram with circles for the class of dogs and the class of friendly things (Figure 10.19).

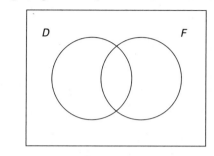

D = dogs

F = friendly things

Figure 10.19

Next, start representing the statements. *Note:* Always diagram general statements before particular ones.

Statement 2 is represented by Figure 10.20.

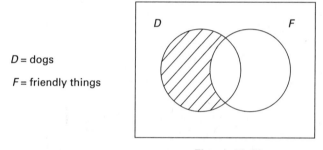

D = dogs

F = friendly things

Figure 10.20

Statements 2 and 3, however, require putting an *m* (for Mandy) in *D* and outside *F,* which is impossible—that region has been shaded in. So, the statements are mutually inconsistent.

Next, consider the statements:

1. Vago is a dog.
2. Some dogs are evil.
3. Vago is not evil.

To determine whether these statements are consistent, again set up the circles (Figure 10.21).

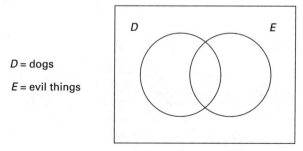

D = dogs

E = evil things

Figure 10.21

We represent statement 2 by Figure 10.22.

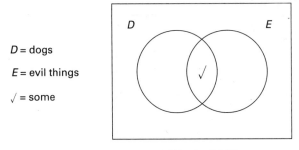

D = dogs

E = evil things

√ = some

Figure 10.22

We represent statements 1 and 3 together by putting a *v* for Vago in D and outside E (Figure 10.23). Clearly, the diagram is coherent so the statements are perfectly consistent.

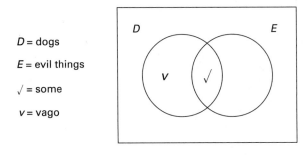

D = dogs

E = evil things

√ = some

v = vago

Figure 10.23

Next consider

1. All dogs are mammals.
2. All cats are mammals.

To represent these claims we need to overlap three circles (for the three mentioned classes) as in Figure 10.24.

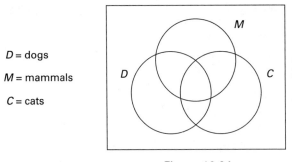

D = dogs

M = mammals

C = cats

Figure 10.24

Statement 1 is represented in Figure 10.25.

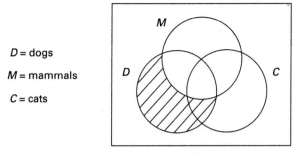

Figure 10.25

Statement 2 is represented in Figure 10.26.

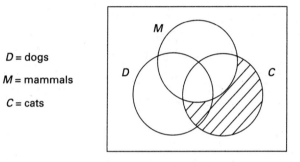

Figure 10.26

Are these diagrams compatible? Certainly—they amount together to Figure 10.27.

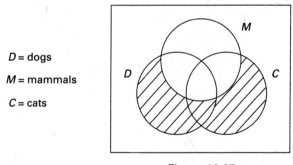

Figure 10.27

So, the two statements are compatible.

Finally, consider these statements:

1. Some dogs are brown.
2. All dogs are mean.
3. No brown things are mean.

Are they consistent? Again, we set up a Venn diagram with three overlapping circles (Figure 10.28).

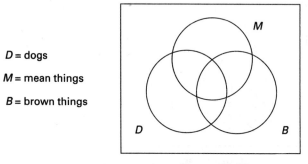

D = dogs

M = mean things

B = brown things

Figure 10.28

We represent statement 2 by Figure 10.29 and statement 3 by Figure 10.30. Putting the two together yields Figure 10.31.

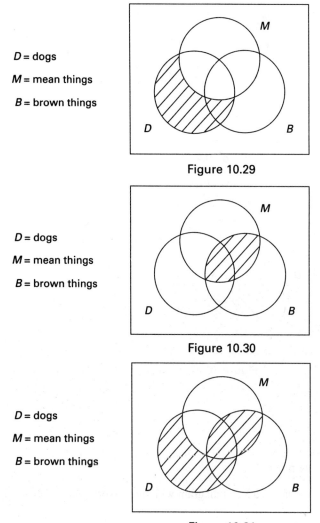

D = dogs

M = mean things

B = brown things

Figure 10.29

D = dogs

M = mean things

B = brown things

Figure 10.30

D = dogs

M = mean things

B = brown things

Figure 10.31

But now notice that the area of overlap between D and B is completely shaded, which rules out putting a check mark there—thus, ruling out representing statement 1. The three statements, therefore, are inconsistent.

Exercise 10.3

For each of the following sets of statements, determine by means of Venn diagrams whether they are consistent.

1. {John is happy; John is a pilot; all pilots are happy.}
2. {Alicia is a dancer; all dancers like coffee; Alicia doesn't like coffee.}
3. {All people are friendly; some people are not friendly.}
4. {All trucks are expensive; some trucks are yellow; some yellow things are expensive.}
5. {All frogs are green; all pigs are green.}
6. {Some Pigs can dance; Porky is a pig; Porky cannot dance.}
7. {All cats are evil; Suzie is a cat: Suzie isn't evil.}
8. {All pigs are friendly; all pigs are talented; Porky is an untalented but friendly pig.}
9. {Some dogs are nice; some dogs are not nice; all dogs are evil.}
10. {All dogs have fur; anything that has fur is nice; no dogs are nice.}

4   Venn Testing for Implication and Validity

Logical implication among class statements is also easy to determine by Venn diagrams. The rule is: ***Class statement C_1 logically implies class statement C_2 if and only if diagramming C_1 represents C_2 as well.*** Again, we can explain by working some examples. First, does "Freddy is a pig" logically imply "There are some pigs" (that is, "Pigs exist")? Diagram "Freddy is a pig," and you get Figure 10.32.

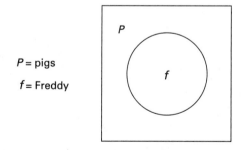

P = pigs

f = Freddy

Figure 10.32

The fact that f occurs in the P circle means that something is there, which is just the diagram for "There are some pigs" (Figure 10.33).

Next, does "All cats are animals" logically imply "Some cats are not animals?" Diagram the first statement, and you get Figure 10.34. But that excludes anything from the area within C but outside A, which is just where you have to place a check mark to express "Some cats are not animals." Thus, the first statement does *not* logically imply the second.

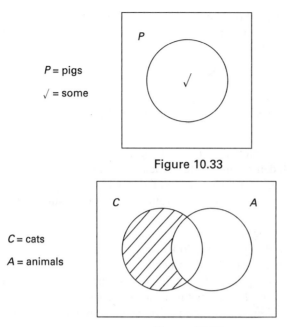

P = pigs

√ = some

Figure 10.33

C = cats

A = animals

Figure 10.34

We can also use Venn diagrams to determine whether a given class argument is valid. In what follows, we will confine ourselves to class arguments of just three terms. The rule is ***A class argument is valid if and only if in diagramming the premises the conclusion is diagrammed as well.***

Again, examples will make this clear.

Example 1: Is the following argument valid?

1. All frogs are green.
2. Kermit is a frog.
∴   Kermit is green.

Diagramming the general premises first yields Figure 10.35. Add the diagram for the second premises, and you get Figure 10.36. Clearly the conclusion is represented, for *k* occurs within the *G* circle.

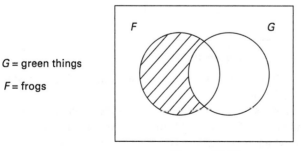

G = green things

F = frogs

Figure 10.35

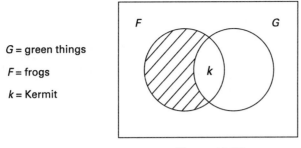

G = green things

F = frogs

k = Kermit

Figure 10.36

Example 2: Is the following argument valid?

1. Some dogs are brown.
2. Some cats are brown.
∴ Some dogs are cats.

Diagram the first premises (Figure 10.37).

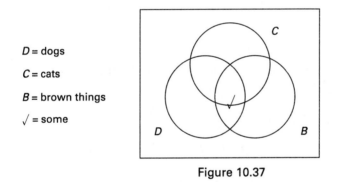

D = dogs

C = cats

B = brown things

√ = some

Figure 10.37

We put the check mark (representing some brown dog) within the overlap between *D* and *B*, but on the border of *C*, because we don't know whether it is a cat. We diagram the second premises similarly (Figure 10.38).

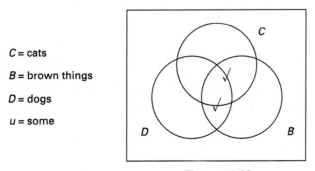

C = cats

B = brown things

D = dogs

u = some

Figure 10.38

Does Figure 10.38 represent the conclusion? No, because the conclusion "Some dogs are cats" would require a check mark *clearly* in the overlap of *D* and *C*. The argument therefore is not valid.

We can also use Venn diagrams to draw relevant inferences about classes. The rule is: ***To draw an inference from premises, diagram the premises and read off what follows.***

For example, what follows from

    1.   All cats are evil.
    2.   Garfield is a cat.

relevant to Garfield?

Diagram the premises (Figure 10.39). (Do the general premise first.)

C = cats

E = evil things

g = Garfield

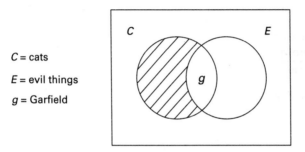

Figure 10.39

What can we say about *g?* It is within the circle for *E;* thus, "Garfield is evil" follows from the premises.

Exercise 10.4A

For each of the following pairs of class statements, use Venn diagrams to determine whether the first implies the second.

1.   All people are evil; no people are evil.
2.   Some pigs can dance; all pigs can dance.
3.   Some pigs are evil; some pigs are not evil.
4.   Some pigs are not evil; not all pigs are evil.
5.   All people are evil; all nonevil things are nonpeople.

Exercise 10.4B

For each of the following, use Venn diagrams to determine whether the argument is valid or invalid.

  1. 1. Some people are evil.
      2. Sam is a person.
      ∴ Sam is evil.
  2. 1. All dogs love cheese.
      2. Mandy is a dog.
      ∴ Mandy loves cheese.

3. 1. Some dogs are evil.
   2. Some cats are evil.
   ∴ Some dogs are cats.
4. 1. All pigs are happy.
   2. Socrates is a pig.
   ∴ Socrates is happy.
5. 1. Some pigs are happy.
   2. Any happy thing is evil.
   ∴ Some pigs are evil.
6. 1. All pigs are happy.
   ∴ No pigs are happy.
7. 1. All pigs are happy.
   2. Any happy thing is evil.
   ∴ Some pigs are not evil.
8. 1. Some pigs are happy.
   2. Any happy thing is evil.
   ∴ Some pigs are not evil.
9. 1. All pigs are happy.
   2. All pigs are evil.
   ∴ Any happy thing is evil.
10. 1. All pigs are happy.
    2. Some happy things are silly.
    ∴ Some pigs are silly.

Exercise 10.4C

For each of the following premise sets, determine what follows relevant to Mandy using Venn diagrams.

1. 1. All dogs are evil.
   2. Mandy is a dog.
   ?
2. 1. Some dogs are evil.
   2. Anything that is evil is happy.
   ?
3. 1. No dogs are evil.
   2. Mandy is a dog.
   ?
4. 1. Some dogs are not evil.
   2. Mandy is a dog.
   ?
5. 1. All pigs are happy.
   2. Mandy is a dog.
   3. All dogs are pigs.
   ?

+5   *Venn Testing for Other Concepts*

In the last chapter we discussed the notion of logical equivalence among pairs of statements. We said that two statements are logically equivalent if and only if they must always have the same truth value. The easiest way to test for this for class statements is by Venn diagrams. The rule is: ***Two class statements A and B are equivalent if and only if they have the same Venn diagram.***

Let's work through an example. Are the class statements

1. All dogs are evil.
2. No dogs are nonevil.

equivalent? Construct the Venn diagrams for each side by side (Figure 10.40). Comparing the two diagrams, we see that they are identical, so the statements are equivalent.

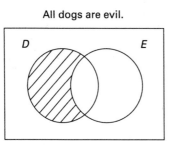

Figure 10.40

Let's work another example. Are the statements

1. No cats like cheese.
2. Some cats don't like cheese.

logically equivalent?

Again, construct the Venns for the statements side by side (Figure 10.41). Comparing the diagrams, we see that they are not identical; hence, the statements are not logically equivalent.

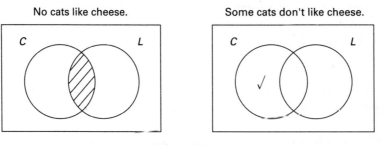

Figure 10.41

Recall from the last chapter that besides logical equivalence, several other logical relations can hold between statements. Specifically, pairs of statements can be contradictories, contraries, and subcontraries. When we are dealing with pairs of class statements, can we use Venn diagrams to check for these other three logical relations? The answer is yes, but there is a simpler procedure: we can simply apply a couple of tables, called **squares of opposition.**

Consider first one-class statements. Figure 10.42 puts the four basic forms "in opposition."

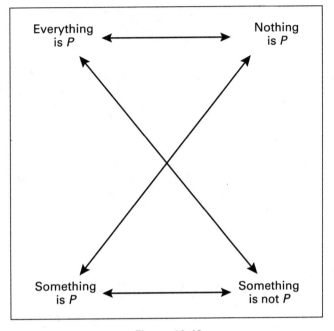

Figure 10.42

We begin with the diagonals. If everything is *P*, what can we say about the statement that something is not *P?* Clearly, that it is false. By the same reasoning, if something is not *P*, then the statement that everything is *P* is wrong. In short, the statements "Everything is *P*" and "Something is not *P*" are contradictories (cannot both be T and cannot both be F).

Next, consider the other diagonal. If nothing is *P*, then the claim that something is *P* is false. Similarly, if something is *P*, then the statement that nothing is *P* is false. Those statements are also contradictories.

Now consider the pairs directly opposite each other. Start with the top pair: "Everything is *P*" and "Nothing is *P*." Could those both be true? No. But could they both be false? Yes, if some things are *P* and some others aren't. So the pair of statements are contraries.

Now look at the lower pair: "Something is *P*" and "Something is not *P*." Could these both be true? Yes. But could these both be false? No. So they are subcontraries. Figure 10.43 summarizes this.

Next, put the four basic two-class statement forms, the categorical syllogisms, in a square of opposition (Figure 10.44). We begin with the diagonals. If all *S* is *P*, what can we say about the statement "Some *S* is not *P*"? Clearly, that it is false. If all *S* is *P*, the things in *S* are all inside *P*, so none can be outside it. Similarly, if some *S* is not *P*, then that

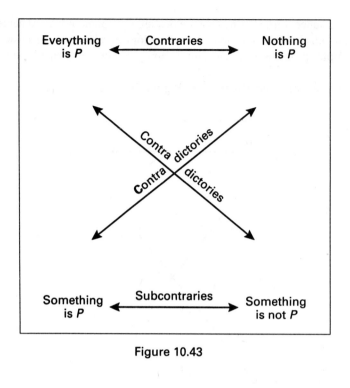

Figure 10.43

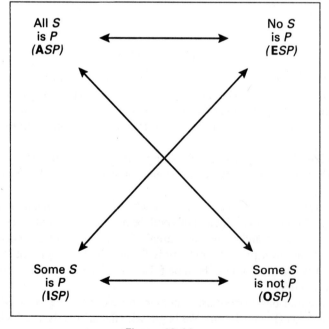

Figure 10.44

means that the statement "All *S* is *P*" must be false. Where both subject and predicate are the same in both statements, the **A***SP* and **O***SP* statements are contradictories.

Look next at any **E** statement and its associated **I** statement. Again, we see contradiction. If no *S* is *P*, then no *S* thing is in the class of *P* things—so the statement that some *S* things are in the class of *P* must be F. Similarly, if some *S* is *P*, then the claim that no *S* is *P* must be F. So again, **E***SP* and **I***SP* are contradictories.

Next, consider the relation between an **A***SP* claim and its associated **E***SP* claim—for example, "All men are Republicans" and "No men are Republicans." Clearly, it is possible for both statements to be F (if, in this example, some men were Republicans but some were Democrats). But the two statements cannot both be true at the same time. Hence, they are contraries.

At the bottom of the square are **I***SP* and **O***SP*. Consider, for example, "Some women are magicians" and "Some women are not magicians." Can both these statements be T? Certainly—so they aren't contradictories or contraries. But they can't both be F: if "Some women are magicians" is F, then "No women are magicians" follows (**I***SP* and **E***SP* are contradictories). But if we assume that there are women (that the class of women is not empty), then "No women are magicians" will entail that "Some women are not magicians"—which is just **O***SP* in this case. Upshot: **I***SP* and **O***SP* cannot both be F. Hence, they are subcontraries. Figure 10.45 summarizes this discussion.

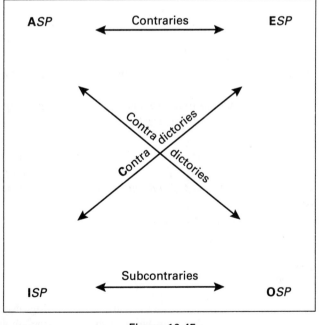

Figure 10.45

To answer whether statements are contraries, contradictories, or subcontraries, you can apply the squares of opposition, although you might have to construct a Venn to determine whether two statements are equivalent.

Example: Are the statements

1. All mice love cheese.
2. No mice love cheese.

contradictories? To answer this, apply the transformation pattern to statement 1: "All mice love cheese" turns into the contradictory "Some mice do not love cheese," which is not equivalent to statement 2 (which you can verify by Venn diagrams).

Example: Are the statements

1. Some pigs are green.
2. No pigs are green.

contradictories? To answer this, apply the transformation pattern to statement 1: "Some pigs are green" turns into the contradictory "No pigs are green," which is exactly statement 2. Notice that had statement 2 been "All pigs are nongreen," you would have had to construct a Venn diagram to see the logical equivalence of "No pigs are green" and "All pigs are nongreen."

Example: Are the following statements contraries?

1. All mice love cheese.
2. Some mice do not love cheese.

Apply the relevant rule to statement 1, and you get "No mice do not love cheese," which (you can verify by a Venn diagram) is not equivalent to statement 2; hence, the original statements are not contraries.

We want next to use Venn diagrams to test for necessary truth, logical equivalence, and contingency. Let's start with necessary truth. The basic rule here is

A class statement is necessarily true if and only if you cannot possibly diagram its denial, and a class statement is necessarily false if and only if you cannot possibly diagram it. A class statement is contingent if and only if you can diagram it and you can diagram its denial.

A few examples will make this clear. Consider:

1. All dogs are dogs.
2. No dogs are dogs.
3. There are some dogs.

Intuitively, statement 1 seems necessarily true: if something is a dog, it is a dog! Similarly, statement 2 seems necessarily false: how can something be a dog yet not be a dog at the same time? And statement 3 seems clearly contingent: we happen to know that there are dogs, but the species could die out tomorrow. What do Venn diagrams tell us? Start with the first statement. To deny it is to say that some dogs are not dogs. Consider the Venn in Figure 10.46.

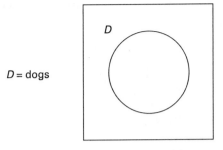

Figure 10.46

To diagram "Some dogs are not dogs" is impossible, because any arbitrary individual dog denoted by a check mark that you put inside *D* cannot lie outside *D*. You might think to try using a check mark both inside *D* and outside *D* (Figure 10.47).

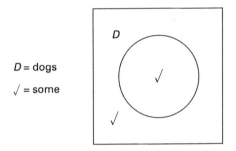

Figure 10.47

But the Venn diagram in Figure 10.47 only says "There are some dogs, and there are some things that are not dogs," which is not at all the same as "There are some things that are both dogs and not dogs!"

Now consider statement 2: "No dogs are dogs." To diagram that you would have to take a symbol for an arbitrary non-dog, call it "*N*," and put it outside the *D* circle. But that would automatically exclude it from being *inside* the circle! So again, it is impossible; thus the statement is necessarily false.

Finally, consider statement 3: "There are some dogs." Can we diagram that? Yes, and easily (Figure 10.48).

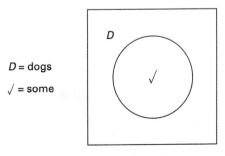

Figure 10.48

Since this statement is diagrammable, and its denial is easily diagrammable (as you can see for yourself), it is contingent. (Whether it is true in fact is a matter of biology, not logic!)

Exercise 10.5A

Use Venn diagrams to determine of each of the following pairs whether they are logical equivalents.

1. All people are friendly; some people are friendly.
2. Everything is beautiful; nothing is not beautiful.
3. Someone is at the dance; nobody is not at the dance.
4. All pigs love cheese; no pigs love cheese.
5. All pigs love cheese; no pigs are non–cheese lovers.

Exercise 10.5B

Use the tables of opposition and (if necessary) Venn diagrams to determine of each of the following pairs whether they are contradictories, contraries, or subcontraries.

1. All pigs are evil; some pigs are evil.
2. No pigs are evil; all pigs are evil.
3. All cats can dance; some cats cannot dance.
4. Some cats can dance; some cats cannot dance.
5. Not everyone likes music; someone likes music.

Exercise 10.5C

Use Venn diagrams to determine whether the following statements are contingent, self-contradictory, or necessarily true.

1. Pigs like cheese.
2. Pigs who like cheese like cheese.
3. Everybody is either friendly or not.
4. Nobody likes sports.
5. Everybody likes sports.

6   *Summary of Concepts*

In this chapter we have used Venn diagrams to explore deductive concepts as they pertain to class statements. Table 10.2 summarizes what we have found.

7   *The Limitations of Truth-Functional and Class Logic*

While truth tables and Venn diagrams are certainly useful as tools for investigating validity, consistency, necessity, logical implication, and other deductive notions, these tools are

TABLE 10.2

Term	Definition	Put in Terms of Consistency	Venn Diagram Test
$A_1, \ldots, A_n$ consistent	$A_1, \ldots, A_n$ can all be T		The diagrams for $A_1, \ldots, A_n$ are compatible
$A_1, \ldots, A_n$ inconsistent	$A_1, \ldots, A_n$ cannot all be T		The diagrams for $A_1, \ldots, A_n$ are not compatible
$A_1, \ldots, A_n$ entail/ imply B	It is impossible for $A_1, \ldots, A_n$ to be all T and B be F	$\{A_1, \ldots, A_n, -B\}$ is inconsistent	Diagramming of $A_1, \ldots, A_n$ diagrams B as well
A_1 . . . A_n ∴ *B* is valid	It is impossible for $A_1, \ldots, A_n$ to all be T and B be F	$\{A_1, \ldots A_n, -B\}$ is inconsistent	Diagramming $A_1, \ldots, A_n$ diagrams B as well
A, B equivalent	A and B cannot differ in truth value	$\{A, -B\}$ and $\{-A, B\}$ inconsistent	Diagrams of A and B are identical
A, B contradictories	A and B must have opposite truth values	$\{A, B\}$ and $\{-A, -B\}$ inconsistent	N/A
A, B contraries	A and B cannot both be T (but can both be F)	$\{A, B\}$ inconsistent $\{-A, -B\}$ consistent	N/A
A, B subcontraries	A and B cannot both be F (but can both be T)	$\{-A, -B\}$ inconsistent $\{A, B\}$ consistent	N/A
A is a tautology	A can't possibly be F	$\{-A\}$ is inconsistent	Cannot diagram $-A$
A is a self-contradiction	A can't possibly be T	$\{A\}$ is inconsistent	Cannot diagram A
A is contingent	A can be T and can be F	$\{A\}$ and $\{-A\}$ are inconsistent	Can diagram A and $-A$

limited. For example, just looking at validity, there are many valid arguments whose validity cannot be proven by truth tables or Venn diagrams. There are arguments involving relations between things, such as

1. All horses are animals.
   _____
   ∴ All heads of horses are heads of animals.

There are arguments involving identity:

1. Sue Smith is the teacher of this class.
2. Sue Smith is happy.
∴ The teacher of this class is happy.

And there are yet other types of argument whose validity does not turn on truth-functional or class connections. For this reason logicians have devised far more powerful approaches to deductive logic. But this is not a text on formal deductive logic, so such approaches are beyond what we can examine here.

InfoTrac College Edition

You can locate InfoTrac College Edition articles about this chapter by accessing the InfoTrac College Edition Web site (www.infotrac-college.com/wadsworth/). Using the InfoTrac College Edition subject guide, enter the search terms relevant to this chapter, and then read abstracts for relevant articles.

Chapter 11

Observation, Memory, and Testimony

---

1   *Sensing, Observing, and Reporting*

In this chapter we begin looking at the chief varieties of inductive reasoning. As we indicated in Chapter 5, induction is a tool for justification but also for explanation and prediction. We begin with observation. It is surely a mark of strong explanatory power of a belief system that it can organize and direct our observations about the world. In what follows, we will explain the errors that can arise in observation and testimony.

Before we turn to specifics, however, let us get clear on some terminology. I want to define four concepts: sensing, perceiving, reporting, and accepting testimony. To **sense** is to experience the world through one or more of the human senses (sight, smell, touch, hearing, and taste). The type of sensing that we most think of is seeing, and we will focus on that. Passive seeing is just receiving images. For example, merely passively seeing a small cloud over your toaster is sensing.

When we interpret what we sense, that is perception. To **perceive** is to recognize, to observe—that is, not just to sense, but *to make sense of.* For example, seeing the cloud above your toaster *as* something burning is perception. You observe your toast burning. You might say that the difference between seeing and observing is the difference between seeing and seeing *as* or seeing *that.*

When we put a perception into words, when we make a statement about our observation either in our mind or by uttering it aloud, we are making a **perceptual report.** To use our earlier example, a perceptual report (or observation statement) would be "My toast is burning up!" Perceptual reports can be of ongoing perceptions. But perceptual reports can also be of past perceptions, in which case we call them **memories.**

Table 11.1 illustrates by several examples the difference among sensing, perceiving, and reporting. Errors arise at the level of sensation, of interpretation, and of reporting, and these we will discuss in the next section of this chapter.

One last concept needs definition. **Testimony** is the reports of other people. Many things you believe on the basis of what you observe yourself. But most things you believe you believe at least partly on the basis of what other people testify they observed. Testimony, since it involves other people with their own biases, presents separate problems

TABLE 11.1

Sense	Perceive	Report
Have an image of a streak of narrow white cloud.	Observe a vapor trail from an engine.	"There's a plane's vapor trail."
Have a sour rancid taste as you drink some milk.	Perceive that the milk tastes spoiled.	"This milk tastes spoiled."
Feel a sharp pain as you rub your fingers across your back in a narrow spot.	Perceive that you have a cut on your back.	"Hey, I've been cut."

that we will discuss in Section 3 of this chapter. One especially important form of testimony is that of experts or authorities (for example, doctors or scientists). We take up the peculiarities of expert testimony in Section 4.

Exercise 11.1

Classify each of the following as sensing, perceiving, or reporting.

1. You have an image of a large, brownish, furry patch.
2. You see a bear.
3. You scream, "Watch out! There's a bear in the cafeteria!"
4. Under questioning by a therapist, you talk about your memory of the day your college cafeteria was invaded by a bear.
5. Fred is listening to Mozart with appreciation.
6. Sue is telling the class about her years as a lifeguard.
7. The rat jumped when it touched its electrified cage.
8. The rat felt pain when it got shocked.
9. Yolanda says she's seasick.
10. Yolanda feels a dull, throbbing pressure as the dentist drills.

2   *Assessing Observation*

We have seen that observing involves having an image and interpreting it, and putting that interpretation into words. We will focus here on seeing; the points we make will apply to perceiving by the other senses as well. Let's get clearer on the process and the pitfalls.

Examine Figure 11.1. If you look long enough, you can view the figure either as two faces looking at each other, or as a chalice. You have the same image but can interpret it in different ways. We interpret our images in two ways: first, based on our innate "brain wiring"; second, based on our cultural and educational upbringing.

To convince yourself that you innately interpret images, conduct the following simple experiment. Take a blank page of white paper, and put a dot in the middle of it. Put a

Figure 11.1 *Two faces or a chalice?*

penny down on the edge of the paper, cover one eye, and focus your other eye on the dot. Push the penny toward the dot with the tip of your pencil or pen. You will see the penny "disappear" temporarily as it approaches the dot and then become visible again. The mind automatically interprets or fills in the gap in visual perception. Much of our sensory interpretation is done automatically.

Besides innate interpretation, perception involves education, both by culture and by formal institutions. For example, we are culturally conditioned to interpret someone nodding his head up and down as indicating answering yes to some question; in other cultures such a gesture would be interpreted differently. Or what you interpret as a vapor trail of a jet plane to someone of a different culture might be seen as merely a curious thin cloud. Within our own culture, formal training changes how we interpret what we sense. For example, consider what a chemistry lab looks like on the first day a chemistry student steps into it and then what that student sees after many years of graduate study.

At the level of putting our observations into words—that is, making observation statements—the main challenge is finding the right words to describe what we see. I may correctly interpret the image in my field of vision as a warplane, without having the exact terminology to express it; I might not have learned the term *fighter-bomber*. Again, as I approach my TV to turn it on, I fully well interpret my visual images that I am approaching the screen, even though I may not know the technical term *cathode ray tube*.

How, then, do we assess the veracity of our observations? By seven criteria. The first two criteria apply at the level of sensation.

First, the better the physical conditions under which the observation occurs, the more likely that the observation is accurate. Is the lighting adequate? Do I have time enough to inspect whatever I am looking at, or am I just catching a glance of it? Is my angle of view good enough to get a clear look? Am I close enough to get a good look?

Second, the better the sensory acuity of the observer, the more likely it is that the observation is accurate. Am I nearsighted? Am I tired or under the influence of some chemical? Am I hysterical or subject to psychological disorders?

The next three criteria apply at the level of interpretation. *Third, the more normal the perceptual situation, the more likely it is that the observation is accurate.* Am I facing an unusual perceptual situation? Optical illusions such as mirages (Figure 11.2) occur when we automatically interpret our sensations in an incorrect way because of some unusual physical conditions. Are my emotions or desires such that they make me misinterpret what I see? This can occur in a host of ways. Fear may make the object of fear look bigger. Hatred may make a smile look like a sneer. Desperate desire to arrive at a destination may make it look closer. And, is my attention properly focused? Especially with riveting events such as crimes and natural disasters, our attention may not be properly focused to interpret all that we sense. In an earthquake, we may focus on our beloved clock toppling over and not notice what else is happening.

Fourth, the more adequate the background of the observer is, the more likely it is that the observation is accurate. Am I experiencing something commonly experienced in my culture and hence easily grasped? Am I subject to cultural prejudice or biases? When I look at a person of another ethnic group, do I see them a certain way because of my conditioning? Do I have gender stereotypes that lead me to interpret behavior inappropriately?

Fifth, the more adequate the formal training of the observer, the more likely it is that the observation is accurate. At the basic level, you cannot see that a goal has just been scored in soccer unless you know a bit about the rules of the game. At a higher level, you cannot see that cathode ray tube is not working if you don't know a bit about electronics.

The next criterion applies at the level of verbalization. *Sixth, the more adequate the vocabulary in the observation domain, the more likely it is that the observation report is accurate.* In practice, of course, we acquire vocabulary as we learn to interpret what we see—informally as we are enculturated and formally as we are formally educated.

These six criteria apply to ongoing observation. Where the observation is past—that is, where we are dealing with the memory of an observation—another criterion applies: *Seventh, the more reliable the memory, the more likely it is that the observation is accurate.* It is not uncommon to "remember" something that in fact never happened or to forget that which in fact did happen. So we need to ask how recently the observation we think we remember occurred, whether our biases are distorting what we are trying to remember, and whether we are subtly "filling in" or "adding to" our recollections.

The reliability of memory has become a very important research topic in cognitive psychology and holds tremendous legal interest as well. For example, Dr. Elizabeth Loftus has conducted experiments in which a completely false memory can be induced in a person merely by prompting from trusted relatives. As an instance, Loftus and her friend were able to prompt her friend's young daughter Jenny to vividly remember being lost in a nearby shopping mall. As a matter of fact, Jenny had never been lost there, but she was

A duck or a rabbit?   An old woman or a young girl?

Figure 11.2   *Optical illusions.*

Two optical illusions from *101 Amazing Optical Illusions* by Terry Jennings,
© 1996 by MacDonald Young Books, illustrations © by Alex Pang, used
courtesy of Sterling Publishing Co., Inc., NY, NY.

able to describe vividly and sincerely her pseudomemory. Later scientifically rigorous
studies confirmed this phenomenon (see Loftus and Ketchum 1994: Chapter 7).

Exercise 11.2A

For each of the seven criteria for accurate observation discussed in this section, describe a
case in which you or someone you know observed something inaccurately because of a
violation of that criterion.

Exercise 11.2B

Each of the phenomena listed here have been widely doubted—and widely believed! Placing
yourself as a skeptic, indicate what questions can be raised about the observations of each.

1. Extraterrestrials
2. The Loch Ness Monster
3. Ghosts
4. The Abominable Snowman

3   *Assessing Testimony*

When other people report their observations to us, we have all the issues surrounding observation discussed in the last section to consider, plus some additional concerns. Four

basic criteria apply to evaluating what other people report: credibility, privilege, consistency, and corroboration.

First, the more credible the witness, the more likely it is that the testimony is accurate.
A witness's **credibility** grows out of a number of factors. First, is the witness biased? It would be silly, say, to believe an eyewitness to a crime who alleges that Fred committed the crime if it turns out that the eyewitness is in fact having an affair with Fred's wife. Second, does the witness have the sensory acuity and mental stability to make reliable observations? Using our earlier example, if Fred's attorney got the eyewitness to concede that she was drinking or using drugs at the time the crime occurred, the jury would be entitled to take her testimony less seriously.

An important clue to the credibility of a witness is his or her **demeanor**—the way in which the witness presents him- or herself. Lawyers often employ consultants who are experts in reading the body language of possible jurors and witnesses. These experts refine and add to the innate ability we all have to detect (to some degree) when others are lying. Perhaps the most famous such body language consultant is Jo-Ellen Dimitrius (1998), who gives us some tips of her trade in her book *Reading People.* For example, about spotting lies, she gives the following rough rule: "Honest people are generally relaxed and open. Dishonest people aren't. Any trait that shows tension, nervousness, or secretiveness indicates possible dishonesty" (63). She lists as examples such traits as shifty or wandering eyes; any type of fidgeting; rapid speech; change in voice; shifting back and forth on one's feet or in a chair; any signs of nervousness; an exaggerated version of the "sincere, furrowed-brow look"; sweating; shaking; hiding eyes, face, mouth; licking lips; running the tongue over the teeth; leaning forward; and inappropriate familiarity (such as backslapping).

Second, the better position the witness is in, the more likely it is that the testimony is accurate. A witness is **positioned well** if he or she is in a position to observe clearly, and the physical conditions are such that clear observation is possible. Reverting to our stock example, it would be silly to place great weight on the testimony of the eyewitness if she were half a mile away from the crime when it occurred.

Third, the more consistent the testimony, the more likely it is to be accurate. A witness's testimony has to be **consistent** for us to take it seriously. If the eyewitness says that Fred committed the murder with a gun, but yesterday he said that he saw him commit the murder with a knife, we are entitled to be skeptical.

Fourth, the more corroborated the testimony, the more likely it is to be accurate. A witness's testimony is **corroborated** if it is supported by other physical (nonobservational) evidence or by the testimony of others. If the eyewitness to the murder says Fred committed the crime with a knife, and near the scene of the crime a knife is found with Fred's fingerprints on it, the testimony is corroborated. If several other people also testify that they saw Fred do it, the testimony becomes even more corroborated.

To see how these criteria function in practice, let's look at an important historical case. In 1998, President Bill Clinton was accused of having an affair with a White House intern named Monica Lewinsky. A special prosecutor, Kenneth Starr, investigated the matter.

After long negotiations, Ms. Lewinsky agreed to testify about the relationship. There was speculation that Ms. Lewinsky was either delusional or at least greatly exaggerated the degree of the relationship. In a report to Congress, Starr (1998: 32–36) addressed the issue of the reliability of her testimony (footnotes omitted):

B. EVIDENCE ESTABLISHING NATURE OF RELATIONSHIP

Physical Evidence

Physical evidence conclusively establishes that the President and Ms. Lewinsky had a sexual relationship. After reaching an immunity and cooperation agreement with the Office of the Independent Counsel on July 28, 1998, Ms. Lewinsky turned over a navy blue dress that she said she had worn during a sexual encounter with the President on February 28, 1997. According to Ms. Lewinsky, she noticed stains on the garment the next time she took it from her closet. From their location, she surmised that the stains were the President's semen.

Initial tests revealed that the stains are in fact semen. Based on that result, the OIC [Office of the Independent Counsel] asked the President for a blood sample and being given assurances that the OIC had an evidentiary basis for making the request, the President agreed. In the White House Map Room on August 3, 1998, the White House Physician drew a vial of blood from the President in the presence of an FBI agent and an OIC attorney.

By conducting two standard DNA comparison tests, the FBI laboratory concluded that the President was the source of the DNA obtained from the dress. According to the more sensitive RFLP test, the genetic markers on the semen, which match the President's DNA, are characteristic of one out of 7.87 trillion Caucasians.

In addition to the dress, Ms. Lewinsky provided what she said were answering machine tapes containing brief messages from the President, as well as several gifts that the President had given her.

Ms. Lewinsky's Statements

Ms. Lewinsky was extensively debriefed about her relationship with the President. For the initial evaluation of her credibility, she submitted to a detailed "proffer" interview on July 27, 1998. After entering into a cooperation agreement, she was questioned over the course of approximately 15 days.

She also provided testimony under oath on three occasions: twice before the grand jury, and because of the personal and sensitive nature of particular topics, once in a deposition. In addition, Ms. Lewinsky worked with prosecutors and investigators to create an 11-page chart that chronologically lists her contacts with President Clinton, including meetings, phone calls, gifts, and messages. Ms. Lewinsky twice verified the accuracy of the chart under oath.

In the evaluation of experienced prosecutors and investigators, Ms. Lewinsky has provided truthful information. She has not falsely inculpated the President. Harming him, she has testified, is "the last thing in the world I would want to do."

Moreover, the OIC's immunity and cooperation agreement with Ms. Lewinsky includes safeguard crafted to insure that she tells the truth. Court-ordered immunity and written immunity agreements often provide that the witness can be prosecuted only for false statements made during the period of cooperation, and not for the underlying offense. The OIC's agreement goes further, providing that Ms. Lewinsky will lose her immunity altogether if the government can prove to a federal judge—by a preponderance of the evidence, not the higher standard of beyond a reasonable doubt—that she lied.

Moreover, the agreement provides that, in the course of such a prosecution, the United States could introduce into evidence the statements made by Ms. Lewinsky during her cooperation. Since Ms. Lewinsky acknowledged in her proffer interview and in debriefings that she violated the law, she has a strong incentive to tell the truth: If she did not, it would be relatively straightforward to void the immunity agreement and prosecute her using her own admission against her.

Ms. Lewinsky's Confidants

Between 1995 and 1998, Ms. Lewinsky confided in 11 people about her relationship with the President.

All have been questioned by the OIC, most before a federal grand jury: Andrew Bleiler, Catherine Allday Davis, Deborah Finerman, Dr. Irene Kassorla, Marica Lewis, Ashley Raines, Linda Tripp, Natalie Ungvari, and Dale Young. Ms. Lewinsky told most of these confidants about events in her relationship as they occurred, sometimes in considerable detail.

Some of Ms. Lewinsky's statements about the relationship were contemporaneously memorialized.

These include deleted email recovered from her home computer and her Pentagon computer, email messages retained by two of the recipients, tape recordings of some of Ms. Lewinsky's conversations with Ms. Tripp, and notes taken by Ms. Tripp during some of their conversations. The Tripp notes, which have been extensively corroborated, refer specifically to places, dates and times of physical contacts between the President and Ms. Lewinsky.

Everyone in whom Ms. Lewinsky confided in detail believe she was telling the truth about her relationship with the President. Ms. Lewinsky told her psychologist, Dr. Irene Kassorla, about the affair shortly after it began. Thereafter, she related details of sexual encounters soon after they occurred (sometimes calling from her White House office). Ms. Lewinsky showed no indications of delusional thinking, according to Dr. Kassorla, and Dr. Kassorla had no doubts whatsoever about the truth of what Ms. Lewinsky told her. Ms. Lewinsky's friend Catherine Allday Davis testified that she believed Ms. Lewinsky's accounts of the sexual relationship with the President because "I trusted in the way she had confided in me on other things in her life. . . . I just trusted the relationship, so I trusted her."

Dale Young, a friend in whom Ms. Lewinsky confided starting in mid-1996, testified:

> [I]f she was going to lie to me, she would have said to me, "Oh, he calls me all the time. He does wonderful things. He can't wait to see me." . . . [S]he would have embellished the story. You know, she wouldn't be telling me, "He told me he'd call me, I waited home all weekend and I didn't do anything and he didn't call and he didn't call for two weeks."

Documents

In addition to her remarks and email to friends, Ms. Lewinsky wrote a number of documents, including letters and draft letters to the President. Among these documents are (i) papers found in a consensual search of her apartment; (ii) papers that Ms. Lewinsky turned over pursuant to her cooperation agreement, including a calendar with dates circled when she met or talked by telephone with the President in 1996 and 1997; and (iii) files recovered from Ms. Lewinsky's computers at home and at the Pentagon.

Consistency and Corroboration

The details of Ms. Lewinsky's many statements have been checked, cross-checked, and corroborated.

When negotiations with Ms. Lewinsky in January and February 1998 did not culminate in an agreement, the OIC proceeded with a comprehensive investigation, which generated a great deal of probative evidence.

In July and August 1998, circumstances brought more direct and compelling evidence to the investigation. After the courts rejected a novel privilege claim, Secret Service officers and agents testified about their observations of the President and Ms. Lewinsky in the White House. Ms. Lewinsky agreed to submit to a proffer interview (previous negotiations had deadlocked over her refusal to do so), and, after assessing her credibility in that session, the OIC entered into a cooperation agreement with her. Pursuant to the cooperation agreement, Ms. Lewinsky turned over the dress that proved to bear traces of the President's semen. And the President, who had spurned six invitations to testify, finally agreed to provide his account to the grand jury. In that sworn testimony, he acknowledged "inappropriate intimate contact" with Ms. Lewinsky.

Because of the fashion in which the investigation had unfolded, in sum, a massive quantity of evidence was available to test and verify Ms. Lewinsky's statements during her proffer interview and her later cooperation. Consequently, Ms. Lewinsky's statements have been corroborated to a remarkable degree.

Her detailed statements to the grand jury and the OIC in 1998 are consistent with statements to her confidants dating back to 1995, documents that she created, and physical evidence. Moreover, her accounts generally match the testimony of White House staff members; the testimony of Secret Service agents and officers; and White House records showing Ms. Lewinsky's entries and exits, the President's whereabouts, and the President's telephone calls.

Note how Starr argues for the veracity of Lewinsky's testimony:

1. physical evidence corroborates the testimony;
2. the details of the testimony and the demeanor of Ms. Lewinsky make the testimony more credible;
3. the immunity deal (by which Lewinsky would have been hit by criminal charges had she been caught lying) makes the testimony more credible;
4. eleven friends and therapists who talked with Lewinsky during the time of the alleged affair testify that she told the same story to them along the way, which shows consistency in her testimony;

5. numerous documents written by Lewinsky during the relevant period confirm the consistency of her testimony;
6. details of her testimony (names, dates, times of visit) were corroborated by the testimony of Secret Service agents, White House staff members, and White House phone logs and visitor logs.

All of these points fall within the general criteria given earlier.

The eminent psychologist Elizabeth Loftus has done considerable work on the psychology of eyewitness testimony. I recommend in particular her survey work *Eyewitness Testimony* (Loftus 1996). In this work, Loftus explores how crucial such testimony is in courtroom proceedings, but also just how error-prone it is. She views eyewitness testimony as part of a three-stage process:

Stage 1: Memory acquisition, or perception
Stage 2: Memory retention
Stage 3: Memory retrieval

At all three stages errors can and do occur.

Consider the first stage, initial perception. Psychological experiments show that the longer the exposure to the incident, the better the memory recall. Similarly, the more frequent the exposure, the better the memory recall. Again, the more salient the detail—the more colorful, extraordinary, or interesting the detail—the better the recall. Moreover, initial memory storage is shaped by expectations and knowledge. Expectations are set by culture, past experiences, personal prejudices, and contextual biases. For example, during hunting season, a number of hunters get shot by other hunters, because the shooters see movement and (mis)perceive elk, which is what they expect to see. Knowledge also affects initial storage. For example, people who are told that a purse has something valuable in it will pay closer attention when it is stolen than if told it has nothing valuable.

Regarding the second stage of memory, again various factors can affect memories. First, time enters in—experiment has shown that memory degrades over time. More interestingly, experiments have shown that postevent information (that is, exposure to information about the witnessed event after the event) can influence later recall. For example, in one experiment, a group of people were shown a video of an accident in which two cars collided. The group was divided into two, and after a period of time, each group was asked questions about the accident. One group was asked, "How fast were the cars traveling when they smashed into each other?" The other group was asked, "How fast were the cars traveling when they hit each other?" The group asked the question using the loaded term *smashed* estimated the speeds of the cars significantly than did the group asked the question with the more neutral term *hit*. (You may recall our discussions of loaded questions in Chapter 3 and loaded language in Chapter 6.) Moreover, the group asked the question using the loaded term *smashed* had significantly higher rate of false memories that there was broken glass at the scene than the group asked the question using the neutral term *hit*.

More generally, people differ in their eyewitness ability. Anxious, neurotic, or preoccupied people tend to make slightly worse eyewitnesses than others. Children, especially very young children, are very suggestive, and so can be led by loaded questions into "remembering" that which did not occur or misremembering that which did occur. In addition, males and females differ in what details of a scene they remember most accurately.

Also, the remarks concerning eyewitness testimony apply to memories as well. If an accuser "remembers" that her father was a member of a satanic cult, raped her, and later forced her to sacrifice her baby, we evaluate that memory (and hence her testimony) by whether she is credible, consistent, and corroborated. Did her memory come back to her in a highly emotional group therapy meeting, or has it been there all along? Is her memory the same in its essential details today as it was yesterday, or does it radically vary with every retelling? Do local police report satanic cult activity, or is there no evidence that such cults exist where she grew up? Does the medical examination by her physician show signs of rape, childbirth, and so forth?

These issues are of more than theoretical interest. Over the last decade there has been an explosion of lawsuits by people who allege their parents molested them on the basis of suppressed memories supposedly recovered during therapy sessions. Also on the rapid rise have been lawsuits by accused parents against therapists who draw out supposedly repressed memories. Jurors typically find that judging which memories are accurate and which are fantasies or distortions is by no means easy. To get an idea of the complexities involved, I recommend the gripping book *Spectral Evidence,* by Moira Johnston (1997). Johnston's book tells the story of the first case in which "memory recovery" therapists were successfully sued by a third party.

Exercise 11.3

Imagine you are sitting on a jury in a murder case. Suppose an eyewitness has just testified that he saw the defendant shoot the victim. Imagine some features of the testimony that would undermine its credibility for you.

4   *Assessing Expert Testimony*

In this section we want to discuss appeals to authority. Some controversy exists about the fallacy of "(bad) appeal to authority," a controversy nicely explored in Douglas Walton's (1997) book *Appeal to Expert Opinion* (see especially Chapter 3). To begin with, there is no uniform agreement on what to call this fallacy: appeal to authority, appeal to expert opinion, *argumentum ad vercundiam,* and bad appeal to authority have all been used. The Latin term *argumentum ad vercundiam* was apparently coined by the seventeenth-century philosopher John Locke, meaning "argument directed to modesty"—the idea being that the arguer appealing to some authority is hoping the listener will defer to that authority out of modesty.

Next, there is controversy as to what constitutes the fallacy. Some logicians define it as invoking the authority of church or state to cow people into accepting a belief, rather than giving evidence to persuade those people rationally. The paradigm case of this was the case of the Renaissance scientist Galileo, who was forced by the church under the threat of arrest and torture to recant his belief in the Copernican theory (that the Sun is at the center of the planetary system), because it contradicted Scripture (such as the passage where Joshua commands the sun to stand still). Another reason Galileo's views were repugnant was because they fundamentally challenged the Aristotelian philosophy held by most influential church figures at the time. For example, an early opinion of the matter was given by the Consultors of the Sacred Congregation of the Holy Office (Langford 1998: 89).

> The first proposition [that the sun is the center of the planetary system] was declared unanimously to be foolish and absurd in philosophy and formally heretical inasmuch as it expressly contradicts the doctrine of Holy Scripture in many passages, both in their literal meaning and according to the general interpretation of the Fathers and Doctors.

But such a definition seems to conflate two quite different fallacies: appeal to fear (discussed in Chapter 8) and bad appeal to authority. In the Galileo case, the church authorities were using an appeal to fear on Galileo: stop advocating the Copernican theory or we will torture you to death! (Unsurprisingly, he gave in.) On the other hand, the zealous church authorities based *their* opinion on the Bible and the physics of Aristotle. But the Bible is not a text on physics, and the works of Aristotle were rapidly becoming outdated during this period.

We can be clearer on this point if we notice that the word *authority* is ambiguous. *Authority* often is used synonymously with *expert* as when we say that a doctor is an authority on medicine. But *authority* also is often used to mean "a person with legal or governmental powers," as when we say that a drug dealer was arrested by the authorities. We can refer to these two different types of authorities respectively as **epistemic authorities** (or **experts**)—that is, authorities because of what they know—and **deontic authorities**—that is, authorities because of the power they possess. Arguments from deontic authority are relatively uncommon. The only logically worthwhile arguments from deontic authority are cases where the authority is in a legal position to issue commands. For example, when a minister says to a couple "I now pronounce you man and wife," his very utterance performs the task of marriage by the power vested in him by the state. Another example would be a police officer who orders you to pull over on the freeway—her position allows her to legitimately order you to do so if she has "probable cause" that you have violated the law. Logically worthwhile arguments from deontic authority are cases where someone has a legal right to issue you a command in the context of utterance and where that command is within the scope of the authority. Let us focus here on arguments from epistemic authority.

Some have argued that a fallacy of appeal to authority comes, not so much when a person cites a bogus authority but when he or she cites the words of an authority in such a way as to stop other people from continuing to raise questions about some issue. (For example, Walton [1997] defends this view in Chapter 8.) But again, that seems to me to conflate two fallacies. Pooh-poohing is the fallacy of choking off legitimate debate, and it can be done by any number of techniques: insults, emotional appeals, sneers and snickers, not just by appealing to authority. So, in our view, "appeal to authority" specifically refers to some flawed appeal to expert testimony.

In this age of increasing specialization, we must often appeal to the testimony of experts. We decide whether to stop smoking or stop eating greasy food on the basis of what our doctor says about these practices. We decide to acquit the defendant as insane on the basis of what the psychiatrists say about the accused. We decide how to vote on nuclear power on the basis of what engineers say about it. Such testimony can be logically worthwhile, but when certain requirements are not met, the testimony should be rejected. We will use the label **bad appeal to authority** (in Latin, **argumentum ad verecundiam**) to refer to such a case.

The rules governing the acceptability of expert testimony are obvious, falling under those same broad headings of credibility, privilege, consistency, and corroboration we discussed in the previous section. I will list these criteria (there are eight of them) and under each give some of the critical questions we must ask of a given appeal to expert testimony to see whether it passes that criterion.

First, the more clearly identified the authority, the more likely it is that the testimony is accurate. To even begin taking an expert seriously, we need to know who he or she is. Where do they work? Advertisements for many products commit fallacious appeals to authority by using expressions such as "experts agree that . . . ," "doctor-tested," and "studies prove the effectiveness of this product." Advertisers call this device *the faceless expert.*

The need to have experts be identified is especially clear when you consider the damage that can be done by rumors (that is, testimony spread from anonymous sources). A delightful look at some recent major rumors that have been widely accepted is to be found in Bob Tamarkins's (1993) book *Rumor Has It.* For example, in 1976 leaflets were circulated in France citing research by unidentified researchers at some unidentified hospital in Paris who had shown citric acid causes cancer. In fact, citric acid is a harmless food additive, but eventually those leaflets reached half of France's general population (Tamarkin 1993: 79) and caused widespread alarm.

Second, the more qualified the expert, the more likely it is that the testimony is accurate. Admittedly, spelling out exactly what makes someone an expert in an area is difficult, but just reading a few books on the subject does not suffice. Does the expert have the most advanced degree appropriate to the field (M.D., J.D., Ph.D.)? Does the expert rank high among his or her peers? Does the expert have relevant publications or a history of successful practice? Is the expert a member in good standing of all relevant professional organizations?

The physicist Michael Friedlander (1995: 171) talks about the notion of an "expert" as scientists typically view it:

> In many places I have talked about the experts. . . . [J]ust who qualifies as an "expert"? Expertise or authority do not automatically accompany a doctoral degree. Colleagues judge expertise on the basis of the accumulation of respected professional publications. A graduate degree usually helps but is not essential. Some scientists become widely accepted as authorities because of the importance and continuity of their scientific contributions.

Third, the more personally reliable the expert, the more likely it is that the testimony is accurate. Is the expert biased regarding the topic under consideration? For instance, the testimony of a doctor employed by a tobacco company who testifies that cigarettes are harmless should be questioned. Was the research done by the doctor done prior to being hired by the tobacco company or paid for by that company? Does this doctor have a track record of research outside the area of tobacco research? Does the expert have a history of lying or stretching the truth (say, to get his or her name in the headlines)? Is this expert conscientious, basing judgments always on detailed study, or is this person prone to off-hand or snap judgments?

Fourth, the more closely relevant the expertise of the expert is to the topic at hand, the more likely it is that the testimony is accurate. We want the expert to testify in his or her field of expertise, or area of competence. Hard as it is for some people to believe, a philosopher's or a physicist's word on economic matters deserves no more credence than anybody else's, unless that person happens to be an expert in both fields (which seldom is the case). Unfortunately, there is a **halo effect** regarding experts: when people know that a person is a famous expert, they tend to give that person credence for whatever he or she says, even if it is totally unrelated to the expert's area of training. I recall a particularly silly instance of this: one time a panel of "experts" was called to testify on farming problems before the House Subcommittee on Agriculture. These "experts" were several famous actresses who played either farmers or farmers' wives in major motion pictures! Famous actors are experts on acting, but not necessarily anything else. People often erroneously equate being glamorous with being knowledgeable.

Fifth, the more current the authority, the more likely it is that the testimony is accurate. Aristotle was once the world's greatest authority on physics, but using his word now in that field would be ridiculous.

Sixth, the more the expert's opinions are based on evidence open to the inspection of other experts, the more likely it is that the testimony is accurate. The medical opinion of even the finest doctor about what ails you is of little value if it isn't base on a complete exam of your body. Expert testimony should be based on direct evidence, which should then be open to evaluation by other experts. This is crucial, because we nonexperts are *not* in a position to evaluate that evidence directly, so we must be able to have other experts evaluate it. An expert's opinion is worth more if it is corroborated by other experts. (In medicine, a good doctor will typically encourage his patient to "get a second opinion.")

Seventh, the more representative the views of the expert is of the views of similar experts, the more likely it is that the testimony is accurate. Oftentimes, even in the most established sciences, areas of deep controversy persist. Some theories may be novel, untested, or not generally accepted. There is nothing wrong with that; indeed, the most widely accepted truths in any science typically started as controversial theories. But if the expert testifying is basing his or her views on theories or practices controversial in the field, that fact should at least be made clear to the listeners. The more unanimous the experts are on a view, the more likely it is to be worthwhile.

This criterion is of more than abstract interest. At one time, it was strictly codified in American law as the **Frye rule:** any scientific theory or practice used as the basis for expert testimony in a courtroom must be generally accepted in the field, not merely be experimental or in the process of being firmly established. In recent years courts have loosened the rules of evidence away from the Frye rule, and some have argued that as a consequence juries now hear even crackpot theories presented as legitimate science. For example, Peter Huber (1991) argues this view in *Galileo's Revenge: Junk Science in the Courtroom.*

Eighth, the more accurately the expert is reported, the more likely it is that the testimony is accurate. Is the expert quoted in full, accurately, and not distorted? And is that quotation fully footnoted? Is what the expert said in plain English, or are there technical terms that must be restated in ordinary language?

The eight criteria listed here fall under the four general criteria given in section 3 for evaluating any testimony. The requirements that the expert cited be identified, quoted in full, qualified, personally reliable, current, and testifying in his or her field of expertise all fall under the heading of the credibility of a witness. The requirements that the expert's testimony be based on evidence open to inspection by other experts and that the testimony be representative of the prevailing views of relevantly similar experts fall under the heading of the corroboration of the testimony.

As always with inductive evidence, these rules are matters of degree. For example, when trying to decide who the better auto mechanic is, do we choose the young person with a community college degree in automotive technology or the person who got her training working in an auto shop for ten years? It can be hard to say.

Again, as always with inductive evidence, our assessments of the strength of evidence of a given inference is open to revision in the light of new evidence. For instance, we might base our decision to follow a certain therapy on what a Freudian psychoanalyst recommends, but we might later decide to reject that advice if we come to the conclusion that Freudian psychoanalytical theory is not scientifically credible but is in fact pseudoscience.

Here are a few faulty appeals to authority:

> New university super "crash-loss" diet turns ugly fat into harmless water and it flows right out of your system by the gallons! Works so fast, you shrink your waistline as much as a full size smaller in just 24 hours (a full inch in a single day), and 4 sizes smaller in just 14 days! That's right! Four inches gone in just 2 weeks!

Which university? Who developed the diet?

> SKINNY LEGS—Try this new amazing scientific home method to ADD SHAPELY CURVES at ankles, calves, thighs, knees, hips! Skinny legs rob the rest of your figure of attractiveness! Now, at last, you can try to help yourself improve underdeveloped legs, due to normal causes, and fill out any part of your legs you wish, or your legs all over as many women have by following this new scientific method. This tested and proven scientific course was prepared by a well-known authority on legs with years of experience.

To what well-known authority on legs is the advertisement referring?

By the way, if you take too much of the skinny-leg formula, we have this.

> FAT LEGS—Try this new amazing scientific home method to reduce ankles, calves, thighs, knees, hips for SLENDERIZED LEGS. Beautifully firm, slenderized legs help the rest of your figure look slimmer, more appealing! Now, at last, you too can try to help yourself to improve heavy legs due to normal causes and reduce and reshape ANY PART of your legs you wish . . . or your legs all over . . . as many women have by following this new scientific method. This tested and proven scientific course was prepared by a well-known authority on legs with years of experience.

You wonder whether it's the same well-known authority on legs!

ACTOR: My doctor wants me to switch to a decaffeinated coffee, because caffeine makes me nervous, but I only like real coffee.

ROBERT YOUNG (who played Dr. Marcus Welby on TV): Phil, Sanka Brand Decaffeinated coffee is 100 percent real coffee and tastes it! Try it.

Robert Young is not a doctor, so why accept his prescription?

Richard Whately (1826: 185) offers the following observation:

> One of the many contrivances employed for this purpose is what may be called the "fallacy of references"; which is particularly common in theological works. It is of course a circumstance which adds great weight to any assertion, that it shall seem to be supported by any passages in Scripture:
>
> > How when a writer can cite few or none of these, that distinctly and decidedly favor his opinion, he may at least find many which may be conceived capable of being so understood, or which, in some way or other, remotely relate to the subject; but if these texts were inserted at length, it would be at once perceived how little they bear on the question; the usual artifice therefore is to give merely references to them;
>
> trusting that nineteen out of twenty readers will never take the trouble of turning to the passages, but, taking for granted that they afford, each, some degree of confirmation to what is maintained, will be overawed by seeing every assertion supported, as they suppose, by five or six Scripture-texts.

The point Whately is making can be generalized. Often, a kind of *ad verecundiam* is committed when a point is buttressed by a mass of footnotes, where the authorities cited in the notes do not really agree with the point the author is trying to make. Indeed, scholars who assume that the absence of copious footnotes in an article or book somehow indicates the lack of scholarly merit commit this fallacy in reverse.

A similar point can be made with regard to the presentation of numerical data and statistics. Often, the data will be presented by some stern-looking figure in a white lab coat, with elaborate charts and digital displays. All such rigmarole serves to lend an air of authority to the data. Such tactics can also be viewed (as we observed earlier) as a kind of positive *ad hominem* argument in that someone is arguing for a point on the basis of the alleged expertise of the person who plumps for it.

Exercise 11.4A

Describe what is fallacious about the following appeals to authority, by showing which criterion or criteria are broken.

1. A famed research team of sensitive psychologists, plus computer technology, create the amazing new "Astral Sounds."

2. "For the first time in 25 years, I passed my driver's test without glasses!" (C. Smith, CT) Exercise your eyes! Without glasses or contacts. Doctor-approved program shows you simple exercises to build up clear eyesight at home. Call for free brochure.

3. Lose Weight and Keep It Off with the Physicians' Clinical Diet Plan! It's simple! It's easy! It works! Written by a physician and based on sound medical principles! No pills or protein supplements. Rush $5.95, check or money order, for prompt delivery.

4. YES—see the amazing proof in your own mirror! With the New TotaLoss Fat Burn-off Program, just one powerful pill in the morning launches you on the most incredible 24-hour fat-burning blitz. Doctors, studies at universities, and leading magazines hail the awesome effectiveness of the TotaLoss capsule formula.

5. You deserve good health—and we want to help you get it by offering you our BEE POLLEN at a reduced rate only with this coupon. Try our BEE POLLEN NOW AND SAVE MONEY. Bee Pollen has been acclaimed by athletes, health experts, and scientists all over the world as a fantastic natural food supplement that provides increased energy, extra stamina, and better health. Now you can try it at no risk! Read all the facts below from the Medical Front thoroughly, then order today with this coupon!

    • German research indicates that Bee Pollen may be helpful in reducing the bad effects of stress of all kinds, from arguments with your spouse, to the after effects of radiation therapy.
    • A Russian scientist reported good results in the treatment of chronic colitis with Bee Pollen. Bee Pollen taken daily has been shown to reduce the number of harmful bacteria in the digestive tract and may work to correct both constipation and diarrhea.
    • Bee Pollen is being used effectively in building immunities to 90% of all allergies.
    • Swedish physicians regularly give Bee Pollen in the treatment of prostate problems. Hundreds of U.S. doctors are now doing the same.

6. POLLY BERGEN: No Singer machine has ever saved you more and given so much. This Touch and Sew II machine has Soft-Touch Fabric Feed for smooth feeding of all fabrics, a Flip and Sew panel for easy sewing of armholes, cuffs and sleeves, and exclusive slant needle that's easy on your fabrics, a two-step built-in buttonholer, and more! Made in the U.S.A.

    Polly Bergen is a member of the Singer board of directors.

7. Stay younger longer! Kungpao powder helps reverse aging! At last, you can live life to the fullest. Recent scientific research reveals Kungpao can

    • increase sexual potency,
    • increase mental ability,
    • improve blood circulation, and
    • help you sleep better.

    Twenty million people use Kungpao powder daily—20 million people can't be wrong! Send your check today.

8. An expert's approval—Supa Tweez has been clinically tested by a university professor of dermatology and proven to be safe and effective. One of his patients had previously been tweezing hairs from her chin every day for 15 years. After treating herself with Supa Tweez, she has eliminated this time-consuming chore for the rest of her life! Over fifteen thousand instruments in use by doctors.

9. If your skin is bothered by oiliness and acne, then you need BUF kit for Acne. Developed by a leading dermatologist, it has a super cleansing sponge—BUF-PUF—and a soap-less cleanser—BUF Acne Cleansing Bar—in a neat little tray for sink or vanity.

10. In fact, we have gone to a lot of expense and trouble proving the Bust Expander does what we say it does. During a medical test using six women who were supervised by two prominent doctors, it was discovered that changes caused by the Bust Expander were phenomenal.

11. Doctors and nutritionists discover certain vitamins can stop and reverse gray hair! It may be possible for you to restore and retain your natural hair color and prevent further graying without dyes, rinses, or other coloring agents . . . the natural way. Medical doctors and nutritionists claim that it is possible to return hair to its natural color simply by adding special high-potency nutrients to the diet. . . .

    Scientists believe it is the inability of the body to process certain vitamins as we grow older that causes hair to turn white.

    A medical doctor had an amazing 82% success ratio treating 460 patients with a vitamin supplement returning hair to its natural color, as reported in "Vitamins and Hormones II."

12. The research results are overwhelming. New National Smoker Study provides solid evidence that "Enriched Flavor" Dormans offer a satisfying alternative to higher-tar cigarettes.

13. Doctor Tested. Here are just a few of the incredible results obtained by actual Slim-Skins users in a special slimming test conducted by a prominent American Physician.

    "I lost 4 inches from each thigh, $2\frac{1}{2}$ inches from my hips, $6\frac{1}{2}$ inches from my tummy, and over 5 inches from my waist in just 3 days with Slim-Skins."—I.Z.

    "Actually trimmed my abdomen 8 full inches and my waist nearly 7 inches while my hips came down about $3\frac{1}{2}$ inches and each thigh 4 inches, for a total loss of over 26 inches all in 3 days with truly astonishing Slim-Skins."—C.D.

    "The final solution in instant figure slimming. I lost $5\frac{1}{2}$ inches from my waist, 5 inches from my tummy, $2\frac{1}{2}$ inches from my hips, and over 3 inches from each thigh—an overall loss of $19\frac{1}{2}$ inches in just one 25-minute period with Slim-Skins."—M.M.

    These "fantastic" inch losses are now documented fact. The famous "fat-burning" diet claims a 3-inch waist loss in 7 days. In the doctor's Slim-Skins test, the waist losses were over 3 inches in just one day—actually in just 25 minutes.

14. This vitamin helps thicken your hair! Hair thinning? Scientific research shows that Panthenol (Vitamin B-5) may give your hair the fuller look you want. This amazing B-vitamin has the unique ability to penetrate the shaft and moisturize from within—providing a lovely natural sheen and fullness as it helps strengthen each strand. Repairs split ends and brittleness, and makes your hair easier to manage, too. Try Mama's Panthenol "F" Hair Thickener for Women.

15. Now, Doctors at leading universities first in Europe and now worldwide have found substances where mere aroma can be used to make you appear more attractive, more impressive, and even more desirable. Scientists first described the incredibly

powerful sexual attractants in insects as Pheromones. For years, many Musk Fragrances have used Pheromones from animals. Now, Pheromones have been found in humans, too! American scientist and researcher, William Borneo, has captured the secret in two new formulas utilizing male and female pheromones to create the ultimate perfume.

16. Pam Poco's whole life has suddenly changed, since she lost an amazing 16 lbs. in seven days and then quickly lost 99 lbs. more. As she describes it: "I was always overweight and tried everything to lose, but the Super-Loss Capsule Program is the only thing that ever worked. It's truly the #1 weapon against fat."

    What is the Super-Loss Diet Program? It's a remarkable weight loss plan with an amazing Clinically Proven Pill. This incredible program can actually make your body burn off the maximum amount of fat . . . in record time. It can help you quickly lose all the weight you need to—without torturous starvation and without battling hunger pangs. Weight loss is fast and dramatic.

17. Omoro—The only one you need! Millions of people have counted on Omoro for their vitamins and mineral protection. Omoro is the only one you need. With 31 vitamins, minerals and other important nutrients, it's the multivitamin that looks out for your well being. Try this exclusive master formula and get the healthful vitamin and mineral insurance you deserve.

18. Enlarge your bosom three full cup sizes in only seven days! What is the secret of larger breasts? The lush, big, round, firm bosoms that get all the love, admiration, and attention of men everywhere! The only permanently easy and safe answer is a "New" active energizer enlarger "Big Bosom Pill" called Aero-plus 3! Developed after 20 years of extensive scientific and medical research and a quarter century of interplanetary and computer experience by a famous lab. If we helped put a man on the moon, we surely can put a big beautiful bosom on a deserving lady. Know the pleasure and fulfillment of going from an A to a D cup. Only $20.00 complete.

19. Announcing the amazing doctor-tested formula that is three times stronger than other diets. This incredible breakthrough that attacks overweight three ways is your key to total weight loss.

    This doctor-tested, medically proven formula is based on published reports form professors at leading medical schools. This three-way punch is the most advanced weight loss method known to medical science.

    With this doctor-tested formula, you can lose even more—like 20, 30, even 50 lbs., till you reach your ideal weight level.

20. "I've been a World Class gymnast for 11 years and competed in 42 major international events. To stand out in top competition, I created my own special moves. That's the critical difference.

    "I believe in demanding the most of myself. Even with a big headache, I have to give more. So now I take Wundaprin. Two Wundaprin give me more pain relief than Extra Strength Tylenol. And that makes a critical difference to me."

    Medical evidence shows what Matt Bungie experienced. In a nationwide study of headache sufferers the results were impressive: two Wundaprin gave more pain relief than Extra Strength Tylenol. That's Wundaprin strength. And remember with all its strength, Wundaprin is gentler to your stomach than aspirin. Use only as directed. Take one Wundaprin tablet. Two tablets may be used if pain does not respond. Do not exceed 6 tablets in 24 hours.

Discover the critical difference with Wundaprin strength.

Exercise 11.4B

Characterize each of the following appeals to authority as prima facie ("on the face of it") reasonable or prima facie fallacious.

1. Sam Field advises you to invest heavily in stock mutual funds. Sam is your family physician.
2. Sue Snappy advises you to lose weight, exercise more, and eat food lower in fat. Sue is a cardiologist you have consulted.
3. Sam Snappy advises you to support free trade legislation. Sam is an economics professor at the University of Chicago, who has recently won the Nobel Prize for Economics.
4. Sue Field advises you to use Magic Cream beauty cream. Sue is a world-famous model paid $1,000,000/year by Magic Cream Corporation for product endorsements.
5. Sam Field advises us that smoking causes cancer. Sam is an oncologist paid $1 million/year by the North American Tobacco Company.
6. Sue Snappy advises you that your car needs a new transmission. Sue is a friend of yours who is a mechanic for the U.S. Army.
7. Sam Snappy advises us to improve relations with Communist Cuba. Sam is an Oscar-winning actor and a well-known political activist. He has taken a number of trips to Cuba and has spoken to the many members of the Cuban Communist Party.
8. Sue Field advises that you quit smoking. Sue is the head of a large chiropractic clinic and is also a record-setting marathon runner.
9. Sam Field advises that we support the American Socialist Party. Sam is a professor of philosophy and has written many articles on the evils of capitalism. Also, he is as poor as a church mouse.
10. Sue Snappy advises that you look for a new career. She is a psychic who has studied your aura for days.

+5   *Observation in Natural Science*

Before leaving the general topic of observation, we ought to think for a few moments about the role of observation in the natural sciences. For the natural sciences have been and are of tremendous importance to modern civilization, and observation is the cornerstone of natural science. Let's make a series of points about scientific observation.

First, observation in science is grounded in sensory input, but it is usually quite distant from the sensory level. For example, an astronomer may talk about what she has observed with the radio telescope, but the sensory-level images are the readings from dials and the sound from an amplifier. When a radiologist observes a tumor on the X-ray film of the patient's lung, at the sensory level the images are of light regions on a dark background. The scientist must undergo quite a lot of training to make correct observations from the low-level sensory input.

Considering the distance between low-level sensory input and high-level scientific observation, it comes as no surprise that scientific observations are very fallible—that is, open to revision in the light of new experience. Quite a bit of routine scientific work consists of rechecking (verifying, corroborating) past scientific observations.

Scientific observations can be randomly or accidentally made. But far more often they are the result of experimental manipulation or at least directed search. For example, to see whether the sun's rays bend around a planet as they pass, the astronomer needs an eclipse. This cannot be set up experimentally, but the astronomer knows when the next eclipse is due and can set up telescopes accordingly. In most sciences, the researcher can set up experiments to observe in a productive way. For example, to test the results of using a new baldness drug, the medical researcher might set up two groups of bald men, give one group the drug and the other group a fake pill (called a *placebo*), and observe whether hair loss slows more in the group using the drug than in the group using the placebo.

Because scientific observation is so high level, directed, and dependent on experimental apparata, we say that scientific observation is theory laden. That is, a scientist observes the work in a manner structured by the theory he/she holds. To revert to the earlier example of the radiologist, it is because he believes that the X-ray machine emits X rays, that X rays are absorbed by denser material, and that tumors are denser than the surrounding tissue that the radiologist observes that the light regions on the film picture are tumors. We touched on the idea of "theory-ladenness" back in Chapter 6; in this example, note that to understand the very word *X ray* involves knowing a good many things about X rays. Our theories thus help shape the world we see—which is one reason this text was given the title it has.

Another characteristic of scientific observation is its precision. Rather than resting content with the observation that gold weighs a lot, the chemist tries to precisely measure just how heavy a given amount of gold is. Observation in science is precise and, where feasible, *quantified.* A very big feature of most natural sciences is the development of various scales of measurement, units of measure, along with the equipment needed to do the measurements. This is all part of the enterprise of seeing the world scientifically.

Finally, it should be stressed that scientific observation is intersubjective or "community based." The standards of measure, experimental apparatus, areas of observational focus, and the whole collection of theories that inform all of these, are seldom if ever the creations of one mind. These things evolve under the collective work of a community of researchers over extended periods of time. Whether a given researcher gets credited with a crucial observational discovery involves the intersubjective agreement of other researchers in the field that he or she did indeed observe what was claimed.

Of course, the fact that observation is a theory-laden and intersubjective activity should not incline you to the crazy view that we "create" the world by our theories. Radiation exists outside our ability to conceptualize, theorize, and measure it—as people can find out to their dismay if, say, they get too near a big jar of plutonium.

Exercise 11.5

Pick any experimental observation in any science you have some knowledge of, and describe in general terms the theories involved in the measurements.

InfoTrac College Edition

You can locate InfoTrac College Edition articles about this chapter by accessing the InfoTrac College Edition Web site (www.infotrac-college.com/wadsworth/). Using the InfoTrac College Edition subject guide, enter the search terms relevant to this chapter, and then read abstracts for relevant articles.

Chapter 12

Inductive Generalization and Inductive Instantiation

---

1 *The Pervasiveness of Inductive Generalization*

You often hear it said that we shouldn't "generalize." This is a puzzling claim. First, generalizing on the basis of experience seems automatic, not just for people but for all other higher animals as well. Just think how quickly a dog will learn to avoid people who are cruel to it. Moreover, it seems only right that we do so. Would a child that couldn't learn, say, to avoid hot stoves after being burned once or twice ever survive to reach adulthood? Finally, the claim "We should never generalize" is itself a generalization!

But we can see a point to the claim that you shouldn't generalize. How often do we see someone judge us based on one mistake we happen to make or judge a whole group of people based on the behavior of one of its members? The point is, we cannot avoid generalizing, but generalization carries the risk of reasoning fallaciously. In this chapter we want to explore the criteria for logical inductive generalization.

To begin to delineate the criteria for assessing generalizations, let's think about some examples.

From ordinary life
1. You try a number of Chinese restaurants and all of them serve rice with dinner. You infer that almost all Chinese restaurants do so.
2. You and most of your friends, all young adults, like a certain movie star. You conclude that most American young adults do so.
3. You check your records and find that nine out of the last ten times your mother borrowed your car, she returned it with the gas tank empty. You figure that in the future, 90 percent of the time when she borrows it again she'll return it with the gas tank empty.

From science
1. Psychologists study several hundred ten-year-olds and find that 73 percent of them are math-phobic. The psychologists conclude that 73 percent of all ten-year-olds are math-phobic.
2. Pollsters interview 1,523 voters in California and find that if the next gubernatorial election were held today, 58 percent would vote Republican. So the political

pollsters conclude that if the election were held today, 58 percent of the voters would vote Republican.

3. Biologists capture several hundred coyotes in the area around Santa Fe, New Mexico, and find that 12 percent of them carry a certain disease. The biologists conclude that 12 percent of all coyotes in that vicinity carry that disease.

In each of these examples, the person or people doing the generalizing examine a group of individuals of a certain type. The group of individuals actually examined we call the **sample.** The entire group of individuals of that type we call the **population.** Generalization is reasoning from sample to population. We observe that some fraction of the sample (all, most, *x* percent) has a certain property, and we conclude that a similar fraction of the whole population has that property. The inference is

1. *x* percent of the sample has *P.*
∴   *x* percent of the population has *P.*

Since we are in effect projecting the property *P* from the sample to the population, let us call it the **projected property.**

Generalization is obviously a valuable, if fallible, tool in our intellectual toolbox. First, generalization enables us to move beyond the limitations of our narrow experiences to come up with better *descriptions* of the world around us. For example, my narrow experience of a dozen or so dogs enables me to have some understanding of the world of dogs. Second, generalization enables us to move from our experiences of the past to *predictions* about the future. Generalizing thus has descriptive uses and predictive (also called "projective") uses. For example, my past experience of dogs is a valuable tool in enabling me to deal with my new pet dog.

Be careful to distinguish generalization from enumeration or census. An **enumeration** (or census) involves checking every individual in a population to see whether it has some property of interest. For example, if I checked every dog in a kennel for distemper, I would be enumerating rather than sampling them. Another example: Every four years the U.S. government conducts a census, in which supposedly every family is contacted to get (among other information) an exact count of the citizenry.

The difference between enumeration and generalization is the difference between deduction and induction: enumeration is *deductive* generalization, while generalization (loosely so-called) is *inductive* generalization. The argument forms given in Table 12.1 make this clear. Conclusion of enumerations thus follow with necessity from the observed premises; conclusions of generalizations are inductive leaps beyond the observed premises.

2   *Criteria for Assessing Generalizations*

Generalization is projection from sample to population, so it stands to reason that the strength of the inference depends in great part (though not entirely) on the quality of the sample. We say a sample is **representative** if it likely has the same proportion of the projected property as does the population as a whole. The quality of a sample is just how representative it is. What then makes a sample representative (that is, logically good)? Three things: the size of the sample, the degree of match between the sample and the population, and the randomness of the sample.

TABLE 12.1	
Enumeration (Deductive Generalization)	Generalization (Inductive Generalization)
1. Every *A*-individual has been found to have property *P*. ∴ All *A*'s are *P* This argument is valid.	1. Every *A*-individual *in this sample* has been found to have property *P*. ∴ All *A*'s are *P* This argument is invalid but may be strong.

First: The larger the sample, the more representative it is, so the stronger the inference is. Generalizing on the basis of too few cases is clearly fallacious. To think that all Etrangians are thieves because you knew one Etrangian and he was a thief is silly. To think that Ford makes a good car because you owned a Ford and your cousin owned a Ford and both were good cars is silly. We need to observe a sufficiently large number of cases to be confident in our generalization. For example, professional political polls often involve samples of about 1,500 people.

Determining exactly how many cases are needed for a generalization to be reliable to a given level is a tricky matter but one of great practical importance, because sampling is time-consuming and expensive. Thus, for example, it would be unrealistic to expect a political pollster to interview several million voters to see how they are going to vote. First, it would cost an outrageous amount. Worse, it would take so long that by the time the pollster finished interviewing the sample, people's opinions may have changed!

Since this is not a text in statistics, we can only make a couple of remarks about sample size. First, the size you need for a reliable sample depends on the underlying variability of the population. For example, suppose you are examining bars of pure gold to determine how well gold conducts electrical current. Since all pure gold is chemically identical, you need only sample one bar. But when examining animals or people, the samples must be much larger because species have tremendous variability. Second, while it is true that the bigger the sample size, the more reliable the generalization, this isn't a matter of direct proportionality. That is, you cannot say that a generalization based on a sample of 3,000 cases is twice as strong as one based on a sample of 1,500 cases.

Second: The more the sample matches the population in relevant respects, the more representative it is, so the stronger the inference is. Besides requiring that the sample be sufficiently large, we need to make sure it is not **biased,** tilted—that is, that it reflects the relevant characteristics of the population as a whole. For example, suppose you wanted to determine who is going to win the presidency in the next election. You decide to interview 1,500 people (to ensure a reasonable sample size) as they come out of a very ritzy jewelry store in Beverly Hills (a wealthy area of California). Will your poll be reliable? No, because the customers of a ritzy jewelry store are not representative of the country as a whole—they are not going to vote in the same way as the rest of us. Wealth is relevant to voting behavior—specifically, wealthier people tend to vote Republican to a greater degree than less wealthy people.

Let's define a couple of terms. A property *R* is **relevant** to a generalization if individuals with *R* are more likely (or less likely) to have the projected property *P* than the average for that population. We say a sample is (fully) **stratified** or **matched to the general population** if it shares all properties relevant to the project property with the population. Thus, the more matched the sample is, the more representative it is, and so the more reliable the inference is.

Several more points need to be made here. First, knowing what properties are relevant to the projected property is a matter for empirical research. We know that ethnicity and income are relevant factors in voting behavior. We know that astrological sign isn't—Virgos don't vote Democrat in larger numbers than Libras. But we have to learn this by studying actual voting patterns.

Second, relevance is a matter of degree. For example, both ethnicity and gender are relevant to voting behavior, but while the voting pattern of, say, African Americans is strongly different from that of European Americans, the voting pattern of women is usually only mildly different from that of men. This means that there is a law of diminishing returns governing sample matching: It would be impractical to try to match *every* known relevant factor in devising the sample, and usually pollsters have a good idea which relevant factors are relatively unimportant for the poll at hand.

Third, all generalizations—like all inductive inferences—are open to revision in the light of new experience. In particular, researchers in a given area may discover new relevant factors that refine and improve our power of generalization.

Fourth, there is a practical difficulty in finding a sufficiently large number of individuals with just the right match of relevant factors, especially when time is a factor. Consider voting behavior again. If I want to stratify my sample accurately, I must locate, say, a specific number of male African American Catholics with incomes of $100,000 a year or more. For this professional pollsters utilize computers.

Finally, even with a good idea of what factors are relevant to a given generalization does not imply that spotting bias in the sample is easy. Spotting bias can still be a tricky matter. A classic case of sampling gone awry occurred in 1936. A popular magazine of the time, *The Literary Digest,* wanted to predict the results of the upcoming presidential election (between the Republican Alfred Landon and the Democrat Franklin Roosevelt). It sent sample ballots to people taken from phone books from all over the country. It got over two million responses and on the basis of that huge sample confidently predicted that Landon would win decisively. In the election, however, Roosevelt won by a large margin. The subsequent loss of prestige caused the magazine to go out of business. The reason for the bad generalization was clear only in retrospect: In the 1930s owning a phone was a luxury many poor and working-class people could not afford. So the sample was skewed in favor of the wealthier-than-average people, who tended to vote disproportionately Republican. Hindsight is always clearer than foresight.

Third: The more randomized the sample, the more representative it is, so the stronger the inference is. Another technique for achieving a representative sample is to select the individuals randomly. A **randomly selected sample** is one in which every individual in the population has an equal chance of being selected for the sample. For example, suppose you are a quality assurance engineer for a computer chip manufacturer. Among other duties, you sample chips that come off the production line. You want to select the chips randomly. You might think to select every fiftieth chip for your sample, but whether that would truly give you a random sample is questionable. Let's say there are ten chip-making machines, and they spit out chips onto a conveyor belt in order. Then every fiftieth chip—hence your sample as a whole—would in fact come from one particular machine, which may be more or less reliable than the other nine. Probably a better procedure (that is, one more likely to give you a representative sample) would be to use a random number generating program (standard software on any personal computer) to spit out numbers and pick the chips accordingly (the third chip, then the seventh, then the second, and so on).

Here again, we need to make a few points. First, don't equate "random" with "haphazard." You might choose a sample of shoppers in a market haphazardly by just casting your eyes around the store and selecting, say, the first twenty people you observe. But that would not necessarily give you a random sample, because you might have unconscious biases that make you notice some people before others—for example, maybe you notice people who dress in bright colors.

Second, knowing whether a given randomizing technique really works to produce a random sample is a matter of empirical research. For example, random number generators in fact come up with numbers by applying some mathematical function to, for instance, the date you run the program, and you might need to know that function to be sure in a given context of generalization that it is not resulting in a biased sample.

Third, again, all generalizations are open to revision in the light of new experience. In particular, researchers in a given area may discover new information that shows a common randomizing technique in fact doesn't produce random samples.

Fourth, randomness is a matter of degree. A random number generator is less truly random than, say, pulling slips of paper from a bucket blindfolded, but it will do for most generalizations. This point reinforces the notion that the strength of any inductive inference is a matter of degree.

Fifth, stratification and randomization can be done together. For example, to project winners in an election shortly after the polls close, the major TV networks will hire pollsters who select precincts to stratify the sample and then randomly interview voters exiting those polling precincts. This allows very accurate and very quick generalizations—which are then broadcast often only minutes after the polls close.

Sixth, sometimes we don't know ahead of time what factors are relevant; that is, there are times when we cannot stratify our samples. Randomization still applies in those cases. Random nonstratified samples of sufficient size will still tend to produce accurate results.

The three criteria given here—size, stratification, and randomness—determine the quality of a sample at a given time. But a sample reliable at one time (say, early in a political campaign) may not be reliable at a later time. For this reason, pollsters and statisticians often employ time-lapse samples. A **time-lapse sample** consists of two or more samples taken at various times and then compared. This is certainly common in political campaigns, during which voter sentiment can shift dramatically as the campaigning unfolds. A polling organization might sample voters on a once-a-month basis during a presidential campaign.

Of course, when conducting a time-lapse sample, it is important that the size and method of selections of the samples remain constant. Otherwise, a shift in the projection may only be due to a change in bias of the sample rather than a real change in the population.

Besides wanting our sample to be representative, we want it to fit the conclusion; that is, we want the conclusion to be an appropriate one for a sample of that sort to justify. To see what fitness refers to, consider an example. Suppose 62 percent of the voters in a representative sample say they are going to vote for Jones in the upcoming election. Should we conclude that *precisely* 62 percent of all voters are going to vote for Jones? Hardly. It is much more likely that *roughly* 62 percent will—that is, that 62 percent plus or minus a few percent will. Put another way, statisticians state generalizations with a margin of error built into the conclusion:

> 1. x percent of the sample has P.
> ∴   Between $(x - m)$ percent and $(x + m)$ percent of the population has P.

where m is the margin of error. This leads us to the last criterion for assessing generalizations.

Fourth: The greater the margin of error stated in the conclusion, the stronger the inference.
Thus, the generalization

> 1.   50 percent of the sample has P.
> ∴   50 percent plus or minus 10 percent of the population has P.

is stronger than

> 1.   50 percent of the sample has P.
> ∴   50 percent plus or minus 2 percent of the population has P.

However, we should note that there is a trade-off here: Although the first inference is stronger (that is, in the first inference the premise gives more support to the conclusion), its conclusion is less informative. To go to the extreme, the generalization

> 1.   50 percent of the sample has P.
> ∴   50 percent plus or minus 50 percent of the population has P.

is very strong (indeed, it is valid), but the conclusion tells us nothing!

The concepts of sample size, randomness, and margin of error are all linked. Statisticians refer to the **level of confidence** of a method of sampling. The level of confidence is a measure of how often that polling result will be within the margin of error of the true value. It can be mathematically shown that a random sample of 1,500 individuals gives a result with a margin of error of 3 percent has a confidence level of 95 percent, no matter how big the underlying population (see Chapter 10 in Baird 1992 for a demonstration).

One last point, tying this chapter with previous ones. All generalizations are based on observed samples; therefore, the confidence we have that the conclusion is true in part depends on the quality of the observation of the sample. Determining whether the sample has been observed correctly requires many of the critical thinking skills discussed earlier. To begin with, we typically rely on the fact that the poll, say, was conducted by a reliable expert, such as a person or an organization like Gallup, Zogby, or Roper. The rules for assessing expert testimony thus apply. Were the people who conducted the questioning trained in mathematical statistics? If so, where and how recently? Is the organization biased? Who sponsored (paid for) the poll?

At the level of actually asking the questions (that is, interviewing the sample), yet more of our critical thinking skills enter in. First, are the questions asked loaded or more neutrally formed? For example, the question "Are you going to vote for Smith for governor?"

is fairly neutral. The question "Given Smith's poor performance as governor, are you going to reelect her?" is clearly biased. Second, are the questions asked framed in vague or ambiguous language, or are they fairly precise? A question such as "How often do you watch movies?" is very vague—does it mean watch TV movies, or rent videos, or actually go out to movie theaters? Third, are the questions reasonably broad and thorough, or too narrow? For example, the sole question "Do you approve of Smith's performance as president?" by itself will not allow the respondent to communicate his or her feelings about Smith. On the other hand, a series of questions would be better: "Has Smith conducted himself with dignity as president?" "Has Smith done a good job with foreign affairs?" "Did Smith work well with Congress?" "Were Smith's economic policies good for the country?"

At the level of the interaction between the interviewer and the interviewee, more issues arise. Was the interviewer off-putting to the person being questioned? A classic example is given by Darrell Huff in *How to Lie with Statistics* (1952: 24). Huff notes that in a study conducted during World War II, African Americans were asked whether they would be treated better or worse if the Japanese conquered the United States. The respondents gave quite different answers to white interviewers than to black ones: 45 percent of those interviewed by white interviewers said blacks would be treated worse by the Japanese, while only 25 percent of those interviewed by black interviewers held the same view. Second, can we be confident that the people interviewed feel free to be candid or that they even know their own feelings? A question such as "How many books do you read each month?" asked by a well-dressed, educated-looking and -sounding interviewer is apt to elicit exaggerated answers from the person on the street.

Exercise 12.2A

In each of the following generalizations, discuss what is wrong with the sample.

1. You are trying to figure out whether most elderly people like Medicare, so you ask your grandfather whether he does.
2. You are trying to decide what percentage of people will vote in the election, so you interview voters at your local shopping mall.
3. You are trying to decide whether you will like sushi (which you have never tried), so you go to dinner at Joe's Discount Sushi Restaurant once.
4. You are trying to decide whether most dogs are friendly, so you try petting dogs at 1,500 houses displaying "Beware of Dog" signs.
5. You want to determine whether most people like pizza, so you decide to ask hundreds of your friends whether they like pizza.

Exercise 12.2B

Consider the following research questions. Describe how you might develop a representative sample to answer each.

1. Do most dogs bark?
2. Are most Americans satisfied with their health care system?
3. Do most people in Poland support membership in NATO?

4. Did most people who have seen movie *X* like that movie?
5. Did most passengers on a certain cruise ship enjoy the cruise?

Exercise 12.2C

Consider the following interview questions. Each is flawed; explain how.

1. Will you try to improve your education next year?
2. Will you punish Senator Jones's bad performance by voting against her next year?
3. How often do you get drunk?
4. Has the president exerted himself in office?

3   *The Fallacy of Hasty Generalization*

Gathering the evidence needed to adequately support a generalization is hard work. Sometimes we get lazy and generalize badly. When we do so, we are committing the fallacy of **hasty generalization.** In a nutshell, a hasty generalization involves generalizing on an insufficient sample or a biased one. For example, consider this report of great interest to those of us concerned about hair loss:

> Baldness is caused by tight neckties and collars and by combing the hair improperly, says a barber who has studied the problem throughout his 50-year career. Fred C. Boor, of St. Louis, Mo., says his theories are proven by the fact that he takes his own advice and still has a full head of hair at the age of 77.

Note that Mr. Boor bases his generalization on only one case: his own. There is a natural psychological tendency to take our own personal life experiences and generalize on them, but arguments from just one case are typically hasty.

Biased samples are also common, as this report illustrates:

> More women prefer a male doctor than a female doctor, a surprising poll reveals. Of 150 women questioned in Washington, D.C., New York, Los Angeles, and the Chicago area, 61 said they preferred men physicians, 46 said women doctors and 43 had no preference.

Here, the "surprising" result that women prefer male to female doctors is based solely on a sample of women *from big cities.* Biased samples are especially common in advertising, where you often find the advertiser giving only the positive testimonials for the product. For instance:

> Doctor Tested. Here are just a few of the incredible results obtained by actual Slim-Skins users in a special slimming test conducted by a prominent American Physician.
> "I lost 4 inches from each thigh, $2\frac{1}{2}$ inches from my hips, $6\frac{1}{2}$ inches from my tummy and over 5 inches from my waist in just 3 days with Slim-Skins."—I.Z.
> "Actually trimmed my abdomen 8 full inches and my waist nearly 7 inches while my hips came down about $3\frac{1}{2}$ inches and each thigh 4 inches for a total loss of over 26 inches all in 3 days with the truly astonishing Slim-Skins."—C.D.

"The final solution in instant figures slimming. I lost $5\frac{1}{2}$ inches from my waist, 5 inches from my tummy, $2\frac{1}{4}$ inches from my hips, and over 3 inches from each thigh—an overall loss of $19\frac{1}{2}$ inches in just one 25-minute period with Slim-Skins."—M.M.

These "fantastic" inch losses are now documented fact. The famous "fat-burning" diet claims a 3-inch waist loss in 7 days. In the doctor's Slim-Skins test the waist losses were over 3 inches in just one day—actually in just 25 minutes.

Notice that only three cases are cited, and all are from positive letters. It is very likely that in addition to favorable letters that the company has received many unfavorable letters ("This stuff is junk!"; "I want my money back!"), yet none are cited in the ad.

Be careful not to confound *hasty* generalization with *sweeping* generalization. A hasty generalization is a type of bad argument: a generalization based on an insufficient or unrepresentative sample. A **sweeping** (or "glittering" or "blanket") **generalization,** such as "All politicians are crooks!" is an overstated, unqualified general statement. One is an argument of insufficient evidence; the other is an overstated statement. The two are distinct: you can, for example, have a hasty generalization in which the conclusion is not a sweeping generalization. For example,

1. My dog Mandy loves bones.
∴ Most dogs like bones.

The conclusion in this example is quite modest, hardly sweeping, but is still inadequately supported by the meager evidence.

Exercise 12.3

The following passages contain hasty generalizations. For each, put the generalization in standard argument form, and then state why it is fallacious.

1. In fact, we have gone to a lot of expense and trouble proving the Bust Expander does what we say it does. During a medical test using six women that were supervised by two prominent doctors, it was discovered that changes caused by the Bust Expander were phenomenal.
2. Most female university students own at least one stuffed animal—and today's college coeds talk over their personal problems with the cuddly creatures.

    That's the result of a survey of 245 women students at Florida State University. All but 10 of the women surveyed had a stuffed animal, and 75 percent of them admitted that they talked to it to relieve tensions, or hugged it for comfort, warmth, and security.
3. Here's my two cents' worth: Crossing guards should be used only for the first three grades of school. Who herds the rest of the kids across streets all summer?

    Secondly: Free meals should be done away with in the schools. Where do the kids eat all summer? Some of these programs are fine, but only when there is an unlimited supply of money.

    Thirdly: Busing should not be mandatory but should be for small fry who must walk more than a mile and a half.

Fourthly: No classes need to begin before 9 A.M. for the first three grades. I went through all the public school system this way and I was OK.

4. An Expert's approval—Supa Tweez has been clinically tested by a university professor of dermatology and proven to be safe and effective. One of his patients had previously been tweezing hairs from her chin every day for 15 years. After treating herself with Supa Tweez, she has eliminated this time-consuming chore for the rest of her life! Over fifteen thousand instruments in use by doctors.

5. "Fantasy Island's" Hervé Villechaize is telling pals never to trust a raccoon. Hervé offered a morsel of chicken to his pet raccoon, and the ungrateful beast not only bit the hand that fed him—he hung on painfully. Hervé suffered a two inch gash on his left index finger. No stitches, but the doc told him it'll be three months before he'll have full use of his hand.

6. "I lost 57 Pounds AND 6 Inches off my Waist in 8 months with the **FINAL DIET PLAN.** I didn't Count Calories and I Was Never Hungry!"

FINAL DIET PLAN

Before	After
• Expensive Diets	• No Counting Calories
• Always Hungry	• No Diet Pills
• Time-Consuming Meetings	• No Packaged Foods
• Results Didn't Last	• No Yo-Yo Diets
• Total Frustration	• Reduced Risk of Chronic Disease

7. I read your editorial about how college students didn't know who Stalin was, what is the Warsaw Pact, etc. Well, when I was in high school, I knew what the Warsaw and NATO pacts were: I knew who Stalin, Churchill, de Gaulle, and Roosevelt were. I knew at least 85 percent of the world's capitals, and if I was given a blank map of the United States or world, I could fill in all the states and most of the world's countries. I enjoyed and was interested in it.

But, unfortunately, I knew very little about math and other subjects. I am 29 years old and have held only menial jobs and am unemployed today. The knowledge I had one can't use. Math, computers, science you can use to become a success. Geography, history, etc. are useless. I found out the hard way.

8. Well, I remember when I lost everything we had: my job, our savings, my pension . . . and we had to borrow money from our relatives to pay the rent and keep food on the table for our little ones. Now I am one of the highest paid executives in my field, my wife has her own business, our kids go to the finest schools, all the bills are paid, and we have money in the bank.

How did this all happen? Just when I was in the depths of despair, my wife read what Jesus said about the mustard seed to me:

"If ye have faith as a grain of mustard seed . . . nothing shall be impossible unto you."
Matthew 17:20

I thought to myself, "if only I had something to hold on to, that I could see and touch." So, I acquired some mustard seeds from the Holy Land, encased them in a credit card–size metallic prayer card, and began carrying it with an affirmation of faith. I was amazed at how my life changed. Not only did I begin to prosper, but my mental and physical health improved.

Are you or someone close to you having problems? I know what it's like to be desperate. I know what it's like to have what you need and want. And I know that you can decide which one it's going to be. What does it require? Faith. Faith and commitment enough to carry your mustard seed from the Holy Land and follow a few simple instructions. I guarantee it. If you will send a check or money order for $4.00 plus $0.70 postage and handling, I will send you a mustard seed from the Holy Land encased in the "Seed of Faith" prayer card with instructions for its use. If you return your "Seed of Faith" prayer card for any reason within 30 days after you received it, I will return your check or money order to you. Can your future wait?

9. Researchers have come up with an ensemble for men that will discourage advances from coeds as surely as bug repellent keeps off mosquitoes.

The outfit—an earring, a tank-top, a fur coat, bell-bottom blue jeans and tire-tread sandals—topped the list of most repulsive clothing compiled on the basis of interviews with 56 college women.

"Tank tops are worn by men who try to show off muscles they don't have," sneered a shapely senior form Southern Methodist University in Texas. "And tire-tread sandals make a guy look like a holdover from Woodstock."

The women, who came from four Texas colleges, were asked to finish the sentence, "An item I particularly detest is . . . ." Items mentioned by more than half the coeds were put on a most-hated list.

10. Kids who skip the prom aren't missing very much. I was quietly amused when I read the letter from the teenager who had a date to the prom. She wrote, "everyone had a terrific time." That girl is living in fantasy-land. The truth is most people have a lousy time.

I am 48 years old. My prom was in 1951. I can't recall a worse evening in my entire life. Five days before prom time I didn't have a date, so I asked a senior if he would take me. He said OK, but I'd have to "go all the way." (That was how they put it in those days.) I refused and finally got an 11th grader to be my escort. (I had to pay his expenses.)

We triple-dated with two couples I didn't know very well. My date couldn't dance and no one else asked me. So I dragged around in agony half the evening and spent the other half in the powder room with six girls who were also having a rotten time.

When our own son asked if he should spend the money to go to his prom, I said it wasn't worth it but he decided to go anyway. Afterward he said, "You were right, Mom. I should have gone bowling."

This is to let the girls who don't get asked know that they aren't missing much.

11. Thirty-six percent of Americans believe they have been reincarnated, an ENQUIRER survey reveals-and some say they've even had flashbacks of their past lives.

In our survey—conducted in New York, Philadelphia, Washington, D.C., Chicago and Los Angeles—we asked a total of 50 men and 50 women this question: "Do you believe you've lived before in a previous life?" The results: 64 percent said "no," while 36 percent said "yes." And as many men as women believe they've been reincarnated.

12. THREE OUT OF FOUR DENTISTS WON'T TREAT AIDS PATIENTS

More than three-fourths of dentists won't treat a patient with a bad toothache if he has AIDS, a recent survey shows.

We called a total of 25 dentists—five each in New York City, Los Angeles, Milwaukee, Dallas, and Fort Lauderdale, Fla. In each case our reporter said, "I have a bad toothache and I'd like to make an appointment. However, I have to be honest—I have AIDS. Will you treat me?"

Nineteen out of 25 dentists, or 76 percent, refused to make an appointment. Only six dentists, or 24 percent, agreed to treat a person who admits he has AIDS.

13.   WHO SHOPLIFTS?

Kim Vogelman of Prism Asset Protection Consultants in Dallas, whose business it is to prevent shoplifting and employee theft, speaks form time to time about his avocation to high school students and other groups. Prior to his talks, Vogelman often conducts surveys. Not long ago, he polled about 200 students on these three questions and obtained the following responses:

	Yes	**No**
Have you ever shoplifted?	32 percent	68 percent
Have you ever been caught shoplifting?	13 percent	87 percent
Do you know anyone who shoplifts?	71 percent	29 percent

On the basis of his experience and questionnaires, Vogelman believes that about a third of high school students (slightly more girls than boys) will shoplift at least once before graduation. "In so many cases," he says, "it seems to have become a rite of passage."

14.   The article on New Schoolteachers (*Times,* Sept. 6) conveniently excludes a whole group of the highest-qualified teachers, those who would exult with a starting salary of $26,000, those with decades of experience in practical, applied math and science, some with 10 to 20 years as part-time teachers, some who would out perform even Jaime Escalante himself—the older aerospace engineers.

No school district dares to utter the words, but age discrimination seems to be the only apparent reason for choosing younger teachers over the older set. Regardless of the popularity of elderly substitute teachers in the eyes of the students themselves, the political dealing of the front office carries the main weight in hiring practices.

This writer has over 15 years teaching, over 20 years of engineering, over 370 college credits, repeating the calculus series to ensure professionalism, a substitute math/physics teacher in nearly 20 school districts, yet is still waiting for the first serious offer. In 1982, L.A. Unified begged this engineer to teach electronics in the district while volunteering at Narbonne High in the Adopt-A-School Program. Today, the phone is strangely quiet.

Charles A. Smith
Huntington Beach

15.   NATURAL CRYSTALS HELPS YOU LOSE WEIGHT!!!
             STOP FOOD FROM DESTROYING YOUR LIFE!

Take a good look at yourself today and ask yourself if you wish to go through the rest of your life looking like you do. If your answer is No, then read on.

This is your chance to lose weight once and for all and to have the kind of body you have always wanted for the rest of your life.

By now you have probably tried many different diets. Some of them worked and some didn't, but in the end you find yourself back to where you started feeling helpless to control your situation. Now you will be able to finally take charge of your life once and for all.

I myself suffered for years being fat—feeling helpless to stop myself from over-indulging. I WAS WEAK!! I had no power to control my weight problem. I felt like a runaway freight train heading helplessly toward Fat City. I looked older than I was and felt it too. I lacked energy to do things I wanted to do and I was putting my health at risk as well.

Then I came upon The Natural Crystals which saved me from my fate. I discovered that these High Energy Natural Crystals gave me the Will Power to put the brakes on once and for all. The helpless feeling disappeared and was replaced by an inner strength and confidence to become master of my own fate.

I researched these wonderful crystals and discovered that these Natural Crystals have been around since the dawn of time and have been used since the beginning of civilization. I was so impressed by these crystals that I had to share them with others who had a similar problem. I have collected a quantity of these Natural Crystals and am offering them to anyone who would like to be Slender, Healthy, and Youthful, but lacks the Will Power to do it.

To order your own Natural Crystal send $12.95 plus $2.00 for postage, handling and immediate delivery to Happy Crystal, P.O. Box 99, Wahoo, TX.

16. There's an epidemic sweeping through medical schools: alcoholism. And the only way it's going to be stopped is if med school staff members are trained to detect it early, say Drs. Anderson Spickard and Tremaine Billings.

All too often excessive alcohol use is overlooked by faculty members and colleagues or is written off to the stress and rigors of the profession, they note.

But all the excuses in the world won't change the fact: Alcoholism is a disease that needs urgent attention.

Over the last ten years, Spickard and Billings have successfully helped seven doctors at Vanderbilt University Medical School who were alcoholics.

"They represent only some of those on the faculty who are impaired by alcoholism and other forms of chemical dependency," they explained.

17. INTERVIEWER: How do you square voluntary school prayer with no change in the Bill of Rights?
FALLWELL: The same way we squared it for 180 years of American history. I feel that the atheist or any objecting child should have the right to leave the classroom during a time of voluntary prayer.
INTERVIEWER: Do you know how traumatic that can be?
FALLWELL: It would be no problem for me.

18. Pam Poco's whole life has suddenly changed, since she lost an amazing 16 lbs. in seven days and then quickly lost 99 lbs. more. As she describes it: "I was always overweight and tried everything to lose, but the Super-Loss Capsule Program is the only thing that ever worked. It's truly the #1 weapon against fat."

What is the Super-Loss Diet Program? It's a remarkable weight loss plan with an amazing Clinically Proven Pill. This incredible program can actually make your body burn off the maximum amount of fat . . . in record time. It can help you quickly lose all the weight you need to—without torturous starvation and without battling hunger pangs. Weight loss is fast and dramatic.

4 *Defeasibility and General Rules*

Throughout this text, we have emphasized that critical thinking is geared toward developing an accurate worldview and using it, applying it, to decide what to do. At the heart of your worldview or belief system are your general beliefs, your generalizations. In Chapter 11 and in the previous sections of this chapter, we examined in detail the two most common ways you learn your general rules: testimony and inductive generalization. Early in life you acquire your general beliefs from what your teachers and parents tell you: Be kind to others; share; don't tell lies. Later on in life, you acquire more and more such beliefs by your own observation, as well your own research into expert sources. In this chapter we want to learn how to apply those generalizations reliably.

Recall from Chapter 5 that we call the process of applying a general rule to a particular case (or cases) *instantiation.* In that chapter we distinguished universal or *deductive* instantiation from *inductive* instantiation. In deductive instantiation, you apply a rule that is true *without any exceptions* to a given case in front of you. This is an error-free process: If a generalization is absolutely universally true, it must apply to every case. But, alas, such generalizations are rare (outside of mathematics). More common is **inductive instantiation,** or *case reasoning,* in which you are applying a *rule* that is true only of typical cases or, as we say in common language, is true *but with exceptions.* For example, it is true that pigs are four-legged animals, but there are exceptions. Table 12.2 makes the point.

We can explain inductive instantiation more clearly if we borrow a concept from the philosophy of law, the concept of defeasibility. Any law is **defeasible** if it can be rendered null and void by exceptional circumstances. Any law legislators devise is understood to be inherently defeasible. A law stating that you are not allowed to drive more than sixty-five miles per hour on a given highway can be defeated by all kinds of exceptional circumstances—a car-jacker has a gun to your head, your wife is in labor, your friend is having a heart attack, and so on. The concept of defeasibility is not only found in legal contexts but in ethical ones as well. It is notoriously hard to formulate ethical principles that are exceptionless. For example, the principle "You should return what you borrow," while generally quite sound, admits of all kinds of exceptions. (Can you think of some? That is, can you think of cases in which the moral thing is not to return what you borrowed?)

To demand of any generalization that it hold without exceptions is usually to demand the impossible. The critical thinker has to know how to apply generalizations—to know to what sorts of cases the general rule was meant to be applied and how it was meant to be applied.

Exercise 12.4

The following statements are true generalizations. Imagine an exceptional case for each (that is, a situation in which the rule would not apply).

1. You should not lie.
2. When driving you must buckle your seat belt.
3. You should return what your borrow.
4. People like fresh food.
5. Criminals should be punished.
6. You should exercise regularly.
7. You should eat a low-fat diet.
8. You should be kind to other people.
9. Always brush your teeth.
10. Respect your elders.

TABLE 12.2	
Deductive Instantiation	Inductive Instantiation
1. All *A*'s without exception ("universally) have *P.* ___ ∴ This *A* has *P.* This argument is valid.	1. Most *A*'s are *P.* ___ ∴ This *A* has *P.* This argument is invalid but may be strong.

5 *The Statistical Syllogism*

Let's analyze inductive instantiation more precisely. The argument form representing inductive instantiation is called **the statistical syllogism,** which we state as the converse of generalization:

If we are talking about single individuals
1. *x* percent of *A*'s have property *P.*
∴ [Probably] This *A* will have *P.*

or

1. *x* percent of *A*'s have *P.*
2. This is an *A.*
∴ [Probably] This has *P.*

If we are talking about subgroups or samples
1. *x* percent of *A*'s have property *P.*
∴ [Probably] *x* percent of this sample of *A*'s has *P.*

or as well

1. *x* percent of *A*'s have *P.*
2. These individuals are *A*'s.
∴ [Probably] *x* percent of these individuals have *P.*

We again call the class of *A*'s the population, and property *P* the projected property. The first premise may state a precise percentage, as in

1. 98 percent of graduates of St. Margaret's Academy go on to college.
2. Susie just graduated from St. Margaret's Academy.
∴ [Probably] Suzie will go on to college.

Or it may use a nonnumerical expression such as *most, often, usually, almost always,* or *almost never,* as in

1. Most dogs like cheese.
2. Vago is a dog.
∴ [Probably] Vago likes cheese.

In what follows, let's assume we are dealing with percentages.

Please note that statistical syllogisms are often formulated in a negative fashion, as in these examples:

1. Almost no pigs can dance.
2. Porky is a pig.
∴ [Probably] Porky cannot dance.

1. Only 2 percent of chickens are pink.
∴ [Probably] This group of chickens is not pink.

We will assume in what follows that negatively formulated statistical syllogisms have been converted to the positive. For the two prior examples, then, we have the following:

1. Almost all pigs cannot dance.
2. Porky is a pig.
∴ [Probably] Porky cannot dance.

1. 98 percent of chickens are not pink.
∴ [Probably] This group of chickens is not pink.

What criteria do we use to assess statistical syllogisms? Three commonsensical rules come to mind.

Rule 1: The closer x is to 100, the more likely the conclusion. Clearly, the premises of the argument

1. 99.99 percent of all pigs like Brie.
2. Porky is a pig.
∴ Porky likes Brie.

make the conclusion more likely than the premises in

1. 55 percent of all pigs like Brie.
2. Porky is a pig.
∴ Porky likes Brie.

Rule 2: The individual or the sample instantiated to should be a representative or typical case (or sample) of the population. For example, consider the argument:

1. 90 percent of all frogs are green.
2. Kermit is a frog.
∴ Kermit is green.

If Kermit is in fact an atypical frog, some special type of frog—say, a Barstow horned frog, which is usually yellow—then of course the premises would not make the conclusion likely. That is, considered merely as a frog, the premises would support the inference that Kermit is green. But considered as a Barstow horned frog, the premises would be

1. Most Barstow horned frogs are yellow.
2. Kermit is a Barstow horned frog.

which would support the conclusion that probably Kermit is yellow.

How can we ensure that the individual or sample instantiated to is a typical case or representative sample? We can try to ensure that the population chosen for the statistical syllogism be the one that shares all relevant characteristics of *x*. If Kermit is a Barstow horned frog, then we need to know what percentage of all Barstow horned frogs are green. If Kermit is a Barstow horned frog suffering from jaundice (a disease that turns skin yellow), then we need to know what percentage of all jaundiced Barstow horned frogs are green.

The point here is just the mirror image of a point made in the last chapter (on generalization). A generalization is reasonable only if the sample on which it is based is representative—that is, has all relevant characteristics of the population as a whole. An instantiation is reasonable only if the individual (or sample) instantiated to shares all relevant characteristics of the population.

Of course, which properties are relevant to a given instantiation—just like to a given generalization—is something we learn empirically and is always open to revision in the light of later experience. We know, for example, that ethnic identity and income level are relevant to voting behavior. So to judge the argument

1. 60 percent of all men vote Democratic.
2. Fred is a man.
∴ Fred will vote Democratic.

we need to ask whether we know anything about Fred's income or ethnic identity. If all we know is that he is a man (that is, if the only relevant population we can place him in is that of men), then the argument is reasonable. But, if we know Fred is wealthy, then the argument becomes weak, because while it might be true that 60 percent of all men vote Democratic, perhaps 70 percent of all wealthy men vote Republican.

Rule 3: The greater the margin of error state in the conclusion, the stronger the inference.

1. 90 percent of men like football.
∴ 90 percent of these 100 guys sitting in this bar like football.

is weaker than

1. 90 percent of men like football.
∴ 90 percent (plus or minus 5 percent) of these 100 guys sitting in this bar like football.

Again, as noted earlier, there is a trade-off here: Although in the second inference the is stronger (that is, the premise gives more support to the conclusion), its conclusion is less informative than in the first argument.

Exercise 12.5

For the following arguments, (1) put the argument in standard form; (2) identify the individual or the sample, the general population, and the projected property; and (3) relying on your general background knowledge, indicate what properties are relevant to determining whether the individual or sample is typical of that population.

1. Most winters in Tahoe see more than ten feet of snowfall. So this winter, Tahoe will see that.

2. The statistics are that 85 percent of all people like hamburgers. So Suzie will.
3. Larry probably likes cheese. After all, he is French American, and 85 percent of French Americans like cheese.
4. Of the freshmen students who registered at Cow U. this fall, virtually all had taken algebra in high school. Al is a freshman registered at Cow U., so he probably took algebra in high school.
5. Only 2 percent of dogs have yellow eyes. So I suspect that the puppy Jamie just got from the pound does not have yellow eyes.
6. Polls show that 78 percent of Californians intend to vote for Jones for governor. Fred is a Californian. So Fred will probably vote for Jones.
7. It is known that 92 percent of all Americans eat beef. Lori is an American, so she probably eats beef.
8. Very few people dislike cheese, so Sue will probably like the cheese platter at the party.
9. I am pretty sure chemotherapy will work on my cancer. After all, it works on 85 percent of people with similar cancers.
10. Almost all dogs can't dance. So probably Mandy, my dog, is a nondancer.

6 *The Fallacy of Accident*

When a person applies a rule to an atypical case, we say he or he or she has committed the fallacy of **accident.** Notice that accident is the converse of hasty generalization. People commit this fallacy in three different ways. First, a person can simply misapply the general rule, overlooking relevant special features of the case at hand. For example, someone might not report a robbery because he believes that people shouldn't be informers. That is a fallacious argument because being an informer means intentionally spying on people and reporting what they do. The term *informer* hardly applies to a person who happens upon a major crime in progress. A similar fallacy would be to allow a friend to drive home after getting drunk at a party, for the reason that you do not want to tell other people what to do. That is a laudable sentiment, but it hardly applies to someone too drunk to rationally decide what to do and drunk enough to kill others.

The second way a person can commit the fallacy of accident is by attempting to refute someone else's general rule by pointing out counterexamples, but where those counterexamples are atypical. For example,

> Ms. A: I doubt that people will readily accept mass transit. After all, cars give people freedom of movement, something they prize highly.
>
> Mr. B: That's absurd. How can you speak about cars giving us "freedom of movement"? Haven't you ever been stuck in a traffic jam?

Here, Mr. B attempts to refute Ms. A's general rule—that cars allow us to move around freely—by citing the atypical situation of being stuck in a traffic jam.

The third way a person can commit the fallacy of accident is by citing **anecdotal evidence**—that is, by citing only one or two cases as counterexamples to overturn a generalization. For example,

> They say that women tend to live longer than men, but it's not true: heck, my grandpa outlived my grandma by nearly two years.

Here, only one case is cited.

Take care not to confound hasty generalization with the second and third kinds of accidents. In hasty generalization, the arguer tries to establish a generalization by looking at atypical, or few, cases. In the second and third sorts of accidents, the arguer attempts to refute someone else's generalization by citing atypical, or few, cases, without necessarily going on to make a new (contrary) generalization.

Exercise 12.6

The following passages contain fallacies of accident. Explain how.

1. People like fresh food. So my guests will love fresh rat meat on their pizza tonight.
2. People shouldn't tell lies. So I guess we should tell our little girl that she is terminally ill.
3. We should be kind to elderly ladies. So we shouldn't put old Mrs. Badger in jail for poisoning those thirty Boy Scouts.
4. People who argue that carrying a gun deters criminal attacks are all wrong. On several recent occasions, U.S. presidents have been the targets of assassins, even though any president is surrounded by gun-toting Secret Service agents.
5. Man is a social animal. So this guy will be sociable even though I just threw a rat at his wife.
6. I disagree that Smith is a good hitter. After he broke his hand he didn't get many hits, now did he?

+7   *Authority and Attacking the Person Reconsidered*

In Chapter 11 we discussed legitimate appeals to expert testimony, as well as fallacious appeals. We can deepen our understanding of the matter if we recast appeals to testimony as statistical syllogisms.

Consider, for example, the testimony of an expert Dr. *X,* who is testifying that a certain medicine is effective in treating colds. We saw in Chapter 11 that such testimony would be credible to the extent that Dr. *X* is a medical doctor, trained in infectious diseases, current, not biased in his advocacy of medicine, and so on. Why is that so? Presumably because most statements about infections diseases by relevantly trained, unbiased, current (and so on) medical doctors are true. That is, a statistical syllogism:

1. Most claims made about infectious diseases by trained, unbiased, current (and so on) medical doctors are true.

2. Dr. *X* is a relevantly trained, unbiased, current (and so on) medical doctor,
    and he claims that this medicine will be effective in treating colds.

∴ [Probably] This medicine will be effective in treating colds.

That argument is strong. Notice that it would cease to be strong if Dr. *X* were *not* a relevantly trained, unbiased, current (and so on) medical doctor, for then it would be virtually impossible for most of his or her statements about infectious diseases (a subject he or she would know little about) to be true.

We can generalize the point to all arguments from expert testimony. Underlying them is a general statistical syllogism:

1. Most statements made by genuine experts (current, unbiased, relevantly
    trained, and so forth) in their field of expertise are true.
2. Statement *S* is such a statement.

∴ [Probably] statement *S* is true.

Similarly, we can see that underlying appeals to any observational testimony is a general statistical syllogism:

1. Most observation statements made by observers who are unbiased, in a position
    to observe clearly, not under the influence of drugs (and so on) are true.
2. Statement *S* is such a statement.

∴ [Probably] statement *S* is true.

Turning now to attacking the person, we saw in Chapter 8 that we cannot dismiss a person's claim/proposal/idea simply because he or she is biased, possessed of bad character, ugly, or such (unless he or she is testifying). The reason becomes clear if we put the fallacy of attacking the person as a syllogism:

1. Most statements made by biased (or hypocritical or repellant or crooked)
    people are false.
2. Statement *S* is such a statement.

∴ [Probably] statement *S* is false.

But it is ridiculous to say that *most* statements made by bad people are false—even bad people usually tell the truth about most things, if only because most things are not worth lying about. Even a filthy pervert is going to tell the truth about what time it is, what foods he or she likes, and so on. So the statistical syllogism that would "justify" attacking the person is fatally flawed.

One last point. When we discussed attacking the person, in Chapter 8, we specifically exempted testimony. We said that a person's character, motives, lifestyle, and so forth, were irrelevant unless we are examining his or her testimony, in which case those considerations *would* be relevant. Knowing that a witness is biased (or has bad character or whatever) does indeed logically undermine that person's testimony. But when a witness's testimony is undermined by discovering flaws in that person, we don't conclude that the claim that the witness is testifying to is *false*—only that the testimony is not good evidence for it. For example, if a medical doctor testifies that cigarettes do not cause cancer, and we discover that he or she is biased (say, paid millions by some tobacco company), we cannot conclude that cigarettes *do* cause cancer—only that we have been given no compelling evidence that they don't.

We can (again) explain this point by considering general statistical syllogisms. To discover relevant flaws in witness *X* only shows that the argument

1. Most things *X* says about this matter are true.
2. *X* says *S*.
∴ [Probably] *S* is true

is a bad one. It does not allow us to infer

1. Most things *X* says about this matter are false.
2. *X* says *S*.
∴ [Probably] *S* is false

Exercise 12.8

Recast arguments from memory as a general statistical syllogism.

InfoTrac College Edition

You can locate InfoTrac College Edition articles about this chapter by accessing the InfoTrac College Edition Web site (www.infotrac-college.com/wadsworth/). Using the InfoTrac College Edition subject guide, enter the search terms relevant to this chapter, and then read abstracts for relevant articles.

Chapter 13

Analogies

---

1 *The Uses of Analogy*

In this chapter we will look at a common mode of inductive reasoning: analogy. An **analogy** is a comparison of two things. Consider these two examples:

> Where does all of this leave us? Economics is in a state of turmoil. The economics of the textbooks and of graduate schools not only still teaches price-auction model but is moving toward narrower and narrower interpretations. The mathematical sophistication intensifies as an understanding of the real world diminishes. Nevertheless, one can see signs of countercurrents beginning to develop. Economic models are being constructed that are designed to better reflect the world as we can see and measure it and also enhance possibilities of exercising economic control. . . . The transition from one mode of thought to another is difficult, since it involves abandoning a beautiful sailing ship—the equilibrium price-auction model—that happens to be torn apart and sinking in a riptide. So a raft must be built to catch whatever winds may come by. That raft won't match the beauty or mathematical elegance of the sailing ship, although it has one undeniable virtue— it floats.
>
> Lester Thurow, *Dangerous Currents*

> The human understanding is like a false mirror, which receiving rays irregularly, distorts and discolors the nature of things by mingling its own nature with it.
>
> Francis Bacon, *The New Organon*

In the first example, we do not have to follow the technical details to see the analogy being made or why it is being made: a specific economic model is compared to a beautiful ship breaking up, and the author is urging us to adopt a less elegant but more workable model much as we would jump on an inelegant but functional raft. In the second example, Bacon compares human understanding to a distorting mirror.

An analogy compares one thing, called the **subject,** to one or more other things, called the **analogs.** In the first example given, the subject is an economic theory and the analog is a beautiful ship. In the second passage, the subject is the human under-

standing and the analog is a distorting mirror. Any analogy can be put in explicit analogical form:

> <Subject> is like <analog(s)>

In evaluating reasoning by analogy, we must explicitly state the analogy. This helps us
focus on the key issues—namely, the similarities and dissimilarities of the two things
compared.

Analogies have four basic uses. The **descriptive** use is the use of that analogy to describe a situation or state of affairs. The **definitional** use is to define a word or phrase. The
argumentative use is as a premise in an argument. Finally, the **heuristic** use is to aid in
research. We will explore each of these uses in turn.

Exercise 13.1

For each of the following passages, determine whether it contains an analogy, and if so,
put the analogy in explicit form: <subject> is like <analogs>.

1. Karla danced all night, then she went home an made an omelet. After eating the
   omelet, she tuned up her car and went for a drive.
2. The way I look at it, the liver is like a muscle. Just like you keep a muscle in shape
   by exercising it, so you must exercise the liver by drinking lots of booze.
3. Margo and Kelly are identical twins, and grew up together. I know Margo, and she
   is brilliant: three earned Ph.D.'s, a multimillionaire stockbroker, and she's a whip at
   fixing diesel engines. So I figure that maybe Kelly is bright too.
4. My dog is a veritable Einstein among dogs. I mean, she is amazingly smart.
5. People can be so cruel. My girlfriend just told me that she thinks I'm stupid.
6. I've dined at that restaurant many times and always had good food, so I think we
   may as well eat there tonight.
7. The Cowboys have defeated the Chargers the last four times they played each other.
   Moreover, this Cowboys team has even better players than it did before. So I'm betting that they will win again.
8. Sue has watched actor *A* in four movies, and she thought he gave a poor
   performance in all of them. So she is reluctant to see his latest movie.
9. Both Luisa and Audrey are successful. Luisa is a major corporate attorney who has
   published over five hundred articles in respected law journals, and Audrey built a
   multibillion-dollar business from scratch.
10. The way Lorenzo sucked up that pizza, you'd think he was a vacuum cleaner.
11. Science can make a bulldozer. But it cannot train the emotions of the driver so that
    he will stop it before a crawling baby and not run over it. This point has been
    brought out succinctly by Bertrand Russell, when he says: "Science can tell him
    how certain ends might be reached. What it cannot tell him is that he should pursue
    one end rather than the other."

    Sampooran Singh, *The Dynamic Interplay between Science and Religion*
12. It was my ambition to make a difficult subject accessible to the general reader, but stu-
    dents familiar with it will, I hope, nevertheless find some new information in these
    pages. This refers mainly to Johannes Kepler, whose works, diaries and correspondence

have so far not been accessible to the English reader; nor does a serious English biography exist. Yet Kepler is one of the few geniuses who enables one to follow, step by step, the tortuous path that led him to his discoveries, and to get a really intimate glimpse, as in a slow-motion film, of the creative act. He accordingly occupies a key position in the narrative.

> Arthur Koestler, *The Sleepwalkers*

13. How do political reformers get away with continuing to use the whole population as guinea pigs, despite a trail of failures and broken promises that would embarrass a used-car dealer?

Whether it is the environmental protection racket today or the Prohibition amendment sixty years ago, it has been one disastrous "noble experiment" after another. It took us more than a decade to face the fact that Prohibition was not prohibiting. It was just corrupting. There are already studies showing that "environmental protection" doesn't protect the environment, that criminal "rehabilitation" programs don't rehabilitate, and that school "integration" programs don't integrate.

Like Prohibition, these other experiments did not simply fail. They have created massive new problems of their own. Prohibition was the greatest boost ever given to organized crime. We are still paying for that today. There are so many bureaucrats protecting the environment that it is literally a federal case to try to drill for oil, dig some coal, or build a hydroelectric dam. All the while, we keep wringing our hands over not having enough energy.

> Thomas Sowell, *Pink and Brown People*

14. Similar in its impulse, like the old thumbs-down of the Roman amphitheatre, is the aggressive booing of the opposing pitcher when he shows signs of weakening.

> *The Freeman Book*

15. Canada is not, as has been often stressed, an entirely precise mosaic of nations; in fact, it is, like the U.S.A., gradually becoming a melting pot of nationalities, the difference between the two countries being that whereas the United States and the individual provinces of Canada allow their various national groups to exist and develop their national cultures, only Canada has recently begun meagerly to assist them materially in their specific endeavours.

> J. R. C. Perkin, *The Undoing of Babel*

16. Now let's consider the universe. The universe resembles the skin of a balloon and the surface of the earth, except that the universe is three-dimensional, while the skin and the surface are essentially two-dimensional objects curved through a third dimension. The universe is a three-dimensional object curved through a fourth dimension.

> Isaac Asimov, *The Roving Mind*

17. Glaser and Pellegrino, also working with inductive reasoning tasks, are concerned with both the strategic and factual knowledge necessary to solve a variety of analogy problems. Their approach differs somewhat from that of Sternberg *et al.* in that they use more difficult problems, thereby increasing the likelihood of errors. As a result, they must be concerned not only with the sequencing of component executions and the efficiency with which they can be carried out, but also with the factors that may affect the subjects' likelihood or ability to carry out the components

correctly. Glaser and Pellegrino share with Sternberg *et al.* the approach of carefully delineating various potential methods of dealing with the items. Whereas Sternberg *et al.* begin with a set of analytic models, their approach is somewhat more data-driven. Glaser and Pellegrino are guided by the various solutions attempted by their subjects. These observations are then used to construct a theoretical framework within which to view individual differences. Armed with such a theoretical framework, it is possible to design instruction based on areas of particular difficulty for problem learners. Thus, the framework not only provides a description of individual differences, it also suggests the potential form and focus of remediation.

> Douglas Detterman and Robert Sternberg, eds., *How and How Much Can Intelligence Be Increased*

18. Just as once Turgenev in his *Hunter's Sketches* made readers acquainted with his native Orel region, in the same way Belov has introduced them to the region roundabout Vologda where he was born and still lives.

> V. Belov, *Morning Rendezvous*

19. France was the leader in noncommercial avant-garde film. Directors like René Clare, Marcel L'Herbier, Jacques Feyder and Abel Gance all made films of individual importance.

> John Martin, *The Golden Age of French Cinema*

20. Hence Descartes framed his famous theory of vortices in a primary matter or aether, invisible but filling all space. As a straw floating on water is caught in an eddy and whirled to the center of motion, so a falling stone is drawn to the Earth and a satellite towards its planet, while the Earth and the planet, with their attendant and surround vortices are whirled in a greater vortex round the Sun.

> Sir William Dampler, *A History of Science*

2   *Descriptive and Definitional Analogies*

Often we use analogies in description. For instance, someone might say that Kelly "ran like a roach across a griddle" to describe how quickly she ran. Analogies are valuable in description for two reasons. First, a well-chosen analogy can condense several literal descriptions into a single short phrase. For example, the description

> Jerry is short, squat, hirsute, with arms longer than are normal for a person his size, and he has very close-set eyes.

can be expressed economically (though pejoratively) by the analogy

> Jerry looks like a baboon.

A second reason that analogies are useful in description is that they can increase the aesthetic quality of the description. An analogy can be moving, amusing, disturbing, or vivid. Compare the following pairs of descriptions. The first of each pair is literal, the second analogical.

1a. John is pleased with his current situation.
1b. John's as happy as a clam!
2a. Helen, you look good.
2b. Helen, thy beauty is to me like those Nicaean barks of yore, that gently o'er a perfumed sea, the weary, way-worn wanderer bore, to his own native shore.

In (1a), John is described literally as happy; in (1b), the description is made by a humorous analogy. In (2a), Helen is described literally; in (2b), the description is made by Edgar Allan Poe's evocative and beautiful analogy.

As we saw in Chapter 6, analogies are expressed explicitly by means of similes (using the terms *like* or *as*), and implicitly by means of metaphors. For example, both the simile

Gary ran off like a rat.

and the metaphor

Gary, a rat, ran.

both express the analogy is like a rat.

A second use of analogy is in definition. We discussed analogical definitions in Section 6 of Chapter 7.

Exercise 13.2

For each of the following literal descriptions, find a shorter analogical description.

1. Maurice is vicious, aggressive, and enjoys hurting people.
2. Sue is quiet, focused on her work, and has intense concentration.
3. That summer was exceptionally hot, with no breeze.
4. The people were running around in all directions, murmuring angrily and moving quickly.
5. The fire was intense, burning many houses quickly, with the wind gusting, and sounding a loud roar.

3 *Analogical Arguments*

Often an analogy is employed as a premise in an argument. For example,

Pudding is very much like cheese, but cheese is nutritious, so pudding is probably nutritious.

When an analogical premise is used in an argument, we speak of the argument as an **argument by analogy.** An argument by analogy has the form

1. A is like $B_1, B_2, B_3, \ldots$.
2. $B_1, B_2, B_3, \ldots$ all have property P.
∴ A has P.

Again, A is the subject, $B_1, B_2, \ldots, B_3$ the analogs. We call P the **projected property.**

Arguments by analogy are inductively strong or weak, depending on whether criteria are met.

First, all things being equal, the more numerous the B cases (the analogs), the higher the degree of strength. For example, the argument

  1. The Toyota I own now is like the ten Toyotas I owned previously.
  2. Those others lasted 100,000 miles.
  ∴ This one will last 100,000 miles.

is stronger than

  1. The Toyota I own now is like the two Toyotas I owned previously.
  2. Those others lasted 100,000 miles.
  ∴ This one will last 100,000 miles.

We cannot really say that since the first argument invokes five times the number of Toyotas as does the second, it is therefore five times as good. We can say only that, all other things being equal, the first presents stronger evidence.

Second, all things being equal, the more numerous the relevant similarities that hold between the analogs B and the subject A, the stronger the inference. By "relevant" here we mean relevant to the projected property. Again, by way of example, the argument

  1. This Toyota is like the other one I owned in that both have the same engine size and power equipment, and it was or will be driven in the same environment.
  2. The other I owned lasted 100,000 miles.
  ∴ So this Toyota will last 100,000 miles.

is stronger than

  1. This Toyota is like the one I owned in that both have the same size engine.
  2. The other Toyota lasted 100,000 miles.
  ∴ This Toyota will last 100,000 miles.

The key word here is *relevant:* a property is **relevant** to *P* if we have reason to think that its presence or absence has something to do with the presence or absence of *P*. For instance, the presence or absence of red body paint has nothing to do with engine life.

Third, all things being equal, the more numerous the relevant disanalogies, the weaker the argument. For example, the argument

  1. The Toyota I own now is like the other Toyota I owned in engine size and power equipment, but I am using this one to haul a trailer every day.
  2. The last Toyota I owned lasted 100,000 miles.
  ∴ This one will last 100,000 miles.

is weaker than

  1. The Toyota I now own is like the other Toyota I owned in engine size and power equipment.
  2. The last Toyota I owned lasted 100,000 miles.
  ∴ This one will last 100,000 miles.

You might wonder what the difference is between the last two rules—if two things do not share a relevant similarity, does that not mean they have a relevant dissimilarity? The answer is that an inductive argument can be made stronger or weaker by the addition of extra premises. And explicitly stating a disanalogy is different from omitting a statement of analogy.

Fourth, the more the property attributed to the subject precisely matches the one attributed to the analogs, the less likely the inference. For example, suppose Lori and Anne are identical twins raised in similar conditions and that Lori has an IQ of 125. The inference that Anne has an IQ of *precisely* 125 is going to be weaker than the inference that she has an IQ of more than 120, which in turn is going to be weaker than the inference that she has an IQ of more than 110. Inductive evidence typically supports conclusions that merely specify ranges much more strongly than conclusions that specify exact numbers.

Fifth, the less numerous the other similarities between the analogs, the stronger the inference. For our analogical inference to be strong, we need to be sure that the property Q that the analogs all share is indeed the one we want to project (that is, attribute to the subject). For example, suppose we know that Suzie, Eddie, Manny, and Yoshi all went to Wilson High School, all had B+ grade averages, and all did well at Orange Coast College. Suppose we know also that Terry went to Wilson, had a B+ average, and is now attending Orange Coast. It would be reasonable to infer that Terry also will do well at Coast. But the inference would be weaker if we knew that Suzie, Eddie, Manny, and Yoshi all were physics majors (at Wilson), whereas Terry was a philosophy major, because for all we know physics majors at that school are more academically adept than philosophy majors. Maybe they are; maybe they aren't—in other words, how do we know that the major taken is not relevant in this case? A stronger inference would be if we took several Wilson students *who had different majors* at Wilson (who had B+ averages at Wilson and who have done well at Coast) and on that basis inferred that Terry would do well.

We have examined the five criteria for assessing the strength of an analogical argument. When such an argument is too weak even to be plausible, we call it a *fallacy of false analogy*. Typically, we say an analogy is a **false analogy** when it overlooks a key relevant significant difference between the subject and the analog(s). That is, in a false analogy, the project property is more closely connected with the differences between the subject and the analogs than with their similarities. Here are a few examples of the fallacy of false analogy:

> Recently, the media covered the near-collision of a small private plane with a large commercial airliner. Despite the fact that there is no evidence that the pilot of the private plane was at fault in any way, everybody seems to be suggesting that we ought to ban or restrict small plane operations at major airports. This suggestion ignores the fact that airports are public property, paid for by all taxpayers, just like we pay for highways. After all, no doubt there are bus and truck drivers who would like to see private cars banned or restricted on major highways. But just as we can all use the freeways, we should all be able to use the airports.

A key difference exists between private autos and private planes that bears on the issue at hand. Air traffic must be centrally controlled and channeled, whereas motor vehicle traffic need not be.

Editor:

I believe that the fraternity system should be abolished on all college campuses. The reason for my belief is simple. The behavior of many fraternity members is spiritually reminiscent of Nazis and Communists. This may sound extreme, but I think it is completely rational in view of the facts.

For example, what about those pledges who tore down all the palm trees last semester? And the continued use of hazing, a practice that has killed a number of students over the years?

This analogy is ridiculous, because of the major differences between the intentions and actions of fraternity students and totalitarians. If fraternities ever start setting up death camps, then the analogy might work.

Bumper sticker: "Guns don't cause crime any more than flies cause garbage."

However, flies do not play a role in the creation of the garbage, while guns do play a role in creating crime.

Determining whether an analogy is a false one or not often requires knowledge of the subject of discussion. Consider this argument:

Why do we support the right to strike of government workers in communist countries, but not in the United States itself? Aren't we being inconsistent?

What this argument overlooks is that in a communist country, *all* workers are government workers, whereas in our country, only a few categories of workers are government employees, such as teachers, police, and the like. Without inconsistency you might support the right to strike of government workers in a communist country and not in ours, as long as the categories of workers meant were different. However, this point would be overlooked by someone who did not know much about the nature of a communist economy.

Exercise 13.3A

Each of the following passages contains an analogical argument. For each, put the argument into the following form:

1. A is like $B_1, \ldots, B_n$.
2. $B_1, \ldots, B_n$ have P.
∴   [Probably] A has P.

1. Assault, murder, and other crimes against another person are both immoral and illegal in our society. Why, then should someone with a bad habit like smoking, be allowed to slowly murder those around him?
2. I don't understand why people are so upset that corporate chief executive officers are getting paid millions in salaries and bonuses. Don't we pay movie stars and rock stars millions? And what about sports stars?
3. Mencius said to King Hsuan of Ch'i, "Supposing one of your ministers had gone on a journey to Ch'u, leaving his wife and children with a friend, and upon returning found his family starving, what do you think he should do?" The King said, "He should cut off all relations with that friend." Mencius said, "Suppose now that the

Leader of the Knights had no control over the knights, then what would you do?" The King said, "I should dismiss him." Mencius said, "Suppose now the kingdom to be ill-governed, what then should be done?" The King turned to his courtiers and spoke of other things.

> *Mencius,* translated by W. A. C. H. Dobson

4. As in prospecting for gold, a scientist may dig with skill, courage, energy, and intelligence just a few feet away from a rich vein, but always unsuccessfully. Consequently in scientific research the rewards for industry, perseverance, imagination, and intelligence are highly uncertain.

> Lawrence S. Kubie, "Some Unsolved Problems of the Scientific Career," *American Scientist* (1954)

5. It is the maxim of every prudent master of a family, never to attempt to make at home what it will cost him more to make than buy. The tailor does not attempt to make his own shoes, but buys them from the shoemaker. The shoemaker does not attempt to make his own clothes, but employs a tailor. The farmer attempts to make neither the one nor the other, but employs those different artificers. All of them find it for their interest to employ their whole industry in a way in which they have some advantage over their neighbors, and to purchase with a part of its product, or what is the same thing, with the price of a part of it, whatever else they have occasion for.

   What is prudence in the conduct of every private family can scarce be folly in that of a great kingdom. If a foreign country can supply us with a commodity cheaper than we ourselves can make it, better buy it of them with some part of the produce of our own industry employed in a way in which we have some advantage.

> Adam Smith, *The Wealth of Nations*

6. It is true that science has become so specialized, even a good education in basic science does not prepare one to be expert in all science. But the same is true of nonscientific pursuits. That historians, for example, have become experts in particular periods or areas (the history of the military, perhaps, or of science or economics) has not dissuaded us from teaching history.

> Bruce J. Sobol, *Current Issues and Enduring Questions*

7. If man can, with almost complete assurance, predict phenomena when he knows their laws, and if, even when he does not, he can still, with great expectation of success, forecast the future on the basis of his experience of the past, why, then, should it be regarded as a fantastic undertaking to sketch, with some pretense to truth, the future destiny of man on the basis of his history? The sole foundation for belief in the natural sciences is this idea, that the general laws directing the phenomena of the universe, known or unknown, are necessary and constant. Why should this principle be any less true for the development of the intellectual and moral faculties of man than for other operations of nature? Since beliefs founded on past experience of like conditions provide the only rule of conduct for the wisest of men, why should the philosopher be forbidden to base his conjectures on these same foundations, so long as he does not attribute to them a certainty superior to that warranted by the number, the constancy, and the accuracy of his observations?

> A. N. de Condorcet, *The Progress of the Human Mind*

8. Look around the world: Contemplate the whole and every part of it: You will find it to be nothing but one great machine, subdivided into an infinite number of lesser ma-

chines, which again admit of subdivisions, to a degree beyond what human senses and faculties can trace and explain. All these various machines, and even their most minute parts, are adjusted to each other with an accuracy, which ravishes into admiration all men, who have ever contemplated them. The curious adapting of means to ends, throughout all nature, resembles exactly, though it much exceeds, the productions of human contrivance; of human design, thought, wisdom, and intelligence. Since therefore the effects resemble each other, we are let to infer, by all the rules of analogy, that the causes also resemble; and that the Author of nature is somewhat similar to the mind of man; though possessed of much larger faculties, proportioned to the grandeur of the work, which he has executed.

David Hume, Dialogues Concerning Natural Religion

9. Unfortunately, the diary [of H. L. Mencken] reveals a man who was shockingly anti-Semitic and racist, to the point where his stature as a giant of American letters may be in danger. . . . I would draw a comparison with Richard Wagner, a virulent anti-Semite. One can still listen to Wagner's operas and appreciate their artistic beauty. The work is separated from the man. Or is it?

Gwinn Owens, "Mencken—Getting a Bum Rap?" New York Times, December 13, 1989

Exercise 13.3B

Each of the following passages contains a false analogy. For each, explain why the analogy is false.

1. A doctor in South Dakota had a remedy for rape, which he symbolically attached to a note scrawled on paper from a prescription pad. "All farmers know how to prevent violence in the barnyard," he wrote. "Their method, used for thousands of years all over the world, is easy, cheap and 100% effective. They transform potentially vicious bulls into socially useful oxen. . . . This method would put the fear that is like no other fear into potentially lawless adolescents."

2. This ballot proposition would result in a 30 percent reduction in the county budget. Could your household budget stand a cut like that?

3. Patients with such diseases as heart disease and diabetes can refuse treatment if they wish. A heart patient has the right to refuse digitalis, and a diabetic can refuse insulin. Why, then, shouldn't a psychiatric patient also have the right to refuse medications?

4. Ban is more effective than Right Guard, Secret, Arrid, and Sure. In fact, Ban Roll-On is more effective than all leading aerosols.

5. It is difficult to understand why college athletes and fans cannot support their own activities. Professional sports teams pay their players millions of dollars a year and manage to get by without a tax on the citizens of their home towns. Certainly collegiate teams, which pay their players only through scholarships, should be able to survive without squeezing money out of already hard-pressed students.

6. I can understand why unemployment is a major problem facing us today. And I can understand why it has become a political football. But I can't understand the idiocy of blaming the president for the unemployment. It is the equivalent of blaming the pope for the increasing crime rate.

7. Charles Smith, who is so concerned about guns killing people ("Letters," October 5), failed to mention a worse killer. Thousands of adults and children are killed or injured for life by autos. Let's start a "ban-the-car" movement. The right to life is more important than the right to drive a car. We can all go back to riding horses.

8. A married woman in her late twenties says she has been going topless for the last four years when the weather is pleasant, when she is working in her yard, driving her car, or riding a motorcycle with her husband. Sunday, State Highway Patrolman T. L. Wolfe stopped her and her husband while she was riding topless on the back of their motorcycle. Wolfe said he later let her go because there is no law prohibiting her from being topless in public. "I guess it's not legally indecent to do that," he said, "but I still believe it's improper. It could cause accidents." The woman's husband supports her action. "You can't have one set of moral values, one for men and another for women," he said. In support of her own actions, the woman said, "If a man can go without a shirt, then so can I. There's not much difference between the chest of a man and the chest of a woman. The only difference I can see is there's a little more fat on a woman's, and a little more hair on a man's."

9. As the mother of a freshman at Henning High School, my stomach turns every morning when I take him to school and see the demonstration by the "teachers." Whatever happened to the dedicated teacher who was only interested in educating and forming the minds of young people? Does such a creature exist anymore or are they all in the teaching profession for money?

    Granted, we all like and need raises from time to time, but can't this be worked out while on the job? The teachers say they have a right to strike. Do police and firefighters have the right to strike and deny the public their right to protection? Do soldiers have the right to strike? Certainly not!

10. Many of my neighbors and I are disgusted with the current practice of towing cars off of private property. For example, on September 3, our houseguests parked in front of our garage. Within minutes, a meter maid passing by stopped, issued a ticket and then had the car towed. This deplorable act, in a society that espouses justice for all, makes me ask, justice for whom? We can do with less of these Gestapo tactics.

Exercise 13.3C

Each of the analogies here is followed by several alternative pieces of information. For each, state whether it strengthens or weakens the core argument. Justify your answer by citing one of the criteria listed for assessing analogies given earlier.

1. Sue has eaten at Jim Jones's Steakhouse five times in the past and the food was great. So she figures the food will be great there tonight.
    a. Jim Jones's Steakhouse has come under new management since she ate there last.
    b. Sue ate different dishes on her previous visits.
    c. Sue ate the same dish on her previous visits, but tonight she is going to try something different.
2. In the past four presidential elections, our state has voted for the Republican candidate. So I figure that it will do so in the upcoming election.

    a. This state had Republican governors before; now the governor is a Democrat.

    b. The unemployment rate and other economic indicators are very nearly the same now as in those previous elections.

    c. In recent years the ethnic makeup of the state has changed dramatically.

3. Leslie has made a lot of money at real estate over the last twenty years. So she figures that she will make money from real estate investments this year.

    a. Leslie has made seventy investments in the past twenty years in real estate and made money from every one.

    b. The investments she made in the past were in rental properties; she is now considering undeveloped land.

    c. Leslie has averaged 20 percent returns on her past investments. She figures she will make 20 percent this year.

4. The Gilman family has eaten at Burger Biggies, a chain of burger joints, many times over the last two years and liked the food. They have moved to a new city and are going to try the Burger Biggie there, expecting to like the food.

    a. Burger Biggie restaurants are all independently owned and managed.

    b. The Gilman family has eaten at Burger Biggies across the country.

    c. The Gilmans have always eaten burgers, but tonight they are going to try the new fish sandwich.

5. Tim is trying to decide what to major in. He knows five people who majored in computer science and went on to become millionaires. So he figures that he should major in it.

    a. Tim figures that if they all became millionaires, he will, too.

    b. Tim is going to attend Podunk University, whereas the five other people all went to Wizard Institute of Technology.

    c. The five people Tim knows all specialized in retro packet switching, and that is what Tim intends to specialize in.

+4   *The Heuristic Use of Analogies*

We have seen how analogies can be used to describe, to define, and to argue, but analogies can be used also to aid the process of research and discovery. Thus, analogies can be used as **heuristic** aids. To see how, let us rethink the nature of analogical statements.

We can view any analogical statement

    A is like *B*

as saying implicitly three things:

1. *A* and *B* share properties $P_1, P_2, P_3, \ldots$.
2. *A* and *B* do not share (differ in) properties $N_1, N_2, N_3, \ldots$.
3. *A* and *B* may or may not share properties $O_1, O_2, O_3, \ldots$.

We will call the shared properties $P_1, P_2, \ldots$ the **positive analogy;** the unshared properties $N_1, N_2, \ldots$, the **negative analogy;** and the open properties (that is, the properties that *A* and *B* may or may not share) $O_1, O_2, \ldots$, the **neutral analogy.** (This terminology is from Hesse 1963). As an example, consider the analogy "Jason ran like a bug across a griddle." The analogy involves

1. The positive analogy: Jason and the bug share the properties of having legs, and moving quickly by means of those legs.
2. The negative analogy: Jason and the bug differ in size, shape, and intelligence.
3. The neutral analogy: Jason and the bug may or may not both be in pain and desperate.

In research of any kind (scientific, legal, philosophical, or anything else), we can use an analogy to point out new areas for investigation. If, for example, we visualize computer software as a kind of product, say, by viewing the programs produced by a software company as being like the cars produced by an automobile company, then many areas are open to investigation. Should the software company be as legally liable for the damage caused to the consumer by their defective software, as is the automobile manufacturer for the damage caused by its defective cars? That is an important area of legal research.

Put in terms we have just discussed, when we set up an analogy on the basis of the positive analogy, we have at our disposal a whole range of possible further positive analogy—namely, the neutral analogy. A good heuristic strategy is thus to set up an analogy with a strong positive analogy and weak negative analogy, and then systematically explore the neutral analogy to discover any new properties that the subject and analog might have in common.

Exercise 13.4

For each of the following analogies, indicate the most obvious positive analogy, negative analogy, and neutral analogy.

1. Cats are like tigers.
2. People are like animals.
3. Her kisses were like wine.
4. Hatred is like a corrosive poison.
5. Football is like war.
6. Life is like poker.
7. Writing is like playing tennis.
8. Business is like war.
9. Dancing is like singing.
10. College is like prison.

+5   Models in Science

We have discussed the use of analogies to describe, define, argue, and discover. As a special case, we will discuss the use of analogies in science.

Analogies are usually termed "models" in science. You run across phrases such as the "liquid-drop model of the atomic nucleus," "the planetary model of the atom," "the equilibrium model of the economic system" and so on in scientific literature. What is the purpose of models in science? Models are used by scientists for all four basic functions discussed earlier.

An excellent discussion of the use of models is found in Keith Holyoak and Paul Thagard's (1996: Chapter 8) book *Mental Leaps: Analogy in Creative Thought.* They mention a number of highly successful analogies in science (186–88):

> 1. **Sound/water waves** . . . Water waves were first used to suggest the nature of sound by the Greek Stoic Chrysippus around the second century B.C., but our knowledge of his views is fragmentary. In the first century A.D., the Roman architect Vitruvius, in the course of explaining the acoustic properties of Greek amphitheaters, explicitly compared the sound of voices to water waves that can flow out and bounce back when obstructed, just as sound spreads and echoes. Here we have the ancient origins off the modern wave theory of sound.
>
> 2. **Earth/small magnet** In his landmark work *De Magnete,* published in 1600, William Gilbert described important experimental investigations of the nature of magnets, and he is proposed for the first time that the planet earth is a giant magnet. The basis for his hypothesis was a systematic comparison between the properties of the earth, such as how it affects compasses, and the properties of the small spherical magnets on which he had performed many experiments. The earth is like these objects in many respects, so according to Gilbert, we should infer that the earth acts like a magnet, engendering the magnetism of the objects that were part of it. Indeed, since the common properties of the earth and small magnets define what it means to be a magnet, the earth not only acts like a magnet, it is a magnet.
>
> 3. **Earth/moon** Galileo's *Dialogue Concerning the Two Chief World Systems,* published in 1630, contained two analogies that made important contributions to his contention that the earth moves. First, Galileo compared the earth to the moon, both of which are spherical, dark opaque, dense and solid, with similar expanses of light and dark and of land and sea. Since the moon was known to move in an orbit, he argued it was reasonable to suppose that the earth does too.
>
> 4. **Earth/ship** Galileo used a different analogy to rebut an argument that the earth does not move. Opponents of his theory argued that if a rock is dropped form a tower, it lands at the base of the tower, suggesting that the tower, and hence the earth, is not in motion. Galileo countered this argument with a ship.
>
> 5. **Light/sound** In his 1678 *Treatise on Light,* Christiaan Huygens used an analogy between light and sound in support of his wave theory of light. That theory was eclipsed for more than a century by Newton's particle theory but was revived in the early nineteenth century by Thomas Young and Augustin Fresnel. These scientists exploited the analogy between light and sound to develop and defend a wave theory of light.
>
> 6. **Planet/projectile** Toward the end of his celebrated *Principia* (1687), Isaac Newton used an analogy to help bring planetary motion within the scope of his theory of gravitation. He compared a planet to a stone thrown upward from the earth with greater and greater force. He presented a diagram to show with a great enough force the path of the stone would become the path of an object in orbit around the earth. Newton used this analogy to support his hypothesis that the orbits of the planets are governed by gravitational force.

7. **Lightning/electricity** We have already Benjamin Franklin's famous analogy leading to the hypothesis that lightning was a form of electricity. Like the earth/small magnet example, this comparison became more than an analogy. Following Franklin's work, the definition of electricity has expanded to include the natural phenomenon of lightning.

8. **Respiration/combustion** During the 1770's when Antoine Lavoisier was developing his oxygen theory of the role in animal respiration. Much of his thinking was guided by an analogy between respiration and combustion, both of which involve a change of oxygen into carbon dioxide and a provision of heat.

9. **Heat/water** In 1824, Nicholas Leonard Sadi Carnot provided a thorough discussion of the motive power of heat, drawing heavily on an analogy between heat and waterfalls. He argued that heat acts on substances, just as water acts on waterfalls, with the power depending in the former case on the amount of caloric (heat substance) and in the latter on the height of the waterfall. The idea of heat as a fluid was already well established by this time, but Carnot put it to much more systematic use.

10. **Animal and plant competition/human population growth** Charles Darwin reported that he arrived at the basic idea of natural selection in 1838 by fortuitous reading of Malthus's tract on human population growth. Darwin had been searching for a mechanism that could produce the evolution of species, and he realized from Malthus that rapid population growth in the face of limited food and land could lead to a struggle for existence. Darwin noticed the analogy between potential human strife (produced by population growth's outstripping resources) and competition among animals and plants for survival.

11. **Natural selection/artificial selection** A different analogy played a much greater role in the development and evaluation of Darwin's theory of evolution by natural selection. He often compared natural selection to the artificial selection performed by breeders, who exploited the inherent variability in animals and plants to choose desired features. Natural selection leads to different species, Darwin argued, just as artificial selection leads to different breeds. Darwin used this analogy in the *Origin of Species* (1859) and elsewhere, both in developing explanations and in arguing for the acceptability of his overall theory.

12. **Electromagnetic forces/continuum mechanics** James Clerk Maxwell was explicit and enthusiastic about the use of mechanical and mathematical analogies. The most important application in his own thinking was the construction in the 1860's of a diagrammed mechanical model for electrical and mechanical forces, consisting of a fluid medium with vortices and stresses. He was able to abstract from this mechanical analog a general mathematical description that could be applied directly to electromagnetism.

13. **Benzene/snake** . . . Friedrich Kekulé proposed in 1865 a new theory of the molecular theory of benzene. According to Kekulé, he was led to the hypothesis that the carbon atoms are arranged in a ring by a reverie in which he saw a snake biting its own tail. This example, like those of Maxwell, Newton, and Morgan, illustrates how visual representations can contribute to creative thinking using analogy.

14. **Chromosome/beaded string** In 1915, Thomas Morgan and his colleagues explained complex phenomena of inheritance by comparing chromosomes to a

string containing beads corresponding to the various factors leading to inheritance. Within a few years, those factors had come to be called "genes." The beaded-string analogy was most useful for describing how novel linkages could arise from breaking and recombining the string.

15. **Bacterial ion/slot machine** In 1943, Salvador Luria was trying to find experimental support for his view that phage-resistant cultures of bacteria arise because of gene mutations, not because of action of the phage on the bacteria. (A phage is a viral organism that destroys bacteria.) None of his experiments worked, but at a faculty dance at Indiana University he happened to watch a colleague putting dimes into a slot machine. He realized that slot machines pay out money in a very uneven distribution, with most trials yielding nothing, some yielding small amounts, and rare trials providing jackpots. He then reasoned that if bacteria become resistant because of gene mutations, then the numbers of resistant bacteria should vary like the expected returns from different kinds of slot machines. This reasoning led to an experiment and theoretical model, for which he was awarded a Nobel prize.

16. **Mind/computer** Numerous analogies have been used over the centuries in attempts to understand the nature of mind and thinking. By far the most fertile has been the use since the 1950's by Alan Turing and many others, of comparisons between thinking and computation. Computational ideas have suggested hypotheses about the nature of mind that have led to much psychological and computational experimentation. . . . [T]his analogy is very dynamic and complex; ideas about computation have influenced conceptions of the mind, which have in turn had an impact on the evolution of new types of computers.

Consider the Bohr ("planetary" or "solar") model of the hydrogen atom. In this model, the hydrogen atom structure is likened to that of the solar system, with the proton at the center, and the electron orbiting it. That model serves to describe the atom. The model stipulates that the electron can travel only in particular orbits, although the electron can jump from one orbit to another. That image serves to define the concept of a "transition" from one state of the atom to another. Analogy serves in an argument to explain why light emitted or absorbed by hydrogen is always at a fixed wavelength (the electron can only move from one set orbit to another, with a particular unit of energy being given off or absorbed). Finally, the model serves to direct research (for example, can we extend it to cover the helium atom, an atom more complex than the hydrogen atom?).

Analogies are valuable, not just in ordinary contexts of reasoning, but in science as well.

+6   *Analogies in Legal Reasoning*

Analogical reasoning is even more common in legal work than in scientific research. Indeed, legal reasoning is almost entirely reasoning by analogy. Cases are decided not by the deductive application of absolutely precise laws but instead by analogies between the case at hand and past adjudicated cases (or **precedent**). In this way, laws grow and often change in meaning as new cases are decided.

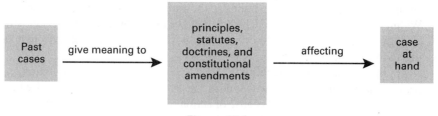

Figure 13.1

This brings out certain differences between the legal and scientific enterprises. To begin with, the concepts in a legal system are intended to be somewhat vague, to permit their application in ever-changing social circumstances. Vagueness is inherent in legal concepts. (We say of legal concepts that they are **porous** or **open textured.**) But scientific concepts are intended to be absolutely precise, or at least as precise as possible. We tolerate more vagueness in legal than scientific enterprises because of the difference in their purposes.

Moreover, laws in a legal system admit of all kinds of exceptions. Or, as we shall put the matter, laws of society are highly **defeasible.** Again, this is in marked contrast to science: In science, we seek exception-free, absolutely valid laws—although whether we find them is up to nature.

We need to flesh out these remarks. The sort of analogical reasoning employed in law is best illustrated in case law. Case law is characterized by the rule or doctrine of precedent.

Precedent works in a three-stage process. First, similarity is discerned between the case at hand and some past case or cases; second, a statement that is descriptive of the important features of those past cases is made into a rule of law; third, that rule is used to adjudicate the case at hand. In case law, the judge is the sole arbiter of which similarities will rule in this case—he or she is not constrained by statute (laws enacted by the legislature) or even the decisions of prior judges as to which factors are important. Quite often, in reaching the decision he or she will emphasize facts thought unimportant in past cases or ignore what was held to be important or even crucial. This is the **doctrine of dictum:** The judge's statement (about which similarities of which precedent cases rule in the case at hand) makes law.

Fairness is guaranteed by the competition of ideas about what is relevant or what similarities ought to govern the judgment regarding the case at hand. The lawyers represent more than their clients—they represent the necessary ingredients for fair decision making. A great part of the research done by a lawyer in the course of his work consists of hunting out cases with similarities to the case at hand that are favorable to his clients and finding reasons that the similarities discovered by the opposing lawyer shouldn't apply in this case. Figure 13.1 summarizes the points we have discussed.

But keep in mind that any current decision is grist for later decisions as well. Thus, the law evolves from cases to principles to cases to revised principles. Figure 13.2 brings this point out.

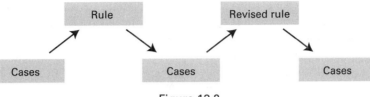

Figure 13.2

Evolution of Legal Concepts

Let's consider an example of the evolution of a set of legal concepts (Levy 1949: 9–27). The general issue involved is the liability of the seller of an article for injury that the article causes to someone who did not buy that article from that seller. The evolution begins in 1816, with the case *Dixon v. Bell.* Bell sent his servant girl to fetch his loaded gun, and while she was carrying the gun it went off, injuring Dixon's son. Dixon sued Bell. The judge ruled in favor of Dixon with the simple understanding that a loaded gun is inherently dangerous when handled carelessly.

In 1837, in *Langridge v. Levy,* Langridge sued Levy because a gun Levy sold Langridge's father blew up in Langridge's hand. The judge ruled in Langridge's favor, because the judge felt that Levy knew the gun to be defective and that even though he was selling the gun to the father, the son would be using it too.

So the concept of "object the damage for which the seller is liable" originally included only objects that are directly dangerous to the buyer or second party through negligence of the seller or first party. But with the 1837 ruling, the concept now included objects that are known by the seller to be defective and known to be used by a third party. In *Langridge v. Levy,* the judge explicitly warned against enlarging this concept to hold *any* seller liable for the damage that his or her goods—even if inherently dangerous—cause later owners who happen to come upon those goods.

This concept again figured into a case in 1842. In *Winterbottom v. Wright,* a coachman (Winterbottom) sued Wright, the manufacturer of coaches, because he (the coachman) was injured by a defective coach manufactured by Wright. But the court ruled that since Wright had sold the coach in question under contract to the Postmaster General, and since Wright had never even heard of Winterbottom, and since Wright did not know that the coach was defective, Winterbottom could not recover damages. Note the acceptance of some analogies and the rejection of others: The court was impressed by the contention (by Winterbottom's attorney) that in this case the seller had to know that *someone* would be driving the coach, whereas in *Langridge v. Levy* the seller couldn't know about the existence of the buyer's son (the attorney was urging the rejection of some of the "facts" of the earlier case).

The next stage in the evolution of the concept came under discussion in 1851, in *Longmeid v. Holliday.* Longmeid had purchased a lamp from Holliday (called by Holliday "Holliday's Patent Lamp") for his household use. When Longmeid's wife tried to light the lamp, it exploded and burned her. Longmeid sued, but the court ruled against him. The judge determined that it had not been shown that Holliday knew the lamp was defective when he warranted it to be sound and that the lamp was not inherently dangerous. Thus, the judge made the concept more precise by including things dangerous in themselves (such as loaded guns), as was held in the first case mentioned, but excluding things (such as coaches and, by dictum in this case, lamps) that had latent defects. In so ruling, the judge choose to ignore an analogy between the man buying a gun for the use of himself and his sons, and the man buying a lamp for the use of himself and his wife.

Now came a period of applying the concept involved in the *Longmeid* case. In 1852, in *Thomas v. Winchester,* a customer in a drugstore was sold a bottle labeled as extract of dandelion but was in reality belladonna. This poisoned Mrs. Thomas, and she quite naturally sued. The bottle was purchased at the store of Dr. Ford, but the poison had been bottled and erroneously labeled at Winchester's shop, so she sued Winchester.

The court held in Mrs. Thomas's favor. The court viewed the mislabeled poison as being akin to a loaded gun (but not a latently defective wagon). In 1869, the court held a chemist liable for negligently preparing shampoo, but in 1870 it did not hold liable the manufacturer of a defective flywheel.

And so it went. The categories of "imminently dangerous" versus "merely latently dangerous" (read: "not dangerous enough to be liable for third-party injuries") were fleshed out by a number of other rulings. By 1915 these rulings were viewed as a law, stated by a federal court as follows:

> One who manufactures article inherently dangerous, e.g. poisons, dynamite, gunpowder, torpedoes, bottles of water under gas pressure, is liable to tort to third parties which they injure, unless he has exercised reasonable care with reference to the articles manufactured. . . . [O]n the other hand, one who manufactures articles dangerous only if defectively made, or installed, e.g., tables, chairs, pictures, or mirrors hung on the walls, carriages, automobiles, and so on is not liable to third parties caused by them, except in cases of willful injury or fraud.

Using this principle, the court denied recovery to someone suing the manufacturer of a defective wheel on the car he had just purchased from a dealer.

But that isn't the end to the story. In a virtually identical case in 1916, *MacPherson v. Buick,* the New York Court of Appeals allowed the person injured in a car with a defective wheel to recover damages from manufacturer of the wheel. The judge explicitly recognized the principle (enunciated explicitly in 1915 but stretching back to *Thomas v. Winchester*), but he held that not all the precedents from the days of horse and buggy could still apply (he probably had in mind the coachman who was injured by the defective carriage). In fact, he considerably broadened the concept of "imminently dangerous" to include much of what was excluded before. It came to mean simply "probably dangerous." The net effect was to bring the law more into line with societal reality, for it became much easier to sue manufacturers for defective products. At a time of an explosion of assembly line manufacturing and mass consumption, this put the law on a new path of evolution.

InfoTrac College Edition

You can locate InfoTrac College Edition articles about this chapter by accessing the InfoTrac College Edition Web site (www.infotrac-college.com/wadsworth/). Using the InfoTrac College Edition subject guide, enter the search terms relevant to this chapter, and then read abstracts for relevant articles.

Chapter 14

Causal Inference

---

1   *The Relation of Cause and Effect*

Our knowledge of cause and effect is crucial to our worldview, and we spend a good deal of effort acquiring that knowledge. As individuals, we are often trying to figure out what causes success, health, wealth, and so on. As a society, we support medical and scientific research of all kinds, aimed at finding the causes of diseases and all manner of other things. In this chapter we will explore reasoning about cause and effect. We will first get clear on the concept of cause and types of causal claims. We will then discuss causal arguments in very general terms. Finally, we will look at specific strategies for determining causes.

To say that something *A* **causes** something *B* (called the **result** or the **effect**) means that *A* produces or brings about *B*. Causes and effects are usually taken to be events, but we also talk about causes as being factors, conditions, or states. In what follows we will use all of these terms. A **causal claim** is a statement that something *A* causes something *B*. Causal claims can be particular, like "Fred's stroke caused his paralysis," or general, like "Bacteria cause infections."

We will take the view that causes precede their effects—that is, that causes occur before the effects, not after. This gives rise to an ambiguity in the word *cause* centering around the temporal closeness of the cause and the effect. Consider the following sequence of events. A car is parked on a hill. The parking brake cable snaps, the brake gives way, and the car rolls down the hill and hits a pig, which subsequently dies. What is the cause of the pig's death? In one sense, being hit by the car was the cause of the pig's death. But in another sense, the cable snapping was the cause. When a finite sequence of events is linked by cause-and-effect relations, we call the sequence a finite **causal chain.** The **remote** cause of an event in a causal chain is the first event in the chain; the **proximate** cause is the event immediately prior to it.

Obviously, causal chains can be infinitely long, in which case what event one takes to be "the" remote cause depends on one's point of view. In the prior case of the unfortunate pig, we can trace the causal chain back indefinitely far: pig crushed; prior to that, car hits pig; prior to that, car rolls downhill; prior to that, the brake fails; prior to that, the metal-fatigued cable snaps; prior to that, the cable is put under tension by the car owner; and so on, back to the building of the car and even earlier to the mining of the ore from which the car metal was extracted. What one picks as the remote cause depends on the context of discussion: A lawyer might focus on the parking brake failure, whereas a mechanical engineer might focus on the metal fatigue of the cable. In what follows, we will have in mind proximate rather than remote causes.

Again, we ought to distinguish causally sufficient conditions from causally necessary conditions. A **causally sufficient condition** for a given effect is a factor that by itself alone produces the effect. For example, sitting on top of a hydrogen bomb when it explodes is certainly a sufficient condition for a person's death. On the other hand, a **causally necessary condition** for a given effect is a factor in whose absence the effect cannot occur.* For example, being exposed to the flu virus is (causally) necessary for getting the flu—you cannot get the flu unless you first somehow come into contact with the virus. But clearly, coming into contact with the flu virus is not sufficient to give you the disease, because you might have built up immunity to it by vaccination or prior illness.

Sometimes a factor is both a necessary and a sufficient condition for the occurrence of a given effect. For example, brain death is a necessary condition for death, but it is also sufficient. Then again, sometimes we find a group of factors, each one of which is necessary for a given effect and which together are jointly sufficient for producing the effect. For example, giving a plant water, nutrients, and sunlight might be (depending on the plant) individually necessary and jointly sufficient for the plant to grow.

A third distinction we need to make is between simple and compound causes. A **compound cause** (also called a **multiple cause**) is one with component factors that work together to produce the effect. For example, if a driver hits a tree after missing a turn in a poorly lit area, on his way home in a hurry after a party at which he had several drinks, we would say that the cause was compound: His drinking and speeding, together with the poor lighting, worked to produce the accident. When a cause is compound, we call each of the components a **partial cause** (also called a **contributing factor**). In the example here, the speeding, drinking, and poor lighting were all partial causes or contributing factors in the accident. When a cause is not compound it is simple. A **simple cause** is one that does not contain components.

Don't confound partial causes with necessary conditions or compound causes with sufficient conditions. A given compound cause might be a necessary condition or both a necessary and a sufficient condition for its effect. Similarly, a simple cause might be a necessary condition, or a sufficient condition, or both a necessary and a sufficient condition for its effect. What is true (by definition) is that, by itself, a partial cause cannot be a sufficient condition for its effect. Of course, a partial cause *can* by itself be a necessary condition, though it need not be. In the prior example, the poor lighting was a partial cause of but not a necessary condition for the accident.

One last distinction ought to be made. Compare the following two full causal claims:

---

*You should not confound causally necessary/sufficient conditions with logically necessary/sufficient conditions. For example, being a married man is logically sufficient for being a man; that is, the statement "If you are a married man, you are a man" is necessarily true. But being a married man is not the cause of being a man. Similarly, being a woman is logically necessary for being a married woman. But it is not causally necessary.

1. Decapitation causes death.
2. Smoking causes cancer.

In the first statement, we are saying that in every case, decapitation is sufficient to produce death. In the second statement, we are not saying that each and every smoker will get cancer but that smoking tends to produce cancer in the population at large. Put another way, it says that smoking is a causal agent of cancer, that a population that smokes will have more cases of lung cancer than if did not smoke. We accordingly define two terms. A **deterministic** cause is one that produces its effect in all cases. A **statistical** cause (also called a *stochastic* cause) is one that tends to produce its effect in populations.

To sum up: Causal statements can be particular or general. We tend to focus on proximate rather than remote causes. Causes can be necessary or sufficient, simple or compound. And causes can be deterministic or statistical. The next exercises should give you some practice in distinguishing causal statements.

Exercise 14.1A

For each of the following statements, determine whether it is causal.

1. Fred is dead.
2. Angela killed her pet snake.
3. Yoshi's cowardice led to his disgrace.
4. People love enchiladas.
5. The depression in Germany in the late 1920s and early 1930s resulted in the rise of Adolf Hitler.
6. The explosion was due to gas being released near an open flame.
7. Monica hates her husband, except when he dances.
8. His heart problems were made worse by his excessive drinking.
9. If you are a murderer, you are by definition evil.
10. If you shoot a person, he or she will bleed.

Exercise 14.1B

For each of the following causal claims, determine whether it is particular or general.

1. Fred died because of poisoning.
2. Gun fights were a major source of deaths.
3. The flu is caused by the influenza virus.
4. Alana got the flu because she was taking care of her brother when he had the flu.
5. Envy causes conflict.

Exercise 14.1C

For each of the following causal statements determine whether it is proximate or remote.

1. The spark caused the explosion.
2. Suzanne's degree in computer science led to her lifetime of high income.
3. Sam died when the missile hit his plane.

4. Sam's death is ultimately due to the decision of the trucking company he worked for to cut back on the budget for inspection and maintenance of the truck fleet.
5. Suzanne crashed because one of her tires blew out when she was driving around the curve.

Exercise 14.1D

For each of the following claims, determine whether it is a statement of causally sufficient or necessary conditions.

1. Breathing is required to live.
2. You won't grow unless you eat protein regularly.
3. Drowning is a leading cause of death.
4. Your computer needs electricity to run.
5. Your car won't run without gas.

Exercise 14.1E

For each of the causal statements below, determine whether the cause is simple or compound.

1. Dropping a fifty-ton stone on a pig will kill it.
2. The match lit because it was struck in the presence of oxygen and was dry.
3. Alcoholism leads to liver disease.
4. Watering your lawn will make it grow, if you feed your lawn and there is ample sunlight.
5. Changing the oil in your car will prolong your engine's life, unless you overheat it.

Exercise 14.1F

For each of the causal statements here, determine whether it is deterministic or statistical.

1. Obesity is a major cause of heart attacks.
2. In this century, all major wars have arisen from ideological disputes.
3. Every one of my dogs died from old age.
4. Excessive drinking can lead to liver disease.
5. Speed kills.

Exercise 14.1G

The following article is from *The Economist* (October 3, 1998). It discusses a number of possible causes or partial causes for a drop in the American crime rate. Identify the causal factors mentioned. Can you think of any other possible cause for the drop in crime not mentioned?

CRIME IN AMERICA
Defeating the Bad Guys

America's plunging crime rates have attracted attention across the world, not least in Britain. What's the secret?

For the past six years, crime rates have been falling all over America. In some big cities, the fall has been extraordinary. Between 1993 and 1997 in New York City violent crime fell by 39% in central Harlem and by 45% in the once-terrifying South Bronx. The latest figures released by the FBI, for 1997, show that serious crime continued to fall in all the largest cities, though a little more slowly than in 1996.

Violent crime fell by 5% in all, and by slightly more in cities with over 250,000 people. Property crimes have fallen, too, by more than 20% since 1980, so that the rates for burglary and car-theft are lower in America than they are in supposedly more law-abiding Britain and Scandinavia. And people have noticed. In 1994, 31% of Americans told pollsters that crime was the most important challenge facing the country. In 1997, only 14% thought so. Some cities' police departments are so impressed by these figures it is said, that they have lately taken to exaggerating the plunge in crime.

Why this has happened is anyone's guess. Many factors—social, demographic, economic, political—affect crime rates, so it is difficult to put a finger on the vital clue. In March this year, the FBI admitted it had "no idea" why rates were falling so fast.

Politicians think they know, of course. Ask Rudy Giuliani, the mayor of New York, why his city has made such strides in beating crime that it accounts for fully a quarter of the national decline. He will cite his policy of "zero tolerance." This concept, which sprang from a famous article by two criminologists in *Atlantic Monthly* in March 1982, maintains that by refusing to tolerate tiny infractions of the law—dropping litter, spray-painting walls—the authorities can create a climate in which crimes of more dangerous kinds find it impossible to flourish. The *Atlantic* article was called "Broken Windows": if one window in a building was left broken, it argued, all the others would soon be gone. The answer: mend the window, fast.

The metro system in Washington, DC, was the first place where zero tolerance drew public attention, especially when one passenger was arrested for eating a banana. The policy seemed absurdly persnickety, yet it worked: in a better environment, people's behavior improved, and crime dropped. Mr. Giuliani, taking this theme to heart has gone further. He has cracked down on windscreen-cleaners, public urinators, graffiti, even jaywalkers. He has excoriated New York's famously sullen cabdrivers, and wants all New Yorkers to be nicer to each other. Tony Blair, visiting from London, has been hugely impressed. But is this cleanliness and civility the main reason why crime has fallen? It seems unlikely.

"Zero tolerance" can also be a distraction, making too many policemen spend too much time handing out littering tickets and parking fines while, some streets away, young men are being murdered for their trainers. It is localized too: though lower Manhattan or the Washington Metro can show the uncanny orderliness of a communist regime, other parts of the city—the areas of highest crime—may be left largely untreated.

William Bratton, New York's police commissioner until Mr. Giuliani fired him for stealing his thunder, has a different explanation for the fall in crime. It came about mostly, he believes, because he reorganized the police department, and restored its morale: giving his officers better guns, letting them make more decisions for themselves, and moving them away from desk jobs and out into the streets. Mr. Bratton made his precinct commanders personally responsible for reducing crimes on their own beats. There was no passing the buck, and those who failed were fired. Within in a year, he had replaced half of them.

On the Street

In most cities, reorganization of the police force has been accompanied by an increase in the number of policemen, which had dwindled in the 1970s and 1980s. The extra numbers have usually been accompanied by a collection of policies known as "community policing." This means encouraging officers to get out from behind their desks and on to the beat, where their visibility will reassure the public. In some cities it has also meant officers becoming more actively involved with residents, youth organizations, schools and other local groups. Community policing has two clear advantages.

A strong police force can deter crime, or get officers speedily to a crime scene; and the police themselves get to know their patch thoroughly enough to prevent crimes, not just pursue the criminals.

Community policing has become so popular that it was the pillar of the 1994 crime bill, in which President Clinton promised 100,000 more policemen on the streets (and eventually provided money for about 70,000). This played heavily to Mr. Clinton's advantage in the 1996 presidential election; and many mayors will bear witness that a heightened police presence has plainly produced lower crime rates.

In Los Angeles, the addition of more than 2,000 policemen since 1993 seems precisely to track the fall in the murder rate. In other parts of the country, the connection can be harder to make. Because money was spread widely and thinly, in many places the extra police were hardly enough to account for drops in crime. The proof will come when the money runs out; the crime bill provided money for these extra cops on the understanding that within three years, local governments would meet the cost themselves. Many of them may not.

In some cities, community policing is taken so seriously that it has turned into something not far from social work. The Boston Police Department is widely credited with the most successful campaign in the country against juvenile crime. This includes co-operation between officers and civilians to scrub off graffiti, run youth clubs, provide tutoring and counselling services and keep an eye open for truants. As a direct result (so the police believe), only two juveniles have been killed with a gun in Boston since July 1995, compared with ten in 1990 alone (juveniles are the most common victims of other juveniles).

As long ago as 1985, a study by Michigan State University into the future of community policing predicted that a force much like Boston's would become the national model: the officer on the beat would also become "the sponsor of the youth team, the community advocate, the block club organizer, the community problem solver. . . ." And occasionally make an arrest, too.

Community policing of this intensity seems hard to fault. But some civil-rights campaigners complain that it is too intrusive; in New Orleans, after more intensive policing methods were introduced last year, citizen complaints of verbal or physical abuse by officers went up by 11%. And the policy has occasionally increased crime, rather than reduced it. Officers who have become involved in their "patch" sometimes grow so intimate with criminals that they cross over to the other side; it happened a few years ago in Philadelphia. Because human beings, even in blue, are so corruptible, some crime-fighters argue that the most dependable new ingredient in the police armory is not human leg-power but computerized intelligence.

On the Screen

The man behind this notion, Jack Maple, is a dandy who affects dark glasses, homburgs, and two-tone shoes; yet he has become something of a legend in America's police departments. For some years, starting in New York and moving on to high-crime spots such as New Orleans and Philadelphia, he and his business partner, John Linder, have marketed a two-tier system for cutting crime.

First, police departments have to sort themselves out: root out corruption, streamline their bureaucracy, and make more contact with the public. Second, they have to adopt a computer system called Comstat which helps them analyze statistics on all major crimes. These are constantly keyed into the computer, which then displays where and when they have occurred on a color-coded map, enabling police to monitor crime trends as they happen and to spot high crime areas. In New York, Comstat's statistical maps are analyzed each week at a meeting of the city's police chief and precinct captains.

Messrs Maple and Linder ("specialists in crime-reduction services") have no doubt that their system is a main contributor to the drop in crime. When they introduced it in New Orleans in January 1997, violent crime dropped by 22% in a year; when they merely started working informally with the police department in Newark, New Jersey, violent crime fell by 13%. Police departments are now lining up to pay as much as $50,000 a month for these two men to put them straight.

It is probable that all these policies and bits of technical wizardry, added together, have made a big difference to crime. But there remain anomalies that cannot be explained, such as the fact that crime in Washington, DC, has fallen as fast as anywhere, although the police department has been corrupt, and hopeless and, in large stretches of the city, neither police nor residents seem disposed to fight the criminals in their midst.

The larger reason for the fall in crime rates, many say, is a much less sophisticated one. It is a fact that crime rates have dropped as the imprisonment rate has soared. In 1997 the national incarceration rate, at 645 per 100,000 people, was more than double the rate in 1985, and the number of inmates in city and county jails rose by 9.4%, almost double its annual average increase since 1990. Surely, some criminologist argue, one set of figures is the cause of the other. It is precisely because more people are being sent to prison, they claim, that crime rates are falling. A 1993 study by National Academy of Sciences actually concluded that the tripling of the prison population between 1975 and 1989 had reduced violent crime by 10%–15%.

Yet cause and effect may not be so obviously linked. To begin with, the sale and possession of drugs are not counted by the FBI in its crime index, which is limited to violent crimes and crimes against property. Yet drug offences account for more than a third of the recent increase of the number of those jailed; since 1980, the in-carceration rate for drug arrests has increased by 1,000%.

And although about three-quarters of those going to prison for drug offences have committed other crimes as well, there is not yet a crystal-clear connection be-tween filling the jails with drug-pushers and a decline in the rate of violent crime. Again, though national figures are suggestive, local ones diverge: the places where crime has dropped most sharply (such as New York City) are not always the places where incarceration has risen fastest.

The Larger Picture

Statistically, each of these new changes in law-enforcement has made some differ-ence to the picture. Yet it seems probable that the factors that have really brought the crime-rates down have little to do with policemen or politicians, and more to do with cycles that are beyond their control.

The first of these is demographic. The fall in the crime rate has coincided with a fall in the number of young men between the ages of 15 and 21, the peak age for criminal activity in any society, including America. In the same way, the rise in the crime rate that started in the early 1960s coincided with the teenage years of the baby-boomers. As the boomer generation matured, married, found jobs, and shoul-dered mortgages, so the crime rate fell.

This encouraging trend was quickly overshadowed, starting in the mid-1980s, by a new swarm of teenagers caught up in a new sort of depravity: the craze for crack cocaine. Crack brought with it much higher levels of violence and, in particular, soaring rates of handgun murders by people less than 25 years old. Yet the terror became too much, and the young began to leave crack alone. Within a few years, at least in most big cities, the drug market had stabilized and settled, even moving indoors; the turf-wars were over, and crack itself had become passé. Studies of Brooklyn by Richard Curtis, of the John Jay College of Criminal Justice, show the clear connection: around 1992, many young bloods decided to drop the dangerous life of the street in favor of steady jobs. In direct consequence, the local crime rate fell.

Murder rates among Americans older than 25 had already been declining since 1980. Here, according to Alfred Blumstein, a professor of criminology at Carnegie Mellon University, there may be even longer-term social factors involved. In an age of easy divorce and more casual relationships, men and women are less likely to murder their partners: between 1976 and 1996, such murders fell by 40%. The de-cline in alcohol consumption, too, means that fewer bar-room brawls leave a litter of corpses on a Friday night.

It sometimes seems that changing social trends also sometimes lie behind the fall in property crime. Burglars tend not to steal television sets now because almost everyone has one; value on the street has plummeted. At the same time, the fact that people stay in watching their sets, rather than going out, deters would-be burglars. Extra garages are standard in the suburbs, to safeguard extra cars; credit cards mean that shoppers carry less cash in their pockets; people working from home, by means of computers, can keep a closer watch over their streets.

Lastly, people are going to greater lengths to protect themselves and their property than they did in the past. This is partly because of the huge fear of crime that preceded the present decline, and partly because—even with recent increases in the number of policemen—the ratio of police to violent crimes reported is still way below what it was in the 1960s.

One American home in five now has a burglar alarm, up from around 1% in 1970; sales of car alarms have risen 40 times over; spending on private security, including private guards, has risen ten times (to $80 billion) since 1975. There are indications that all this may do more for citizens' confidence than it does for crime; that property criminals, being mostly opportunists, will merely move to a place where potential victims are less diligent. Yet the police are happy to attribute a 53% decline in the burglary rate in Washington's inner suburbs, between 1977 and 1997, to Neighborhood Watch and car alarms.

Some people suppose that increasing prosperity may affect crime in more fundamental ways. When people are better and unemployment is low (it is 4.5% at present), there is simply less incentive to rob others, and perhaps less incentive even to hurt them. Historically, crime rates tend to fall in boom years; the lowest recorded point for murder occurred in the mid-1950s. Yet research has also shown that local economic booms (especially when caused by the introduction of gambling casinos into a depressed region) can actually cause certain sorts of crime to rise.

The Inevitable Upturn

The "social-trend" explanations are bothersome not only because they are ambiguous. Each of them is also reversible. This is why the news of falling crime rates has been greeted with only muted joy. The economy may sometimes seem to be breaking free of old cycles, but sooner or later there will probably be a downturn. And demography is fairly predictable. So is the tendency of drug dealers to find some new kick to sell to the young once their current wares go out of fashion. The police are well aware of this. As Boston's police commissioner said, immediately after noticing how juvenile murders had fallen to zero in his city, "There is only one way the statistics can go."

Within a few years, the numbers of 15–21 year olds in the country will be rising again. Yet the point is not the sheer number of teenage boys; it is the number leading messy lives. More ominously, by 1999 the first generation of babies born when their mothers were addicted to crack will start to reach puberty. By 2000, three-fifths of black youths turning 15 will have been born to single mothers. Police departments are expecting a wave of "super-criminals"—at worst drug-addicted, at the least deprived of paternal discipline, and probably heavily armed—to hit the streets then. The scourge will be compounded if then the economy is looking worse.

Police departments also know that some sorts of crime—especially juvenile crime and property crime—have not fallen back to anywhere near the levels of the post-1945 years; and they know besides, that crime has not fallen everywhere. There are signs that it may merely have moved to new terrain. Because the big cities, wired and well-policed have become difficult for criminals to work in, or because the drug market there is saturated, they have moved to more modest-sized cities in areas that were once relatively crime-free. Drug gangs are now found in small towns throughout the mid-west and the Rockies; crack, once a plague of the ghettos, is now devastating the poorer parts of the rural South.

The numbers tell the story. Whereas the biggest cities—New York, Chicago, Los Angeles—congratulate themselves on plummeting rates of crime, crime rates have risen since 1993 in places like Nashville, Phoenix, Milwaukee and Charlotte, North Carolina: pleasant cities, which no one would call deeply troubled, but whose population has been growing rapidly.

In fact, crime rates are rising in most medium-sized towns across the country. And, though crime in central Washington, DC, has fallen, in some parts of that city's suburbs crime rates have doubled since the 1970s, growing much faster than the population. The irony is that there are signs that refugees from city centers, driven out to the suburbs by fear of crime, have drawn the criminals after them.

In short, crime seems to behave much as a flu virus does. It adapts itself to new factors, and new forces, and inoculation against one strain does not guarantee any immunity for the next one. It moves around as people do and, like most social activities, follows fashions. For at its base, of course, is flawed human nature: which is, unfortunately, a statistical constant.

2 *Evidence for Causal Claims: Temporal and Statistical Linkages*

We have examined the various kinds of causal claims that we meet. Given that causal claims are very important components of our worldviews, how do we establish them? What sorts of evidence go into establishing causal claims? In this section we will examine the general nature of causal influence, leaving it for the next two sections to lay out some specific argument forms.

In general terms, two sorts of connections are part of the evidence for a causal claim: temporal linkage and statistical correlation. Temporal linkage applies to deterministic causal claims, while statistical correlation applies to statistical causal claims. **Temporal linkage** is connection in time. If we are talking about particular events *A* and *B,* when *A* occurs shortly before *B,* we say that *A* **precedes** *B*; when *A* and *B* occur together, we say that *A* and *B* are **simultaneous.** If *A* and *B* are always temporally linked, we say *A* and *B* are **constantly conjoined.**

Examples of precedence/simultaneity:

> The bombing of Pearl Harbor immediately preceded the declaration of World War II by the U.S.A.
> My headache immediately followed consuming several glasses of red wine.

Examples of constant conjunction:

> Whenever someone is decapitated, he or she dies shortly thereafter.
> My chest pains occur whenever I exercise.

Correlation is a statistical linkage between factors or features of populations. Two features F_1 and F_2 are correlated in a population if the percentage of those with F_2 is higher or lower among those with F_1 than with those lacking F_1. For example, to say heart disease is correlated with coffee consumption is to say that the incidence of heart disease is higher or lower among coffee drinkers than people who don't drink coffee. Correlation is a two-way relation: if A is correlated with B, B is correlated with A. Examples of correlations follow:

> The chances of success in college is correlated with your score on the SAT.
> The accident rate among drivers is correlated with the number of traffic tickets they receive.
> The rate of heart disease among people is correlated to the amount of fat in their diets.

Correlations can be positive or negative. F_1 is **positively correlated** with F_2 if the percentage of those with F_2 is higher among those with F_1 than among those without F_1. F_1 is **negatively correlated** with F_2 if the percentage of those with F_2 is lower among those with F_1 than those without F_1. Some examples are:

> High SAT scores are positively correlated with graduation rate in college; that is, students with high SAT scores have a higher rate of graduating college than those with lower scores.
> Drug abuse is negatively correlated with graduation rate in college; that is, students who abuse drugs have a lower rate of graduating college than those who do not abuse drugs.
> A high-fat diet is positively correlated with heart disease; that is, people who eat a lot of fatty foods have a higher rate of heart disease than those who do not eat a lot of fatty foods.
> Exercise is negatively correlated with heart disease; that is, people who exercise have a lower rate of heart disease than those who do not exercise.

Note that if A is negatively correlated with B, then A is positively correlated with the lack of B. Because of this, we can simplify the rest of this discussion if we just talk about *positive* correlations. From here on, I will mean by "correlation" positive correlation.

To get back to causal inference, then, we now see that such an inference has at least one premise about two things being temporally or statistically linked and a conclusion that one of these things causes the other.

1. A and B are temporally or statistically linked (that is, A precedes B, or A and are simultaneous, or A and B are correlated).

∴ A causes B.

Is that all there is to causal argument?

It's easy to see that the answer is no, that we need to have at least one more premise. This is because there are many possible explanations for a linkage between A and B besides that A causes B. Consider the following candidates to explain, say, the correlation of A and B:

> *Explanation 1:* A and B are constantly conjoined/correlated because A causes B. For example, studying is correlated with academic success because studying causes you to learn.

Explanation 2: A and B are constantly conjoined/correlated because B causes A. Heart disease is correlated to stress not because heart disease causes stress, but the reverse.

Explanation 3: A and B are constantly conjoined/correlated purely by chance—that is, are **accidentally correlated.** For example, over the last twenty years there has been a perfect correlation between hair loss on my head and the growth of population on the planet Earth—but clearly there is no causal connection between the two!

Explanation 4: A and B may be constantly conjoined/correlated because something else (C) causes both A and B. For example, my shortness of breath and chest pains may be correlated not because chest pain causes my shortness of breath, or because shortness of breath causes chest pains, but because arteriosclerosis causes both.

Explanation 5: A and B are constantly conjoined/correlated because they are **reciprocal effects**—that is, they cause each other. For example, A and B might directly mutually cause each other, as when children are playing on a seesaw. When child A is pushing her end of the seesaw up, she is pushing child B down, and vice versa. Another example: A and B might form what is called a "positive feedback loop." Suppose A is success and B is self-confidence. Success in any venture will increase your self-confidence. But strong self-confidence will then increase your ability to succeed, which will then add more to your self-confidence.

    There are also negative feedback loops. You are depressed. You drink too much as a consequence. Being drunk makes you feel physically lousy and lowers your self-esteem. That depresses you so you drink too much. We colloquially call this a "downward spiral."

Explanation 6: A and B are constantly conjoined/correlated because A together with some other factor C causes B; that is, A is a partial cause of B. For example, taking birth control pills is correlated with a lower rate of pregnancy among people, because taking birth control pills together with being female causes a lower rate of pregnancy. (The pill has no effect on men!)

Explanation 7: A and B are constantly conjoined/correlated because B together with some other factor C causes A; that is, B is a partial cause of A. For example, lower rate of pregnancy is correlated with birth control usage because birth control pill usage together with being female causes a lower rate of pregnancy.

So the crucial second premise of a causal argument is one that asserts that the best explanation for the linkage in the first premise is that A causes B. We thus see that causal inference is a special case of the IBE:

1.   A and B are temporally or statistically linked.
2.   That A causes B is the best explanation for that linkage.
∴   [Probably] A causes B.

So good causal reasoning will consider and rule out other possible explanations for an observed correlation besides the obvious immediate causal explanation.

Exercise 14.2

Discuss the possible explanations for the following temporal and statistical linkages.

1. Positive correlation between income level and amount of higher education
2. Positive correlation between grade point average and self-esteem
3. Positive correlation between the rate of heart disease and the amount of fat in the diet
4. Negative correlation between the rate of heart disease and amount of exercise
5. Positive correlation between the accident rate among drivers and the number of traffic tickets received

3   *Establishing Deterministic Causes*

In this section we will look at how it is we can establish deterministic causal claims. While deterministic causal claims are less common in ordinary life than are statistical causal claims, we can get a good sense for establishing statistical causal claims by first considering deterministic claims.

Probably the best place to start is by looking at the approach for determining caused formulated by the nineteenth-century logician John Stuart Mill. He put forward five methods for determining causes, but we will focus on just two (see Mill 1967: 255*ff.*).

Let's begin with Mill's method of agreement. The method of agreement states that if two or more instances of the phenomenon under investigation have only one circumstance in common, the circumstance in which alone all the instances agree is the cause (or effect) of the given phenomenon (Mill 1967: 255*ff.*). For example, if we investigate baldness and find that potassium shortage is the only circumstance that all bald men have in common, then we may conclude that potassium shortage causes baldness (or that baldness causes potassium shortage).

Now, this rule needs to be clarified. To begin with, the rules as stated talk about possible causal factors without limitation. For example, the method of agreement tells us that to discover, say, the cause of baldness, we need only find the factor that all bald men have in common. But the number of potential factors is infinite. Do we have to check every imaginable property? Color of eyes? Toenail length? Favorite music? Amount of sardines consumed? Distance between the man's scalp and Venus?

The point is that to even begin searching for a cause of a given phenomenon, we must first have an idea, a *hypothesis,* about which properties are *relevant.* And the number of potentially relevant factors is indeterminate. We must remember that we are in the realm of the inductive: No matter how sure we are we have examined all relevant factors, it is always possible that we have overlooked one.

So let us put the rule thus:

Rule 1: ("Agreement") The more we can be sure that **A** *is the only relevant common factor in all occurrences of* **B,** *the more likely it is* **A** *that caused* **B.** The rule of agreement is eliminative in nature. In practice, we start with a list of possible relevant factors to examine as candidates for the causes and examine the cases one by one to eliminate candidates that are not present in all cases.

Consider an example. Suppose we are trying to find the cause of a disease called chokosis. We suspect that one of the following factors is the cause: alcohol consumption, potassium shortage, lack of exercise, and smoking. We examine four people with chokosis and find the following:

1. Mr. *A* doesn't drink, does have a shortage of potassium, exercises a lot, but smokes.
2. Ms. *B* drinks, has a potassium shortage, doesn't exercise at all, but doesn't smoke.
3. Mr. *C* drinks, has a potassium shortage, exercises, and smokes.
4. Mrs. *D* drinks, has a potassium shortage, doesn't exercise, but does smoke.

What does this information show?

Case 1 rules out alcohol consumption and lack of exercise as common factors. Case 2 rules out smoking as a common factor. That leaves potassium shortage as a possible common factor, and neither case 3 nor case 4 rule that out. Our conclusion: *If* one of the hypothetical causes we chose to investigate (alcohol, potassium shortage, lack of exercise, and smoking) is a *deterministic* cause of chokosis, then the four cases examined eliminate all but potassium shortage as candidates. If we kept examining more cases and potassium shortage was found in every case, we could grow ever more confident that it is a cause, but we could never be certain. It is also possible that further examination of chokosis patients might find one without potassium shortage, which would rule that factor out as a (deterministic) cause. We would then have to come up with new hypothetical causes to investigate.

The second of Mill's methods we want to examine is the "joint method of agreement and difference." The joint method of agreement *and* difference states that if two or more instances in which the phenomenon occurs have only one circumstance in common, while two or more instances in which it does not occur have nothing in common except the absence of that circumstance, then the circumstance in which alone the two sets of instances differ is the cause (or effect, or part of the cause) of the phenomenon. For example, if we examine a number of cases of those who live past seventy-five and a number of those who do not, and we find that the one factor that the former have in common that all the latter lack is regular exercise, then we may conclude that regular exercise is the common (part or full) cause of longevity.

Now, again, this rule is inductive and eliminative. In practice, we are examining a small number of cases relative to the totality of such cases, and we look only at relevant possible causes (candidate causes). So let us put this as a second rule, the rule of difference:

Rule 2: ("Difference") The more we can be sure that A is the only relevant difference between cases in which B occurs and those in which B does not occur, the more likely it is that A caused B. By "only relevant difference" we mean that only *A* is such that it occurs when *B* occurs and does not occur when *B* does not occur.

Let's consider an example. Suppose we want to find the cause of Booboo fever, a dread new ailment. We start with a list of suspected causes: high fat diet, a parasite called "fluke *X*," a bacterium *X*, and chocolate consumption. We examine four cases, two who have the fever and two who don't, and we find the following:

Case 1 (has Booboo fever): has a high-fat diet, has the parasite, has the bacterium, and eats lots of chocolate.

Case 2 (has Booboo fever): has a high-fat diet, has the parasite, has the bacterium, and never eats chocolate.

Case 3 (does not have Booboo fever): has a high-fat diet, has the parasite, does not have the bacterium, and does eat chocolate.

Case 4 (does not have Booboo fever): has a high-fat diet, does not have the parasite or the bacterium, and eats chocolate.

What can we conclude?

Case 1 rules out nothing. Case 2 rules out chocolate. Case 3 rules out high-fat diet (since the person *has* the factor but does not have the disease), and rules out the parasite and chocolate. Case 4 adds nothing new. Thus, if any of the initial suspected causes is the cause, bacterium X is. The examination of the further cases, both with and without the disease, would either increase the confidence we have that the bacterium is the cause of the fever or rule it out, forcing us to look for new hypotheses.

A classic case of the use of the rule of difference is found in experiments conducted by U.S. Army doctors Walter Reed, James Carroll, and Jesse Lezear in November 1900. The doctors were attempting to determine the cause of yellow fever.[*]

> Experiments were devised to show that yellow fever was transmitted by the mosquito alone, all other reasonable opportunities for being infected being excluded. A small building was erected, all windows and doors and every other possible opening being absolutely mosquitoproof. A wire mosquito screen divided the room into two spaces. In one of these spaces fifteen mosquitoes, which had fed on yellow fever patients, were liberated. A non-immune volunteer entered the room with the mosquitoes and was bitten by seven mosquitoes. Four days later, he suffered an attack of yellow fever. Two other non-immune men slept for thirteen nights in the mosquito-free room without disturbances of any sort.
>
> To show that the disease was transmitted by the mosquito and not through the excreta of yellow fever patients or anything which had come in contact with them, another house was constructed and made mosquitoproof. For 20 days, this house was occupied by three non-immunes, after the clothing, bedding and eating utensils and other vessels soiled with the discharge, blood and vomitus of yellow fever patients had been placed in it. The bed clothing which they used had been brought from the beds of the patients who had died of yellow fever, without being subjected to washing or any other treatment to remove anything with which it might have been soiled. The experiment was twice repeated by other non-immune volunteers. During the entire period all the men who occupied the house were strictly quarantined and protected from mosquitoes. None of those exposed to these experiments contracted yellow fever. That they were not immune was subsequently shown, since four of them became infected either by mosquito bites or the injection of blood from yellow fever patients.

---

[*]This example is found in Copi and Cohen (1998: 509) and was taken from Paul Henle and William K. Frankena, *Exercises in Elementary Logic* (1940).

Notice the rule of difference being used twice. In the first experiment, it was set up that the key relevant difference between the volunteers was the presence of mosquitoes: the volunteer who was bitten by the mosquitos got yellow fever; the volunteers who did not get bitten did not get the fever. In the second experiment, the volunteers came into extensive contact with all sorts of materials from yellow fever patients but only got the disease after they were bitten by mosquitoes or were injected with the blood of yellow fever patients.

Note again that we put the first two rules in terms of relevant factors, and inductively: We can *never* examine *all* possibly relevant factors of all cases of *B*, but the more relevant factors we examine, the stronger the inference. And the more *B* cases we examine, the stronger the inference. It is very important to see that this feature of eliminating competing relevant factors is central to strong inference. Otherwise, fallacies can occur—called, appropriately enough, **false cause** fallacies.

Consider a fallacious form of argument, **post hoc ergo propter hoc** (Latin for "after this, therefore because of this"). This is the fallacy of concluding that *A* caused *B* solely on the basis of the fact that *A* happened before *B*. For example, to conclude that President Smith caused a recession simply because the recession occurred shortly after Smith assumed office is to commit this fallacy. What is fallacious about post hoc ergo proper hoc is that the information given in the premise (that *B* followed *A*) doesn't rule out other possible explanations for *B* besides *A* causing *B*. There are many other relevant factors to be looked at besides who got elected to the presidency to figure out what caused a recession. Post hoc ergo propter hoc is a case of the rule of difference gone awry: One *B* case is examined, and no other relevant factors are considered besides the occurrence of *A*.

The post hoc argument form is thus a degenerate case of difference. In post hoc ergo propter hoc, all the premise tells us is that *B* followed *A*. But by the rule of difference, to conclude with any reasonable degree of confidence that *A* caused *B* would require us to know in addition that the *only* relevant change before *B* happened was the occurrence of *A*. That stated, we have a case of difference, to be evaluated accordingly. That absent, we simply have a fallacy.

Politicians habitually commit the fallacy of post hoc ergo propter hoc by taking credit automatically for whatever good things happened while they were in office and charging their opponents as responsible for the bad things that happened while those folks were in office. Consider these examples, taken from the Carter-Ford debates of 1976:

> CARTER: As a matter of fact since the late 60's, when Mr. Nixon took office, we've had a reduction in the percentage of taxes paid by corporations from 30% down to about 20%. We've had an increase in taxes paid by individuals. Payroll taxes from 14% up to about 20% and this is what the Republicans have done to us. Which is why tax reform is so important.

> FORD: I think the record should show, Mr. Newman, that the Bureau of Census, we checked it just yesterday, indicates that in the four years that Gov. Carter was governor of the state of Georgia, expenditures by the government went up over 50%. Employees of the government of Georgia during his term of office went up over 25%. And the figures also show that the bonded indebtedness of the state of Georgia during his governorship went up over 20%.

Carter's claim that the Republicans are responsible for the "bad" changes in the tax system is backed only by a temporal link. He needs to give more evidence—say, by showing that Republicans are the ones who passed the relevant tax laws. (Ford pointed out that the Democrats controlled Congress during that period.) Ford's implicit claim (that Carter was responsible for the increase in the cost and size of Georgia's state government while he was governor) again rests on too little evidence. Did Carter's party control the Georgia legislature, which controls spending? Does the governor in Georgia have the power to veto spending programs at will? Was there a large increase in Georgia's population during that period (thus requiring a commensurate growth in size of government)? These questions need to be answered for the temporal linkage to indicate responsibility.

Another form of false cause is the **correlation fallacy,** in which someone infers that *A* causes *B* just because *A* and *B* occur together. The correlation fallacy is a degenerate form of the rule of agreement. We need to know more than that *A* and *B* occur together; we need to have good evidence that *A* is the only relevant factor that the *B* cases share to have any confidence *A* is the cause of *B*. Absent that, the inference is very weak. For example, consider this silly story:

> THE TERRIFYING DOG OF DEATH—Four years ago, Turruzzu (this devil-dog) was sitting outside my aunt's home. Shortly afterward, she collapsed and died from a heart attack. "It is uncanny," Anna Carioto, 17, eldest daughter of bricklayer Pasquale Carioto, said. "On October 26, 1977, my father died in a car crash. That same morning, that dog was sitting outside our house." Antonio Carchivi, chief of the traffic police said "Everyone feeds the dog, but nobody wants to see him sitting outside their house. Everybody is afraid, grown men included. Nobody wants to kill the dog, they are too scared. Last year when the dog had eczema, the local veterinarian treated him very carefully with lots of love and attention." The Major, an elementary school teacher, said, "There have been accidents and a murder in which the dog was seen outside the victims' houses beforehand.

Here, all we are told is that the appearance of this dog was followed repeatedly by accidents or death. But we don't have any information that shows that the dog's appearance is the only relevant common factor.

Exercise 14.3A

For each of these passages, determine whether the method of agreement or the method of difference is being employed (or both). All passages are from Konner (1982).

1. In every culture there is at least some homicide, in the context of war or ritual or in the context of daily life, and in every culture men are mainly responsible for it. Among the !Kung San of Botswana, noted for their pacifism as well as for equality between the sexes, the perpetrators in twenty-two documented homicides were all men. Fights over adultery or presumed adultery were involved in several cases, and a majority of the others were retaliations for previous homicides. In a sample of 122 distinct societies in the ethnographic range, distributed around the world, making weapons was done by men in all of them. There are of course, exceptions, certainly at the individual level and, in rare cases—such as modern Israel or nineteenth-century Dahomey—transient partial exceptions at the group level. What we are dealing with, to be sure is a difference in degree, but one so large that it may as well be qualitative. Men are more violent than women.

2. One of the most impressive experiments of the kind produced "pseudohermaphro-
    dite" monkeys by administering male gonadal hormones to female fetuses before
    birth. As they grew, these females showed neither the characteristic low female level
    of aggressive play nor the characteristic high male level, but something precisely
    between.

3. In 1874, Carl Wernicke, a then obscure twenty-six-year-old neurologist, described a
    new aphasic syndrome characterized by fluent and rapid but largely meaningless
    speech, with most of the content words missing, and almost total loss of comprehen-
    sion of speech despite normal hearing. These patients often had lesions in a quite
    different region—now called Wernicke's area—behind and adjacent to the area of
    the cerebral cortex involved in the first-level interpretation of auditory patterns.
    (Wernicke's area would be approximately above the ear, although this association
    with hearing is purely coincidental.) In his impressive paper on the subject, Wernicke
    went on to advance a theory of the brain mediation of language, taking into account
    his own findings as well as Broca's. According to this theory, the area he identified,
    adjacent to the primary higher processing center for hearing, was responsible, for the
    analysis of sound patterns at the level of speech comprehension.

4. Nineteen of the subjects appeared at birth to be ambiguously female, and were
    viewed and reared as completely normal females by their parents and other relatives.
    At puberty they first failed to develop breasts and then underwent a completely mas-
    culine pubertal transformation, including growth of a phallus, descent of the testes
    (which had previously been in the abdominal cavity), deepening of the voice, and the
    development of muscular masculine physique. Physically and psychologically they
    became men, with normal or occasionally hyper-normal sexual desire for women and
    with a complete range of sexual functions except for infertility due to abnormal ejac-
    ulation (through an opening at the base of the penis). After many years of experience
    with such individuals, the villagers identified them as a separate group, called
    "guevedoce," ("penis at twelve"), or "machihembra," ("man-woman").

    The physiological analysis undertaken by Imperato-McGinley and her colleagues
    revealed that these individuals are genetically male—they have one X and one Y
    chromosome—but lack a single enzyme of male sex-hormone synthesis, due to a de-
    fective gene. The enzyme, 5a-reductase, changes testosterone into another male sex
    hormone, dihydrotestosterone. Although they lack dihydrotestosterone almost com-
    pletely, they have normal levels of testosterone itself. Evidently these two hormones
    are respectively responsible for the promotion of male external sex characteristics at
    birth (dihydrotestosterone) and at puberty (testosterone). Despite the presence of
    testosterone, the lack of "dihydro" makes for a female looking newborn and pre-
    pubertal child. The presence of testosterone makes for a more or less normal mas-
    culine puberty.

5. Testosterone promotes aggression, certainly in males and possibly in females, in a
    much more specific way. Indeed, generalized stress is more likely to decrease the level
    of testosterone. Yet, in members of various species, especially in males, testosterone
    injections can increase aggressiveness in various situations and male castration can
    decrease it. Naturally occurring variations in testosterone level can accompany fight-
    ing behavior, and fighting can in turn affect that level. For example, in an experiment
    in which two groups of rhesus monkeys were made to fight, the losers experience a

large decrease after the fight (actually in two stages, the second perhaps corresponding to the final acceptance of the loss), while the winners did not.

Exercise 14.3B

The following passages contain false cause fallacies. Explain why.

1. Baldness is caused by tight neckties and collars and by combing the hair improperly, says a barber who has studied the problem throughout his 50-year career.

   Fred C. Boor, of St. Louis, Mo., says his theories are proven by the fact that he takes his own advice and still has a full head of hair at the age of 77.

2. Your boss has a bigger vocabulary than you have. That's one good reason why he's your boss.

3. Not long ago a poll of pregnant U.S. high school students revealed that of the 1,000 unmarried girls questioned, 984 had become pregnant with suggestive pop music as a background.

4. Well, I remember when I lost everything we had: my job, our savings, my pension . . . and we had to borrow money from our relatives to pay the rent and keep food on the table for our little ones. Now I am one of the highest paid executives in my field, my wife has her own business, our kids go to the finest schools, all the bills are paid, and we have money in the bank.

   How did this all happen? Just when I was in the depths of despair, my wife read what Jesus said about the mustard seed to me:

   If ye have faith as a grain of mustard . . . nothing shall be impossible unto you. Matthew 17:20

   I thought to myself, "if only I had something to hold on to, that I could see and touch." So I acquired some mustard seeds from the Holy Land, encased them in a credit card–size gold metallic prayer card, and began carrying it with me as an affirmation of faith. I was amazed at how my life changed. Not only did I begin to prosper, but my mental and physical health improved.

   Are you or someone close to you having problems? I know what it's like to be desperate. I know what it's like to have what you need and want. And I know that you can decide which one it's going to be. What does it require? Faith. Faith and commitment enough to carry your mustard seed from the Holy Land and follow a few simple instructions. I guarantee it. If you will send a check or money order for $4.00 plus $.79 postage and handling, I will send you a mustard seed from the Holy Land encased in the "Seed of Faith" prayer card with instructions for its use. If you return your "Seed of Faith" prayer card for any reason within 30 days after you received it, I will return your check or money order to you. Can your future wait?

5. Talisman Changes Lives for Millions—An extraordinary phenomenon is sweeping the North American continent, it was learned from reliable sources here recently. A well-known but little understood woman who calls herself Madame Labonga is possessed by a power that allows her to dispense most of life's good things to whomever owns her specially designed Talisman.

   Money, wealth, happiness, love, and prosperity unfold the moment the famous Labonga's Talisman is worn or carried. What is this Talisman? It is a specially minted coin that mysteriously confers upon the wearer or carrier an almost certain propensity for happiness and success in every venture of life. There is only one stipulation, however. Instructions must be followed meticulously because for some peculiar reason the effectiveness of the Talisman is dependent on them. A set of these instructions is enclosed with each Talisman.

People who have worn or carried this mystical Talisman have reported an almost immediate reversal of their luck. Most report that sooner or later their lives are radically changed.

Others report a gradual, though definite, change. Madame Labonga is not available for comment though reporters have been dogging her footsteps for months now. Maybe that's the key to her success: Complete secrecy. And inaccessibility.

Now for those of you out there who are straining at the bit to change your luck here's how to do it. Simply send $2.50 for each Aluminum Talisman, $4.50 for each Bronze Talisman, or $9.45 for each Electro-Plated Gold Talisman.

6. One of the "intellectual" arguments advanced by those who oppose the death penalty is that it is not a deterrent. Then how in the world can we account for the monstrous increase in armed robbery and murder since our ten-year moratorium on that penalty? Or is that too simplistic for "intellectuals " to understand?

7. People who follow the news are more successful, friendly, and responsible than those with no interest in current events, a university study has discovered.

But if you haven't been keeping informed, you can easily change, says an expert.

"Those who don't keep up with current events tend to be more hostile, more defensive, less sociable and less likely to accept blame," says psychology professor Dr. Henry H. Schmo.

"They are the foot-stompers, the people who shake their fists at stop-lights and scream at salesladies."

However, people in the know about the news tend to be "all-around high achievers," said Dr. Schmo, who conducted a study of 63 people at Long Island University (LIU).

"They are easier to be around because they are more secure."

"If you don't keep up with the news, you can change," said Dr. Sherman Blatz, LIU professor of psychology.

"You can too be more successful, more sociable, more willing to accept responsibility and generally more fun to be around simply by making yourself more aware of current events."

How? Read at least one newspaper a day, watch TV news at least twice a week, watch a TV talk show at least once a month and discuss current events with other people as often as possible, he suggested.

8. Princess Di has that magic touch! Her delicate hands have the miraculous power to heal the sick, say many grateful men, women and children who've been freed from pain and disease just by a touch from the caring Di.

"She has a great, unusual talent," says Raffaele Curi, organizer of Italy's famed Spoleto music festival.

"When I told her I suffered from arthritis in the shoulder, she told me to stand still and held her hands for a few minutes over my shoulders.

"The pain disappeared miraculously and never returned.

"She is a natural-born healer. She has an exceptional power in her hands, and I know she has cured many children and others suffering from persistent pains."

4   *Establishing Statistical Causes*

In the last section we examined strategies for examining deterministic causes. Let us turn now to strategies for establishing statistical causes. My treatment relies on that of Giere (1979) and Baird (1992).

Recall that statistical causes are causal factors in populations. Scientists have specific types of tests to determine causes in populations. The three forms of argument (or studies) we will examine are experimental cause-to-effect studies, nonexperimental cause-to-effect studies, and nonexperimental effect-to-cause studies. We will examine these in turn. Each assumes a **target population** within which we seek to find the causal factor or factors responsible for a phenomenon of interest to us (that is, the effect). The examples I will focus on are cases from medical research. In such research, the target population is either human beings or a species held to be physiologically analogous to humans in some respect (rats, dogs, rabbits, pigs, or other species, depending on the research). The effect being investigated is usually some disease or malady. And the suspected cause under investigation is often a proposed medicine or some physiological factors (such as diet, exercise, or genetic structure) that can be controlled.

Remember that we are in the domain of the induction. We don't inspect the entire target population; instead, we deal with samples.

With this in mind, let's state the causal argument forms. First, in a **controlled cause-to-effect experiment,** a sample of the target population is divided into two subgroups, the **experimental group** and the **control group.** The experimental group is subjected to the suspected causal factor being tested, while the control group is treated the same way as the experimental group except it is not subjected to the suspected causal factor. Subsequently, both groups are checked to observe the frequency of the effect. If the difference in observed frequency is large enough, we can conclude that the causal factor is indeed the cause of the effect. Figure 14.1 illustrates this experimental design.

Consider an example. Suppose we want to test whether a new cholesterol-lowering drug is effective. We take a sample of people and divide them into the experimental and the control group. We give the experimental group the drug and the control group a **placebo**—that is, an inert sugar pill. We then (after an appropriate period of time) measure the serum cholesterol levels of members in each group. We discover that the experimental group has average cholesterol levels 50 percent lower than the control group. That would be good evidence that the drug works; that is, it indeed causes a lowering of cholesterol.

Consider a classic example, a test for the effectiveness of the Salk polio vaccine done in the 1950s. To set the scene: Polio was a terrible disease, because it afflicted mostly children and came in unpredictable epidemics. An early vaccine developed in the 1930s showed promise in lab tests but had to be withdrawn because it brought on the disease more often than it prevented it. So when the Salk vaccine was developed, researchers

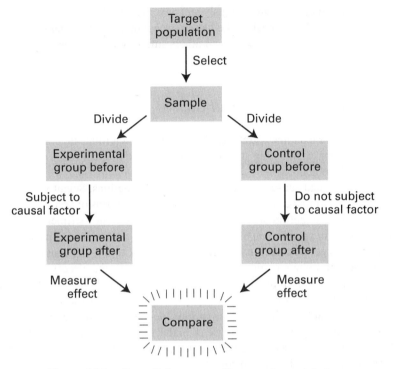

Figure 14.1   *Controlled cause-to-effect experimental design*

wanted to test it. They did not want to just vaccinate a large group of children and observe the results, because no drug or vaccine is 100 percent effective, and polio cases fluctuated wildly from year to year naturally. For example, in 1931 there were about 18,000 cases, while in 1932 there were about 5,000 cases (Baird 1992: 113). So even if you vaccinated a large group of children and saw a major drop in polio incidence, you would have no way of knowing whether the drop was due to the vaccine or would have occurred naturally anyway.

So a control group experiment was set up. A large group (over 400,000) of first-, second-, and third-graders were selected. Of these, roughly half were vaccinated, and the rest not. The rates of polio were then compared, and it was found that the vaccinated group had a polio rate of 28 per 100,000 while the unvaccinated group had a polio rate of 71 per 100,000 (Baird 1992: 115). The results were considered decisive, since the vaccine cut the rate of polio by more than half.

A number of rules apply, however, to distinguish strong from weak control group experiments.

Rule 1: The more representative the initial sample, the stronger the inference. Remember that control group experiments involve two major inductive steps: first, a selection of an initial group of subjects, second, the division of that group into two subgroups and subsequent tests. That first step is a prelude to a generalization. We need (as discussed in Chapter 12) to ensure the initial sample should be sufficiently large, randomly chosen, and (if feasible) matched with the target population in all relevant respects. In the polio example, the initial sample was large (400,000). A possible source of bias is that the sample was entirely of schoolchildren, because perhaps schoolchildren are healthier than children not attending school. In fact, although in some countries only wealthy children go to school, in the United States of that period (as now) education was mandatory and virtually universal. And the schools chosen were from different areas of the country.

Rule 2: The experimental group should be matched to the control group in all relevant respects. We want to set the experiment up in such a way as to eliminate **confounding variables**—that is, any differences aside from the causal factor we are testing that would result in a difference in the effect. In practice, the best way to do this is by randomly assigning individuals to the experimental and control groups. For example, in the polio experiment, children could have been assigned numbers from a random number table, and then those with odd numbers would have gotten the vaccine, while those with even numbers would not have. (Something like this was, in fact, done, but only with about half the students, for reasons made clear later.)

Rule 3: Where feasible, the experiment should be double-blind. You should recall from Chapter 11 that observation has its own dangers, so it is no surprise that control group experiments, which are, after all, based on observation, need to be done with an eye to the pitfalls of observation. In particular, patients and doctors often perceive things differently when they know whether they are receiving the experimental drug. Reverting to our polio case, a patient who knows he or she is getting the vaccine might then be more inclined to shrug off a mild case of polio as being influenza. A doctor who knows which patients were vaccinated might diagnose symptoms in those patients in a subtly different way. For this reason, many control group experiments are **single-blind,** meaning that while the researchers and the doctors know who gets the experimental protocol, the patients do not. And many experiments are **double-blind,** meaning that neither the patients nor the doctors who administer the experimental drugs know which patients are receiving the real drug and which are receiving a placebo. All things being equal, double-blind experiments are preferable.

In many cases, double-blind experiments may not be feasible. In the polio case, while the researchers were able in many of the schools to do the test double-blind, in the other schools the parents objected to not knowing whether their children were receiving the vaccine. In those schools, the vaccine was administered to all the second-graders, whereas the first- and third-graders went unvaccinated.

Rule 4: The larger the observed frequency difference of the effect between the experimental and control groups, the stronger the inference. Suppose we took a large group of people, divided them into two groups, and measured average cholesterol levels in both groups. Let's suppose the difference between the averages of the cholesterol levels of the two groups is *x*. Now suppose we do absolutely *nothing* to either group for a year and then measure the average cholesterol levels again. Would you expect the difference between those averages to still be exactly *x?* No, of course not—there would be some slight natural variation over that year, no matter how closely matched the groups. For this reason, we look for the observed frequency of the effect to be sufficiently large to be statistically significant. All things being equal, a frequency difference of 80 percent allows a more confident inference than one of 2 percent. (Note that such an observed frequency difference doesn't mean that we can be forty times more confident of the conclusion in the second experiment than we are in the first!)

As we saw in Chapter 12, determining significance levels is a sophisticated mathematical matter. A significance level of 95 percent would mean that the observed frequency difference would be a matter of chance in five experiments out of one hundred. Significance levels depend on the size of the randomly assigned experimental and control groups and the size of the observed frequency difference of the effect. The higher level of significance we want, the bigger the groups need to be or the bigger the frequency difference needs to be. Thus, there is a trade-off in the size of sample needed and the size of difference observed: All things being equal, the larger the sample, the smaller the frequency difference needed to be significant at a given level.

We have focused so far on controlled cause-to-effect studies. Let us briefly review the other two statistical causal inference patterns.

The second form of inference used to determine stochastic causes is a **nonexperimental cause-to-effect study.** In this research, a sample of the target population is divided into two groups, one composed of individuals who have been exposed to the suspected cause (the subject group), and the other consisting of individuals who have not been exposed to the suspected cause (the control group). The groups are then examined for the frequency of the effect. If there is a sufficiently large difference in observed frequency, we infer that the suspected cause is a real cause.

For example, suppose we want to know whether smoking causes lung cancer. We might take a sample of people and divide them into smokers and nonsmokers. We might then do a follow-up study after some years to compare the incidence of lung cancer among the subject people (the smokers) and the control people (the nonsmokers). If we observe a sufficiently higher frequency of lung cancer among the smokers than among the nonsmokers we can infer that smoking is a cause of cancer.

Note that the difference between the first type of study and the second is whether we (the researchers) administer the suspected cause to the subject group or not. It would hardly be ethical to deliberately expose a group of people to a suspected carcinogen to see the effects! (We might well do that to a group of rats, of course.)

The third type of study for determining stochastic causes is the **nonexperimental effect-to-cause study.** In this type of research, a sample of the target population is taken and divided into those who already have the effect being investigated, the subject group, and those who don't have the effect, the control group. These groups are then examined for the frequency of the presence of the suspected cause. Again, if there is a significantly greater frequency of the suspected cause among the subject members than among the control members, we can infer that it is a real cause.

For example, we might take a sample of people and divide it into those who have heart disease (the subject group) and those who don't (the control group). We might then check for frequency of high cholesterol (the suspected cause). Again, if there is a significantly greater frequency of elevated cholesterol among those with heart disease than those without, we can infer that the suspected cause is a real cause.

Again, it is important to keep in mind the highly inductive nature of these patterns of argument. In particular, the nonexperimental studies are inherently less reliable than experimental studies. This is because in an experimental study, we can be more sure that the only relevant difference between the subject and control groups is the suspected cause (because we administer it), assuming we took care in choosing representative samples. But in nonexperimental studies, we are dividing group members into groups based on whether they were exposed to a suspected cause (in nonexperimental cause-to-effect studies) or have the effect (in nonexperimental effect-to-cause studies). And there may well be other relevant factors in common. For example, in our study of heart disease, perhaps those with heart disease may have higher levels of stress compared with those without heart disease, and maybe stress causes high cholesterol as well as heart disease. The chance of confounding variables is accordingly higher.

One last point about statistical causal experiments needs to be mentioned. We need to remember that often the target population consists of animals that are analogized with humans. In such cases, the reliability of the inference depends not only on the rules mentioned earlier but also on the rules for evaluating analogies given in Chapter 13. For example, it has been reported that most animal tests on prescription drugs are performed on young rats, rather than older ones, because young rats cost less. But this biases research results because the metabolism of young rats is more similar to younger people than to elderly people. Thus, such tests on rats can result in drugs being approved that have more side effects for the elderly than for the young.

You might wonder why researchers bother with doing experiments with animals at all. Why not just set up control group experiments on people? The reasons are two: cost and moral considerations. On the cost side, setting up control group experiments on people is very expensive. Researchers have to do expensive follow-ups (people are less willing to live in cages than are rats!), researchers often have to pay for people to participate, people can sue researchers for damages, and so on. Certainly, large drug companies have lots of money for research, but even for them it is most cost-effective to first test drugs on animals. After all, only about one out of fifty experimental drugs proves to be safe and effective enough to obtain FDA approval.

More important, testing on humans entails moral considerations. For example, if we suspect that a certain metal is carcinogenic, it would be immoral to force a group of people to ingest it as part of a study. Most of us (though not all) would view it as much more ethical to test the hypothesis on rats.

InfoTrac College Edition

You can locate InfoTrac College Edition articles about this chapter by accessing the InfoTrac College Edition Web site (www.infotrac-college.com/wadsworth/). Using the InfoTrac College Edition subject guide, enter the search terms relevant to this chapter, and then read abstracts for relevant articles.

Chapter 15

Explanation, Hypothesis, and Prediction

---

1   *Key Concepts*

In Chapter 5, we indicated that a common inductive argument form is the inference to the best explanation (IBE). We formulated the argument roughly as

    1.   Facts $F_1, \ldots, F_n$.
    2.   The best explanation of $F_1, \ldots, F_n$ is H.
    ∴   [Probably] H is true.

In this chapter we want to explore this argument form (and more generally the topic of explanation) further. To start, we need to define a few core concepts.

Let's begin with the most central concept, the concept of explanation. What is it to explain something? Consider some examples.

    1.   The detective explains who murdered the victim.
    2.   You explain why your friend looks so tired and depressed and is suffering from weight loss.
    3.   A medical researcher explains why the women in a certain delivery ward experience a higher incidence of childbed fever.
    4.   Your mechanic finds the cause of your car's rough idling.
    5.   An astronomer finds the reason for the slight wobble in a planet's orbit.

The first thing to notice about these explanations is that they are all responses to questions. Specifically, explanations are answers to why-questions.

Let's be a bit more careful. Recall from Chapter 3 that a pertinent question can be responsively answered by giving a direct or a corrective answer. Consider the following why-question and two responses to it:

QUESTION: Why is the suicide rate among computer programmers going up?

ANSWER 1: Computer programmers are facing a huge wave of layoffs, and unemployed people tend to be more suicidal.

ANSWER 2: The suicide rate among computer programmers has not in fact gone up.

Answer 1 is clearly an explanation of the alleged fact (namely that the suicide rate among computer programmers has gone up); Answer 2 is a denial of the alleged fact to be explained. So to be more precise, an **explanation** is a direct answer to a why-question, while a **debunking** is a corrective answer to a why-question.

A nice example of a debunking is given by the sociologist and priest Father Andrew Greeley (1986) in his *Confessions of a Parish Priest.* He tells of trying to pick a topic for his doctoral dissertation. He wanted to pick a topic of use to his religion, and a friend of his who was the superintendent of Catholic schools suggested Greeley investigate why Catholic students don't go on to graduate school as frequently as Protestants. Greeley started his research, as is common, with a literature search and found that, indeed, many sociologists had put forward the view that Catholic students were less likely than Protestants to attend graduate school. So he set about doing the research on the problem. He describes the results (Greeley 1986: 206):

> One Saturday morning in the summer of 1961, as I was finishing my first full year at the university, I stopped by NORC to see if the first run for my doctoral dissertation had come up from the machine room. I was eager to see the extent of Catholic deficiency in graduate school attendance in the 1961 graduates we were studying.
>
> Everyone knew that Catholics were less likely to go on to graduate school. My doctoral challenge was to learn why. . . .
>
> I found a cross-tab[ulation]. . . . Catholics from the June 1961 class were more likely to attend graduate schools the following autumn than their Protestant classmates. Across the top of the printout, Davis had written, "It looks like Southern Methodist loses this year to Notre Dame!"
>
> It was my first delightful experience of discovering that what everyone knows to be true is not necessarily true.

Greeley's research debunked the notion that Catholic college graduates went on to graduate school less often than their Protestant peers.

A second clarification is needed. We often use the term *explanation* to mean "correct explanation." But many, if not most, proposed explanations are eventually found to be incorrect, so we ought to distinguish between *true* explanations and *proposed* explanations. In practice, we are devising and evaluating proposed explanations so it would be wise to have a term for this. A **hypothesis** is a proposed explanation. We also often use the term *theory* to mean hypothesis, as when Watson says, "What's your theory about this case, Holmes?" But be careful, because scientists often use the term *theory* to mean an established or proven or received theory (as in "the special theory of relativity," which is at this point not hypothetical but proven). Then again, scientists sometimes use the term *theory* to refer to a whole field of study, as in the "theory of electromagnetism" or "quantum theory."

Now, an explanation (be it hypothetical or established) is a direct answer to a why-question. But what does that mean, exactly? Recall from Chapter 3 that this means providing statements that, together with relevant background facts, would (if true) establish the statement to be explained. Again, consider an example. You might explain why your friend looks tired and depressed and is losing weight by hypothesizing that he or she is worried. The specific hypothesis that your friend is worried, together with the unspoken assumption that worry causes lack of sleep, depression, and weight loss, establishes the observed fact that your friend looks tired, depressed, and so on.

Notice that in this example, the full explanation consists of the specific hypothesis (namely, that your friend is worried) together with background generalization (namely, that worry causes sleeplessness, depression, and weight loss). We can thus view a full explanation as an enthymeme: What is explicitly stated is the specific hypothesis or explanatory factor or cause for the alleged fact to be explained, and what is unstated but no less crucial are the background generalizations that tie that hypothesis to the explained fact.

I will borrow some terminology from Carl Hempel (1966: 50). The phenomenon we are trying to explain is the **explanandum;** put another way, the explanandum is the fact presupposed by the why-question. The statements we use to answer the question we call the **explanans.** The explanans is the explicit answer plus the background material.

One last concept needs to be explored. We explain what is happening now or in the past. But we also answer questions about the future. To **predict** is to answer a question about the future. For example, in answer to the question

When will the comet be nearest to Earth?

we expect a prediction of the form

The comet will be nearest to Earth on July 1, 2090.

Pretty clearly, being able to predict events is important in our daily lives, not to mention in science. If we couldn't predict how the frozen pizza will behave when we put it in the microwave oven—that is, if we had no way of saying whether it would cook, explode, or metamorphose into a large spider—we wouldn't plan to have pizza for dinner! Nor could rocket scientists dare to launch satellites if they couldn't predict trajectories based on physical laws and facts about rocket thrust and burn times.

As defined earlier, predictions are not explanations. Predictions are answers to which- and whether-questions about the present or future. However, they are related in the sense that if you attempt to establish or justify your prediction, you will be explaining your answer.

2   *Types of Explanation*

In the last section we defined the concept of explanation very broadly as an answer to a why-question. We want not to get clearer on some types of explanation—that is, on some types of why-question.

Consider first the question "Why did the bridge collapse when the truck drove onto it?" An answer to that question will take the form of citing certain specific initial conditions (such as the weight of the truck, the age and the type of materials used in the construction of the bridge, the weather conditions at the time, and so on) together with the relevant causal laws of engineering (about how stress can deform metal and so on), from which the fact that the bridge collapsed when it did could be established. This pattern of explanation crucially involves the citing of deterministic causal generalizations as part of the answer, and it is very common in the physical sciences and engineering. We call this accordingly **deterministically causal** explanation.

Consider next the question "Why did Smith get the flu?" An answer to that question will take the form of citing certain initial conditions (such as the fact that Smith had not had his flu shot, that his wife and children had earlier had the flu, and so on) together with statistical claims about some group or groups (such as the claim that the probability is high that a person unimmunized against the flu living in close proximity with people who have the flu will him- or herself contract the disease). This pattern of explanation crucially involves the citing of statistically causal generalizations as part of the answer, and it is very common in medical science. We call this accordingly **statistically causal** explanation.

Consider now a third question: "Why did Kim major in computer science?" An answer to that question will take the form of enumerating the reasons, goals, or purposes Kim had in mind for choosing that major, together with Kim's belief about the usefulness of majoring in computer science in achieving those goals. Here, the explanandum is the choice or action taken; the explanans, the reasons for the choice and the agent's beliefs about the relation between the choice and the goals. This pattern of explanation, so common in social science and elsewhere, we will call **intentional** explanation.

Consider now a fourth question: "Why do mammals have lungs?" An answer to that question will take the form of indicating the function or role that lungs have or play in the mammalian body. This pattern of explanation, so common in biology and elsewhere, we will call **functional** explanation. In functional explanation, the explanandum is the presence of some feature or component of an organism, structure, or system, and the explanans is a statement about its role in that system or structure.

Intentional and functional explanations are similar in appealing to purposes or goals. For that reason they are often lumped together under the labels "purposive" or "teleological." We ought to be clear on the difference, however. An intentional explanation makes reference to *mental* purposes (intentions), whereas functional explanations make reference to *nonmental* purposes.

Finally, consider the question "Why did civil war erupt in the United States in 1861?" An answer will involve sketching out how the outbreak of the Civil War evolved from prior conditions. This pattern of explanation, so common in history, biology, and elsewhere, we will call **historical** explanation. In historical explanation, the explanandum is a later state of a system, and the explanans consists of statements about the prior events or state of that system, together with general assumptions about how the state of that type of system developed or evolved over time.

Exercise 15.2

For each of the question-and-answer sets here, determine whether the proposed explanation is deterministically causal, statistically causal, intentional, functional, or historical.

1. QUESTION: Why do ducks have webbed feet?
   ANSWER: It enables them to swim faster.
2. QUESTION: Why did that large earthquake in Turkey occur?
   ANSWER: Turkey is on a line under which the large plates that form the land masses rub up against each other, and these plates slipped.
3. QUESTION: Why did Senator Smith suddenly change his mind on the labor bill before Congress?
   ANSWER: The NEA and the AFL-CIO, both large labor unions, threatened to support Smith's opponent in the upcoming election unless he changed his position on that bill.

4. QUESTION: Why do birds have feathers?
    ANSWER: Birds evolved from flying dinosaurs, and along the way scales developed on the dinosaurs, which mutated into feathers.
5. QUESTION: Why did Jones develop heart disease?
    ANSWER: Because he smoked, drank heavily, ate a high-fat diet, and didn't exercise regularly, and those are proven risk factors in heart disease.
6. QUESTION: Why did Senator Smith vote for more gun control?
    ANSWER: Her daughter was killed by an attacker with a handgun.
7. QUESTION: Why did that comet smash into Mars?
    ANSWER: The trajectory of the comet came within the gravitational pull of the planet.
8. QUESTION: Why did the American Civil War occur?
    ANSWER: The power sectors in the southern economy wanted to maintain the institution of slavery, but the North was growing in power, and northerners opposed slavery.
9. QUESTION: Why do societies develop religions?
    ANSWER: Religion serves as a vehicle for inculcating moral habits necessary for the stability of a society.
10. QUESTION: Why did Oedipus kill his father?
    ANSWER: Unconsciously, he desired to replace his father so he could sleep with his mother.

3   *A Closer Look at Causal Explanations*

Given their extraordinary importance in physical science, we should look at deterministic and statistical explanations more closely.

Consider a typical elementary explanation from a beginning physics class. We want to explain why a solid iron ball released from a height of sixteen feet hits the ground after one second. To do this, we employ a law of physics: any object released near the Earth in a vacuum will fall a distance in feet equal to sixteen times the time of fall (in seconds) squared. We apply this law to the initial conditions: The object dropped is an iron ball, so its density is much higher than that of air, so we can ignore the fact that we are conducting the experiment in air (rather than a vacuum). The height from which it is dropped is sixteen feet. We apply the equation

$$h = 16t^2$$

plugging in $h = 16$ to find that $t^2 = 1$, or $t = 1$ second—which was the fact to be explained.

In deterministic causal explanations, then, the answer involves stating a deterministic causal law or laws and initial conditions, which, against the background of accepted facts, establish the explanandum. It is worth emphasizing the importance of the role of background facts here. This point was emphasized very well by the physicist Pierre Duhem (1954) around the turn of the century, explaining that the soundness of any such explanation depends on **auxiliary** or **background hypotheses.** In our simple example, we assume for one thing that iron has a far greater density than air, so that the air can be dismissed as a "near vacuum." We also assume that sixteen feet above the ground in the area in which we are conducting the experiment counts as "near" enough to the surface of the Earth (which it wouldn't be if we were, say, floating in a space station high above the Earth).

The deterministic causal generalizations used in deterministic causal explanations are established by the methods we discussed in Chapter 14.

Let us turn next to statistical causal explanations. We gave as an example earlier of some guy Smith who probably got the flu because he had not gotten a flu shot and was in proximity to his wife and kids. Here, the answer cites initial conditions and works against a background statistical causal generalization that exposure to flu in the absence of the relevant immunization is a cause of flu in populations.

Again, the statistical causal generalizations utilized in statistical causal explanations are established by the methods discussed in the last chapter.

4   *Rules for Forming Hypotheses*

We have a better grasp of the terms used in the statement of the IBE; now we need to spell out the pattern of inference more carefully. As it stands, we understand the IBE

1. Fact *F* is true.
2. Hypothesis *H* is the best explanation for *F.*
∴   *H* is probable.

to mean

1. we believe some fact or facts about *F* to be true, which we desire to explain. If the facts are *not* true, this calls for debunking, not explaining;
2. we have some candidate hypothesis *H* that explains *F* better than any other hypothesis;
3. to even be considered as a candidate hypothesis, by the very meaning of the word *hypothesis, H* together with relevant background information must establish the facts *F* to be explained.

Now, the next issue is, Where does the hypothesis come from? This is a matter of considerable debate among cognitive scientists and philosophers of science. I will adopt the model elaborated by Peter Lipton (1993, especially Chapter 4) in his book *Inference to the Best Explanation.* Under this view, the IBE starts with a set of plausible candidate hypotheses, and then selects the best one. A further restriction on the IBE is suggested by Erwin (1996: 70). We need to have some reason to believe that the set of proposed explanations contains the correct one. That is, we formulate or devise possible hypotheses and try to do so exhaustively, discarding immediately those that are implausible in the context of our background beliefs. Then, of those that remain, the plausible ones, we pick the best. This may involve conducting further tests.

Let's take a simple example. Suppose you come out in the morning, go to your car, and notice cat prints on the hood. What is the best explanation for those prints? You can immediately discount such "hypotheses" as these: An earthquake occurred in China, some dogs in Chile burst into flames spontaneously, or the prime minister of Britain has a cold. You can do this because none of those "hypotheses" even remotely explains the prints—they are not even relevant so are not even genuine hypotheses. Instead, you develop a list of genuine candidates, such as a cat walked on the hood of my car; a mischievous child with a fake cat paw made prints on my car; and a passing car hit a cat, whose body flipped through the air and impacted my car's hood, feet first. We then choose the best—in this case, absent knowledge that there is a young prankster or dead cat nearby, the first hypothesis.

Let us then try to formulate a few very rough rules regarding hypothesis generation.

Rule 1: To even count as a candidate hypothesis, any hypothesis must at least account for the facts to be explained. By the very nature of a hypothesis, it needs to explain the facts—it must be relevant to what it is meant to explain. Again, that means that the hypothesis, together with the background material, entails or provides inductive support for the facts.

Rule 2: The more plausible hypotheses formed to examine, the better. Faced with a fact to be explained, you should try to formulate as many reasonable or plausible (as opposed to merely possible) hypotheses as you practically can. There are good logical as well as psychological reasons for this practice. Logically, the IBE sanctions inference to the *best* explanation, which means that we need to examine several hypotheses to compare their merits to the point where you have good reason to think that the correct one is among those you have considered. Psychologically, we need to avoid the human tendency to entrench; that is, once a provisional hypothesis is selected we have a tendency to commit to that hypothesis and "quit there." Instead we need to generate several hypotheses, to see where each leads, to learn new facts through the testing process.

Of course, the number of hypotheses, even plausible ones, that explain a phenomenon is in principle limitless. We must limit ourselves to the plausible ones, not the far-fetched ones.

Rule 3: The hypotheses formed should be testable. We might view this rule as just a gloss on rule one, but it is important to dwell on testability for a moment. Crucial to critical thinking is being open to counterevidence. If you formulate hypotheses that are so vague, ambiguous, loaded, or hedged that they can't be tested, you defeat critical thought. For example, to hypothesize that invisible fairies tipped over your trash cans is to hypothesize that which cannot be tested.

The German psychologist Dietrich Dorner has studied problem solving among adults (for a review of his work, read his book *The Logic of Failure: Why Things Go Wrong and What We Can Do to Make Them Right* [1966]). He finds that the willingness to test hypotheses is the big difference between successful ("good") participants in problem-solving experiments and unsuccessful ("bad") participants. Dorner (1996: 24) notes, "The good participants differed from the bad in how often they tested their hypotheses. The bad participants failed to do this. For them, to propose a hypothesis was to understand reality; testing that hypothesis was unnecessary. Instead of generating hypotheses, they generated 'truths.'"

Rule 4: Unpleasant or unsettling hypotheses should be formulated along with the others. We have a psychological tendency to avoid formulating hypotheses that are unpopular, unpleasant, unsettling, or disturbing. A person will pass blood in his or her urine and will often not want to consider the hypothesis that he or she has bladder cancer. And scientists throughout history have had to struggle to get unpopular hypotheses tested. So the critical thinker makes an extra effort to formulate unpleasant hypotheses.

You might view rule 4 as being part of rule 2, but it is worth separate mention.

5   *Rules for Assessing Hypotheses*

A number of factors go into judging one hypothesis better than another. Without pretending our list is complete, the virtues of hypotheses are empirical adequacy, generality, fruitfulness, conservatism, simplicity, and accuracy. Since these are all matters of degree—as usual with inductive inference—we will state these as rules. We assume that we are faced with competing hypotheses, each of which, if true, would explain a specific phenomenon.

Rule 1: All things being equal, the more tests a hypothesis has survived, the more probable it is. A hypothesis that has been experimentally tested over and over is more likely than one that has only been tested a few times. We say of such a hypothesis that it is very **empirically adequate.** You might think that this rule is false in such cases where a researcher conducts the same experiment over and over again. But even in such cases, things change every time the experiment is run (the position of the moon, the time of day, the outside temperature, and so on), so the fact that the hypothesis being tested continues to pass muster tells us something. Of course, it is much better if we vary the conditions of the test.

Rule 2: All things being equal, the wider the scope of the hypothesis, the more probable it is. Scope is a measure of how much a hypothesis explains. One theory has wider scope (also called "greater generality") than another if it explains more classes or kinds of facts, facts taken from different domains. For example, a doctor is investigating an outbreak of illness in her town. The doctor also hears that a large number of rodents are dying. She considers two hypotheses:

> H_1: The people all got sick eating bad food at the local restaurant.
> H_2: The people and rodents have all been infected by a microbe.

H_2 is at least initially more plausible, because it explains both the people's and the rodents' disease.

Two cautionary notes. First, a hypothesis with wider scope must still relevantly explain the facts in the different areas. Second, trade-offs can be involved in using rules 1 and 2: A broad hypothesis may explain facts from different areas but may do so only weakly, whereas a more narrow hypothesis may have been tested more thoroughly in its narrow domain. Empirical adequacy typically trumps generality.

Rule 3: All things being equal, the more compatible a hypothesis is with other well-established hypotheses, the more probable it is. Remember that consistency is one of the qualities we desire in our worldviews. We want our hypotheses to be consisted with our other beliefs, especially when those other beliefs or hypotheses are well established. Conversely, to the extent a hypothesis conflicts with well-established theory that fact counts as initial evidence against it. For example, suppose your guests become ill shortly after eating your world-class BBQ chicken. One hypothesis is that they got food poisoning from bacteria on the chicken (you should have cooked the chicken longer!). Another hypothesis is that the chicken you cooked in fact became highly radioactive from the heat of the grill. But the latter hypothesis conflicts with what we know about radioactivity.

Again, there are trade-offs. The history of science is full of scientific revolutions, in which a new theory conflicted with existing theories but eventually won out because of its other virtues, most especially empirical adequacy.

Rule 4: All things, being equal, the more fruitful a hypothesis is, the more probable it is. A hypothesis is **fruitful** if it predicts and explains new facts. Fruitfulness differs from generality and scope in that generality and scope deal with antecedently known or believed facts. For example, suppose two hypotheses both explain why large numbers of people became ill this year. But suppose one hypothesis predicts that next year the same number of people will become ill again with the same symptoms, while the other hypothesis does not. Suppose further that a year rolls by and, sure enough, the same number of people become sick with the same symptoms. Clearly, the hypothesis that predicted the new outbreak is (all things being equal) more probable than the one that didn't.

Rule 5: All things being equal, the simpler a hypothesis is, the more probable it is. A hypothesis is **simpler** than another if it references fewer things or has fewer terms. Again, although spelling that out is no easy matter, the concept is intuitively easy to grasp. For example, faced with a patient who has fever, chills, sore throat, and sniffles, it would be simple for the doctor to hypothesize that the patient has been infected by one virus rather than a combination of two viruses at once.

Rule 6: All things being equal, the more accurate a hypothesis is, the more probable it is. Suppose we are trying to explain an outbreak of a disease afflicting 10 percent of the population. Suppose one hypothesis entails that somewhere between 0 and 30 percent of the population will get the disease, whereas a second hypothesis entails that between 8 and 12 percent of the population will get the disease. The second hypothesis more accurately entails the explicandum and so is more likely—again, all things being equal.

It is important to reiterate that in evaluating hypotheses, things are seldom all equal. That is, in comparing two candidate hypotheses, you might find, for example, that the first is simpler but the second has wider scope or that the first is more accurate but the second is more general. In such cases, reasonable people will differ in which hypothesis to adopt, and only further new research can determine who was correct.

Exercise 15.5

Each of the following problems presents a fact and a pair of candidate hypotheses. Based on the six criteria listed earlier, choose the more plausible one. Justify your choice.

1. *Fact:* You go to your parked car after spending the day shopping and find the side window smashed in.
   Hypothesis 1: A large bird hit the window.
   Hypothesis 2: A thief smashed in the window.
2. *Fact:* Your pet hamster, Napoleon, has died.
   Hypothesis 1: Napoleon died from a disease.
   Hypothesis 2: Napoleon died from poison gas.

3. *Fact:* You hear noises outside during the night, including rustling about, growling, and trash cans clanging. You live in an area where bears are common.
   Hypothesis 1: A bear has been going through your trash.
   Hypothesis 2: Your neighbor has been going through your trash.
4. *Fact:* You see a squirrel disappear behind a tree.
   Hypothesis 1: The squirrel has entered a time/space warp and gone to a remote part of the universe.
   Hypothesis 2: The squirrel has hidden in a hole or in some rocks.
5. *Fact:* You have been out partying for ten nights in a row. You feel completely exhausted.
   Hypothesis 1: You are tired from the partying.
   Hypothesis 2: You have suddenly developed leukemia.

InfoTrac College Edition

You can locate InfoTrac College Edition articles about this chapter by accessing the InfoTrac College Edition Web site (www.infotrac-college.com/wadsworth/). Using the InfoTrac College Edition subject guide, enter the search terms relevant to this chapter, and then read abstracts for relevant articles.

Part Three

Chapter 16

Applications of Critical Thinking: Decisions in a Democratic Market Economy

Decision Making: A General Model

---

1 Decisions, Decisions

Our lives are full of decisions: where to eat, what car to buy, what movie to see, what profession to choose, and so on. If critical thinking is useful anywhere, it should be useful in decision making. And it is.

Roughly speaking, decision making (choosing) involves selecting a course of action from a group of alternatives based on criteria of choice (goals, considerations, objectives). For example, choosing a profession involves selecting from the alternatives in your society (education, law, medicine, entertainment, business, and so on) the basis of your goal or goals (financial reward, prestige, ease of work, and so on).

All decision making takes place in a context, a real-world environment involving facts about which alternatives are really available, what costs and benefits pertain to each alternative, and what chances of success apply to each alternative. To revert to our earlier example of deciding what profession to enter, my social circumstances dictate the alternatives. I can't very well choose engineering in a society without engineers. More subtly, my context affects the chance of success for each alternative. Genetically, if I am bereft of musical ability, the option of being a concert violinist, while theoretically open to me, is practically closed. The chances of a person of no musical ability becoming a concert violinist are virtually zero. Socially, if I am born into a group forbidden to enter a particular profession, and I cannot leave or alter that society, again, my chances of successfully entering that profession are low. Economically, if I am born into poor surroundings, my chances of success in entering a profession may be inhibited. For instance, your ability to become a high-achieving theoretical physicist depends in part on whether your talents are spotted early and your schooling is intense and well directed. Being so poor that you never get to attend school makes it tough, though not impossible, to become a physicist.

By "context," I mean to include social factors and genetic factors. But in decision making, character enters in as well. The world is full of people who, by dint of character, have overcome social and genetic limitations to succeed in what they choose to do in life. William Faraday, despite poverty and lack of formal education, became one of the greatest

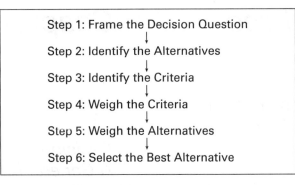

Figure 16.1   *Decision cycle*

theoretical physicists ever to have lived. Art Tatum, despite early blindness, became a pre-eminent jazz pianist. Ramanujan, despite poverty and social discrimination, became a great mathematician. Rick Dempsey became a fine football player despite having a disability (his foot was burnt half off in childhood). Character—effort, will, desire, perseverance, hustle—can change the odds dramatically for the better. Lack of character, sadly, can change the odds for the worse.

We will view logical decision making as following a general model, which we will call the **decision cycle,** laid out in Figure 16.1 (this model is derived from that found in Halpern 1989: Chapter 8). Let us go through each step of the cycle, discussing what thinking is reasonable and what is fallacious in each.

2   *Framing the Decision Question*

The first important step in effective decision making is to get clear on what your decision really is. Consider purchasing a house. To frame the question "Which house should I buy?" is to set yourself up for trouble. You need to be clear on the time frame: Is this house supposed to be the house you spend the rest of your life in? Or are you looking for a place for the next few years only (because, say, you anticipate having to move when you move up in your career, or because you plan to marry and have children in a few years)? Again, consider the question of what car you are going to buy. If you phrase the question "What car would project the best image of me?" you will bias the choice toward the flashy cars. The initial decision question biases the decision in the direction of the sexiness of the car, as opposed to its practicality.

You should recall from earlier chapters the concept of a fallacy. We have used the term broadly to mean any mistake in reasoning. So we have discussed fallacies of questions, fallacies of language, and fallacies of argumentation. It should be no surprise, then, that a number of fallacies arise in decision making as well. We have just met one: In framing the decision question, we need to avoid the **fallacy of loaded question**—building in presuppositions that bias your decision making in the direction of some choices rather than others.

Exercise 16.2

For each of the following decisions, select the best-framed question. Justify your answer.

1. Deciding what to do after college:
    a. What should I do that will lead to the best career?
    b. What should I do that will lead to earning a good living?
    c. What should I do that will make me feel less lonely now?
    d. What job should I take?
2. Deciding where to shop for school clothes:
    a. What mall should we go to?
    b. Which discount store should we go to?
    c. Which store should we go to?
3. Deciding what to do over the weekend.
    a. Which book should I read?
    b. Which party should I attend?
    c. What should I watch on TV?
    d. What recreational activities should I pursue?
    e. What activities should I pursue?

3   *Identifying the Alternatives*

Once you have framed the decision question, the next step in rational decision making is to identify your alternatives, your options or choices.

The context of the decision and your character determine the real alternatives. If you are a college student, deciding what to major in, your alternatives are set by the college catalog—unless you are free to transfer elsewhere, or your college allows you to "design" your own major. If you come to a fork in the road, you must either drive left or right, unless you have an off-road vehicle or a helicopter. Be clear: In listing the alternatives open to you in the context of a decision, you should consider all *relevant* possible options. And knowing which options are "viable" (that is, realistically available) is again a matter of judgment.

When you have overlooked options that are realistically open to you, we say that you have committed the **fallacy of false dilemma.** For instance, if you reasoned as follows (having just graduated high school):

> I can get a job or go to college. But I really need money now, so I guess I'll get a job.

you would be setting yourself a false dilemma. You have other choices: You could work part-time and go to college part-time; you could join the army; or you could try to get a scholarship.

False dilemmas are found in public life as well as our own private lives. We occasionally hear such false dilemmas as

> America—love it or leave it!
> Should we raise taxes and increase services, or cut taxes and slash services?

Exercise 16.3A

List your options for each of the following (consult the phone book, newspaper, or other sources).

1. Choosing a movie for tonight (without renting a video)
2. Choosing a Chinese restaurant within a five-minute drive of where you live
3. Choosing a four-wheel drive vehicle
4. Choosing a college in your home town
5. Choosing a major at your college

Exercise 16.3B

The following are false dilemmas. Explain how.

1. You should believe in God. If God doesn't exist, all you've lost is a few Sundays, but if God does exist, then you've gained eternal bliss.
2. You shouldn't go to college. After all, either you know what will be taught or you don't. If you know what will be taught, then you don't need to go. And if you don't know what will be taught, you won't know what to take.
3. Either we start publicly funding elections, or we allow politicians to get unlimited amounts of money from anybody or anything. But unlimited, unregulated money would lead to unlimited corruption. So we need to fund elections publicly.
4. Either we routinely enforce the death penalty, or else we let murderers spend a few years in jail and then just parole them. Do you want murderers surrounding your family? No? Then support the death penalty!
5. Either we pass an amendment outlawing abortion, or we allow unrestricted abortion on demand.
6. I read your editorial about how college students didn't know who Stalin was, what is the Warsaw Pact, etc. Well, when I was in high school I knew what the NATO and Warsaw Pacts were; I knew who Stalin, Churchill, DeGaulle, and Roosevelt were. I knew at least 85 percent of the world's capitals, and if I was given a blank map of the United States or world, I could fill in all the states and most of the world's countries. I enjoyed and was interested in it.

    But, unfortunately, I knew very little about math and other subjects. I am 29 years old and have held only menial jobs and am unemployed today. The knowledge I had one can't use. Math, computers, science you can use to become a success. Geography, history, etc., are useless. I found out the hard way.
7. As the mother of a freshman at Henning High School, my stomach turns every morning when I take him to school and see the demonstration by the "teachers." Whatever happened to the dedicated teacher who was only interested in educating and forming

the minds of young people? Does such a creature exist anymore, or are they all in the teaching profession for money?

4   *Identifying the Criteria*

The next step in rational choice is to get clear on the goals or criteria of choice. The goals in a situation may involve general considerations such as income, social esteem, personal fulfillment, or happiness. Or they may be specific, such as achieving a high grade point average, finding the lowest price, or locating the closest theater.

Several points need to be made here. First, it is a matter of considerable dispute among moral philosophers, economists, political scientists, and psychologists whether all goals ultimately can be defined by one basic goal (say, pleasure) or can be measured by one standard (say, money). For example, the eminent nineteenth-century moral philosopher Jeremy Bentham held that the value of all activities was simply the pleasure they produce, and he developed a "hedonic calculus" to balance pleasures and pains in choosing activities. Again, many economists argue that, in balancing goals at tension, we can always use money to measure our desire for various outcomes; thus, we are able to quantify subgoals and determine balance.

Clearly, it is often possible to measure outcomes on a single scale, and in what follows we will assume that we can state our goals so that we can do so. Whether it is always possible to do so we will leave an open question.

Second, it is important to realize that the criteria governing a decision are often "at tension," often conflict. Choices almost always involve trade-offs, and the clear thinker is aware of those trade-offs.

Third, it is extremely important to list as one consideration your chances of success. The **fallacy of wishful thinking** occurs when you greatly overestimate your chances of success in an option. For example, people often engage in wishful thinking when they buy lottery tickets. They greatly overestimate their chances of winning—which, of course, the companies running the lotteries count on!

Exercise 16.4

For each of the following choices, identify the criteria of choice involved. If there is more than one subgoal, explain how they conflict.

Example: Choosing a restaurant

Goals involved: Low cost; extensive menu; close location; high-quality food. Conflicts possible: Cost may be higher for higher-quality food; cheapest restaurants may be the farthest away.

1. Choosing a car
2. Choosing a stereo system
3. Choosing a treatment for cancer
4. Choosing a company for a contract to manufacture a new type of rifle
5. Choosing a congressperson

5   *Weighing the Criteria and Alternatives*

The different criteria in a given decision have to be weighed against each other. You not only have to figure out what criteria are going to govern your choice but also how these criteria rank against each other. How much weight do you attach to income, as opposed to the desire to help others or the desire to spend a lot of time with your family?

Finally, for each criterion, you need to weigh the alternatives. For example, suppose we are deciding which new car to buy. One criterion is likely to be cost, and we can rank the cars we are considering accordingly as very expensive, expensive, moderately priced, and inexpensive.

Another phrase for weighing the alternatives is "assigning the costs and benefits." Costs and benefits should be calculated over the long run. We need to avoid the fallacy of **short-term thinking** and the desire for "immediate gratification."

6   *Putting It All Together: Selecting the Best Option*

We can finish the decision cycle by calculating (in a crude way) the best decision. We do this by systematically filling out a decision table, whose general structure is given in Table 16.1.

Let's work through a simple example. Suppose you are trying to decide which restaurant to go to tonight. First, list your alternatives—what restaurants are there reasonably open to you? Let's imagine there are only five: Luigi's, Charlie's Hash House, the Chinese Panda Restaurant, McDonald's, and Chateau LeDough. Put them on top of the table:

	Charlie's	Chinese		Chateau
Luigi's	Hash House	Panda	McDonald's	LeDough

Next, what criteria govern your choice? Cost, of course. Closeness is another—all things being equal, you don't want to drive too far. Third, quality of food needs to be considered. Also, there is "ambiance"—that is, how enjoyable the restaurant is to be in. Oh, and of course there is service—you don't want to be yelled at by the waiters! Put these on the side of the table (Table 16.2).

Next, you need to weigh the criteria. Here tastes vary, and also cases vary: usually ambiance may not be important to you, but it might be if you are on a romantic date. Let's use a five-point scale for each factor: 5 indicates that the criterion is very important; 4 that it is important; 3 that it is less so; 2 that it is only moderately important; 1 that the crite-

---

TABLE 16.1   Alternatives

Criteria	Weights of Criteria	Weights of Alternatives
Overall scores		

TABLE 16.2	Selecting a Restaurant					
Criteria		Luigi's	Charlie's Hash House	Chinese Panda	McDonald's	Chateau LeDough
Cost						
Closeness						
Quality						
Ambiance						
Service						

TABLE 16.3	Weighing the Criteria					
Criteria	Weight	Luigi's	Charlie's Hash House	Chinese Panda	McDonald's	Chateau LeDough
Cost	5					
Closeness	4					
Quality	4					
Ambiance	1					
Service	2					

rion is of slight importance. In our example, let us suppose that tonight's dinner is not a special occasion, just a convenient dinner out, and that you are on a tight budget. In such a case, cost would be highly important, maybe a 5. Closeness and quality of food are moderately important, maybe 4 each. Ambiance is of virtually no importance—just a 1— and service is of not much more importance—say, a 2. We fill in the values in Table 16.3.

Now, you need to determine how well or poorly each alternative fits the criteria. We can weigh the alternatives on a slightly different scale +2, +1, 0, −1, −2, where +2 means the alternative satisfies the criterion well, +1 means the alternative satisfies it moderately well, 0 is neutral, −1 means the alternative moderately fails the criterion, and −2 means it strongly fails the criterion.

Let's go over the restaurants. Luigi's is a nearby mom-and-pop pizzeria, with cheap, good food. No ambiance, and the service is mediocre. So we score Luigi's a +1 on cost, +1 on quality, +2 on closeness, 0 on ambiance, and a −1 on service. Charlie's is a nearby coffee shop, with bad food, but reasonable prices. The service is okay, but it is a dive. So we score Charlie's a +1 on cost, −2 on quality, a +2 on closeness, −2 on ambiance, and +1 on service.

Next we look at the Chinese Panda and McDonald's. Both are a fair distance away. The Chinese Panda is moderately priced with great food, a quiet atmosphere, and friendly service. So we score the Chinese Panda +1 on price, 0 on closeness, +2 on quality, +1 on ambiance,

TABLE 16.4   Scoring the Criteria

Criteria	Weight	Luigi's	Charlie's Hash House	Chinese Panda	McDonald's	Chateau LeDough
Cost	5	+1	+1	+1	+2	−2
Closeness	4	+2	+2	0	0	−2
Quality	4	+1	−2	+2	0	+2
Ambiance	1	0	−2	+1	−2	+2
Service	2	−1	+1	+1	−2	+2

and +1 on service. The McDonald's is very inexpensive, the food so-so, the service minimal (you get your own food), and it has very sparse surroundings. So we score the McDonald's +2 on price, 0 on closeness, 0 on quality, −2 on service, and −2 on ambiance.

Finally, there is Chateau LeDough. This is a very fancy French restaurant all the way across town. The food is incredible but insanely high priced. The service is tremendous—the waiters and waitresses absolutely jump up if a customer even arches an eyebrow. And the ambiance is extraordinarily romantic. So we score Chateau LeDough −2 on price, −2 on closeness, +2 on quality, +2 on ambiance, and +2 on service. In Table 16.4, we have entered the scores.

Finally, we compute the overall scores. We do this by multiplying the weight by the individual scores and adding them.

> Luigi's: $5 + 8 + 4 + 0 - 2 = 15$
> Charlie's: $5 + 8 - 8 - 2 + 2 = 5$
> Chinese Panda: $5 + 0 + 8 + 1 + 2 = 16$
> McDonald's: $10 + 0 + 0 - 2 - 4 = 4$
> Chateau LeDough: $-10 - 8 + 8 + 2 + 4 = -4$

Our rough calculation indicates that the Chinese Panda is the best choice, with Luigi's a close runner-up.

Keep in mind that these calculations are very inexact and of course dependent on the assignment of values to the various alternatives. In the imaginary scenario we discussed earlier, you were choosing a restaurant for an ordinary night's dinner; thus, your decision was dominated by cost, quality, and closeness. But now imagine that tonight you're choosing a restaurant to which to take a very important date—in fact, the date of your life. You want this person to experience dining at its finest, and price is no object. You don't care how far the drive is because you enjoy his or her company.

In this scenario, the weights would change. Cost and closeness might be weighted 1 or even 0, while quality, ambiance, and service all are now weighted 5. Let's redo the calculations with these new weights (weighting cost and closeness as 1):

> Luigi's: $1 + 2 + 5 + 0 - 5 = 3$
> Charlie's: $1 + 2 - 10 - 10 + 5 = -12$
> Chinese Panda: $1 + 0 + 8 + 5 + 5 = 19$

McDonald's: $2 + 0 + 0 - 10 - 10 = -18$
Chateau LeDough: $-2 - 2 + 10 + 10 + 10 = 26$

Under this new scenario, Chateau LeDough is the way to go.

7   *Common Psychological Pitfalls*

One would like to think that human beings reason more or less rationally in most situations, at least those of an economic nature. But recent work by cognitive psychologists and economists has cast doubt on that belief. I don't wish to devote extensive space to review the myriad ways in which people act irrationally even in purely economic contexts, but a brief review is in order. For a fuller review, I recommend the survey article "Rethinking Thinking," in *The Economist* (1999).

To begin with, people tend to be inordinately influenced by the fear of *regret*—they will pass up large benefits if they think there is even a small chance of feeling they have failed. Moreover, people have a *status quo bias:* they will risk more to keep something they have than they would to get it in the first place. Third, people are typically *overconfident;* that is, they routinely overestimate their chances of success.

People also tend to *anchor* their beliefs to outside suggestion; that is, they tend to be overly influenced by others, even when they know that those other people are no better informed about the matter at hand. People tend to *compartmentalize:* They divide aspects of their lives into compartments and then make decisions about things in one compartment without taking into account the implications for things in another compartment.

People often engage in *magical thinking,* too: They will often believe that their actions are caused by something that in fact has nothing to do with them. For example, a person who picks a stock more or less by guessing, who then sees the stock rise, will often conclude that his or her choice was due to great skill as an investor.

Moreover, people tend to be *loss-averse:* They attach more weight to losing something than to gaining it. For example, taxi drivers have been shown to follow the practice of setting a daily target income, and quitting for the day when they hit that goal. This results in them quitting early on busy days (when fares are easier to get) and working longer on slow days. Of course, they would work fewer hours for the same or even more money if they put in fuller shifts on the busy days and shorter shifts on the slow days. But they are afraid of not making their quota on the slow days.

Finally, people often make decisions out of *spite.* They will often take a worse deal for themselves in order to see others get a bad deal as well.

InfoTrac College Edition

You can locate InfoTrac College Edition articles about this chapter by accessing the InfoTrac College Edition Web site (www.infotrac-college.com/wadsworth/). Using the InfoTrac College Edition subject guide, enter the search terms relevant to this chapter, and then read abstracts for relevant articles.

Chapter 17

Application I: Advertising and Consumer Choice

---

1   *The Pervasiveness of Consumer Choice*

We live in a consumer economy. Our demands for goods and services drive the economy and set prices. We spend a great deal of time working throughout our lives to get the money to buy things because we think them either necessary for survival or (in our wealthy society) useful in achieving happiness. For example, in deciding to buy a car, we aim to solve our basic need for transportation, but also—and often more importantly—we believe that by buying an expensive car we will become admired and respected and (again we believe) that doing so will make us happier.

Now, purely rational consumer choice would be simply a case of the decision cycle discussed in Chapter 16. We would begin with the goal of purchasing something—say, a widget. We would examine each brand of widget, determining its price and qualities (both positive and negative). We would then try to select the one with the most desirable characteristics (quality of construction, warranty, energy efficiency, and the like) and the least undesirable characteristics (side effects, energy inefficiency, and so forth) for the best price. In a phrase, we would try to get the most widget for the buck.

However, advertising and other sales tactics distort rational consumer choice at all points in the decision cycle. The advertiser (and the salesperson) are in what is called an **adversary position** with respect to the consumer. As a matter of economic reality, the advertiser/salesperson is going to put forward the best case to convince you the consumer to buy. So it would be useful review some of the ways in which advertising and other sales tactics can defeat critical thinking in purchasing. We will focus on two major areas: the role of advertising in manipulating demand (that is, deforming the original choice to purchase) and the role of advertising in misinforming the buyer regarding costs and benefits of the product or service. Before we do, let's first look at the psychological mechanisms that salespeople and marketers exploit to move their products.

2   *Psychological Mechanisms Exploited by Sales Agents*

In this section, I am going to rely heavily on the work of the psychologist Robert Cialdini, who has studied how compliance specialists get us to do what they want (see especially

Cialdini 1993). By **compliance specialist,** we mean a person who gets paid to make people comply with the wishes of the person who pays him or her. I divide compliance specialists into two broad groups: sales agents and political agents. **Sales agents** include salespeople, advertisers, marketing executives, telemarketers, and con artists. **Political agents** include political handlers, publicity agents, captive pollsters, spokesmen, and so forth. These categories are not mutual exclusive: Politicians often employ the same ad agencies as do commercial companies. In this chapter we will focus on the tactics of sales agents, leaving it for the next chapter to examine political operatives.

Psychologists have studied consumer behavior scientifically, often in the employ of marketing agencies. Cialdini's own research has included "participant observer" work, in which he has worked as a trainer alongside skilled sales agents to observe just how it is that they are able to do their craft so well.

Let's begin by talking about what the term *psychological mechanism* means. A **psychological mechanism** (also called a *fixed-action pattern*) is a sequence of behaviors that occur in virtually the same fashion and in the same order whenever a specific feature (the "trigger feature") of the environment is encountered. Cialdini's favorite example is the mothering behavior of mother turkeys (warming, cleaning, and huddling chicks beneath them). This behavior is triggered by a specific "cheep-cheep" noise: Whenever the mother turkey hears that noise, even if from a tape recorder attached to a stuffed skunk (a natural enemy of the turkey), she will exhibit that behavior—mother the skunk!

All animals, including people, have psychological mechanisms, and for good reason. These patterns of behavior typically work well in the animal's natural environment—in behavioral terms, they have survival value. But because they are automatic behaviors. the animal can be "tricked" by researchers into exhibiting that behavior in situations that are not advantageous to the animal. Well, when it is done by a scientist studying animal behavior, even though the animal is tricked, it isn't harmed and it is done for a noble cause (the advancement of science). However, sometimes an animal gets preyed upon by "mimics"—other animals who trigger automatic responses to the detriment of the animal. For example, females of one firefly species have learned to mimic the mating signals of another species, luring males of that species to their deaths. And when humans trick other humans, it is much more often to prey on them than to study them.

Let's review, then, some of the most common psychological mechanisms (discussed in detail in Cialdini) that can be exploited by sales agents.

1. **Contrast:** People tend to judge things in contrast. If two things are presented one after another, and they are fairly different, people will judge the difference as being greater than it really is. For example, a classic experiment in psychophysics labs is to have a student put one hand in a bucket of cold water, and the other hand in a bucket of hot water, then put both hands in a bucket of lukewarm water. Invariably the student is puzzled to find that the same water feels warm to the hand that was in the cold water, and cold to the hand that was in the hot water.

2. **Reciprocity:** People tend to reciprocate—that is, return favors for favors. Thus, people who are given something tend to feel obligated to give something in return. For example, Cialdini cites the case of a professor who tried the following experiment: He sent Christmas cards to a sample of perfect strangers, and, sure enough, cards came flying back to him from those perfect strangers.

3. **Entrenchment:**[*] People tend to stay in a course of action once they have committed to it, even if the consequences are unexpectedly bad. For example, two Canadian psychologists discovered that people are more confident of their horse's chance of winning after placing a bet than they are immediately before placing it, even though the objective odds are the same.

4. **Social proof:** People tend to judge what is correct or proper by looking at what other people think is correct or proper. For example, if you are at a dinner with people you don't know well, and chicken is served, you will probably look to see whether the other guests start eating the chicken with their hands before you do so. As Cialdini notes, this is why TV sitcoms have laugh tracks: When you hear other people laughing, you feel as if you ought to laugh as well.

5. **Authority:** People tend to obey authorities. A classic experiment (conducted by the psychologist Stanley Milgram) illustrates this mechanism with hellish clarity. In his experiment, student volunteers were told that they were going to participate in a study about how punishment affects learning. The student volunteer would have the job of administering the punishment—an electric shock—to a person sitting in a chair in a room visible to the student volunteer (the "Learner"). What the volunteers (called the "Teachers") didn't know was that the Learner, whom they assumed was just another volunteer for the experiment like themselves, was, in fact, an actor. Each volunteer Teacher was told to put a series of questions to the Learner and, every time the Learner made a mistake, administer an electric shock increasing in intensity. In actuality, the electric shock equipment was a phony—the teacher would turn a dial to a voltage level and push a button, whereupon the actor would act shocked and in pain.

   To Milgram's astonishment, the vast majority of these student "Teachers" would obey the instructions to increasingly shock the Learner, even when the Learner began to scream, demand to be let out, beg the student to stop, scream that he was having a heart attack, and finally slump in his chair, seemingly paralyzed or even dead. The student "Teachers" would often beg Milgram to let them stop, would express concern for the hapless, victimized Learner, but they would continue to obey his direction to keep increasing the shocks. And, keep in mind, these were student *volunteers* free to tell Milgram to go to hell if they wanted, with no chance of themselves being punished. This experiment gives you some insight into how governments can get ordinary citizens to cooperate in setting up concentration camps.

6. **Scarcity:** People value something more highly than they would otherwise when they perceive it as scarce—that is, of limited availability. For example, if we hear that gasoline is in short supply, we will run to the gas station immediately to fill up our tanks.

---

[*] The terms I use for several of these psychological mechanisms differ in some cases from Cialdini's. Also, I have added a couple of mechanisms to the list.

7. **Sympathy:** People tend to want to help others in need (absent some distrust or dislike of those in need). For example, shown a picture of a totally unknown person being attacked by wild animals, we will find ourselves hoping he or she escapes.

8. **Greed:** People tend always to desire more than they possess, even if what they have is adequate for a good life. There is a famous scene in a classic movie, *Key Largo,* in which a criminal, "Rocco," is asked what he wants in life. His reply: "*More!*" That is a succinct expression of the mechanism of greed.

9. **Association:** When two things occur together, people tend to associate them, even if there is no real connection. For example, the eminent Russian physiologist and psychologist Ivan Pavlov conducted a now-famous experiment with dogs. He would ring a bell before feeding them. Very rapidly, the dogs associated food with the bell, so that when he merely rang the bell (with no food around), the dogs would salivate.

    We should distinguish positive from negative association. In **positive association,** we associate one or more positive things with some other thing. In **negative association,** we associate one or more negative things with some other thing. For example, recent psychological research shows that we automatically associate favorable traits such as intelligence, honesty, and kindness with physical attractiveness. One study showed that in criminal trials, handsome men were twice as likely to avoid jail sentences as unattractive ones. This bias was shown by both male and female jurors.

10. **Salience:** People tend to notice and focus on certain features of a situation rather than others, depending on their state of mind. For example, the psychologist Elizabeth Loftus has shown that in armed robberies, people tend (not unnaturally!) to focus on the gun.

Now, these mechanisms are pervasive in people (and other animals) because they generally, in the normal environment, have survival value. With most of them that is obvious. But even a mechanism such as obedience to authority, which might seem at first to be socially dysfunctional, in fact is normally very functional. As Cialdini notes, has there ever been a successful community of anarchists?

But what is normally useful can become harmful in certain contexts. Let's see how advertisers and sales agents can use these mechanisms against us.

3   *The Role of Advertising in Manipulating Demand*

In a rational world, people would always begin by asking, "Do I need a widget at all?" before examining widgets for possible purchase. But in a consumer world, part of what advertisers and sales agents are about is creating a demand for widgets where none exists to begin with. This can be done in many ways. The most common sales pitches used to create or amplify demand are scare ads, assumptive pitches, gift pitches, ads using models and symbols, shills, sympathy pitches, golden opportunity pitches, bait and switch, testimonials, and subliminal ads. Let's examine these in turn and note the psychological mechanisms behind each.

Scare Ads

Many ads attempt to make you buy by making you afraid. I won't belabor this point, as we discussed irrelevant appeals to fear (specifically, scare tactics) in Chapter 8. Suffice it to say that such ads work by salience: We tend to notice first that which appears to threaten us.

Assumptive Pitches

In an **assumptive pitch,** a sales agent tries to build the choice to buy into a loaded question. Consider these examples:

1. Mr. Jason, I can see that you are impressed by this widget. Will this be cash or charge?
2. Mr. Jason, when I show you that this car is the best bargain on the lot, are you in a position to put a deposit down to hold it until you can complete the paperwork tomorrow?
3. Mr. Jason, thank you for sending a check in to us so promptly for those office supplies. I am going to release the rest of your order today.

In the first example, the salesclerk is presupposing that since I am impressed by the widget, I will automatically buy it. In the second case, the salesperson is presupposing that the car in front of me is in fact the best buy and, moreover, that I intend to buy it. In the third, the telemarketer is presupposing that the payment I just made was not for the whole order I placed but only part of it.

Entrenchment is the reason for the success of assumptive pitches. Once you start considering a loaded question, the presupposition gets psychologically entrenched in you.

Gift Pitches

In a **gift pitch,** a sales agent tries to use a prize, gift, or give-away item to sell products consumers wouldn't otherwise consider. This tactic is especially common in telemarketing (that is, telephone sales). An excellent survey of telemarketing fraud in general is Fred Schulte's (1995) book *Fleeced! Telemarketing Rip-Offs and How to Avoid Them*. He gives an example of a case in which a young college student bought overpriced and unnecessary vitamins from a telemarketer offering a prize (29):

> Ginger Ellis, then a twenty-one-year-old college student in Sacramento, California, recalled one such encounter with a friendly female telemarketer for one of the giant Las Vegas prize rooms. The caller implied Ellis would win a Lincoln, one of six prizes highlighted in a letter mailed to her home. Excited at the prospect of winning the luxury car, she called the toll-free phone number on the letterhead. The friendly voice said that all Ellis had to do was purchase some high-potency vitamins for $719, including shipping and handling.
>
> Ellis doubted the deal at first. She asked to speak to the phone agent's supervisor who assured her the sales promotion was legal under Nevada law. The supervisor

praised her intelligence for asking questions, a tactic that allayed her concerns. By dropping her guard, Ellis was hooked.

She bit on further sales calls with new offers of prizes, continuing to buy despite that each prize she received was far less than the telemarketer had promised.

Looking back, Ellis admitted what few victims of the telemarketing scam would concede: her greed got in the way of good judgment. In the end she did not get something for nothing.

Schulte notes that prize boiler rooms keep track of the people who fall for the prize scam and sell these "sucker lists" to other boiler rooms.

One psychological mechanism here (as Schulte mentions in the prior quote) is simple greed. If you have a strong desire to get something for nothing, you can be exploited by the con artist. There is an old adage among con artists that expresses this point well: "You can't con an honest man." Most cons involve exploiting greed. In fact, the telemarketers themselves are often quite aware of the role of greed. Schulte (1995: 62) recounts the following story:

> One long-time operator of the racket held hour-long sales sessions with new hires in which he bluntly explained: "We are selling greed." He also would storm through the sales room daily yelling at employees to close more sales and make him richer faster.
>
> The soldiers in these scam brigades have their own language, code of conduct, and hierarchy. They refer to their customers with contempt, calling them "mooches," or people who deserve to get cheated because they tried to get something for nothing.
>
> "People want money to fall out of the sky, and we make it sound easy and comfortable," says one master of the ad specs swindle who requested anonymity. "We don't care if they ever get their products or if they spend their last dime on it. They bought the story and they deserve what they get."

To try to educate the public about the phoniness of the prize scams, U.S. Postal Service inspectors mailed out postcards with a "You are a Winner!" pitch on it, with an 800 number for people to call. On the 800 number was a recorded message warning the gullible to beware of such gimmicks. Schulte (1995: 258) describes the result:

> Unfortunately, the pink-postcard stunt was a hit beyond all expectations. More than three hundred thousand people called the number, apparently thinking they would win a prize.
>
> For postal regulators the experience reflected their frustration after years and years of issuing alerts and fighting for new laws to crack down on the problems. No matter what they do or say, many people don't seem to get the message to avoid these scams, and postal inspectors find themselves in the unenviable position of trying to regulate human greed.

While the prize rooms run by telemarketers are an extreme, they are not rare (in fact, they are a big business). But even more legitimate business use giveaways and prizes to boost sales.

The second mechanism behind gift pitches is reciprocity. Cialdini gives the examples of the Hari Krishna sect. In the 1960s and 1970s, members of the Krishna Society were out in great numbers in airports, soliciting charitable deductions. Before asking for money, the member would give his or her target a flower. By this simple mechanism, the Krishnas were able to make most people feel obligated to them and thus more inclined to hand over money.

The next two pitches we met earlier in our discussion of fallacious appeals to emotion, especially appeals to the crowd and appeals to pity.

Ads Using Models and Symbols

Many ads feature attractive **models** or national **symbols** such as the flag, the Lincoln Memorial, the Statue of Liberty, and so on, featured near the product being pitched. Such ads we classified earlier as appeals to the crowd. Figures 17.1 and 17.2 show attractive models used to advertise products. In the first example, a model gazes lovingly at a man's shoes. In the second, a handsome actor who exemplifies classiness is pictured above a camcorder.

The mechanism here is association. The models in these ads are attractive, and so we like them and associate them with the product. And when a national symbol is used, people associate the good feelings about their country with the product.

Shills

Another sales tactic is the use of shills. A **shill** is someone who appears to be just another customer or citizen but is in fact paid by the sales agent to appear as a customer. For example, an auction may have shills present to bid up the price on the items being auctioned off.

The mechanism behind the shills is twofold. First, positive association (shills are often young and attractive, not old and ugly). Second, there is social proof: Shills enable genuine customers to feel part of a large group.

A classic use of both symbols and shills is found in Larry Tye's (1998) book *The Father of Spin: Edward L. Bernays & the Birth of Public Relations*. Bernays, ironically a nephew of Sigmund Freud, was an earlier pioneer of modern advertising. One of his most successful campaigns was conducted on behalf of his client, the American Tobacco Company, to persuade women to take up the habit of smoking. Bernays's "brilliant" idea was to make smoking the symbol of emancipation. He first put out stories to the media to the effect that the taboo against women smoking in public was a sign of male domination of women. Then, he organized a march of fashionable young women down Fifth Avenue in New York City, led by a young woman (who just happened to be his secretary) carrying cigarettes (which were called "Torches of Freedom"). Newspapers carried pictures of this charade, and within weeks it had a great effect—theaters changed the rules to allow women into the smoking rooms, sales to women increased, and so on.

Bernays thus used a number of clever ploys: He used a shill, models, and loaded terminology ("torches of freedom") and manipulated the media to publicize all of this. What a guy!

All good tailors recommand Hitachi Hi 8 camcorder because it is the only one which doesn't deform your pockets.

Lightness is good. But more is necessary to make an exceptionnal camcorder. Stereo sound, digital zoom x 20, three possibilities of fading, red colour filter, sepia or B/W, the WMH 37 shoots in Hi 8 **HITACHI** perfectly. Hand-sewn in fact.

VMH 37 CAMCORDER

Figure 17.1

Reprinted with permission of Hitachi Corporation (Tarrytown, NY).

Sympathy Pitches

A **sympathy pitch** is just a pitch that attempts to make the listener or reader feel pity and act on it. Sympathy pitches are just fallacious appeals to pity. As we saw in Chapter 8, some very large charities show pictures of suffering children and lead people to believe that their donations will go to specific children—whereas in reality, the money is pooled and spent for large projects. This is misrepresentation. In the world of telemarketing, you encounter outright fraud. Some charity telemarketers contribute less than 5 percent of the

Figure 17.2

Reprinted with permission of Johnson & Murphy (Nashville, TN).

funds they collect for a target group (orphans, say, or police widows) (Schulte 1995: 155).
Schulte gives an especially disgusting example of boiler rooms called "handicapped sales
rooms" (146). The telemarketer calls people, saying that he or she is disabled and is trying
to earn a living selling household items. These items (such as light bulbs or trash bags) are
grossly overpriced, but the customers buy anyway out of sympathy. It turns out, however,
that the telemarketers are rarely disabled in the ordinary sense of the word. Instead, their

"handicaps" include psoriasis, high blood pressure, asthma, alcohol dependency, and even felony convictions!

Golden Opportunity Pitches

In a **golden opportunity pitch,** the sales agent suggests that the buyer, because of some imminent event, should buy now or lose the opportunity. For example, an Oriental rug store near where I live has a sign that says, "Going out of business! All rugs must be liquidated!!" That sign has been there for five years now. Sales fliers quite often use phrases such as "Buy Now! Quantities Limited," "Clearance Sale! Everything Must Go!" and "Only Two Left at This Price!" Some states now require any business advertising "going out of business" or any equivalent phrase to file proof that it is in fact true, because of so many phony ads.

Of course, these tactics are taken to fraudulent extremes in some telemarketing operations. For example, one area of growing telemarketing fraud is the sale of "biz-opps"— business opportunities. The telemarketer starts by placing ads in the "Business Opportunities" section of the classified ads in various newspapers around the country. The biz-opp can be anything: jewelry, gem sales, payphone routes, investment in bull semen, or ostrich farming. Let's use an example given by Schulte (1995: 164–174). The initial ad for payphone routes might look like this:

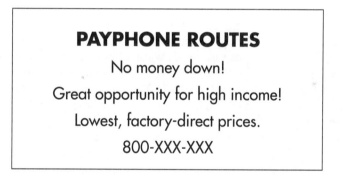

Now, newspapers almost never check up on these ads, although readers often assume the newspapers do. Or the telemarketer will send out mailers by the thousands.

People call the 800 number and get subjected to a sales pitch. Here is an actual telemarketing script, courtesy of the Maryland Attorney General Office:

A WONDERFUL OPPORTUNITY FOR THE SMALL INVESTOR

$ A quarter may seem like a small amount of money, yet many of the largest fortunes in this country have been built on individual sales with profits of no more than a penny, nickel, or dime.

$ The next time you watch someone drop a quarter in a Pay Phone, multiply that person by the hundreds of thousands in this country who do the same thing every day of the year. Then you will begin to realize how much money these little silent mechanical salesmen accumulate for their owners. Yet they are paid no salaries, they hand in no expense account, they work at their jobs night and day and never ask for holidays or vacations.

$ The operating of Pay Phone routes is not confined to large cities. The small investor has, in many cases, equal or better opportunities of making a greater profit. The small operator has the advantage of close personal supervision and minimum operating cost, using the home until he gets the business built up from its own earnings to a point where it demands larger quarters. This business, however, also interests persons with unlimited capital.

The telemarketer proceeds to "**puff**" the pitch by exaggerating the profitability of the investment, and urging that the opportunities are going fast, fast, fast. The telemarketing company may employ "singers"—that is, people paid to act as satisfied past investors. Once the gullible customer has heard the singers' testimony and the puffed-up pitch, the telemarketer closes the deal by having the customer overnight a cashier's check.

The scam lies in the fact that the investor/customer never gets the payphones or whatever else he or she has invested in. The telemarketing company stalls the customers with creative excuses for months and then "goes out of business," taking the customers' money with them!

Another variety of golden opportunity pitches is to be found in the realm of bunco artists. A **Ponzi scheme** is a type of investment scam in which investors are lured in by the promise of high returns on the money they put in. Such schemes (named after the early twentieth-century con artist Carlo Ponzi) work by paying off early investors with the money collected from later investors, rather than investing money in some legitimate profitable enterprise. Eventually, the number of new investors (suckers) is not enough to pay the old, and the pyramid collapses. James Walsh (1998) very thoroughly reviews actual Ponzi schemes in his delightful book *You Can't Cheat an Honest Man: How Ponzi Schemes and Pyramid Frauds Work . . . and Why They're More Common Than Ever.*

What mechanisms underlie these golden opportunity pitches? Scarcity and greed. People are tempted by the idea that there are a dwindling number of openings for these highly profitable ventures and that enormous amounts of money are just there for the picking. As Walsh puts it (1998: 137), "Ponzi perps are moved by greed. In most cases, they'd rather steal money quickly than earn it gradually . . . but they also count on the greed of their investors to make the schemes work."

Bait and Switch

Another common sales tactic is called **bait and switch.** In this ploy, a well-known brand is offered at an incredibly cheap price. When the customer shows up to buy, however, the salesperson claims that the store is all out of that particular item. However, the customer is told that another item is available that is an even better deal. This other item is either a no-name brand for the same price or a different model of the same well-known brand at a higher price.

Bait and switch is very common in consumer electronics and car sales. The psychological mechanism behind bait-and-switch is entrenchment. The customer has driven to the store, already committed to buying, cash in hand, faced with the choice of either buying this unanticipated item or (horror of horrors!) returning home empty-handed. The temptation to buy the unanticipated item is usually irresistible.

Testimonials

Next, let's look briefly at **testimonials.** In a testimonial ad, a product is endorsed by a putative satisfied customer or (more commonly these days) by putative experts. We already looked at fallacious appeals to authority in Chapter 11, so I won't go into extensive details. But testimonials often amplify or create demand. Pretty clearly, testimonials derive their power from the mechanisms of social proof (in the case of "satisfied customer" ads) and authority (in the case of "expert testimony" ads).

We should note that a common type of testimonial is the paid endorsement. As the name implies, a paid endorsement is a testimonial in which the person endorsing (that is, testifying in favor of) a product is paid for that endorsement by the products' manufacturers. Paid endorsements are inherently logically suspicious, because (all things being equal) the credibility of a witness is undermined by his or her biases.

Subliminal Ads

The term *subliminal* means below the level of conscious perception. Advertisers often aim their ads at the subliminal level. This is especially common in advertising for alcohol and tobacco products, because federal law places great restrictions on such advertising. For example, it is illegal to advertise on TV for cigarettes and hard liquor. So the cigarette and liquor companies will sponsor various sports events and put their logos or brand names all over the place. You tune in to see a football game and may not consciously notice that "Kophum Cigarettes" has put its name right on the scoreboard, but you subliminally notice it. Again, advertisers will often pay a movie producer to have the actors starring in his or her movie be shown using the advertisers' products. You are watching the hero enter a bar after saving the universe, and you only subliminally notice that he orders a beer with the "Blotto Beer" label.

Subliminal ads usually work by association. Seeing the product name associated with sports heros or romantic leading actors inclines the viewer to ascribe good qualities to the product.

Like advertising directed at children, subliminal advertising seems especially aimed to get around critical thinking. Ruchlis (1990: 226) puts the point well:

> Subliminal messages are difficult to counteract by means of logical reasoning because they bypass the conscious level of thought and mold opinions about products through subconscious feelings. If people are shown how to detect and analyze subliminal messages in ads and commercials, they would have a better chance to avoid the potentially harmful effects of such campaigns.

The preceding examples are cases in which adults are emotionally manipulated to make them want things they didn't begin by wanting. An especially controversial genre of such advertising is advertising directed at children. Much of the advertising you see on TV, and most of it during children's shows, is aimed at getting children to desire certain brands. The motivation for such advertising is clear. To quote Karen Stabiner (1993a: 10), a journalist who has studied advertising:

> The children's market continues to grow. . . . [A]ccording to James U. McNeal, Texas A&M University professor, children with two working parents have become involved in an increasing number of purchase decisions. He estimates that the 12-and-younger set has a vote on about $147 billion in spending each year.
>
> More to the point, children have decades of buying power ahead of them—and unlike their parents, who carry awareness of 1,500 brand names in their heads, they have no preconceived preferences. They are a blank slate. The combination—money to spend and an open mind—makes children irresistible to American business, and places them at the center of a heated controversy over whether, and how much, to sell an audience whose critical thinking faculties are still in the caterpillar stage.

Advertisers contend that ads targeted at kids are justified by the fact that those ads can induce the children to consume that which benefits them. But this is not always true. Candy and sugary high-fat foods, for example, can hardly be considered a blessing for kids. Moreover, as Stabiner's quote mentions, children are not critically aware enough to comparison shop, to sift through the substance of ads to pick out the truth, and to realize when their emotions are being manipulated.

As an example of such emotional manipulation, consider this description of the rationale behind Kool-Aid (a powdered children's drink) (Stabiner 1993a: 11):

> Andy Bohjalian worked on the Kool-Aid account 10 years ago. . . . When he started working on Dannon 2½ years ago, he remembered the seminal lesson of his days on the fruit-drink account: Make a kid feel like he rules his universe, and he will desire the product that makes him feel that way.
>
> "We discovered that if we had adults doing these slapstick reactions, falling on banana peels, wigs falling off, if we made adults look silly because they saw Kool-Aid Man and were shocked and frightened—the kids loved it because they were in control," says Bohjalian. They called the Kool-Aid Man and he created chaos in the adult world.
>
> "In the real world, kids are at the bottom of the food chain," he says, "and one really successful way to advertise to kids is to give them a sense of power, give them a place where they call the shots, instead of everyone telling them what to eat, and when to go to bed and clean up their room."

Some movement toward curbing children's advertising has occurred. Recently, the cigarette companies agreed to stop advertising cigarettes by using cartoon characters (such as "Joe Camel"). But clearly more needs to be done.

4   The Role of Advertising in Misinforming Consumers about Costs and Benefits

Ideally, having decided to purchase something, we would examine the cost and benefits of each brand and choose the best. But sales pitches and advertising can deform the process in several ways. We can broadly distinguish four ways sales agents can misinform the consumer. First, they can exaggerate positive information; second, they can downplay negative information; third, they can omit negative information; finally, they can misinform about alternate choices.

By "exaggerating positive information," I mean that the sales agent exaggerates the benefits of the product or, in the case of an investment, its chances for success. This is often called **puffing** the product. Telemarketers also have a happy phrase for this: they call it "painting the dream." Typically, sales agents use the methods of overstatement covered in Chapter 6. Weight losses become "fantastic weight losses." Hair growth becomes "incredible, amazing hair growth." A slight chance of making a profit becomes "a sure-fire, guaranteed profit maker."

In a similar fashion, sales agents can downplay negative information, by which I mean downplaying the costs of the product, its limitations, or drawbacks, or—again, if we are talking about investments—the chances of failure. Again, sales agents use the methods of understatement discussed in Chapter 6. A price of $10 becomes "only $10," "a mere $10," or even "the amazing low price of $10." A drug with major side effects is labeled "safe for most people; some may experience slight difficulties."

These techniques for exaggerating benefit and downplaying costs can be augmented (if the sales pitch or ad is printed) by clever accenting, again discussed in Chapter 6. For example,

3 Tapes or CD's

Only $5.00*!!!

*Plus shipping and handling charges of $12.00

Limit 3.

Note that the mechanism behind accenting is the principle of salience—your eye automatically focuses on the big print.

Besides exaggerating benefits and downplaying costs, the sale agent often engages in **special pleading;** that is, he or she states only the information about the case that is favorable to it. In particular, the sales agent often will omit mentioning certain costs or liabilities of the product at hand—often criminally so. Cigarette manufacturers battled for years having to mention in their advertising the health risks associated with smoking. And on a number of occasions, car companies have fought to suppress information about safety problems with various models. The famous consumer advocate, Ralph Nader, first came to public attention when he published a book describing the risks of driving the Chevrolet Corvair. Remember—sales agents are typically in adversary position vis-à-vis the consumer.

Finally, sales agents often work to misinform the consumer about his or her choices—they can describe competing brands misleadingly or omit mention of them. We call these **comparison tricks.** For example, false analogies can be employed to compare the product at hand with other products that are not its real competitors. For instance, an ad for Ban Roll-On deodorant says that it is more effective than "all other aerosols." But it is misleading to compare a roll-on (which is applied directly to the skin) with aerosols (which are sprayed from a distance). A study by an independent lab comparing Ban with other roll-ons would be a more compelling piece of evidence. Another example involves nutritional labeling. By law, food products must have a label telling the consumer how many calories, how much fat, and so on, the product contains. But often a producer will present the data based on a different portion size than other bags of the same size. For instance, one potato chip manufacturer may say its bag has only seven grams of fat per serving, but count that bag as having two servings (for a fourteen-gram total). Another brand with identical bag size may list ten grams but the bag as having one serving.

A recent case of a comparison trick regarding luxury automobiles is described in this article (courtesy of Chris Knap and the *Orange County Register* [1999]).

BMW Says Cadillac Is a Big Fibber

When it comes to Cadillac, what can we believe?

It was just a few weeks ago that Cadillac admitted it fudges its 1998 sales figures, a misguided effort to beat Irvine's Lincoln.

Now BMW of North America is complaining that Cadillac cheated in an "independent" slalom test that is the subject of a new print ad for Cadillac's Seville.

The ad says that Seville STS was faster through the slalom course than "the vaunted BMW 540i."

The fine print notes that the Seville got to wear optional 150 mph Z-rated tires while the BMW had to make do with the standard H-rated tires, good for 118 mph.

"The difference between H-rated and Z-rated tires does make a difference," said BMW's Andrew Cutler. "You are misleading the consumer."

"We met all legal requirements," said Cadillac's Chris Preuss. "If they feel it wasn't a fair comparison, they should do another test with Z-rated tires on both cars."

A special comparison trick worth noting involves the use of contrast. Realtors will often list a "setup" property—that is, an overpriced, dumpy property. They don't expect to sell that property, but they use it as a contrast to sell *other* properties. They will take a customer first to the setup and then talk it down. Next, they will take the customer to a nicer property, which looks even nicer by the comparison with the setup.

False dilemmas can be set deliberately to divert the consumer's attention. The sales agent might say, "There are only two really luxury cars, the Cadillac you see before you and the Mercedes. But Mercedes is ridiculously overpriced, and, besides, the Cadillac is made right here in the good old U.S.A.!" Note that the sales agent has conveniently *not* mentioned other luxury cars, such as BMW, Lexus, or Infinity (to name just a few).

Exercise 17.4

The following imaginary ads contain sales tactics discussed in this chapter. Identify the tactic, and explain what is illogical about the ad.

1. HELP THE CHILDREN!
    These abandoned children are begging for help, as you can see just by looking at their eyes. What can you, an ordinary person, do? You can send money right away. Even a small donation will HELP THE CHILDREN!
2. You can win—FIFTY THOUSAND DOLLARS! Imagine what you could do with the money . . . a new car . . . send your kids to college . . . take a fabulous trip!

    All you have to do to enter our contest is to order one or more magazines from the following list.

3. "My memory improved overnight."
   "I don't forget things anymore the way I used to!"
   "The number one cure for memory loss!"
   The above quotes are from some of the hundreds of letters we get every week raving about our new memory-aide pill "GINKO-BOMB." Just two Ginko-bombs a day, and your memory will be like it was when your were in your early twenties.

4. CUSTOMER: I'd like to buy one of the IBM personal computers you have advertised in today's paper.
   SALESMAN: Oh, those? We sold out of those in three hours—if you read the small print in the ad, there were only five available to be remaindered anyway. But we have just announced a new sale on an even better model, the Supa Clone 44. Let me show you.

5. CUSTOMER: Pardon me, but can you tell me something about this watch?
   SALESCLERK: Certainly! You picked the best one, in my opinion. This is a Swiss-made, hand-crafted beauty. Let's open a charge account for you; that way you will save an extra 15 percent on this purchase!

6. ACT FAST OR KICK YOURSELF LATER!!!
   We have openings for just three telemarketers to help sell our new line of sportswear. TOP COMMISSIONS! DAILY SPIFFS!

7. USED CAR SALESMAN (to prospective customer): Why do I think this is the car for you? First, it has over 150,000 miles on it, so you know that the engine is well broken-in and tested. Second, the tires are bald, which actually increases traction. Also, the car has had a lot of owners, which tells you that it is a popular model!

8. You've promised yourself a new car long enough! Now's the time to buy. Our prices are at *Incredible All-Time Lows!* Fabulous cars at fantabulous low prices!

9. DON'T TAKE CHANCES!
   LACK OF VITAMINS CAN CAUSE
   A SLOW, HORRIBLY PAINFUL DEATH!
   Buy Wonda Vita tablets, which give you 100% of the recommended minimum daily amount of all key vitamins.

10. I can see that this fine crystal decanter set interests you very much. As well it should—it is the perfect holiday gift. Do you want two sets, or perhaps three?

11. It's the ALL AMERICAN RUG SALE—this weekend only at All American Rug Company. Uncle Sam says NOW IS THE TIME FOR ALL GOOD PEOPLE TO BUY A RUG!

12. (Ad mailed to you with a dollar attached.)
    Why are we sending you this monetary gift? Just to thank you in advance for subscribing to our investment newsletter. This dollar is your first step on the way to the million dollars you will eventually earn by following the incredible investment advice every month in the newsletter.

13. Amazing Results! See for yourself! FAT JUST MELTS AWAY LIKE MAGIC! Eat whatever you like, it doesn't matter, so long as you take SUPALOSS diet pills! The weight losses will be AWESOME!

14. Compare our minivan with the Ford and Chevy sport-utility vehicles, and what do you see?
    Our minivan has much more interior space, for less money! A "no-brainer" choice.

15.   Aren't you tired of seeing other people earn big bucks . . .

WHILE YOU LIVE ON PEANUTS?

You deserve big money, and we can help you get it!
How? Easy—a small investment in commodities futures
CAN MAKE YOU FILTHY RICH IN A MATTER OF DAYS!
Get your share! Call now 800-XXX-XXXX.

5   *Overcoming Sales Trickery*

In reading the foregoing, we can see that the essence of the problem is that the consumer is often in an adversary situation with the salesperson or advertiser. That is, the salesperson/advertiser is an advocate of the product he or she is selling/advertising and is paid to the consumer to buy it. So, the temptation is strong to use fallacies and other tricks to create or amplify the initial desire for a product or to mislead the consumer as to costs and benefits. Faced with this, the critical consumer should follow a couple of rules.

Rule 1: Play off sales agents against each other. After listening to salesperson *A* pitch Willie's Widgets to you, go over to the Wonder Widget Showroom and let their salesperson *B* reply. You will find that *B* will be very helpful in counteracting *A*'s tricks.

Rule 2: Research the products you are considering. Serious shoppers devote considerable time to learning which stores have good prices on which products. In that sense, cruising the shopping malls can be said to enhance critical thinking! More seriously, remember that medical care involves consumer choice as well. Researching the alternative treatments to your disease can pay off, and not just monetarily. Several neutral consumer magazines are very useful sources about the costs and benefits of competing products.

In leaving this topic, we should leave on a positive note. Although, indeed, much advertising is manipulative and misleading, much of it is also entertaining and informative or at least logical. Let's explore this idea for a moment. What counts for "logically acceptable" advertising?

Go back to the decision cycle. The reasonable criteria for deciding to purchase any item are, first, you need it (or at least should want it enough to bother buying it.); second, it is cheaper than its competitors (costs less) or superior in some way to its competitors (has more benefits).

"Superior" in a product means higher quality, easier to use, better serviced, more easily obtained, more beautiful, bigger, or whatever. Thus, a rational ad will focus on need, cost, or superiority of product.

Examples abound of rational ads directed at need. For example, insurance ads in parents-oriented magazines often point out rightly the need for young parents to be covered by health and life insurance. Similarly, brokerage houses often advertise to young workers the need to set up retirement stock and bond accounts to provide for their retirements. Again, ads for, say, orange juice often cite the need for vitamin C (found in orange juice). Such advertising is aimed at educating the consumer about real needs as opposed to artificially creating false "needs."

There are also plenty of rational ads directed at cost. Discount brokerages often display the commissions they charge for transactions. Electronics stores frequently show pictures of particular computer systems on sale, fully disclosing prices and specifications, allowing the consumer to comparison shop by paper. The same holds true for many supermarket ads.

Finally, many ads rationally direct their appeal to the superiority of the product advertised. One car manufacturer advertises the 100,000-mile warranty standard on its cars. Another advertises *Consumer Reports'* results of crash tests on its vans. Yet another car manufacturer reports consumer satisfaction surveys by J. D. Power and Associates, an independent consumer sampler. Ads for cruises often display pictures of the ship's cabins or the food served. In fact, it is likely that most ads either are purely logical or contain some rational argument mixed in with the manipulation.

Additionally, advertisers must adhere to government-set standards for the truth of the claims made in their ads. The various "truth-in-advertising" laws are enforced by the Federal Trade Commission, local fraud units, and state attorneys general. Moreover, various consumer watchdog groups, as well as the Better Business Bureau, monitor advertising excesses. These external controls, as well as our intuitive ability to detect manipulation and misrepresentation, aided by a study of critical thinking, enable us to make reasonable consumer choices.

Exercise 17.5

Describe how you would research the costs and benefits of competing brands for the following products:

1. a minivan
2. paper towels
3. a new computer

4. a new pair of skis
5. a new desk

InfoTrac College Edition

You can locate InfoTrac College Edition articles about this chapter by accessing the InfoTrac College Edition Web site (www.infotrac-college.com/wadsworth/). Using the InfoTrac College Edition subject guide, enter the search terms relevant to this chapter, and then read abstracts for relevant articles.

Chapter 18

Application II: Political Rhetoric and Democratic Choice

1   *Political Agents*

In the last chapter we examined choice, and the ways sales agents can defeat rational decision making by exploiting certain common psychological mechanisms. Let's briefly review the major concepts we met in that discussion, as they will be crucial in our discussion of political choice.

First, we introduced the general concept of a "compliance specialist" as being any person who is employed by an entity (corporation, business group, or person) to get some target group to act in a manner desired by that employing entity. We divided compliance specialists into two groups: sales agents, hired to sell products, and political agents, hired to elect politicians or pass laws. These groups are not exclusive; that is, sales agents are often employed as political agents as well. This point is made well by Joe McGinnis (1969: 26–27) in his book, *The Selling of the President:*

> Politics, in a sense, has always been a con game.
>
> The American voter, insisting upon his belief in a higher order, clings to his religion, which promises another, better life; defends passionately the illusion that the men he chooses to lead him are of finer nature than he.
>
> It has been traditional that the successful politician honor this illusion. To succeed today, he must embellish it. Particularly if he wants to be President. . . .
>
> That there is a difference between the individual and his image is human nature. Or American nature, at least. That the difference is exaggerated and exploited electronically is the reason for this book. Advertising, in many ways, is a con game, too. Human beings do not need new automobiles every third year; a color television set brings little enrichment of the human experience; a higher or lower hemline no expansion of consciousness, no increase in the capacity to love.
>
> It is not surprising, then, that politicians and advertising men should have discovered one another. And, once they recognized that the citizen did not so much vote for a candidate as make a psychological purchase of him not surprising that they began to work together. . . .

Advertising agencies have tried openly to sell Presidents since 1952. When Dwight Eisenhower ran for re-election in 1956, the agency of Batton, Barton, Durstine and Osborn, which had been on a retainer throughout his first four years, accepted his campaign as a regular account. Leonard Hall, national Republican chairman said: "You sell your candidate and your programs the way a business sells it products."

The second major concept is that of the psychology of persuasion. We found that all compliance specialists utilize certain psychological mechanisms to augment or even replace rational persuasion. The mechanisms we looked at were contrast, reciprocity, entrenchment, social proof, authority, scarcity, sympathy, greed, association (both negative and positive), and salience. As we review common political fallacies, we will see how these same mechanisms are involved.

Third, we considered the notion of an "incomplete adversary system." That is, unlike a courtroom setting, in which both sides of an issue are represented by professional advocates, the consumer is in a situation in which he or she faces a sales agent alone. That sales agent is an advocate of a certain product and will try to get the consumer to buy by presenting a one-sided case—and a case not always based on good logic and true statements. A similar relation holds between the voter and the political agent: It is an incomplete adversary system. The political agent is an advocate of a particular position and is not typically concerned to present a logical case. To combat the incomplete adversary system in consumer choice, we suggested that the consumer do two things: First, learn the standard fallacious pitches used by hucksters (and understand the psychological mechanisms behind them); second, try to create a more complete adversary system by playing off sales agent against sales agent. Similarly, in this chapter we will suggest that the voter should learn the standard political rhetorical tricks (and understand the psychological mechanisms behind them) and try to create a more complete adversary system by forcing political advocates to debate rather than merely orate.

2   *Common Political Rhetorical Tricks*

Politicians and other political agents use a variety of techniques to influence the voter, such a large variety that we could write a book about those techniques alone. In fact, many such books have been written, from Machiavelli's *The Prince* in 1532 down to some current ones. Three I like in particular are *Hardball: How Politics Is Played Told by One Who Knows the Game* by Christopher Matthews (1988), *The Selling of the President* by Joe McGinnis (1969), and *Spin Cycle: Inside the Clinton Propaganda Machine* by Howard Kurtz (1998). I will be relying on these sources as we review some political tactics.

Warm and Fuzzy Ads

Politicians often seek to associate themselves with positive things, even if they had no role in the creation of those things. They kiss babies, throw out the first ball in ball games, lead parades. They stage **photo ops**—cases in which a politician's handlers arrange for the politician to be photographed in some positive situation. This is a common political trick. Examples come readily to mind. President Ronald Reagan was once filmed at the opening of a Veteran's Hospital, the funding for which he tried to veto. Presidential candidate Walter Mondale was once photographed delivering a speech on national defense, proudly standing aboard an aircraft carrier, the funding for which he had opposed. (Actually, the photo op backfired on him when his opponent pointed out Mondale's inconsistency during a televised debate.) President Bill Clinton bragged about the wonderful effects of a welfare reform bill he signed, but only after vetoing it twice and fighting it bitterly to the last moment. Such ads are especially common on TV. As Kurtz (1998: 105) notes, President Reagan's advisor, Michael Deaver, held that TV pictures mattered more than what the news correspondents said.

The mechanisms behind photo ops and related ads is, of course, positive association. Psychologically, we transfer our good feelings about good news to the messenger of that news. Cialdini (1993: 192) puts the point thus:

> If politicians are relative newcomers to the use of celebrity endorsements, they are old hands at exploiting the association principle in other ways. For example, congressional representatives traditionally announce to the press the start of federal projects that will bring new jobs or benefits to their home states; this is true even when a representative has had nothing to do with advancing the project or has, in some cases, voted against it.

Attack Ads

Just as positive association is exploited in many positive campaign ads, negative association is exploited in many negative political ads. Negative political ads—"attack ads," as they are so aptly called—have always been present in political campaigns but seem to have gotten even more common in recent years. Of course, attacking the person is a common fallacy met in attack ads. For example, in the 1998 primary election in California, an initiative was put on the ballot to outlaw the use of any union member's dues for political contributions without the written consent of that member. This was bitterly opposed by organized labor, which spent many millions in attack ads claiming that the advocates of the initiative were out-of-state big businessmen intent on destroying health care and schools. In another case, in the 1996 California general election, an initiative was put on the ballot to outlaw racial preferences in government hiring, contract letting, and university admissions. Some students at the California State University at Northridge, who were opposed to the initiative, staged a debate, but instead of inviting the authors of the initiative or other prominent spokespeople for the initiative to speak for the "pro" side, chose instead to hire and fly in a Ku Klux Klan–related politician, David Duke, to speak for the initiative. The attempt to manipulate the voters by this artifice was so obvious, however, that it backfired, and the initiative passed handily.

When a political agent fallaciously attacks another politician using abusive language, we call it **name-calling.** When a political agent fallaciously attacks the circumstances or hypocrisy of another politician, we call it **smearing.** But besides smears and name-calling, political agents often attack their opponents by distortions (that is, strawman/ignoring the issue) and false cause blaming. For example, consider this exchange from the 1960 Kennedy-Nixon presidential debate:

> MR. McGEE: Senator Kennedy, yesterday you used the word "trigger-happy" in referring to Vice President Richard Nixon's stand on defending the islands of Quemoy and Matsu. Last week on a program like this one, you said the next president would come face to face with a serious crisis in Berlin. So the question is: would you take military action to defend Berlin?

> MR. KENNEDY: Mr. McGee, we have a contractual right to be in Berlin coming out of the conversations at Potsdam and of World War II. That has been reinforced by direct commitments of the President of the United States; it's been reinforced by a number of other nations under NATO. I've stated on many occasions that the United States must meet its commitment on Berlin. It is a commitment we have to meet if we are going to protect the security of Western Europe. And therefore on this question I don't think that there is any doubt in the mind of any American; I hope that there is not any doubt in the mind of any member of the community of West Berlin; I'm sure there isn't any doubt in the mind of the Russians. We will meet our commitments to maintain the freedom and independence of West Berlin.

> MR. SHADEL: Mr. Vice President, do you wish to comment?

> MR. NIXON: Yes. As a matter of fact, the statement that Senator Kennedy made was that—to the effect that there were trigger-happy Republicans, that my stand on Quemoy and Matsu was an indication of trigger-happy Republicans. I resent that comment. I resent it because th—it's an implication that Republicans have been trigger-happy and therefore would lead this nation into war. I would remind Senator Kennedy of the past fifty years. I would ask him to name one Republican President who led this nation into war. There were three Democratic Presidents who led us into war. I do not mean by that that one party is a war party and the other party is a peace party. But I do say that any statement to the effect that the Republican Party is trigger-happy is belied by the record. We had a war when we came into power in 1953. We got rid of that; we've kept out of other wars; and certainly that doesn't indicate that we're trigger-happy. We've been strong, but we haven't been trigger-happy.

Kennedy started by name-calling (Nixon is "trigger-happy"—that is, overly willing to go to war), to which Nixon responded by a false-cause linkage between Democratic presidents and wars.

We need to be clear that although many positive and negative ads fallaciously exploit association, many do not. Legitimate positive ads cite actual accomplishments of the candidate in past offices he or she has held. Legitimate negative ads point out genuine relevant mistakes made by the candidate in his or her past. If the ads are truthful, not distorted, and relevant, they are, of course, logically worthwhile. But even in such cases, it is crucial to remember that the political agent is only stating one side of the case. You the voter must gather *all* the relevant information pro and con.

Artful Dodging

In Chapter 8 we discussed pooh-poohing—that is, dismissing rather than responding to legitimate questions—and ignoring the issue—that is, talking about an irrelevant subject. We will lump pooh-poohing and ignoring the issue together as **artful dodging.** Political agents often raise artful dodging to an art form. Matthews (1988: Chapter 9) mentions a tactic politicians employ he calls "always concede on principle," by which he means that the clever politician, faced with objections to a pet policy he can't refute, should "surrender not on the substance but on the principle at stake, giving the impression of compromise by telling his adversaries what they want to hear" (149). This approach amounts to elevating pooh-poohing to a major weapon in political fights.

Besides pooh-poohing, politicians of course often ignore issues. For example, then–presidential candidate Ronald Reagan was once posed the question "Just where would you slash the federal budget if you were sitting in the Oval Office today?" He answered:

> Everyone seems to think that the only way to cut government is to eliminate programs. Of course, there are unnecessary programs. My experience in California as governor showed me that some programs do not benefit the people. But—more importantly—virtually everything run by government has an overhead higher than that of the private sector. I found that our greatest savings in California—and they were tremendous—resulted from the elimination of waste and fraud and abuse rather than the elimination of programs. I think it's significant that in the federal department of that used to be HEW—now the department of Health and Human Services—they recently eliminated wasted, fraud and abuse. They eliminated it by having a meeting of all the department heads in which Secretary Patricia Harris made a rule that henceforth they would no longer use the words *fraud, waste and abuse.* Those words won't appear anymore; officials will now refer to mismanagement.

Notice that Reagan never answers the specific question (namely, which programs he would cut); he says there are indeed unnecessary programs (but which ones?); he found as governor that there are unnecessary programs (yes, but which ones?); that savings can be made by eliminating waste, fraud, and abuse (perhaps true, but not the question); and he jokes that his opponent's administration eliminated waste, fraud, and abuse by simply renaming it. It is clear why he ignored the issue: If he named the programs he would have cut, people who benefit from those programs would have been more inclined to vote against him.

Another example of the artful dodger was Mike McCurry, President Clinton's press secretary. At one point, Clinton was being sued by Paula Jones for sexual harassment. McCurry developed a clever technique for dodging questions about the lawsuit (Kurtz 1998): He would tell any reporter asking any question about the suit to address the question to the lawyer in charge of Clinton's defense, Bob Bennett. McCurry knew full well what Bennett would reply to such questions: "No comment!" McCurry called any questions about Clinton's alleged adulterous affairs "sleazy" even when they were relevant to questions of obstruction of justice.

Here is another example of artful dodging, taken from the 1996 Clinton–Dole presidential debate:

President Clinton, my name's Jack Flack. I'm a retired Air Force Pilot. Sir, it's officially forecast that our Medicare and Social Security deficits are measured in the trillions of dollars next century.

Depending upon who you listen to, Social Security will be bankrupt in the year 2025 or 2030. I feel this is grossly unfair, especially to our younger generations who are losing faith in the system. My question is this: assuming you agree that our entitlement programs are on an unsustainable course, what specific reforms do you propose.

CLINTON: First of all they are two different things. Social Security and Medicare are entirely different in terms of the financial stabilities. Let's talk about them separately.

Social Security is stable until, as you pointed out, at least the third decade of the next century. But we'd like to have a Social Security fund that has about 70 years of life instead of 30 years of life.

What we have to do is simply make some adjustments to take account of the fact that the baby boomers, people like me, are bigger in number than the people that went before and the people that come just after us.

And I think what we'll plainly do is what we did in 1983, when Senator Dole served—and this is something I think he did a good job on—when he served on the Social Security Commission, and they made some modest changes to Social Security to make sure that it would be alive and well into the 21st century.

And we will do that. It's obvious that there are certain things that have to be done, and there are 50 or 60 different options. And a bipartisan commission to take it out of politics will make recommendations and build support for the people.

Medicare is different. Medicare needs help now. I have proposed the budget which would put 10 years on the life of the Medicare Trust Fund.

That's more than it's had a lot of the time for the last 20 years. It would save a lot of money through more managed care. But giving more options, more preventive care and lowering the inflation rates in the prices we're paying providers without having the kind of big premium increases and out-of-pocket costs that the budget I vetoed would provide.

Then that will give us 10 years to do with Medicare what we're going to do with Social Security—have a bipartisan group look at what we have to do to save it when the baby boomers retire. But now, we ought to pass this budget now and put tenures on it right away so no one has to worry about it.

To the question what he would do to reform Medicare and Social Security, Clinton replied, (1) we need to make adjustments (yes, but what changes?); (2) we will have another Social Security commission make changes (yes, but what changes?); (3) I've proposed changes to Medicare (yes, but what changes?); (4) we need better care at lower prices with no premium increases (yes, but how?); and (5) we need a bipartisan commission to study it. He gave no specific answer; instead, he just gave general comments.

Spot Ads

You might have wondered at one aspect of campaigning: simple repetition. Telephone poles get plastered with "Vote for Jones!" stickers. Billboards scream "Jones is right for

America!" Bumpers are adorned with bumper stickers "Jones in 2000!" And then there are the endless spot ads: "Jones is best!" repeated in short ads played on TV and radio.

Why are such ads so common? Well, because they work. But why do they work? Because of positive association. As Cialdini (1993: 176–177) puts the point:

> For the most part, we like things that are familiar to us. To prove the point to yourself, try a little experiment. Get the negative of an old photograph that shows the front view of your face and have it developed into a pair of pictures—one that shows you as you actually look and one that shows your reverse image (so that the right and left sides of your face are interchanged). Now decide which version of your face you like better and ask a good friend to make the choice, too. If you are at all like a group of Milwaukee women on whom this procedure was tried, you should notice something odd: Your friend will prefer the true print, but you will prefer the reverse image. Why? Because you *both* will be responding favorably to the more familiar face—your friend to the one the world sees, and you to the transposed one you find in the mirror every day.

> Because of it effect on liking, familiarity plays a role in decisions about all sorts of things, including the politicians we elect. It appears that in an election booth voters often choose a candidate merely because the name seems familiar. In one controversial Ohio election a few years ago, a man given little chance of the state attorney-general race swept to victory when, shortly before the election he changed his name to Brown—a family name of much Ohio political tradition.

> How could such a thing happen? The answer lies partially in the unconscious way that familiarity affects liking. Often we don't realize that our attitude toward something has been influenced by the number of times we have been exposed to it in the past. For example, in one experiment, the faces of several individuals were flashed on a screen so quickly that later on, the subjects who were exposed to the faces in this manner couldn't recall having seen any of them before. Yet, the more frequently a person's face was flashed on the screen, the more these subjects came to like that person when they met them in a subsequent interaction. And because greater liking leads to greater social influence, these subjects were also more persuaded by the opinion statements of the individuals whose faces had appeared on the screen most frequently.

Control the Agenda

We have seen before that politicians and political agents will dodge questions that they feel uncomfortable about, either by pooh-poohing or ignoring the issue. The flip side of that is that political agents strive to control the agenda—that is, to frame the questions so that they control the debate or channel the interview in the way most favorable to them. For example, Richard Nixon's 1968 presidential campaign was almost entirely conducted by TV based on a set format. Nixon would be asked questions by a small panel of people, carefully selected ahead of time, before a small audience of supporters, also carefully chosen by the ad team. The questions were not rehearsed, and Nixon was occasionally caught off-guard. Toward the end of the campaign, the ad team hit upon an improved strategy. During a nationally televised telethon, viewers were invited to call in with questions for Nixon. Here is how those questions were given to him (McGinnis 1969: 149–150):

> Later Jack Rourke was asked how it really would work.
>
> "I understand Paul Keyes has been sitting up for two days writing questions," Roger Ailes said.
>
> "Well, not quite," Jack Rourke said. He seemed a little embarrassed.
>
> "What is going to happen?"
>
> "Oh . . ."
>
> "It's sort of semi-forgery, isn't it?" Ailes said. "Keyes has a bunch of questions Nixon wants to answer. He's written them in advance to make sure they're properly worded. When someone calls with something similar, they'll use Keye's question and attribute it to the person who called.
>
> "Isn't that it?"
>
> "More or less," Jack Rourke said.

Embarrassing questions were discarded, and more likeable questions were rewritten to make them even more useful!

More generally, political agents control the agenda by controlling which reporters get which bits of information. Political agents understand that reporters derive their prestige and income from being the first to publish a story, and they use this power to their advantage. Perhaps the most clever such political agent was Mike McCurry, press secretary for President Clinton. He was a master of quashing questions he didn't like, stonewalling, misleading, and above all controlling the reporters he faced daily. Here is a sample of his "magic" (Kurtz 1998: 31–32):

> Still, [reporter Deborah] Orin believed that there was legitimate material in Aldrich's book, incidents that the ex-FBI man would be in a position to know. He had written that Craig Livingstone, a low-level White House aide who later resigned for improperly obtaining FBI files on Republicans, had once issued a memo chastising White House staffers for writing bad checks. What about that? Either there was a memo or there wasn't. Orin soon pressed McCurry at the gaggle, but he deflected the question. A few days later she tried again to ask about some of the charges by Gary Aldrich.
>
> "Still trying to resurrect him, huh?" McCurry shot back.
>
> Orin pressed on. Was there a Craig Livingstone memo on bad checks? True or not?
>
> "I am not going to check, because most of what he writes in that book has already been proven to be without merit," McCurry said.
>
> "If it's not true, why don't you want to check it?"
>
> "I don't think it's worth my time to check."
>
> A CBS producer, Mark Knoller, piped up. "But Deborah's question is legitimate, isn't it, Mike?"
>
> The book, McCurry told Orin, "was filled with lies. And your newspaper, as I recall, reprinted large portions of it."
>
> "And it printed your denials, Mike. But the question is a question about a memo. Did or didn't he issue such a memo?"

"I do not know."

"Will you check?"

"No."

"Why not?"

"Because I don't want to," McCurry said. Then he threw down the gauntlet. "Does any other news organization want to pose the question?"

It was a tense moment. McCurry was suddenly the playground bully, challenging the rest of the gang to stand up for Deborah Orin. There was an uncomfortable silence. "Okay, hearing none, any other questions?" McCurry said. Another reporter asked about a Pentagon initiative, and the briefing moved on.

Orin felt humiliated. Her whole body was shaking. Afterward, several reporters approached her and apologized for their behavior. "They felt as if their balls had been cut off while my limb was cut off, " Orin said later. "The press corps was totally emasculated."

One reporter told her, "I didn't want to use up any chits for your story." Orin was stunned.

The dirty little secret of covering the White House, she felt, was that there wasn't much that McCurry and his colleagues would do to help you. Oh, you might get an early leak on some budget proposal or presidential appointment, but by and large everyone, whether in favor or not, was fed the same thin gruel. And most of the reporters would not stick their necks out and risk losing what little access they had. They had become too passive. McCurry, she realized, was winning the war.

Spin

Pool players often put spin on a ball as they hit it so that it will wind up where they want it. Political agents "spin" stories so that those stories wind up being as helpful as possible to their clients. Here is a classic example, given by Chris Matthews (1988: 168–171):

> Talk to any Wall Street analyst and you will hear plenty of stories about how much time, effort and creativity companies spend managing expectations and the reaction to their performance. When their stock moves up, it's good news, when it drops, it's "profit-taking"—good news again!
>
> Politicians call that *spin.*
>
> In 1984, Walter Mondale was the early front-runner for the Democratic nomination. His people had pursued a cautions campaign, keyed to winning powerful endorsements and making his nomination seem inevitable. Even in the Iowa caucuses, the first real test of strength, Mondale led with 49 percent to 16 percent for Colorado Senator Gary Hart.
>
> But the strategy fell apart in New Hampshire, where Hart, the young, outdoorsy, "new breed" candidate won a smashing upset. A week later, Hart upset Mondale again, in the Maine caucuses.
>
> It was now two days before Super Tuesday, the big Democratic primary day of 1984, the day Mondale's plan had called for having the nomination wrapped up. But Hart was eating him for breakfast, on his way to overwhelming wins in Massachusetts and Florida. Even Dade County was about to vote against Hubert

Humphrey's Minnesota protege. Mondale would be lucky if he could survive the big March primary day with a win in Alabama and Georgia.

Robert Beckel, Mondale's campaign manager, knew that defeat in Georgia would be disastrous.

There could be no explaining away Jimmy Carter's Vice President losing Jimmy Carter's home state.

Beckel applied spin, a spin, a sophisticated media-wise extension of "Hang a lantern on your problem." First, you admit you have a crisis. Second, while the public is buying your act, you quickly exploit the situation to turn the heat onto your opponent.

Here's the spin that Beckel put on Super Tuesday: If a defeat in Georgia spelled defeat nationally, victory in Georgia could be read as victory nationally. If Mondale took Georgia, then he was on his way to the White House.

For the thirty-six hours before the primary, Beckel talked to every reporter who would listen.

The message: Mondale needed to win in Georgia to keep his campaign alive. If he lost, he was dead; but if he won, he would survive and Hart would have failed.

Beckel had a second plan for primary night. Maybe Mondale was fizzling on the road. Maybe he lacked support in the states that were holding that day's primaries. The networks would still want pictures on primary night. NBC in particular had planned a special hour long program for 10 P.M. Eastern Standard Time on the early results of Super Tuesday.

Beckel wanted to be sure that the pictures looked damned good for Mondale. His candidate might not pull out the voters in the big primary states, but Beckel could still created a crowd for the cameras in the nation's capital. He put out a call to every known Mondale supporter in greater Washington to make sure they were at the Capitol Hilton on primary night. "You've been with Fritz," he told them. "This is one night he needs you. Be there. The whole campaign depends on it."

A respectable "Mondale crowd" gathered. Every paid campaign worker, every Washington lawyer looking for an appointment, every Democratic regular anyone could dig up assembled before the network cameras in the ballroom.

The Mondale rearguard then followed with a tactic that Jerry Bruno had made famous advancing Jack Kennedy in 1960. Partitions were used to make the room as small as possible.

"We just *packed* the joint," Beckel said later. "We threw up a partition that made the room a third the size of the ballroom. You couldn't move in the . . . place."

The video stage was set for what may have been the greatest election-night post-mortem con job in history. Mondale lost seven contests out of nine. But that was just the arithmetic. At a few minutes past ten, campaign director Robert Beckel walked into what looked like a crowded ballroom to tell the faithful that Mondale had just carried Georgia. To the NBC view audience, the event played like a victory statement.

Beckel's spin had succeeded famously. When he arrived for a live *Today* show interview the morning after Super Tuesday, Beckel was enthusiastically congratulated by Bryant Gumbel. "Yup," his elated guest beamed, "it's the comeback of the year."

Beckel had accomplished this miracle of news management in two stages: he built his media credibility by openly admitting the problem, and he built on this immediate authenticity by defining the events in the most self-serving way possible. By telling the press that a defeat in Georgia would spell Mondale's doom, he was able to claim a victory on Super Tuesday by the mere force of his candidate's victory in a single, previously overlooked primary state.

Tom Rosenstiel (1994) gives another example of spin, this time taken from the 1992 Clinton presidential campaign. During the primary campaign, a letter came to light indicating that then candidate Bill Clinton had dodged the draft as a student during the Vietnam War. Rosenstiel (1994: 76–77) tells the story of how Clinton's controllers handled a letter Clinton had written to his draft board:

> While Wooten was interviewing Clinton in New Hampshire, Koppel was calling the Clinton campaign in Little Rock, inviting Clinton onto *Nightline* to discuss the letter. And during that conversation, Koppel indicated that his source for the letter had connections to the Pentagon.
>
> Clinton refused *Nightline* in order to ponder his options. His campaign was in free fall. And he had been contacted by two competing ABC news shows about the letter. James Carville was arguing Clinton had to go on the offensive. He should release the letter himself. And citing Koppel as the source, he said, Clinton should say the Pentagon had leaked it in order to destroy him.
>
> Clinton's candidacy hung in the balance, Carville said. He was that close to being politically dead.
>
> After sleeping on it, Clinton agreed to release the letter. And after hearing Koppel repeat that the Pentagon may have had a role in the letter's release, he agreed to appear on *Nightline*.
>
> The Clinton news conference was a classic. The candidate arrived, released the letter, blamed the Pentagon for trying to get him, and cited Koppel as his source. He was trying to get out in front of a story and put his own spin on it. It was an exercise in damage control. In the political wilderness, where handlers believe perception is reality, Clinton was trying to manage reality. By their clumsiness, ABC had allowed Clinton to steal their scoop and obscure the meaning of the story.

Of course, the psychological mechanism behind spin is contrast. The "spinmeister" usually gets the voters to expect something really bad, and then when the bad story emerges it seems almost good by comparison.

Button Pushing

Politicians are quite adept at pushing emotional buttons, by appealing to fear, pity, and the crowd, especially appealing to patriotic sentiments. Consider Robert Dole's opening statement in the 1996 Clinton-Dole debate:

> MODERATOR: The order for this evening was set by coin toss. We begin now with Senator Dole and his opening statement. Senator Dole.

DOLE: Thank you very much Jim. Let me first give you a sports update. The Braves 1, Cardinals nothing—early on.

I want to thank you, and I want to thank everybody here tonight. And I want a special thanks to my wife Elizabeth, my daughter, Robin, for their love and support, and thank the people who are listening or watching all over America.

In 20 days you will decide who will lead this country into the next century. It's an awesome responsibility, and you must ask yourself, do you know enough about the candidates? You should know as much as possible about each of us.

Sometimes the views have been distorted, and millions and millions of dollars in negative advertising spent distorting my views. But tonight I hope you'll get a better feel of who Bob Dole is and what he's all about.

But I think first, you should—I should understand that the question on your mind is, do I understand your problem? But I understand that if it occurred to me, and I might just say that I come from a large family. I got lots of relatives. And they're good, average middle-class, hard-working Americans. They live all across the country. They're not all Republicans. Maybe all but one.

But in any event, I understand the problems. Whether it's two parents working because one has to pay the taxes and one has to provide for the family, whether it's a single parent who just barely pays the pressing bills, or whether you're worried about an education for your children, going to the best schools, or whether your worried about safe playgrounds, drug-free schools, crime-free schools.

This is what this election is all about.

And hopefully tonight when we conclude this debate you will have a better understanding, and the viewing and listening audience will have a better understanding.

Thank you.

Notice that Dole in rapid succession talked about: baseball (America's favorite sport); his family; his middle-class, hard-working, and numerous relatives; and decent Americans worried about taxes, drug-free schools, and so on. He said nothing about his qualifications, past accomplishments, present projects, or future plans.

Front Groups

Another tactic used by political agents is the formation of "front organizations" or "front groups." A **front group** is a group who covertly represent some special interest while seeming concerned with other issues, typically using innocuous or misleading names. A classic example, is told by Tye (1998) about the pioneer of modern public relations, Edward Bernays. Bernays represented the United Fruit Company, a huge corporation with widespread interests in Central America. A new government took over in Guatemala and apparently intended to nationalize some of the company's plantations. Bernays created "the Middle America Information Bureau," which ostensibly was a neutral group of concerned citizens with the goal of publicizing the "communist penetration" of Central America. Sure enough, the newspapers printed the stories, the public got inflamed, and the CIA backed rebels who overthrew the Guatemalan government. More recently, campaigns for various state initiatives are often paid for by groups with names such as "Americans against High Taxes" or "Americans for Honesty in Government," which are often fronts for various factions or organizations.

The point here is *not* that we should automatically dismiss whatever any front group says. That would be an ad hominem approach on our parts. However, we equally should not automatically grant what a front group advocates credence just because they call themselves some nice thing. Moreover, when they are testifying as experts to some advocated position, we have a right to know their biases.

Focus Groups

The use of focus groups is a device that enables political agents to carry out their various rhetorical tricks. A **focus group** is a sample of voters who are paid to form a discussion group led by a political agent trained in polling and political science. The agent tries phrases with the focus group and observes how they respond. Phrases that get a strong response (be it positive or negative) are noted. The political agent then passes this along to his or her employers to be used in warm and fuzzy ads, or attack ads, or in speeches outlining where a candidate stands. The candidate rattles off all these "wonderful" ideas, which "resonate with the voters"—because the voters were sampled ahead of time to see which buzz-phrases turned them on—and the audience just eats it up.

Exercise 18.2A

The following passages are taken from four sources: the October 17, 1996, Clinton–Dole Presidential debate; the October 13, 1960, Kennedy–Nixon presidential debate; the October 21, 1984, Reagan–Mondale presidential debate; and the 1952 "Checkers" speech by Richard Nixon. Each contains one or more instances of button pushing—that is, fallacious emotional appeals (appeals to pity, the crowd, and fear). Identify and discuss one such fallacy in each passage.

1. NIXON: But then I realized that there are still some who may say, and rightly so—and let me say that I recognize that some that some will continue to smear regardless of what the truth may be, but that there has been understandably some honest misunderstanding on this matter—and there's some that will say, "Well, maybe you were able, Senator, to fake this thing. How can we believe what you say? After all, is there a possibility that maybe you got some sums in cash? Is there a possibility that you may have feathered your own nest?" And so now what I am going to do—and incidentally this is unprecedented in the history of American politics—I am going at this time to give to the television and radio audience, a complete financial history; everything I've earned; everything I've spent; everything I owe. And I want you to know the facts.

    I'll have to start early. I was born in 1913. Our family was one of modest circumstances and most of my early life was spent in a store out in East Whittier. It was a grocery store—one of those family enterprises. The only reason we were able to make it go was because my mother and dad had five boys and we all worked in the store. I worked my way through college and to a great extent through law school.

And then, in 1940, probably the best thing that ever happened to me happened. I married Pat—she's sitting over there. We had a rather difficult time after we married, like so many of the young couples who may be listening to us. I practiced law, she continued to teach school. Then in 1942, I went into the service. Let me say that my service record was not a particularly unusual one. I went to the South Pacific. I guess I'm entitled to a couple of battle stars. I got a couple of letters of commendation, but I was just there when the bombs were falling and then I returned. I returned to the United States and in 1946 I ran for the Congress. When we came out of the war, Pat and I—Pat during the war had worked as a stenographer and in a bank and as an economist for a government agency—and when we came out, the total of our savings from both my law practice, her teaching, and all the time that I was in the war—the total for the entire period was just a little less than $10,000. Every cent of that, incidentally, was in government bonds.

2. MODERATOR: All right now, we go to the closing statement. Senator Dole, your first two minutes, sir.

DOLE: Well let me thank everybody here at the university and, Jim, thank you and all the people may still be watching or viewing.

This is what it's all about. It's not about me. It's not about President Clinton. It's about the process. It's about selecting the President of the United States.

So, we have our differences. We should have our differences. Mentioned other parties. They have their differences. If we all agreed it'd be a pretty dull place. We should have more debates. Maybe we'll have another debate on the economy.

But I would just say this: This is the highest honor that I've ever had in my life. To think that somebody from Russell, Kansas, somebody who grew up in living in a basement apartment, somebody whose parents didn't finish high school, somebody who spent about 39 months in hospitals after World War II, somebody who uses a button hook everyday to get dressed, somebody who understands that there are real Americans out there with real problems, whether they're soccer moms, or the single parents, or families working with seniors or people with disabilities, whoever they may be—but there are very fundamental differences in this campaign.

President Clinton opposes term limits. President Clinton opposes a constitutional amendment to balance the budget. President Clinton opposes a voluntary prayer amendment. He opposes an amendment to protect the flag of the United States of America. People give their lives—a couple of servicemen here, they sacrificed. They give everything for America. We ought to protect the American flag with a constitutional amendment. But beyond that we need to address the economy.

And I would just save my time, I'm running out here. It's a very proud moment for me. And what I want the voters to do is to make a decision. And I want them to be proud of their vote in the years ahead, proud that they voted for the right candidate, proud that they voted, hopefully, for me.

And I'll just make you one promise. My word is good. Democrats and Republican groups have said Bob Dole's word is good. I keep my word. I promise you the economy is going to get better. We're going to have a good economic package and we're going into the next century a better America.

Thank you.

3.   NIXON: My point is this: that once you do this—follow this course of action—of indicating that you are not going to defend a particular area [the small islands Quemoy and Matsu, off the coast of China], the inevitable result is that it encourages a man who is determined to conquer the world to press you to the point of no return. And that means war. We went through this tragic experience leading to World War II. We learned our lesson again in Korea. We must not learn it again. That is why I think the Senate was right, including a majority of Democrats, a majority of the Republicans, when they rejected Senator Kennedy's position of 1955. And incidentally, Senator Johnson was among those who reflected this position—voted with the seventy against the twelve. The Senate was right because they knew the lesson of history. And may I say, too, that I would trust that Senator Kennedy would change his position on this—change it; because as long as he as a major presidential candidate continues to suggest that we are going to turn over these islands, he is only encouraging the aggressors—to press the United States, to press us to the point where war would be inevitable. The road to war is always paved with good intentions. And in this instance the good intentions, of course are a desire for peace. But certainly we're going to defend what has become a symbol of freedom.

4.   MODERATOR: Mr. President [Clinton].

     CLINTON: There's one thing I'd like to say, as I agree with what Senator Dole said. It's a remarkable thing in a country like ours that a man who grew up in Russell, Kansas, and one who was born to a widowed mother in Hope, Arkansas, could wind up running for president, could have a chance to serve as president. So the first thing I want to say is thank you for giving me the chance to be President.

     This election is about two different visions about how we should go into the 21st century. Would we be better off, as I believe, working together to give each other the tools we need to make the most of our God-given potential, or are we better off saying, you're on your own?

     Would we be better off building that bridge to the future together so we call all walk across it, or saying you can get across it yourself.

     If you don't leave this room with anything else tonight, and if the people watching us don't leave the room with anything else, I hope you'll leave with this.

     This is a real important election. The world is changing dramatically in how we work, how we live, how we relate to each other. Huge changes. And the decisions we make will have enormous practical consequences.

     So we've talked about our responsibilities tonight. I want to talk about your responsibility. Your responsibility is to show up on November the 5th because you're going to decide whether we're going to balance the budget now, but protect Medicare, Medicaid, education and the environment.

     You will decide whether we're going to keep fighting crime with the Brady Bill, the assault weapons, and finish putting those 100,000 police. Whether we're going to move a million people from welfare to work.

     Whether we're going to give our families more protection for their kids against drugs and tobacco and gangs and guns. Whether we're going to give our children a world-class education where every eight year old can read, every 12-year old can log on to the Internet, every 18 year old can go to college. If we do those things, we'll build that bridge to the 21st century. And the greatest country in history will be even greater.

Thank you.

5. NIXON: Well, that's about it. That's what we have and that's what we owe. It isn't very much, but Pat and I have the satisfaction that every dime that we've got is honestly ours. I should say this—that Pat doesn't have a mink coat. And I always tell her that she'd look good in anything.

    One other think I should probably tell you because if I don't they'll probably be saying this about me too. We did get something—a gift—after the election [nomination]. A man down in Texas heard Pat on the radio mention that our two youngsters would like to have a dog. And believe it or not, the day before we left on this campaign trip, we got a message from the Union Station in Baltimore saying that they had a package for us. We went down to get. You know what it was. It was a little cocker spaniel dog, in a crate that he had sent all the way from Texas, black and white, spotted, and our little girl, Tricia, the six-year old, named it Checkers. And you know, the kids, like all kids love the dog, and I just want to say this, right now, that regardless of what they say about it, we're going to keep it.

Exercise 18.2B

The following passages are taken from the same sources as the prior ones. Each contains artful dodging (that is, pooh-poohing, shifting the burden of proof, and ignoring the issue). Indicate the question being dodged and the manner in which it is dodged.

1. MR. McGEE: Senator Kennedy, yesterday you used the word "trigger-happy" in referring to Vice President Richard Nixon's stand on defending the islands of Quemoy and Matsu. Last week on a program like this one, you said the next president would come face to face with a serious crisis in Berlin. So the question is: would you take military action to defend Berlin?

    MR. KENNEDY: Mr. McGee, we have a contractual right to be in Berlin coming out of the conversations at Potsdam and of World War II. That has been reinforced by direct commitments of the President of the United States; it's been reinforced by a number of other nations under NATO. I've stated on many occasions that the United States must meets its commitment on Berlin. It is a commitment that we have to meet if we're going to protect the security of Western Europe. And therefore on this question I don't think that there is not any doubt in the mind of any member of the community of West Berlin: I'm sure there isn't any doubt in the mind of the Russians. We will meet our commitments to maintain the freedom and independence of West Berlin.

2. QUESTION: You've been quoted as saying that you might quarantine Nicaragua. I'd like to know what that means. Would you stop Soviet ships as President Kennedy did in 1962, and wouldn't that be more dangerous than President Reagan's covert war?

    MONDALE: What I'm referring to there is the mutual self-defense provisions that exist in the inter-American treaty, the so-called Rio Pact, that permits the nations, our friends in that region, to combine to take some steps, diplomatic and otherwise, to prevent Nicaragua when she acts irresponsibly in asserting power in other parts out-side of her border to take those steps, whatever the might be, to stop it.

The Nicaraguans must know that it is the policy of our Government that those people, that leadership must stay behind the boundaries of their nations, not interfere in other nations. And by working with all of the nations in the region, unlike what the President said [the Administration] have not supported negotiations in that region, we will be much stronger because we'll have the moral authority that goes with those efforts.

3.   MODERATOR: All right, the next question for Senator Dole. Yes ma'am, right there.

QUESTION: My name is Melissa Lydeana. I'm a third-year student at U.C. San Diego. And I just want to say that it's a great honor representing the voices of Amer-ica. And my voice—my question is concerning you, Mr. Dole. All the controversy regarding your age, how do you feel you can respond to the young voices of America today, and tomorrow?

DOLE: Well, I think age is very—you know, wisdom comes from age, experience and intelligence. And if you have some of each, and I have some age and some experi-ence, some intelligence.

That adds up to wisdom. I think it is also a strength. It's an advantage. And I have a lot of young people working my office, working my campaign.

This is about America. This is about, somebody said earlier, one of the first ques-tions. We're together. It's one America. One nation.

I'm looking at our economic plan, because I'm concerned about the future for young people. I'm looking about drugs. The President's been AWOL for four years.

I'm looking about crime. He'll claim credit now for crime going down, but it hap-pens because mayors and governors and others have brought crime down. Rudy Giu-liani, the Mayor of New York, brought crime down 23 percent just in New York City. And, of course, the President will take credit for that.

My view is, we want to find jobs and opportunities and education. This year, the Republican Congress as far as student loans went from $24 billion to $36 billion over the next six years. A 50 percent increase, the highest appropriation ever. Six billion dollars for Pell grants, very, very important.

We also raised the amount of each Pell Grant.

In our economic plan, the $500 child credit can be used for young people, roll over and over and over. You're—of course, not this age. But if you have a child two-years old, seven percent interest would be worth about $18,000 by the time that child was ready for college.

4.   NIXON: It isn't easy to come before a nation-wide audience and bare your life, as I have done. But I want to say some things before I conclude, that I think most of you will agree on. Mr. Mitchell, the Chairman of the Democratic National Committee, made the statement that if a man couldn't afford to be in the United States Senate, he shouldn't run for the Senate. And I just want to make my position clear. I don't agree with Mr. Mitchell when he says that only a rich man should serve his Government in the United States Senate or in the Congress. I don't believe that represents the think-ing of the Democratic Party, and I know that it doesn't represent the thinking of the Republican Party.

5. MR. MCGEE: Uh—Senator Kennedy, a moment ago, you mentioned tax loopholes. Now your running mate, Senator Lyndon Johnson, is from Texas, an oil-producing state and one that many political leaders feel is in doubt in this election year. And reports from there say that oil men in Texas are seeking assurance from Senator Johnson that the oil depletion allowance will not be cut. The Democratic platform pledges to plug loopholes in the tax laws and refers to inequitable depletion allowance as being conspicuous loopholes. My question is, do you consider the twenty-seven and a half percent depletion allowance inequitable, and would you ask that it be cut?

MR. KENNEDY: Uh—Mr. McGee, there are about a hundred and four commodities that have some kind of depletion allowance—different kinds of minerals, including oil. I believe all of those should be gone over in detail to make sure that no one is getting a tax break; to make sure that no one is getting away from paying the taxes he ought to pay. That includes oil; it includes all kinds of minerals; it includes everything within the range of taxation. We want to be sure it's fair and equitable. It includes oil abroad. Perhaps that oil abroad should be treated differently than the oil—er—here at home. Now the oil industry recently has had hard times. Particularly some of the smaller producers. They're moving about eight or nine days in Texas. But I can assure you that if I'm elected President, that whole spectrum of taxes will be gone through carefully, and if there is any inequities in oil or any other commodity, then I would vote to close that loophole. I have voted in the past to reduce the depletion allowance for the largest producers; for those from five million dollars down, to maintain it at twenty-seven and a half percent. I believe we should study this and other allowances; tax expenses, dividend expenses, and all the rest, and make a determination of how we can stimulate growth; how can we provide the revenues needed to move our country forward.

6. QUESTION: This great nation has been established by the Founding Fathers who possessed a very strong Christian beliefs and godly principles. If elected President of the United States, what could you do to return this nation to these basic principles? And also, do you feel that the President, the office of the President, has the responsibility to set role examples to inspire our young people?

DOLE: Well, no doubt about it, our Founding Fathers had a great deal of wisdom. And in addition to what you mentioned, they also were concerned about this all-powerful central government in Washington, D.C. that would in effect confiscate your property. So I carry around in my pocket—I can't pull it out, I'd violate the rules—a copy of the 10th Amendment which says that we ought to return power to the states and power to the people, the people here. You ought to make more decisions, well a few of you. Honor, duty, and country—that's what America is all about.

Certainly the President of the United States, the highest office in the world, has the responsibility to young people, as we talked about earlier, to everyone, by example.

And as when it comes to public ethics, he has a responsibility. And you have 30 some in your administration who have either left or being investigated or in jail or whatever, and you've got an ethical problem.

It's public ethics. I'm not talking about private, we're talking about public ethics. When you have 900 files gathered up by some guy who was a bouncer in a bar and hired as a security officer to collect files—in Watergate I know a person who went to jail for looking at one file. One F.B.I. file.

There are 900 sequestered in the White House—900. People like you. Why should they be rifling through your files? So the President has a great responsibility.

It's one that I understand and certainly will carry out.

7. QUESTION: Mr. President, could I take you back to something you said earlier? And if I'm misquoting you please correct me. But I understood you to say that if the development of space military technology was successful, you might give the Soviets a demonstration and say, "here it is," which sounds to me as if you might be trying to gain the sort of advantage that would enable you to dictate terms, and which I would then suggest to you might mean scrapping a generation of nuclear strategy called mutual deterrence, in which we in effect hold each other hostage. Is that your intention?

    REAGAN: Well, I can't say that I've roundtabled that and sat down with the Chiefs of Staff, but I have said that it seems to me that this could be a logical step in what is my ultimate dream. And that is the elimination of nuclear weapons in the world. And it seems to me that this could be an adjunct, or certainly a great assisting agent, in getting that done. I am not going to roll over as Mr. Mondale suggests, and give them something that could be turned around and used against us. But I think it's a very interesting proposal to see if we can find first of all something that renders those weapons obsolete, incapable of their mission.

    But Mr. Mondale seems to approve MAD—MAD is Mutual Assured Destruction, meaning if you use nuclear weapons on us, the only thing we have to keep you from doing it is that we'll kill as many people of yours as you will kill of ours. I think that to do everything we can to find, as I say, something that would destroy weapons and humans is a great step forward in human rights.

8. QUESTION: President Clinton, my name is Cecily Kelly. Yesterday, Yassir Arafat said in Palestine that he thinks the key to success in the Middle East is the commitment of Americans. Would you, as President, send American troops to Israel or the West Bank as peace keepers?

    CLINTON: Let me just take two seconds of my time because I'm the Commander in Chief to respond to one thing that was said.

    I propose to spend $1.6 trillion on defense between now and the year 2002. And there's less than 1 percent difference between my budget and the Republican budget on defense.

    Now, on the Middle East, as you know, I've worked very hard for peace in the Middle East. The agreement between the Palestinians and the Israelis was signed at the White House.

    And the agreement—the peace treaty with Jordan, I was—went to Jordan to sign that, to be there.

    But—and I think the United States can do whatever we reasonably can. I can say this, I do not believe that Yassir Arafat wants us to send troops to the West Bank. We have never been asked to send troops to the West Bank.

9. QUESTION: Mr. Mondale, two related questions on the crucial issue of Central America. You and the Democratic Party have said that the only policy toward the horrendous civil wars in Central America should be on the economic developments and negotiations with, perhaps a quarantine of, Marxist Nicaragua. Do you really believe

that there is no need to resort to force at all? Are not these solutions to Central America's gnawing problems simply again too weak and too late?

MONDALE: I believe that the question oversimplifies the difficulties of what we must do in Central America. Our objectives ought to be to strengthen the democracy, to stop Communist and other extremist influences and stabilize the community in that area.

To do that, we need a three-pronged attack. One is military assistance to our friends who are being pressured.

Secondly, a strong and sophisticated economic aid program and human rights program that offers a better life and a sharper alternative to the alternative offered by the totalitarians who oppose us. And finally, a strong diplomatic effort that pursues the possibilities of peace in the area.

That's one of the big disagreements that we have with the President, that they have not pursued the diplomatic opportunities either within El Salvador or as between the country and its neighbors and have lost time during which we might have been able to achieve peace.

This brings up the whole question of what Presidential leadership is all about. I think the lesson in Central America, this recent embarrassment in Nicaragua where we are giving instructions for hired assassins, hiring criminals and the rest—all of this has strengthened our opponent.

A President must not only assure that we're tough. But we must also be wise and smart in the exercise of that power. We saw the same thing in Lebanon where we spent a good deal of America's assets, but because the leadership of this government did not pursue wise policies, we have been humiliated and our opponents are stronger.

The bottom line of national strength is that the President must be in command. He must lead. And when a President doesn't know that submarine missiles are re-callable, says that 70% of our forces are conventional, discovers three years into his administration that our arms control efforts have failed because he didn't know that most Soviet missiles were on land—these are things a President must know to command. A President is called the Commander-in-Chief. And he's called that because he's supposed to be in charge of facts and run our government and strengthen our nation.

Exercise 18.2C

The following passages are taken from the same sources as those cited earlier. Each contain political attacks (name-calling, smears, strawman, and false cause). Explain the fallacy in each.

1. REAGAN: I have said on a number of occasions, exactly what I believe about the Soviet Union. I retract nothing that I have said. I believe that many of the things they have done are evil in any concept of morality that we have. But I also recognize that as the two great superpowers in the world, we have to live with each other. And I told Mr. Gromyko we don't like their system. They don't like ours. And we're not gonna change their system and they sure better not try to change ours. But, between us, we can either destroy the world or we can save it. And I suggested that certainly it was to

their common interest, along with ours, to avoid a conflict and to attempt to save the world and remove the nuclear weapons. And I think that perhaps we established a little better understanding.

I think the in dealing with the Soviet Union, one has to be realistic. I know that Mr. Mondale in the past has made statements as if they were just people like ourselves and if we were kind and good and did something nice, they would respond accordingly. And the result was unilateral disarmament. We canceled the B-1 under the previous administration. What did we get for it? Nothing.

2. NIXON: Well, then the question arises: You say, "Well, how do you pay for these [expenses associated with running for the U.S. Senate] and how can you do it legally?" And there are several ways that it can be done, incidentally, and that it is done legally in the United States Senate and in the Congress. The first way is to be a rich man. I don't happen to be a rich man so I couldn't use that way. Another way that it is used is to put your wife on the payroll. Let me say, incidentally, that my opponent, my opposite number for the Vice Presidency on the Democratic ticket, does have his wife on the payroll. And has had it, her, on his payroll for the ten years—for the past ten years. Now, just let me say this. That's his business and I'm not critical of him for doing that. You will have to pass judgment on that particular point. But I have never done that for this reason: I have found that there are so many deserving stenographers and secretaries in Washington that needed the work that I just didn't feel it was right to put my wife on the payroll. My wife's sitting over here. She's a wonderful stenographer. She used to teach stenography and she used to teach shorthand in high school.

3. MR. DRUMMOND: Uh—Mr. Kennedy, Representative Adam Clayton Powell, in the course of his speaking tour in your behalf, is saying, and I quote: "The Ku Klux Klan is riding again in this campaign. If it doesn't stop, all bigots will vote for Nixon and all right thinking Christians and Jews will vote for Kennedy rather than be found in the ranks of the Klan-minded." End quotation. Governor Michael DiSalle is saying much the same thing. What I would like to ask, Senator Kennedy, is what is the purpose of this sort of thing and how do you feel about it?

MR. KENNEDY: Well the que—the—Mr. Griffin, I believe, who is the head of the Klan, who lives in Tampa, Florida, indicated a—in a statement, I think, two or three weeks ago that he was going to vote for Nixon. I do not suggest in any way, nor have I ever, that that indicates that Mr. Nixon has the slightest sympathy, involvement, or in any way imply any inference in regard to the Ku Klux Klan. That's absurd. I don't suggest that. I don't support it. I would disagree with it. Mr. Nixon knows very well that in this—in this whole matter that's been involve with the so-called religious discussion in this campaign, I've never suggested, even by the vaguest implication, that he did anything but disapprove it. And that's my view now. I disapprove of this issue. I do not suggest that Mr. Nixon does in any way.

4. DOLE: Well, I get back to the economic package, because again, I think this is very important. If there's anything that's going to change America, it's get the economy to grow.

The President inherited a good economy, sure. The S & L crisis, then they were selling assets, got a Republican Congress cutting spending finally, and he says, be the best four years ever.

That's not true. We had 1.2 million bankruptcies, set a new record. Credit card debt's never been higher. I just told you about this manufacturing job loss, which is going to increase.

We need a good strong economic package. Let the private sector create jobs, and they can do it.

5. MONDALE: Mr. President [Reagan], I accept your commitment to peace, but I want you to accept my commitment to a strong national defense. I propose a budget, I have proposed a budget, which would increase our nation's strength by, in real terms, by double that of the Soviet Union. I tell you where we disagree. It is true, over 10 years ago I voted to delay production of the F-14 and I'll tell you why. The plane wasn't flying the way it was supposed to be, it was a waste of money.

Your definition of national strength is to throw money at the Defense Department. My definition of national strength is to make certain a dollar spent buys us a dollar's worth of defense. There's a big difference between the two of us. A President must manage that budget. I will keep us strong, but you'll not do that unless you command that budget and make certain we get the strength we need. When you pay $500.00 for a $5.00 hammer, you're not buying strength.

6. KENNEDY: On the question of the cost of our budget, I have stated that it's my best judgment that our agricultural program will cost a billion and a half, possibly two billion dollars less than the present agricultural program. My judgment is that the program the Vice President put forward, which is an extension of Mr. Benson's program, will cost a billion dollars more than the present program, which cost about six billion dollars a year, the most expensive in history. We've spent more money on agriculture in the last eight years than the hundred years of the Agricultural Department before that.

7. MONDALE: One of the biggest problems today is that the countries to our south are so desperately poor that these people who will almost lose their lives if they don't come north, come north despite all the risks. And if we're going to find a permanent, fundamental answer to this, it goes to American economic and trade policies that permit these nations to have a chance to get on their own two feet and to get prosperity so that they can have jobs for themselves and their people.

And that's why this enormous national debt, engineered by this Administration, is harming these countries and fueling this immigration.

These high interest rates, real rates, that have doubled under this Administration, have had the same effect on Mexico and so on, and the cost of repaying those debts is so enormous that it results in massive unemployment, hardship and heartache. And that drives our friends to the north—to the south—up into our region, and the need to end those deficits as well.

8. MODERATOR: Mr. President, your rebuttal.

REAGAN: Well, my rebuttal is I've heard the national debt blamed for a lot of things, but not for illegal immigration across our border, and it has nothing to do with it.

But with regard to these high interest rates, too, at least give us the recognition of the fact that when you left office, Mr. Mondale, they were $22\frac{1}{2}$, the prime rate; it's now $12\frac{1}{4}$, and I predict it'll be coming down a little more shortly. So we're trying to undo some of the things that your Administration did.

9.   NIXON: Why do I feel so deeply? Why do I feel that in spite of the smears, the misunderstanding, the necessity for a man to come up here and bare his soul, as I have, why is it necessary for me to continue this fight? And I want to tell you why. Because, you see, I love my country. And I think my country is in danger. And I think the only man that can save America at this time is the man that's running for President on my ticket, Dwight Eisenhower. You say, "Why do I think it's in danger?" and I say, "Look at the record." Seven years of the Truman-Acheson administration and what's happened? Six hundred million people lost to the Communists. And a war in Korea, in which we have lost 177,000 American casualties. And I say to all of you that a policy that results in a loss of six hundred million people to Communists and a war which cost us 177,000 American casualties isn't good enough for America. And I say that those in the State Department that make the mistakes which caused that war and which resulted in those losses should be kicked out of the State Department just as fast as we get them out of there. And let me say that I know Mr. Stevenson won't do that because he defends the Truman policies. And I know that Dwight Eisenhower will do that and that he will give America the leadership it needs.

3   *Overcoming Political Trickery*

We have seen how political agents can exploit the same psychological mechanisms that sales agents do. How can we resist such rhetorical trickery? Several rules come to mind.

Rule 1: Try to pit one political agent against another. Remember that the political agent who is trying to influence you is in an adversarial position toward you; that is, he or she is advocating a position with no obligation to present the other side. So train yourself to resist agreeing until you listen to agents of contrary views. If you are reading a flyer put out by one candidate, go out of your way to find and read flyers put out by his or her opponent.

Additionally, try to seek out contexts that are more balanced than speeches or ads. Why? Well, with a speech or an ad, the politician can completely control the discourse and not face immediate criticism. But in interviews and debates, the politician is forced to some degree to respond to points made by another. This tends to make such discourse more informative (dialogues tend to be more informative than monologues), but we should still be aware of logical problems.

Consider, first, interviews. Politicians will often ignore the issue/question put to them if they can get away with it. One way to improve the quality of an interview is to structure it so that the questioner can do immediate "follow-ups"—that is, ask the politician to amplify or more adequately respond to a given question. Not surprisingly, many politicians are reluctant to grant one-on-one, no-holds-barred interviews unless they believe that the interviewer is highly sympathetic to their point of view.

Political debates between politicians or political advocates have an advantage over interviews in that each side is overtly representing its position. As such, each opponent has an interest in exposing the fallacies and falsehoods put forward by the other. In fact, however, most American political debates (as opposed to British or Canadian ones) are not true debates but rather tandem candidate interviews with limited power of reply. That is, a question is put to a candidate, and then each candidate replies to the question and makes comments (if time) on the opponent's answer. Even within such a debate, fallacies are common.

Another way to get both sides of the story is to subscribe to political journals on all sides of the political spectrum. If you read a lot of left-of-center publications, subscribe to a couple of right-of-center ones as well; if you read primarily right-of-center publications, try reading some on the other side of the fence.

Remember that while there are truth-in-advertising laws, there are no "truth-in-campaigning" laws. So you need to take special care to listen to both sides of the issue.

Rule 2: Read primary sources as well as secondary ones. Remember that political agents are trained to "spin"—that is, to interpret and present situations in a way that benefits their clients. The best way to defeat spin is to learn the facts yourself. When a political agent interprets a speech for you, read the speech yourself. When a political columnist writes about an event, characterizing it in some slanted way, try to consult more straight news sources (such as wire reports about the event) before agreeing with the columnist's take on things.

One final note to conclude this chapter. There is no way to discuss how to resist the rhetorical trickery of political agents without bringing up the failure of many, if not most, voters to read and learn about the issues and candidates. As the professional political agent Raymond Price said (McGinnis 1969: 38):

> "Voters are basically lazy, basically uninterested in making an *effort* to understand what we're talking about, . . ." Price wrote. "Reason requires a high degree of discipline, of concentration; impression is easier. Reason pushes the viewer back, it assaults him, it demands that he agree or disagree; impression can envelop him, invite him in, without making an intellectual demand. . . . When we argue with him we demand that he make the effort of replying. We seek to engage his intellect, and for most people this is the most difficult work of all. The emotions are more easily roused, closer to the surface, more malleable."

Or, as Harry Treleaven, an advertising expert who specialized in political campaigns, puts the point (McGinnis 1969: 44–45):

> Later in the winter following the campaign to elect George Bush, Treleaven wrote a long report of what he had done. He called it "Upset: The Story of a Modern Political Campaign," and had seven copies made. He had written of himself in the third person: "Treleaven, of course, looked long and carefully at candidate George Bush. What he saw he liked—and more importantly, he recognized that what he liked was highly promotable."
>
> One thing that intrigued Treleaven was that issues would not have to be involved in the campaign. There was no issue when it came to selling Ford automobiles; there was only the product, the competition and the advertising. He saw no reason why politics should be any different.
>
> He wrote in "Upset," "Most national issues today are so complicated, do difficult to understand, and have opinions on that they either intimidate or more often, bore the average voter. . . . Few politicians recognize this fact."

Harry Treleaven went around Houston in the August heat, asking people on the street what they thought of George Bush. He found that Bush was "an extremely likable person," but that there was haziness about where he stood politically."

This was perfect. "There'll be few opportunities for logical persuasion," Treleaven wrote, "which is all right—because probably more people vote for irrational, emotional reasons than professional politicians suspect."

A classic example of voter ignorance is from the 1964 Barry Goldwater campaign for the presidency (Matthews 1988: 198):

There's a great old political story passed down over the years: An elderly woman tells a reporter why she intends to vote against Senator Barry Goldwater, the 1964 Republican candidate for President:

"He's the guy who's going to get rid of TV."

"But madam," interrupts the reporter, "I think you're making a mistake. Senator Goldwater is talking about getting rid of the Tennessee Valley Authority, TVA."

"Well," the elderly woman persists, "I'm not taking any chances."

If you are unwilling to put out the effort to learn where the candidates stand on the issues, you will be an easy voter to manipulate.

InfoTrac College Edition

You can locate InfoTrac College Edition articles about this chapter by accessing the InfoTrac College Edition Web site (www.infotrac-college.com/wadsworth/). Using the InfoTrac College Edition subject guide, enter the search terms relevant to this chapter, and then read abstracts for relevant articles.

Glossary

Abusive form (of attacking the person): Attacking a person's character

Accent: Changing the meaning of a word or phrase by stressing or omitting part of it

Accident: The fallacy of applying a general rule in an atypical way or to an atypical case

Adversary position: A sales or political agent is in an adversary position with respect to the consumer or voter if the agent is solely concerned with persuasion (that is, presents only a one-sided case).

Ambiguous: A word is ambiguous if it has more than one meaning.

Amphiboly: A sentence that is ambiguous due to grammatical construction

Analogy: A comparison of one thing (called the *subject*) to one or more other things (called the *analogs*)

Announcement: A statement about where a person or group stands on some issue

Antecedent: The component that follows the *if* in a conditional

Appeal to fear: To use threats or scare tactics instead of evidence to get a point accepted

Appeal to pity: To invoke the feeling of pity instead of giving evidence to get a point accepted

Appeal to sex: A form of appeal to the crowd in which allusions to sex replace rational evidence

Appeal to the crowd: Arousing feelings of group identity instead of giving evidence to get a point accepted

Apples and oranges: A form of ignoring the issue in which the speaker lumps the real issue *A* in with irrelevant issue *B*, and then directs his argument to *B*

Arguing against the person: Attacking the person

Argument: A set of one or more statements, called the *premises,* taken as evidence for another statement, called the *conclusion*

Argumentum ad baculum: Appeal to fear

Argumentum ad hominem: Attacking the person

Argumentum ad ignorantiam: Arguing that something must be true (or false) because nobody can prove it is not

Argumentum ad misoricordiam: Appeal to pity

Argumentum ad populum: Appeal to the crowd

Argumentum ad vericundiam: Illogical appeal to authority

Artful dodging: Systematically refusing to answer questions responsively; that is, pooh-poohing and ignoring the issue

Association (psychological mechanism): The tendency to assume a causal connection faced with a temporal one

Assumptive pitch: A sales pitch using a loaded question

Attack ads: Political ads that associate a candidate with negative things

Attacking the person: Criticizing a person instead of giving evidence that his or her point is wrong

Authority (psychological mechanism): The tendency to obey authorities

Bad appeal to authority: Using the testimony of an "expert" as evidence for a point, when that expert is not identified, not competent in the area under discussion, not quoted in full, not current, or not unbiased

Bait and switch: A deceptive sales tactic in which an item is advertised for a very low price, but when customers show up to buy it, they are told it is sold out and then shown other less desirable or more expensive items

Bandwagon argument: Arguing that something is true on the basis that everybody or most people believe it

Begging the question: Assuming during the course of your argument the very thing you are supposed to prove

Biased description: Using loaded language to slant evidence

Biconditional: A compound with two components. A biconditional is true if and only if both components have the same truth value.

Binary compound statement: A compound statement with two components

Button pushing: Appealing to emotion

Categorical proposition: A statement of the form "all/some S is/are P"; that is, "[quantifier] [subject term] [copula] [predicate term]"

Causal chain: A finite sequence of events linked by causal connections

Causal claim: A statement that something A causes something B

Causal slippery slope (argument): An argument of the following form:

1. If A_1 occurs, then it will cause A_2, which in turn will cause $A_3, \ldots$, ultimately causing A_n.
2. But A_n has negative consequences.

∴   We should not do A_1.

Causally necessary condition (for a given effect): A factor in whose absence the effect cannot occur

Causally sufficient condition (for a given effect): A factor that by itself produces the effect

Cause: A causes B means that A produces or brings about B

Caviling: A form of ignoring the issue in which petty details are discussed instead of the larger issue at hand

Circumstantial variety (of attacking the person): Accusing a person of bias

Claim: Statement

Class: A group of things

Classify: To group objects into categories depending upon various properties or characteristics of those objects

Coining definition: One that assigns a meaning to a new word

Collective use (of a general term): Use of that term to refer to the members of the group collectively—that is, as a whole

Complement of a set: The set of those members of the universal set that are not members of the original set

Compliance specialist: A person paid to make others comply with the wishes of his or her employer

Composition: Either assuming that what is true of the parts is true of the whole or else using a general term distributively in the premises and collectively in the conclusion

Compound cause: A cause with component factors that work together to produce the effect

Compound question: One that contains one or more questions as components

Compound statement: A statement that contains one or more other statements as components

Conceptual mapping: The classification of meanings

Conclusion indicator: A word that signals that the clause following it expresses the conclusion

Conditional: A statement that if some component statement *A* (called the *antecedent*) is true, then a second statement *B* (called the *consequent*) will be true

Confounding variable: An alternate possible cause of the effect being investigated

Conjunction: A compound of two statements *A* and *B* that asserts that both are true

Consequent: The component that follows the *then* in a conditional

Consistent: A group of statements is consistent if and only if it is possible for all of them to be true.

Constant conjunction (of *A* and *B*): *A* and *B* always occur together.

Context: The passages or conversation surrounding a passage or remark

Contingent: A statement is contingent if it is possible for it to be false and possible for it to be true.

Contradiction: A statement that cannot possibly be true

Contradictories: Two statements are contradictories if they cannot both be false and cannot both be true.

Contraries: Two statements are contraries if they can both be false but cannot both be true.

Contrast (psychological mechanism): The tendency to judge a situation by comparison with what immediately preceded it.

Contributing factor: A partial cause

Control the agenda: To frame questions so as to make them easier to answer

Controlled cause-to-effect experiment: In such an experiment, a sample of the target population is divided into two subgroups, the experimental group and the control group. The experimental group is subjected to the suspected causal factor being tested, while the control group is treated the same way except for not being subjected to the suspected causal factor. Subsequently, both groups are checked to observe the frequency of the effect. If the difference in observed frequency is large enough, we can conclude that the causal factor caused the effect.

Correct answer (to a question): A true, responsive answer to that question

Corrective answer (to a question): A statement that indicates that one or more of the presuppositions to a question is false

Correlation: Two features F_1 and F_2 are correlated if and only if the percentage of those with F_2 is higher or lower among those with F_1 than among those lacking F_1.

Correlation fallacy: The fallacy of concluding that A causes B simply because A and B occur together

Corroborate: To support by physical evidence

Critical thinking: The process of improving your overall worldview and using it more efficiently in understanding the world around you and in making decisions

Debunking: A corrective answer to a why-question

Deductive logic: The study of arguments to determine which are valid and why

Deductive validity: An argument is deductively valid if and only if it is impossible for the premises to be true and the conclusion false.

Defeasible: A law or rule is defeasible if it can be rendered inapplicable by exceptional circumstances.

Definiendum: The word being defined in a definition

Definiens: The word or phrase that defines the word being defined in a definition

Definition: Giving the meaning of a word

Demeanor: The way in which a person presents him- or herself

Deontic authority: An authority because of the power he or she possesses

Describe: To give a set of propositions that characterize a situation

Detensifier: An adverb of degree used to diminish the power of a predicate

Deterministic cause: One that produces its effect in all cases

Direct answer (to a question): A statement that completely answers the question but gives no more information than is needed

Directly relevant (to a question): A statement is directly relevant to a question if and only if it is a responsive answer to that question.

Disjunction: A compound with two components. A disjunction is true if and only if at least one of the components is true.

Distributive use (of a general term): Using that term to refer to members of the group as individuals

Diversion: A form of ignoring the issue in which the speaker changes the subject by joking

Division: Either assuming that what is true of the whole is true of the parts or else using a general term collectively in the premises and distributively in the conclusion

Double-blind experiment: An experiment in which neither the patients nor the doctors administering the experimental drugs know which patients are receiving the real drug and which are receiving the placebo

Empty set: The set containing no members

Entail: A statement A entails a statement B if and only if it is impossible for A to be true and B to be false.

Enthymeme: An argument with unstated premises or conclusion

Entrenchment (psychological mechanism): The tendency to stay in a course of action after an early commitment

Enumeration: Observing every member of a whole population; that is, a sample of 100 percent of the population.

Enumerative definition: Defining the reference of a term by naming the things in it

Epistemic authority: An authority because of what he or she knows

Equivocation: Shifting from one meaning (of an ambiguous word or phrase) to another during the course of an argument, or using an ambiguous sentence to mislead the listener or reader

Erotetic: Having to do with questions

Essence: The essence of something is the set of properties that define or necessarily characterize it

Euphemism: A phrase that is a gentler or more appealing way of expressing a concept

Evaluative statement: A statement about the worth or goodness of something

Exclusive disjunction: A binary compound that is true if and only if one but only one of its components is true

Exemplify: To give an illustration of a claim

Expert: Epistemic authority

Explanandum: The phenomenon we are trying to explain

Explanans: The statements that explain the phenomenon

Explanation: A direct answer to a why-question; that is, a set of statements (called the *explanans*) that jointly entail or establish the statement of the phenomenon to be explained (called the *explanandum*)

Explicit definition: A direct equation of meaning between the definiens and definiendum

Extension (of a term): The class of objects referred to by that term

Extrinsic worth: Instrumental worth

Factual statement: A statement that is intended to describe the world

Fallacy: (1) Broad sense: a mistake in reasoning. We can commit fallacies in questioning, arguing, deciding, and any other area of reasoning. (2) Narrow sense: an illogical argument; that is, an argument that is neither valid nor strong

False analogy: A comparison that overlooks significant differences between the things compared

False cause: Arguing that *A* causes *B* merely on the basis that *A* and *B* are linked in time

False dilemma: A dilemma in which either significant options are overlooked or consequences of stated options are misstated

Figurative language: Language using figures of speech

Figure of speech: A word or phrase used in a nonliteral way to increase the emotional or rhetorical effect of the sentence

Focus group: A sample of voters who meet under the supervision of a political agent. The agent observes what phrases or ideas elicit responses with the group and uses that information to help politicians craft ads and speeches.

Front group: A group who covertly represent some special interest while seeming concerned with other issues

Fruitful: A hypothesis is fruitful if it explains and predicts new facts.

General simple statement: A simple statement that refers to a group of individuals

General term: A term that refers to a group

Genetic fallacy: A case of attacking the person in which an idea is dismissed on the basis of the alleged defects of the group who originated that idea

Gift pitch: A sales pitch involving the promise of a prize or give-away item

Glittering generalities: A form of ignoring the issue in which a general issue rather than the specific issue at hand is talked about.

Golden opportunity pitch: A pitch alluding to some imminent event that allegedly should incline the consumer to buy

Grading: Classification with evaluation

Grammatical ambiguity: Ambiguity arising from the bad grammatical structure of a sentence

Greed (psychological mechanism): The tendency always to want more than we have

Guilt by association: A form of attacking the person in which a person is discredited by attacking the group to which he or she belongs, or his or her associates

Hasty generalization: A generalization made on the basis of an unrepresentative sample

Hedging: The fallacy of changing a statement during an argument by understating it

How-question: A request for the techniques for doing some task

Hyperbole: Overstatement

Hypostatization: Treating an abstraction as if it were a concrete object

Hypothesis: A proposed explanation

Ignoratio elenchi: Ignoring the issue

Ignoring the issue: Arguing about something other than the point at hand

Inclusive disjunction: A binary compound that is true if and only if one or both of its components are true

Inconsistent: A set of statements is inconsistent if and only if it is impossible for all of them to be true.

Indirectly relevant (to a question): A statement is indirectly relevant to a question if and only if it is evidence for some responsive answer to that question.

Inductive logic: The study of arguments to determine their degree of strength and why

Inductively strong: An argument is inductively strong if and only if it is not impossible but it is unlikely that the conclusion would be false given that the premises are true.

Innuendo: A negative suggestion made by disguised or veiled comments about someone

Instrumental worth: Value as a tool to obtain something else

Intension (of a term): The set of properties in virtue of which an object is part of the extension of the term

Interrogative sentence: A sentence ending with a question mark

Intersection (of two sets): The set composed of those objects common to both sets

Intrinsic worth: Desirable in and of itself, ultimate value

Irony: The use of words with literal meaning the opposite of what is really meant

Irrelevant slippery slope: A form of ignoring the issue, in which the speaker changes the issue to some other irrelevant issue by degrees

Jargon: Needlessly long or technical verbiage

Laden: A word is laden if it has emotional or theoretical connotations.

Lexical ambiguity: Ambiguity arising from the multiple meanings assigned to a word in a sentence

Linked support: The support of a conclusion by two or more premises that work together

Loaded language: Using laden words to bias the statement of evidence in favor of a predetermined conclusion

Loaded question: A question with a false or debatable presupposition

Logic: The normative study of the evidential relations between premises and conclusions of arguments

Logical equivalence: Two statements are logically equivalent if it is impossible for them to differ in truth value.

Matched: A sample is matched to the general population if and only if it is stratified.

Meiosis: Understatement

Memory: A perceptual report of a past perception

Metaphor: A word or phrase meaning one kind of thing is applied to another kind of thing for the purpose of suggesting a likeness between the two

Metonym: The use of a word or phrase to stand for something to which it has an important relation

Mob appeal: a form of appeal to the crowd in which feelings of ethnic, national, or religious identity are manipulated

Modality: A claim about the degree of confidence the speaker has in a given statement

Model: (1) Another word for worldview; (2) another word for analogy (used in scientific writings)

Multiple cause: Compound cause

Name: A term that refers to a particular individual

Name-calling: Attacking an opponent with abusive language

Necessarily false: A statement is necessarily false if it is impossible for it to be true.

Necessarily true: A statement is necessarily true if it is impossible for it to be false.

Necessary truth: A statement that cannot possibly be false

Negation: A compound with one component. A negation is true if and only if the component is false.

Negative correlation: F_1 is negatively correlated with F_2 if the percentage of those with F_2 is lower among those with F_1 than those without F_1.

Nit-picking: Caviling

Nonexperimental cause-to-effect study: A study in which a sample of the target population is divided into two groups, one of individuals who have been exposed to the suspected cause (the subject group), and the other of individuals who have not been exposed to the suspected cause (the control group). The groups are then examined for the frequency of the effect. If there is a sufficiently large difference in observed frequencies, we infer that the suspected cause is the real cause.

Nonexperimental effect-to-cause study: A study in which a sample of the target population is divided into those who already have the effect (the subject group) and those who do not have the effect (the control group). The groups are then examined for the frequency of the suspected cause. If there is a significantly greater frequency of the suspected cause in the control group than in the subject group, we infer that it is the real cause.

Observation statement: A statement about what we perceive/observe

Observe: To perceive

Operational definition: Defining a term by giving experimental criteria that must be met for that term to apply

Ostensive definition: Defining the reference of a term by pointing to it

Overstate: To use words that increase the content or force of the claim

Partial cause: A component of a compound cause

Particular simple statement: A single statement that refers to a particular individual

Path: A row in a truth table

Perceive: To comprehend, make sense of, or recognize what is being sensed

Perception: An act of perceiving

Perceptual report: An observation statement

Personify: Treat a nonhuman object as if it were human

Persuasive definition: A definition intended to influence attitudes

Pertinent: Reasonably related to the general context of conversation

Photo op: "Photo opportunity"; a situation contrived to allow a politician to be photographed in a positive context

Physical claim: Factual claim about the physical world

Physical statement: A factual statement about the physical world

Placebo: An inert pill or treatment

Pooh-poohing: Dismissing rather than arguing against your opponent's point

Population: The entire group of individuals targeted by a generalization

Positive assertion: The emphatic assertion of a claim without any warrant or proof

Positive correlation: F_1 is positively correlated with F_2 if the percentage of those with F_2 is higher among those with F_1 than among those without F_1.

Post hoc ergo propter hoc: The fallacy of concluding that A caused B solely on the basis of the fact that A happened before B

Precedent: Past adjudicated cases

Precising definition: One that aims to reduce the vagueness of a term

Predicate: A term that refers to a property of an individual or a relation among individuals

Prediction: An answer to a question about the future

Premise cluster: A group of mutually linked premises

Premise indicator: A word that signals that the clause following it expresses a premise

Presupposition (of a question): A statement that must be true if that question is to have any true answer

Principle of charity: Trying to interpret/fill in unstated premises so as to make the most defensible argument before criticizing it

Projected property: The property of the sample in a generalization that we are inferring to hold of the population

Proposition: A statement

Proximate cause: The event immediately prior to the end of a causal chain

Psychological mechanism: A sequence of behaviors that occur in virtually the same fashion and in the same order whenever a specific feature (the "trigger feature") of the environment is encountered

Psychological statement: A factual claim about the mental world

Puffing: Overstating the quality of something

Qualifier: A phrase that limits the application of the predicate

Quantifier: A word or phrase that refers to a portion of a group

Question: A request for information

Random/randomly selected: A sample is random/randomly selected if and only if every individual in the population has an equal chance of being in the sample.

Reciprocity: The inclination to return favor for favor

Recursive definition: Defining a term by giving a generating function for objects of that kind

Red herring: A highly controversial but irrelevant side issue

Reference: The objects picked out by a term

Referentially unclear: A phrase whose meaning allows several referents and whose actual referent is not made clear by context

Reformative definition: A definition that is intended to establish a new meaning for an existing term

Reification: Treating an abstraction as if it were a concrete object

Relevant (to a generalization): A property R is relevant to a generalization if and only if individuals with R are more (or less) likely to have the projected property than the average for that population.

Relevant (to a question): A statement is relevant to a question if and only if it is either directly or indirectly relevant to that question.

Remote cause: The first event in a causal chain

Repeated assertion: Repeating a claim without offering any proof of it

Rephrase: To restate a point using different words

Reportive definition: A definition that gives the meaning speakers actually assign to the word defined

Representative: A sample is representative if and only if it likely has the same proportion of the projected property as does the population as a whole.

Request (of a question): States how many of the alternatives presented by the question are desired in the answer

Responsive answer to a question: A statement that has the appropriate logical form to be a possible answer to that question

Salience (psychological mechanism): The tendency to focus on some features of a situation rather than others, depending on state of mind

Sample: The group of individuals actually examined/observed in a generalization

Scarcity (psychological mechanism): The tendency to value something more highly if it is seen as scarce

Sense (of a term): The set of qualities that the word connotes

Sense (the world): To experience the world through sight, smell, touch, hearing, and taste

Sentence: A grammatical sequence of words of a language

Set: Any collection of things

Set theory: That branch of mathematics that studies sets

Shifting the burden of proof: Trying to make the other person do the proving, when you ought to be doing so

Shill: A person who is paid to appear as a customer

Short-term thinking: Calculating costs and benefits over the short run

Simile: A stated comparison between different things, using the explicit word *like* or *as*

Simple cause: One that does not contain components

Simple question: One that does not contain any questions as components

Simple statement: A statement that contains no other statements as parts or components

Single-blind experiment: An experiment in which the researchers and doctors know who gets the experimental treatment but the patients do not.

Single support: The support of a conclusion by a premise taken singly

Smearing: Attacking an opponent by accusing him or her of bias or hypocrisy

Social proof (psychological mechanism): The tendency to judge what is good or proper by looking at what other people think is good or proper

Sophistry: Illogical but persuasive argumentation

Sorting: Classification without evaluation

Sound: An argument is sound if and only if it is valid and all the premises are true.

Special pleading: Stating only the evidence favorable to a given position or only the benefits of a given product

Spin: To present a story in such a way as to make it more favorable

Spot ads: Small ads that aim to convince through mere repetition

Statement: Something that may be asserted or denied

Statement of aesthetic value: Judgments about the artistic worth of literary, musical, or artistic works.

Statement of moral obligation: A statement about what people ought to do

Statement of moral worth: A judgment about the moral desirability of people's character traits and motives

Statement of nonmoral worth: A statement about the desirability of objects or sensations

Statistical cause: One that tends to produce its effect in populations

Stipulative definition: Coining definition

Stratified: A sample is stratified if and only if it shares all properties relevant to the projected property with the population.

Strawman: A form of ignoring the issue in which rather than address the issue at hand, the speaker addresses a distortion of it

Subcontraries: Two statements are subcontraries if and only if they cannot both be false but can both be true.

Subject (of a question): The range of alternatives the question presents

Subliminal ad: An ad aimed below the level of conscious perception

Suggestive definition: One that suggests a given meaning be assigned to the word defined

Summary: A set of statements that highlights or repeats points made earlier in a passage

Sweeping generalization: An overstated, unqualified general statement

Sympathy (psychological mechanism): The tendency to want to help others in need

Sympathy pitch: A sales pitch that appeals to pity

Synonymic definition: Defining the meaning of one word by giving another

Synonyms: Words of identical or nearly identical meanings

Tautology: A statement that cannot possibly be false

Taxonomy: The classification of objects

Temporal linkage: A connection in time

Testimonials: Ads in which a putative satisfied customer or an alleged expert endorses a product

Testimony: The observation reports of others

Theoretical definition: A definition intended to bring the meaning of a term closer to current scientific theory

Time-lapse sample: Two or more samples taken at various times and then compared

Truth-functional compound: A compound whose truth value is determined solely by the values of the components

Truth value: Whether a statement is true or false

Tu quoque: A form of attacking the person in which the speaker is accused of hypocrisy

Ultimate worth: Intrinsic worth

Unary compound statement: A compound statement with only one component

Understate: To use words that diminish the content or force of a claim

Union (of two sets): The set composed of all the elements of the two component sets

Universal set: The set containing everything

Unspecific: A word/phrase is unspecific if its reference is unstated.

Vague: A word is vague if it has imprecise meaning.

Verbose: A sentence is verbose if it is needlessly wordy.

Warm and fuzzy ads: Political ads that associate a candidate with positive things

Weasel words: Detensifiers

Whether-question: A question that presents its subjects explicitly and requests the respondent to select among them

Which-question: A question that presents its subjects by means of some description and requests the respondent to select the things that fit the description

Why-question: A request for explanation or proof

Wishful thinking: Overestimating the chances of success for a given option

Worldview: A set of beliefs about the world or some part or aspect of it

Bibliography

Anderson, Lisa. 1998. "Deception Plays Big Role in Kid Charities." *Orange County Register,* March 15, p. 1.

Arnauld, Antoine, and Pierre Nicole. 1996. *Logic or the Art of Thinking.* Cambridge: Cambridge University Press.

Baird, Davis. 1992. *Inductive Logic: Probability and Statistics.* Englewood Cliffs, N.J.: Prentice Hall.

Belnap, Nuel D., and Thomas B. Steel, Jr. 1976. *The Logic of Questions and Answers.* New Haven, Conn.: Yale University Press.

Bennett, James T., and Thomas J. DiLorenzo. 1994. *Unhealthy Charities: Hazardous to Your Health and Wealth.* New York: Basic Books.

Cialdini, Robert B. 1993. *Influence: The Psychology of Persuasion.* New York: Morrow.

Cohen, Morris, and Ernest Nagel. 1934. *An Introduction to Logic and Scientific Method.* New York: Harcourt, Brace & World.

Copi, Irving M., and Carl Cohen. 1998. *Introduction to Logic.* 10th ed. Upper Saddle River, N.J.: Prentice Hall.

Dimitrius, Jo-Ellen. 1998. *Reading People.* New York: Ballantine.

Dorner, Dietrich. 1996. *The Logic of Failure: Why Things Go Wrong and What We Can Do to Make Them Right.* New York: Holt.

Duhem, Pierre. 1954. *The Aim and Structure of Physical Theory.* Trans. P. P. Wiener. Princeton, N.J.: Princeton University Press.

Edwards, Betty. 1989. *Drawing on the Right Side of the Brain.* Los Angeles: Tarcher.

Erwin, Edward. 1996. *A Final Accounting: Philosophical and Empirical Issues in Freudian Psychology.* Cambridge, Mass.: MIT Press.

Flesch, Rudolf. 1946. *The Art of Plain Talk.* New York: Harper.

Frankena, William. 1973. *Ethics.* 2d ed. Englewood Cliffs, N.J.: Prentice Hall.

Friedlander, Michael W. 1995. *At the Fringes of Science.* Boulder, Colo.: Westview.

Giere, Ronald N. 1979. *Understanding Scientific Reasoning.* New York: Holt, Rinehart, & Winston.

Greeley, Father Andrew. 1986. *Confessions of a Parish Priest.* New York: Simon & Schuster.

Green, Jonathan. 1996. *Chasing the Sun: Dictionary Makers and the Dictionaries They Made.* New York: Holt.

Groarke, Leo, Christopher Tindale, and Linda Fisher. 1997. *Good Reasoning Matters! A Constructive Approach to Critical Thinking,* Ontario: Oxford University Press.

Halpern, Diane F. 1989. *Thought and Knowledge.* Hillsdale, N.J.: Erlbaum.

Hempel, Carl G. 1966. *The Philosophy of Natural Science.* Englewood Cliffs, N.J.: Prentice Hall.

Hesse, Mary B. 1963. *Models and Analogies in Science.* London: Sheed & Ward.

Holyoak, Keith, and Paul Thagard. 1996. *Mental Leaps: Analogy in Creative Thought.* Cambridge, Mass.: MIT Press.

Huber, Peter. 1991. *Galileo's Revenge: Junk Science in the Courtroom.* New York: Basic Books.

Huff, Darrell. 1952. *How to Lie with Statistics.* New York: Norton.

Jason, Gary. 1994. *Introduction to Logic.* Boston: Jones & Bartlett.

Johnston, Moira. 1977. *Spectral Evidence: The Ramona Case: Incest, Memory and Truth on Trial in Napa Valley.* New York: Houghton Mifflin.

Knap, Chris. 1999. "BMW Says Cadillac Is Big Fibber." *Orange County Register,* May 25, Business Section, p. 1.

Konner, Melvin. 1982. *The Tangled Wing: Biological Constraints on the Human Spirit.* New York: Rinehart & Winston.

Langford, Jerome J. 1998. *Galileo, Science and the Church.* South Bend, Ind.: St. Augustine's.

Leno, Jay. 1992. *Jay Leno's Headlines Book I, II, III: Real but Ridiculous Headlines from America's Newspapers.* New York: Random House.

Levi, Edward H. 1949. *An Introduction to Legal Reasoning.* Chicago: University of Chicago Press.

Lipton, Peter. 1993. *Inference to the Best Explanation.* London: Routledge.

Loftus, Elizabeth F. 1996. *Eyewitness Testimony.* Cambridge, Mass.: Harvard University Press.

Loftus, Elizabeth, and Katherine Ketchum. 1994. *The Myth of Repressed Memory: False Memories and Allegations of Sexual Abuse.* New York: St. Martin's.

Lunzer, Francesca. 1985. "Bitter Pills." *Forbes,* June 3, p. 203.

Mill, John Stuart. 1967. *A System of Logic.* London: Longmans.

Nagel, Ernest. 1961. *The Structure of Science: Problems in the Logic of Scientific Explanation.* New York: Harcourt, Brace & World.

Neaman, Judith, and Carole Silver. 1995. *The Wordsworth Book of Euphemisms.* Hertfordshire, England: Wordsworth.

Popper, Karl R. 1994. *The Myth of Framework.* London: Routledge.

Purtill, Richard L. 1972. *Logical Thinking.* New York: Harper & Row.

"Rethinking Thinking." 1999. *The Economist* 353, no. 8150 (December 18–30): 63–65.

Reynolds, Quentin. 1950. *Courtroom: The Story of Samuel S. Leibowitz.* New York: Farrar, Strauss.

Ridley, Matt. 1996. *The Origins of Virtue: Human Instincts and the Evolution of Cooperation.* New York: Penguin.

Robinson, Adam, and John Katzman. 1993. *The Princeton Review: Cracking the GRE.* New York: Villard.

Robinson, Richard. 1954. *Definition.* Oxford: Clarendon.

———. 1971. "Arguing from Ignorance." *Philosophical Quarterly* 21, no. 83: 97–108.

Rosenstiel, Tom. 1994. *Strange Bedfellows: How Television and the Presidential Candidates Changes American Politics.* New York: Hyperion.

Ruchlis, Hy. 1990. *Clear Thinking: A Practical Introduction.* New York: Prometheus.

Schulte, Fred. 1995. *Fleeced! Telemarketing Rip-offs and How to Avoid Them.* Amherst, N.Y.: Prometheus.

Stabiner, Karen. 1993a. "Get 'Em While They're Young." *This World* (*San Francisco Chronicle*), October 17.

———. 1993b. *Inventing Desire.* New York: Simon & Schuster.

Smith, Timothy W., Snyder, C. R., and Perkins, Suzanne C. 1983. "The Self-Serving Function of Hypochondriacal Complaints: Physical Symptoms as Self-Handicapping Strategies." *Journal of Personality and Social Psychology* 44, no. 4: 787–797.

Tamarkin, Bob. 1993. *Rumor Has It: A Curio of Lies, Hoaxes, and Hearsay.* New York: Prentice Hall General Reference.

Tye, Larry. 1998. *The Father of Spin: Edward L. Bernays and the Birth of Public Relations.* New York: Crown.

Walsh, James. 1998. *You Can't Cheat an Honest Man: How Ponzi Schemes and Pyramid Frauds Work and Why They're More Common Than Ever.* Los Angeles: Silverlake.

Walton, Douglas. 1992a. *The Place of Emotion in Argument.* University Park: Pennsylvania University Press.

———. 1992b. *Slippery Slope Arguments.* Oxford: Clarendon.

————. 1997. *Appeal to Expert Opinion.* University Park: Pennsylvania State University Press.

Webster's Universal College Dictionary. 1997. New York: Random House.

Whately, Richard. 1826. *Elements of Logic.* London: Mawman.

Wheeler, Kenneth G. 1983. "Perceptions of Labor Market Variables by College Students in Business, Education, and Psychology." *Journal of Vocational Behavior* 22: 1–11.

Williamson, Timothy. 1994. *Vagueness.* London: Routledge.

Youngson, Robert. 1998. *Scientific Blunders: A Brief History of How Wrong Scientists Can Sometimes Be.* New York: Carroll & Graf.

Zinsser, William. 1980. *On Writing Well.* 2d ed. New York: Harper & Row.

Answers to Even-Numbered Exercises

Exercise 2.2A

2. The simplest components are "Mandy is maladjusted" and "Mandy is unfriendly." This is a disjunction.

4. The simplest components are "You are alive" and "You are dead." This is a disjunction.

6. The simple components are "She gets angry" and "You'll see fireworks." This is a conditional.

8. The components are "Quiller is a spy" and "Quiller is a thug." This is a denial of a disjunction.

10. The components are "Sue is happy" and "Sue is rich." This is a biconditional.

12. The components are "Fred is dead," "Wanda is well," and "We should invite them for dinner." This is a conditional.

14. The components are "Fred will die," "Ted will die," and "The bomb detonates." This is a biconditional.

16. The simplest components are "John is careful" and "John passes the test." This is a disjunction.

18. The simplest components are "You will be happy" and "You do work you enjoy." This is a biconditional.

20. The simplest components are "You will win" and "You will cheat." This is a denial of a conditional.

Exercise 2.2B

2. "Each of my students goes through this struggle"; "You will go through this struggle." Conjunction

4. "You attain this smooth integration in drawing"; "All five component skills must be in place." Conditional (first clause is antecedent; second is consequent)

6. "The basic strategy for gaining access to R-mode was stated in the original book"; "The basic strategy for gaining access to R-mode was emphasized in the original book." Conjunction

8. "This ability is difficult perhaps impossible to acquire"; "You have learned to perceive the relationships of lights and shadows through drawing." Disjunction

10. "You gain access to the subdominant visual, perceptual R-mode of the brain"; "You present the brain with a job that the verbal analytic L-mode will turn down." Conditional (first clause is antecedent; second clause is consequent)

Exercise 2.3A

2. General

4. Particular

6. General

8. Particular

10. Particular

Exercise 2.3B

2. Conditional, general components

4. Conditional, antecedent particular, consequent general

6. Conjunction, first conjunct particular, second clause general

8. Conjunction, both components general

10. Disjunction, both components general

Exercise 2.3C

2. Particular; subject is "Winnie the Pooh"; predicate is "yellow."

4. General; quantifier is "most."

6. Particular; subjects are Christopher Robin and "Tigger"; predicate is "dislikes honey."

8. General; quantifier is "everybody."

10. General; quantifier is "a few."

Exercise 2.4

2. Contingent

4. Necessary truth

Exercise 2.5

2. Assuming the word *stupid* is used literally, statement is factual and psychological.

4. Statement is evaluative, a statement of aesthetic worth.

6. Statement is factual and psychological.

8. Statement is factual and physical.

10. Statement is evaluative, a statement of moral worth.

12. Statement is factual and psychological.

14. Statement is evaluative, a statement of moral worth.

Exercise 3.1A

2. a. What movie shall we see?

    b. Presupposes we are going to see a movie

   c. We should see *Dog's Night Out.*

   d. I don't want to see a movie.

4. a. Have you stopped stealing cars?

   b. Presupposes that I have stolen cars in the past

   c. (yes) I stopped stealing cars when I turned eighteen.

   d. I have never stolen cars.

6. a. Why are Americans so unhappy?

   b. Presupposes that Americans are unhappy

   c. They are unhappy because they fear unemployment.

   d. Americans are happy.

8. a. Was it through stupidity or dishonesty that this administration destroyed the independence of the Supreme Court?

   b. Presupposes that this administration has in fact destroyed the Court's independence

   c. It was through stupidity.

   d. The Supreme Court has not lost its independence at all.

10. a. How does one light the furnace?

    b. Presupposes that the furnace can be lit

    c. Push the pilot button for thirty seconds, then light.

    d. Your gas has been cut off, so your furnace cannot be lit.

12. a. Does Santa Claus exist?

    b. No presupposition

    c. Yes, he does.

    d. No corrective answer

14. a. When did Mom say the train would arrive?

    b. Presupposes Mom specified a time of arrival

    c. 10:00 P.M.

    d. Mom died twenty years ago.

Exercise 3.1B

2. Why did you choose to study philosophy?   4. Where are we going?

Exercise 3.2A

2. *Subject:* You believe in magic; you do not believe in magic. *Request:* Select one. Whether-question

4. *Subject:* X is a time at which the burglary occurred. *Request:* Fill in for X a time. Which-question

6. *Subject:* X is a set of descriptions for lowering the roof on this car. *Request:* Fill in for X the appropriate instructions. How-question

8. *Subject:* X is the capital of British Columbia. *Request:* Fill in for X the name of a city. Which-question

10. *Subject:* You want the upper bunk; you want the lower bunk. *Request:* Select one.
    Whether-question

Exercise 3.2B

2. Simple

4. Compound

6. Simple

8. Simple

10. Compound

Exercise 3.3

2. *Responsive:* Unicorns don't exist. *Unresponsive:* Up yours.

4. *Responsive:* You should take Ada. *Unresponsive:* Why do you want to learn that drivel?

6. *Responsive:* I don't know. *Unresponsive:* I don't care.

8. *Responsive:* Seven angels will fit on the head of a pin. *Unresponsive.* You're a pin-head.

10. *Responsive:* You can't get a cat to dance. *Unresponsive:* Why in God's name would anybody own a cat?

Exercise 3.4A

2. Presupposes debatably Southern Mortgage Company is different from its competitors

4. Presupposes debatably that musicians are more illogical than the rest of us

Exercise 3.4B

2. Loaded—presupposes that you committed a crime

4. Not loaded

Exercise 4.2A

2. 1. The Padres have weak pitching.
   2. Their best hitter is injured.
   ∴ The Padres won't win this year.

4. 1. Unemployment is down.
   2. The stock market is up.
   3. The budget deficit is shrinking.
   ∴ The recession is over.

6. 1. Jazz musicians constantly perform.
   2. Jazz musicians don't get much sleep.
   3. Jazz musicians drink and take drugs.
   4. Jazz musicians eat high-cholesterol food.
   ∴ Jazz musicians can be expected to have heart disease.

8. 1. The audience uses drugs.
   2. The audience drinks.
   ∴ You should not attend the concert.

10. 1. The murderer kills one person.
    2. The traitor, if he succeeds, kills a whole nation.
    ∴ Treason is worse than murder.

12. 1. The bacteria can attack oil in fish.
    2. The bacteria could attack oil in human skin.
    3. The bacteria could attack oil-drilling platforms.
    4. The bacteria could survive on the ocean's surface.
    ∴ The bacteria could pose a risk.

14. 1. If we leave the kid home, he will burn the house down.
    2. We don't want him to burn the house down.
    ∴ We should take the kid with us.

16. 1. Laura and Steve have known each other a long time.
    2. Relationships that have lasted for years tend to continue.
    ∴ It is surprising that they have broken up.

18. 1. If Mark was in the car crash, the police would have notified us by now.
    2. The police have not notified us.
    ∴ Mark was not in the car crash.

20. 1. If you come any closer, I'll shoot.
    2. You don't want to be shot.
    ∴ You should not come any closer.

Exercise 4.2B

2. (This is a case in which an argument is reported rather than given.)
   1. Engineers don't allow for curvature of the Earth in building canals or railroads.
   2. The opposite shore of Lake Winnebago is clearly visible from twelve miles away.
   ∴ The Earth is flat.

4. 1. When you sleep, you increase in height.
   ∴ If you are going to take a physical exam and want to appear tall, take the exam in the morning.

6. 1. Dance is a performing art.
   2. At many universities, dance is housed in the fine or performing arts area.
   ∴ Dance courses should be accepted as fulfilling the general education requirements in humanities and fine arts.

8. 1. The people in my seminars report that the win-it-all approach no longer works.
   ∴ The win-it-all style no longer works.

10. 1. To lift the incomes of the poor will also lift the incomes of the rich by greater absolute
    amounts.
    ∴ Inequality may grow as poverty declines.

12. 1. Over many years I have cured my patients who have agoraphobia without using
    psychoanalysis.
    ∴ Psychoanalysis is not needed to cure agoraphobia.

14. 1. We all have a sense of the sacredness of human identity.
    ∴ We recoil from those who would intrude on our privacy.

16. 1. The number of congresspeople has stayed roughly the same over the last fifty years.
    2. The congressional workload has grown exponentially.
    ∴ The work of Congress is increasingly done elsewhere.

18. 1. Much of the good President Eisenhower did was done covertly.
    ∴ Eisenhower has a shabby place in history.

20. 1. Everywhere Geyer went, two kinds conspicuously followed her, assigned by the police.
    ∴ Nobody from the guerillas would talk to her.

Exercise 4.3A

2. c
4. a

Exercise 4.3B

2. Without good pitching and its best hitters, a baseball team won't win often.

4. Low employment, rising stock prices, and shrinking budget deficits are all signs of a good (that is, nonrecessionary) economy.

6. Stress, sleep deprivation, alcohol and drug abuse, and a high-fat diet are risk factors in heart disease.

8. Drugs and alcohol are things you should not be around.

10. Killing a nation is worse than killing a person.

12. None

14. None

16. None

18. The police have not notified us.

20. None

Exercise 4.3C

2. If we can build roads without allowing for the curvature of the Earth, and we can see across small lakes without seeing any curvature, then there is no curvature.

4. None

6. What is done at many other colleges should be done here.

8. None

10. None

12. None

14. To hold human identity sacred is to hold privacy sacred.

16. The exponential increase in work cannot have been done by the fixed number of congresspeople.

18. If a president makes many key decisions covertly, historians will not be able to discover his or her merits.

20. Guerillas won't talk to people are obviously being tailed by agents of the government.

Exercise 4.4A

2. Positive assertion

4. 1. If he had brains, he'd be dangerous.
    2. He isn't dangerous.
    ∴ He has no brains.

6. 1. Health insurance is a must.
    2. The company won't volunteer anything.
    ∴ We have to put health insurance in our contract.

8. Not an argument, but a repeated assertion

10. Not an argument, but a rephrasing

Exercise 4.4B

2. 1. Rising living standards are intertwined with our identities.
    2. We will enter a period of slow growth.
    ∴ We will experience disappointment.

4. 1. AT&T focuses on the U.S. telecommunications market.
    2. The non-U.S. market is twice as large and is growing more rapidly.
    ∴ Unless AT&T becomes a greater force in world exports, its global market share will steadily decline.

6. No argument here, just a series of assertions

8. 1. People are ignorant.
    2. This book teaches the law and eliminates the need to see lawyers.
    ∴ This book is very needed.

10. No argument here, just assertions

12. No argument, just narration

14. 1. Any diversion causes your readers to lose interest in what you have to say.
    2. You shouldn't want people to lose interest.
    ∴ You should avoid introducing irrelevancies.

16. 1. Alcoholism costs society a lot.
    ∴ Anything that might possibly help alcoholism should be investigated.

18. 1. Hitler's description of a lower-class family matches what we know of his family in respect to the drunkenness of the father.
    ∴ Hitler was probably describing his own family life.

20. 1. Japan steals technology.
    2. Japanese industries form cartels that target foreign industries for dumping.
    ∴ Japan is winning the trade war because it cheats.

Exercise 4.5

2. 1. My Ford doesn't run right.
   ∴ You shouldn't buy a Ford.
   Purpose: to persuade

4. 1. Some dog is happy.
   2. My dog is happy.
   ∴ My dog is some dog!
   Purpose: to joke

6. 1. This bill will put more teachers in the classroom.
   2. This bill will put more money into teacher training.
   3. This bill will expand the school lunch program.
   4. Those are good things to do.
   ∴ My support for the bill was justified.
   Purpose: to justify behavior

Exercise 4.6A

2. 1 = People hate and fear snitches.
   2 = People hate Richard.
   3 = Richard is a snitch.
   4 = People fear Richard (enthymeme)

$$\frac{1+3}{}$$
   ↙   ↘
   2   4

4. 1 = Andrea likes cheese.
   2 = Andrea likes something.
   3 = Somebody likes something.

$$\frac{1}{↓}$$
$$\frac{2}{↓}$$
   3

6. 1 = Rhonda's dog is a Pomeranian.
   2 = Pomeranians bark like crazy.
   3 = Rhonda's dog will bark a lot.
   4 = Old man Crandall hates noise.
   5 = Crandall will hate Rhonda's dog.

$$\frac{1+2}{↓}$$
$$\frac{3+4}{↓}$$
   5

8. 1 = Billie is a loner.
   2 = Loners are distrusted.
   3 = Billie will be distrusted.
   4 = People who are distrusted are disliked.
   5 = Billie will be disliked.

$$\frac{1+2}{\downarrow}$$

$$\frac{3+4}{\downarrow}$$
$$5$$

10. 1 = People are basically greedy.
    2 = Communism will fail.
    3 = Communism requires that people be unselfish.
    4 = Capitalism will win.
    5 = If communism fails, then capitalism wins.

$$\frac{1+3}{\downarrow}$$

$$\frac{2+5}{\downarrow}$$
$$4$$

12. 1 = Food shortages in the Third World are increasing in frequency.
    2 = High oil prices have taken their toll.
    3 = The Third World is in desperate economic straits.
    4 = Western nations should greatly increase their aid to the Third World.
    5 = The communist nations are nearly bankrupt.
    6 = The communist nations cannot afford to give any more aid.
    7 = Aid can come only from the Western or the communist countries.

$$\frac{1+2}{\downarrow} \quad \frac{5}{\downarrow}$$
$$\frac{3+6+7}{\downarrow}$$
$$4$$

14. 1 = The use of computers in education is to be welcomed.
    2 = Computers are endlessly patient.
    3 = Computers force students to interact.
    4 = Computers remind students of video games.
    5 = We should be putting more computers into schools.
    6 = We need to start training more teachers in computer science.

16. 1 = Many will be crowding the beach this summer.
2 = We ought to open a hot dog stand at the beach.
3 = It gets hot at the beach.
4 = People get thirsty in the heat.
5 = We should sell cold drinks
6 = We ought to open a hot dog stand that sells cold drinks.
7 = People get hungry at the beach.

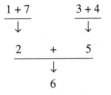

18. 1 = Computers have the power of creative thought.
2 = Computers will eventually be able to replace highly paid workers.
3 = We should no longer treat computers as mere inanimate objects.

20. 1 = Dogs are pack animals.
2 = Cats aren't pack animals.
3 = Dogs are able to work together in hunting.
4 = Cats aren't able to work together in hunting.
5 = Dogs are sociable.
6 = Cats are not sociable.

1   2

↙   ↘   ↙   ↘

3   5   4   6

Exercise 4.6B

2. 1 = The president said he did not want Lewinsky to file a false affidavit.

2 = The president did not want Lewinsky to be deposed.

3 = A true affidavit would have led to Lewinsky being deposed.

4 = The president is lying.

4. 1 = The statements made by the president to Currie were false.

2 = The statements made by the president to Currie were consistent with his testimony at his deposition.

3 = The president was lying when he claimed he was trying to refresh his memory.

4 = You can't refresh your memory by lying to the person you are checking your memory against.

5 = The president was lying in his grand jury testimony when he said he was trying to get a date restriction.

6 = The president never mentioned date restrictions when talking to Currie.

7 = The president said before the grand jury he did not know why he asked Currie those questions.

8 = If the president were trying to influence Currie's testimony, his questions to Currie make sense.

9 = The president was trying to improperly influence Currie's testimony.

$$\frac{1+2+4}{\downarrow} \qquad \frac{6}{\downarrow}$$
$$\frac{3 \quad + \quad 5+7+8}{\downarrow}$$
$$9$$

6. 1 = The president tried to obstruct justice.

2 = The president told Lewinsky to file an affidavit to avoid being deposed.

3 = The president told Lewinsky to file an affidavit to avoid questions at his own deposition.

4 = The president, in getting Lewinsky to avoid being deposed and avoid being questioned, was seeking to impede discovery in the Jones lawsuit.

5 = The president and Lewinsky often used cover stories.

6 = Lewinsky's testimony was unambiguous.

7 = The president had a lack of memory.

8 = They planned to lie under oath.

9 = The president suggested that she continue to use cover stories even after she was named a witness in the Jones suit.

10 = The president never told Lewinsky to stop telling these stories and tell the truth.

11 = The president told those cover stories in his depositions.

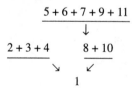

Exercise 5.1

2. Valid

4. Valid

6. Neither valid nor strong

8. Strong

10. Valid (If the dice are not loaded, it follows mathematically that the chances are high that a 7 will not be rolled. The fact that the last twelve rolls were 7's is irrelevant.)

Exercise 5.2A

2. DS

4. HS

6. MT

8. HS

10. MP

Exercise 5.2B

2. Instance of form 3

4. Instance of form 1

6. Instance of form 6

8. Instance of form 4

10. Instance of form 6

Exercise 5.3

2. Argument from analogy

4. Inductive instantiation

6. Argument from analogy

8. Inductive instantiation

10. Inductive instantiation

Exercise 6.2

2. Don't cry over spilt milk.

4. Too many cooks spoil the broth.

6. The KGB was designed to control the Russian people.

8. Free speech benefits the state.

10. Parents are important in the intellectual development of their kids.

12. Children feel more stress when facing inappropriately hard tasks.

14. Many aspects of social phenomena are unconscious.

Exercise 6.4A

2. We should make the most of what remains of our lives before we die.

Exercise 6.4B

2. "savage"; "drastically"; "insulting rubbish"

4. "terror"; "campaign of fear and intimidation"; "seize power"; "exploiting"; "pierce"

6. "lonely"; "destructive"; "personal strength"; "creativity"; "Intimate ties"

8. "oppression"; "corrupt"; "domination"; "surrender"; "conquest"; "trickery"; "exploitation"; "robbed"; "injustice"; "hatred"; "sadism"; " murdered"; "lie"; "betray"; "humiliate"; "crush"; "ignore"

10. "featherbrained"; "wasting"; "outrageous"; "squander"

12. "state"; "fascism"; "democracy"; "one"; "community"; "idea"; "will"

Exercise 6.5A

2. Generally, pizza tastes good.

4. Likely, not everyone can dance.

6. Darwin more or less devised modern evolutionary theory.

8. Education is useful to some degree.

10. People don't always like the truth.

Exercise 6.5B

2. Pizza always tastes great to everybody.   4. Patriots are evil.

Exercise 6.6A

Look up the words in a dictionary.

Exercise 6.6B

2. "After driving for forty years straight, I fell asleep at the wheel and had an accident"; "I have been a driver for forty years without ever falling asleep at the wheel, but recently I fell asleep at the wheel and had an accident." Grammatical ambiguity

4. "The crowd admired the ship's bottom"; "The crowd admired Mrs. Clinton's bottom." Grammatical ambiguity

6. "A motorist on the freeway was wounded by a sniper"; "A motorist was wounded by a sniper who was on the freeway." Grammatical ambiguity

8. "She prefers shopping to being with her husband"; "She likes shopping more than her husband likes shopping." Grammatical ambiguity

10. "Susie plays the piano without having to read music," "Suzie uses her ear rather than her fingers to play the piano." Lexical ambiguity

Exercise 6.6C

2. The print emphasizing what looks like a check amount is large and bold; the print explaining that this is only a coupon is small. Accent

4. Harmless ingredients can interact when mixed to create a harmful substance. Composition

6. Sue is assuming that what is true of people her age taken as a whole is true of her as an individual. Division

8. The qualifier that indicates that this is a coupon (not a check) is separated by asterisks. Accent

10. Just because an average of prices is expected to rise, that doesn't mean that each individual price will. Division

12. The parts of the universe may not have the same properties as the whole. Composition

14. *Bad* is used in the premise to mean "immoral" and in the conclusion to mean "incompetent." Equivocation

16. The parts of the universe may not have the same properties as the whole. Composition

18. The first premise can be read "Different uncommon events happen every day" or "The same uncommon events happen everyday." Equivocation (amphiboly)

20. Does she stretch the jar itself or the honey inside? Equivocation

22. *Lick* can mean lick with the tongue or defeat. Equivocation

Exercise 6.7A

2. Bum   4. Pervert

Exercise 6.8C

2. I do believe this is the finest food I ever ate!   4. Fred is a veritable Pavarotti!

Exercise 6.8D

2. Fred, who is vile, ran away.

4. He welcomed her kisses.

6. The tornado traveled through the town.

8. The children became hyperactive after eating the desserts.

10. Her boyfriend was a burden to her.

Exercise 7.3A

2. Dogs; dogs who have been to the moon; green dogs who have been to the moon; green dogs who have been to college and been to the moon. Reference decreases to zero after first term

4. Unicorns; pink unicorns; pink unicorns that love pizza; educated pink unicorns that love pizza. Reference does not decrease because it starts out zero

Exercise 7.3B

2. People; men; young men; frightened young men

4. Cannot be put in terms of increasing sense, because unicorns and dragons are different sorts of mythical beasts

Exercise 7.4

2. *Physician* means doctor.

4. *Mammal* means an animal that gives birth to live young.

6. Estonia, Latvia, Lithuania

8. *Thesaurus* means a book that lists synonyms.

10. *Proboscis* means nose.

12. *Traffic court* means a court trying cases having to do with the traffic code.

14. *Despicable* means contemptible.

Exercise 7.5

2. Definition is circular.

4. Definition is inaccurate—men can be cooks.

6. Definition is inaccurate—doesn't distinguish cooks from busboys, janitors, and so forth.

8. Definition is negative and inaccurate (a tie is not a win).

10. Definition okay

12. Definition okay

14. Definition figurative and inaccurate

Exercise 7.6A

2. Teachers try to eliminate ignorance (agent and action).

4. Stomach carries out digestion (agent and action, or cause and effect).

6. Bomb causes damage (cause and effect).

8. Greedy people desire money (goal of).

10. Transistor is a part of a radio (part and whole).

Exercise 7.6B

2. A cat is a type of pet.

4. No strong relationship exists—outside France, frogs are not a type of meal, nor do they "have meals."

6. Sanctuary is a place of protection. Type or case of

8. Cattle form herds. Part and whole

10. An *apostate* is a person who has abandoned a religion. Antonym

Exercise 7.6C

2. e

4. d

6. d

Exercise 7.6D

2. c	8. c
4. b	10. d
6. a	

Exercise 7.7A

2. Sorting   4. Grading

Exercise 7.7B

2. Not exhaustive   4. Classification okay

Exercise 8.1

2. a. The American Civil War never ended.

   b. It ended in 1865.

   c. Dogs never make war.

4. a. Dogs don't run in packs.

   b. Because they are group hunters in the wild.

   c. Why are you always talking about animals?

6. a. I never went to college.

   b. I went to UCLA.

   c. Shut up or I'll smack you.

8. a. No corrective answer

   b. Yes, ghosts exist.

   c. I love old cars.

10. a. Dogs never eat grass.

    b. They eat grass as a purgative.

    c. Why don't *you* go eat some grass?

Exercise 8.3

2. *Problem:* No evidence is given that the article in question was unfair, only assertions that it was and a threat to rescind subscription. *Label:* appeal to fear

4. *Problem:* Rather than giving evidence that shows the superiority of Superfone, the ad makes you feel sorry for Mom. *Label:* appeal to pity

6. *Problem:* The picture of death is used to scare the reader into buying vitamins. *Label:* appeal to fear

8. *Problem:* No evidence is given that Jones's article about Morrison is inaccurate; instead, Jones is called a hippie, a plastic person, and a bozo. *Label:* attacking the person

10. *Problem:* The advertisement only talks about the million lasses who use the product. *Label:* appeal to the crowd

12. *Problem:* Mayor Turkle doesn't give evidence that his park program is any good; instead critics have to do the proving. *Label:* shifting the burden of proof

14. *Problem:* A subtle appeal to one's desire not to smell bad. *Label:* appeal to the crowd

16. *Problem:* The editor's reply doesn't give evidence that Smith's comparison is inaccurate; instead, it suggests Smith is hypocritical for not going to the other school. *Label:* attacking the person

18. *Problem:* The ad gives no evident that the guide for sale will help you avoid cancer. And the word *cancer* is in large print. *Label:* appeal to fear

20. *Problem:* The fact that Hitler opposed abortion does not prove that abortion is good—even bad people can occasionally be right. *Label:* attacking the person

22. *Problem:* The ad only talks about how many people read Tony the psychic and does not give any evidence that his views are correct. *Label:* appeal to the crowd

24. *Problem:* The official immediately cuts off the questioner. *Label:* pooh-poohing

26. *Problem:* Mr. Hawk does not give any evidence that the creationists are mistaken; instead, he accuses them of bias. *Label:* attacking the person

28. *Problem:* The opponents of the KKK are said to include all sorts of bad groups. But even "bad" groups can be right. *Label:* attacking the person (and appeal to the crowd)

30. *Problem:* The Nazis offered no evidence of the superiority of their publication and instead offered veiled threats to those who would cancel. *Label:* appeal to fear

Exercise 8.4A

2. The issue is a three-ball walk, not presto boards in Florida.

4. The issue is whether he has in fact changed his position on governmental support for various business to win votes. Reagan only talks in generalities about how consistent he has been for twenty years.

6. The candidate is asked about what he would do to stop Soviet-backed subversion in the Caribbean. He instead replies (a) this administration is doing nothing (yes, but what would *you* do?); (b) the Caribbean is being subverted (yes, but what would you do about it?); (c) the Caribbean is important; (d) the Communists are subverting Central America (yes, but the question is about the Caribbean); (e) we need to develop a North American Accord.

8. The issue is restricting smoking in restaurants, not the number of kids we should be allowed to have or the type of car we should drive.

10. The issue is how certain it is that the economy will turn around by the end of spring. The president instead talks in generalities about the recession ending in the months and years ahead.

12. The issue is how to get interest rates down. The respondent instead talks in general terms about what the problem is.

14. The issue is lowering the speed limit to 55 miles per hour. Instead, the writer talks about seeing accidents occur at 10 miles per hour.

Exercise 8.4B

2. No evidence is given that Whitman's sampler is good, only that it has been given by Americans for many years. Appeal to the crowd

4. No evidence is given that GE makes a better or less expensive product. Instead, the ad evokes patriotic images. Appeal to the crowd

6. No evidence is given that the soap is either better or less expensive. Instead, the ad talks about how popular the soap is. Appeal to the crowd

8. Falwell, when asked whether he supported burning rock albums, replies that he had never done that. That was not the question. Ignoring the issue

10. The ad gives no information about just how your donation will be spent. Instead, it aims to provoke feelings of guilt and pity. Appeal to pity

12. The speaker doesn't give evidence to rebut charges that his or her country violates human rights; instead, he or she accuses the United States of hypocrisy. Attacking the person

14. The coach makes a joke rather than explaining why his whole offense is built around one player. Ignoring the issue

16. The ad presents no information about how and how effectively the pill works to enlarge bosoms; instead, it dwells on how much men admire big bosoms. Appeal to the crowd

18. The ad gives no evidence that the body treatment works, only that a lot of the product has been sold. Appeal to the crowd

20. The letter writer doesn't give any proof that Smith's article was wrong; instead, he calls Smith "pseudointellectual," "pompous," and so on. Attacking the person

22. The ad gives no information about the quality or price of Dodge products but rather merely invokes America. Appeal to the crowd

24. The question was whether to develop solar power, not to convert our power systems immediately to solar. Ignoring the issue

26. The ad insinuates that failing to take vitamin tablets will risk your life. Appeal to fear

28. The issue is not whether national defense is necessary but whether a dramatic increase in defense spending is needed. Ignoring the issue

30. The issue is school lunches, not communism. Ignoring the issue

Exercise 9.2

2. $C \leftrightarrow X$
   T F T

4. $--(X \to -A)$
   T T T T T T

6. $-[(A \to X) \leftrightarrow X]$
   F T T T T T

8. $A \to (-B \vee C)$
   T T T T T T

10. $-A \leftrightarrow (A \to C)$
   T T F T T T

12. $-[-A \& -(B \leftrightarrow -X)]$
   T T T T T T T T T

14. $-(A \leftrightarrow B) \leftrightarrow -(X \leftrightarrow Z)$
   T T T T T T T T T

16. $[-A \to (Z \leftrightarrow X)] \leftrightarrow [-X \to (A \& B)$
   T T T T T T T T T T T T T

18. $-[-A \leftrightarrow (-B \leftrightarrow -X)] \vee Z$
   T T T T T T T T T F T

20. $-\{-[A \to (Z \vee B)] \& - [Z \leftrightarrow (B \vee X)]\}$
   T T T T T T T T T T T T T T

Exercise 9.3

2. $D \& B$

4. $B \rightarrow D$

6. $-A \& (A \rightarrow D)$

8. $-C \rightarrow (D \& A)$

10. $(-A \lor -C) \rightarrow (-D \& -B)$

12. $B \rightarrow (-C \& -D)$

14. $A \leftrightarrow (B \& -D)$

Exercise 9.4A

2.

A	B	A ↔ B	–B	–A	Path
T	T	T T T	F T	F T	M
T	F	T F F	T F	F T	M
F	T	F F T	F T	T F	M
F	F	F T F	T F	T F	T

There is a T path, so the statements are consistent.

4.

H	Z	H & Z	Z ↔ H	–H	Path
T	T	T T T	T T T	F T	M
T	F	T F F	F F T	F T	F
F	T	F F T	T F F	T F	M
F	F	F F F	F T F	T F	M

There are no T paths, so the set is inconsistent.

6.

A	B	C	A & B	B ↔ C	–A	C	Path
T	T	T	T T T	T T T	F T	T	M
T	T	F	T T T	T F F	F T	F	M
T	F	T	T F F	F F T	F T	T	M
T	F	F	T F F	F T F	F T	F	M
F	T	T	F F T	T T T	T F	T	M
F	T	F	F F T	T F F	T F	F	M
F	F	T	F F F	F F T	T F	T	M
F	F	F	F F F	F T F	T F	F	M

There are no T paths, so the set is inconsistent.

8.

M	N	R	M & N	N → R	R ↔ M	Path
T	T	T	↑T↑	↑T↑	↑T↑	T
T	T	F				
T	F	T				
T	F	F				
F	T	T				
F	T	F				
F	F	T				
F	F	F				

There is at least one T path, so the set is consistent.

10.

H	B	R	H → B	-B	-B → R	-R	Path
T	T	T	↑T↑	F↑	↑↑T↑	F↑	M
T	T	F	↑T↑	F↑	↑↑T↑	T↑	M
T	F	T	↑F↑	T↑	↑↑T↑	F↑	M
T	F	F	↑F↑	T↑	↑↑F↑	T↑	M
F	T	T	↑T↑	F↑	↑↑T↑	F↑	M
F	T	F	↑T↑	F↑	↑↑T↑	T↑	M
F	F	T	↑T↑	T↑	↑↑T↑	F↑	M
F	F	F	↑T↑	T↑	↑↑F↑	T↑	M

There are no T paths, so the set is inconsistent.

Exercise 9.4B

2. a. M b. $M \lor A$ c. $-A$

M	A	M	M ∨ A	-A	Path
T	T	T	↑T↑	F↑	M
T	F	T	↑T↑	T↑	T
F	T	F			
F	F	F			

There is at least one T path, so the set is consistent.

4. a. $H \leftrightarrow R$ b. $-H \& R$

H	R	$H \leftrightarrow R$	$-H \& R$	Path
T	T	T T T	T T F T	M
T	F	T F F	T T F F	F
F	T	F F T	T F T T	M
F	F	F T F	T F F F	M

There are no T paths, so the set is inconsistent.

6. a. $F \& (S \leftrightarrow T)$ b. $T \vee (-F \& -S)$

F	S	T	$F \& (S \leftrightarrow T)$	$T \vee (-F \& -S)$	Path
T	T	T	T T T T T	T T F T F T	T
T	T	F			
T	F	T			
T	F	F			
F	T	T			
F	T	F			
F	F	T			
F	F	F			

There is at least one T path, so the set is consistent.

8. a. $B \& -M$ b. $B \leftrightarrow R$ c. $R \leftrightarrow M$

B	M	R	$B \& -M$	$B \leftrightarrow R$	$R \leftrightarrow M$	Path
T	T	T	T F F T	T T T	T T T	M
T	T	F	T F F T	T F F	F F T	F
T	F	T	T T T F	T T T	T F F	M
T	F	F	T T T F	T F F	F T F	M
F	T	T	F F F T	F F T	T T T	M
F	T	F	F F F T	F T F	F F T	M
F	F	T	F F T F	F F T	T F F	F
F	F	F	F F T F	F T F	F T F	M

There is no T path, so the set is inconsistent.

10. a. $C \to K$ b. $-K$ c. $C \to W$ d. $-C \to W$

C	K	W	$C \to K$	$-K$	$C \to W$	$-C \to W$	Path
T	T	T	✝ T ✝	F ✝	✝ T ✝	✝ ✝ T ✝	M
T	T	F	✝ T ✝	F ✝	✝ F ✝	✝ ✝ T ✝	M
T	F	T	✝ F ✝	T ✝	✝ T ✝	✝ ✝ T ✝	M
T	F	F	✝ F ✝	T ✝	✝ F ✝	✝ ✝ T ✝	M
F	T	T	✝ T ✝	F ✝	✝ T ✝	✝ ✝ T ✝	M
F	T	F	✝ T ✝	F ✝	✝ T ✝	✝ ✝ F ✝	M
F	F	T	✝ T ✝	T ✝	✝ T ✝	✝ ✝ T ✝	T
F	F	F					

There is at least one T path, so the set is consistent.

Exercise 9.5A

2.

A	B	A	$A \to B$	$--A$	Path
T	T	T	✝ T ✝	T ✝ ✝	T
T	F				
F	T				
F	F				

Since there is at least one T path, the set is consistent so $\{A, A \to B\}$ does not entail $-A$.

4.

A	B	Z	$A \,\&\, -B$	A	$-Z$	Path
T	T	T	✝ F ✝ ✝	T	F ✝	M
T	T	F	✝ F ✝ ✝	T	T ✝	M
T	F	T	✝ T ✝ ✝	T	F ✝	M
T	F	F	✝ T ✝ ✝	T	T ✝	T
F	T	T				
F	T	F				
F	F	T				
F	F	F				

Since there is at least one T path, the set is consistent, so $\{A \,\&\, -B;\ A\}$ does not entail Z.

Exercise 9.5B

2.

A	B	A ∨ B	–B	– –A	Path
T	T	T T T	F T	T A T	M
T	F	T T F	T F	T A T	T
F	T				
F	F				

Since there is at least one T path, the set is consistent, so the argument is invalid.

4.

A	B	C	A → (B & C)	–(A → C)	Path
T	T	T	T T T T T	F T T T	M
T	T	F	T F T A A	T T A A	M
T	F	T	T F A A T	F T T T	M
T	F	F	T F A A A	T T A A	M
F	T	T	A T T T T	F A T T	M
F	T	F	A T T A A	F A T A	M
F	F	T	A T A A T	F A T T	M
F	F	F	A T A A A	F A T A	M

There are no T paths, so the set is inconsistent, so the argument is valid.

6.

M	T	B	–M ∨ (T & B)	–M ↔ T	–T	Path
T	T	T	A A T T T T	A A F T	F T	M
T	T	F	A A F T A A	A A F T	F T	M
T	F	T	A A F A A T	A A T A	T A	M
T	F	F	A A F A A A	A A T A	T A	M
F	T	T	T A T T T T	T A T T	F T	M
F	T	F	T A T T A A	T A T T	F T	M
F	F	T	T A T A A T	T A F A	T A	M
F	F	F	T A T A A A	T A F A	T A	M

There are no T paths, so the set is inconsistent, so the argument is valid.

8.

A	B	C	$-A \leftrightarrow (B \rightarrow C)$	$-A \,\&\, -C$	$--B$	Path
T	T	T	A T F T T T	A T F A T	T A T	M
T	T	F	A T T T A A	A T F T A	T A T	M
T	F	T	A T F A T T	A T F A T	F T A	M
T	F	F	A T F A T A	A T F T A	F T A	M
F	T	T	T A T T T T	T A F A T	T A T	M
F	T	F	T A F T A A	T A T T A	T A T	M
F	F	T	T A T A T T	T A F A T	F T A	M
F	F	F	T A T A T A	T A T T A	F T A	M

There are no T paths; thus the set is inconsistent; therefore, the argument is valid.

10.

A	B	D	$-[A \lor (B \lor D)]$	$-B \rightarrow -A$	$--B$	Path
T	T	T	F T T T T T	A T T A T	T A T	M
T	T	F	F T T T T A	A T T A T	T A T	M
T	F	T	F T T A T T	T A F A T	F T A	M
T	F	F	F T T A A A	T A F A T	F T A	M
F	T	T	F A T T T T	A T T T A	T A T	M
F	T	F	F A T T T A	A T T T A	T A T	M
F	F	T	F A T A T T	T A T T A	F T A	M
F	F	F	T A A A A A	T A T T A	F T A	M

There are no T paths; thus, the set is inconsistent, thus the argument is valid.

Exercise 9.5C

2. 1. $C \rightarrow R$
  2. $-C$
  ∴ $-R$

C	R	$C \rightarrow R$	$-C$	$-R$	Path
T	T	† T †	F †	F †	M
T	F	† F Å	F †	T Å	M
F	T	Å T †	T Å	F †	M
F	F	Å T Å	T Å	T Å	T

There is a T path, so the set is consistent, so the argument is invalid.

4. 1. $S \& L$
  2. $-A$
  ∴ $A \vee S$

S	L	A	$S \& L$	$-A$	$-(A \vee S)$	Path
T	T	T	† T †	F †	F † † †	M
T	T	F	† T †	T Å	F Å † †	M
T	F	T	† F Å	F †	F † † †	F
T	F	F	† F Å	T Å	F Å † †	M
F	T	T	Å F †	F †	F † † Å	M
F	T	F	Å F †	T Å	T Å Å Å	M
F	F	T	Å F Å	F †	F † † Å	F
F	F	F	Å F Å	T Å	T Å Å Å	M

There are no T paths, so the set is inconsistent, and thus the argument is valid.

6. 1. $S \vee J$
   2. $J \rightarrow W$
   $\therefore S \vee W$

S	J	W	S ∨ J	J → W	¬(S ∨ W)	Path
T	T	T	T T T	T T T	F T T T	M
T	T	F	T T T	T F F	F T T F	M
T	F	T	T T F	F T T	F T T T	M
T	F	F	T T F	F T F	F T T F	M
F	T	T	F T T	T T T	F F T T	M
F	T	F	F T T	T F F	T F F F	M
F	F	T	F F F	F T T	F F T T	M
F	F	F	F F F	F T F	T F F F	M

There are no T paths, so the set is inconsistent, so the argument is valid.

8. 1. $S \rightarrow A$
   2. $A \rightarrow W$
   $\therefore S \rightarrow W$

S	A	W	S → A	A → W	¬(S → W)	Path
T	T	T	T T T	T T T	F T T T	M
T	T	F	T T T	T F F	T T F F	M
T	F	T	T F F	F T T	F T T T	M
T	F	F	T F F	F T F	T T F F	M
F	T	T	F T T	T T T	F F T T	M
F	T	F	F T T	T F F	F F T F	M
F	F	T	F T F	F T T	F F T T	M
F	F	F	F T F	F T F	F F T F	M

There are no T paths, so the argument is valid.

10. 1. $S \rightarrow A$
    2. $A \rightarrow W$
    $\therefore S \vee W$

S	A	W	$S \rightarrow A$	$A \rightarrow W$	$-(S \vee W)$	Path
T	T	T	T T T	T T T	F T T	M
T	T	F	T T T	T F F	F T F	M
T	F	T	T F F	F T T	F T T	M
T	F	F	T F F	F T F	F T F	M
F	T	T	F T T	T T T	F F T	M
F	T	F	F T T	T F F	T F F	M
F	F	T	F T F	F T T	F F T	M
F	F	F	F T F	F T F	T F F	T

There is a T path, so the argument is invalid.

Exercise 9.5D

2.

A	B	$A \vee B$	$-A$	$-(?B)$	Path
T	T	T T T	F T		M
T	F	T T F	F T		M
F	T	F T T	T F		
F	F	F F F	T F		M

We want no T paths. Rows 1, 2, and 4 are not T paths immediately. So we need to make $-(?B)$ false when B is T to block that row. That means $?B$ is to be T when B is T. "B" will do the job.

4.

A	B	C	(A & C) → B	C & A	–(?B)	Path
T	T	T	T T T T T	T T T		
T	T	F	T T T T T	F F T		M
T	F	T	T T T F T	T T T		M
T	F	F	T T T T T	F F T		M
F	T	T	T T T T T	T F T		M
F	T	F	T T T T T	F F T		M
F	F	T	T T T T T	T F T		M
F	F	F	T T T T T	F F T		M

We need to choose –(?B) to block all T paths. But the two premises as they stand rule out all rows but row 1. So –(?B) must be F in row 1, which means ?B must be T in row 1, when ?B is T. So "B" will work.

Exercise 9.6A

2.

B	Q	B & Q	Q ↔ B	Path
T	T	T T T	T T T	T
T	F	T F F	F F T	F
F	T	F F T	T F F	F
F	F	F F F	F T F	M

Answer: none

4.

Q	R	Q ↔ R	–Q ↔ –R	Path
T	T	T T T	F T T F T	T
T	F	T F F	F T F T F	F
F	T	F F T	T F F F T	F
F	F	F T F	T F T T F	T

Answer: equivalent

6.

A	B	C	(A & B) & C	A & (B & C)	Path
T	T	T	↑↑ ↑T ↑	↑T ↑↑ ↑	T
T	T	F	↑↑ ↑F ↑	↑F ↑↑ ↑	F
T	F	T	↑↑ ↑F ↑	↑F ↑↑ ↑	F
T	F	F	↑↑ ↑F ↑	↑F ↑↑ ↑	F
F	T	T	↑↑ ↑F ↑	↑F ↑↑ ↑	F
F	T	F	↑↑ ↑F ↑	↑F ↑↑ ↑	F
F	F	T	↑↑ ↑F ↑	↑F ↑↑ ↑	F
F	F	F	↑↑ ↑F ↑	↑F ↑↑ ↑	F

Answer: equivalent

8.

A	B	C	−A ∨ C	−B & A	Path
T	T	T	↑ ↑T ↑	↑ ↑F ↑	M
T	T	F	↑ ↑F ↑	↑ ↑F ↑	F
T	F	T	↑ ↑T ↑	↑ ↑T ↑	T
T	F	F	↑ ↑F ↑	↑ ↑T ↑	M
F	T	T	↑ ↑T ↑	↑ ↑F ↑	M
F	T	F	↑ ↑F ↑	↑ ↑F ↑	F
F	F	T	↑ ↑T ↑	↑ ↑F ↑	M
F	F	F	↑ ↑F ↑	↑ ↑F ↑	F

Answer: none

10.

A	B	C	−A ↔ (B ∨ C)	A ↔ (B ∨ −C)	Path
T	T	T	F T F T T T	T T T T T T	M
T	T	F	F T F T T T	T T T T T T	M
T	F	T	F T F F T T	T F F T T T	F
T	F	F	F T T F F F	T T F T T T	T
F	T	T	T F T T T T	F F T T T T	M
F	T	F	T F T T T T	F F T T T T	M
F	F	T	T F T F F T	F T F T T T	T
F	F	F	T F F F F F	F F F T T F	F

Answer: none

Exercise 9.6B

2. a. *B & J*

   b. *B & −J*

B	J	B & J	B & −J	Path
T	T	T T T	T F F T	M
T	F	T F F	T T T F	M
F	T	F F T	F F F T	F
F	F	F F F	F F T F	F

Contraries

4. a. *H & C*

   b. *C → H*

H	C	H & C	C → H	Path
T	T	T T T	T T T	M
T	F	T F F	F T T	M
F	T	F F T	T F F	F
F	F	F F F	F T F	F

None

6. a. $A \mathbin{\&} -S$

   b. $-A \vee (S \mathbin{\&} F)$

A	S	F	A & –S	–A ∨ (S & F)	Path
T	T	T	†F A†	A† T ††	M
T	T	F	†F A†	A† F †A	F
T	F	T	†T †A	A† F A†	M
T	F	F	†T †A	A† F AA	M
F	T	T	AF A†	†A T ††	M
F	T	F	AF A†	†A T †A	M
F	F	T	AF †A	†A T AA†	M
F	F	F	AF †A	†A T AA	M

Contraries

8. a. $-A \mathbin{\&} -F$

   b. $(-A \vee -S) \vee -F$

A	F	S	–A & –F	(–A ∨ –S) ∨ –F	Path
T	T	T	A† F A†	A† A† F A†	F
T	T	F	A† F A†	A† †A T A†	M
T	F	T	A† F †A	A† A† T †A	M
T	F	F	A† F †A	A† †A T †A	M
F	T	T	†A F A†	†A A† T A†	M
F	T	F	†A F A†	†A †A T A†	M
F	F	T	†A T †A	†A A† T †A	T
F	F	F	†A T †A	†A †A T †A	T

None

10. a. $(A \& S) \& M$

    b. $(-A \& -M) \vee S$

A	S	M	(A & S) & M	(-A & -M) ∨ S	Path
T	T	T	T T T T T	F T F T T T	T
T	T	F	T T T F F	F T F T T T	M
T	F	T	T F F F T	F T F T F F	F
T	F	F	T F F F F	F T T T F F	F
F	T	T	F F T F T	T F F T T T	M
F	T	F	F F T F F	T T T T T T	M
F	F	T	F F F F T	T F F T F F	F
F	F	F	F F F F F	T T T T T F	M

None

Exercise 9.6C

2.

A	A → -A	Path
T	T F F T	F
F	F T T F	T

Contingent

4.

A	B	(A & B) → -A	Path
T	T	T T T F F T	F
T	F	T F F T F T	T
F	T	F F T T T F	T
F	F	F F F T T F	T

Contingent

6.

A	B	(A & B) → (B & A)	Path
T	T	⚊ ⚊ ⚊ T ⚊ ⚊ ⚊	T
T	F	⚊ ⚊ ⚊ T ⚊ ⚊ ⚊	T
F	T	⚊ ⚊ ⚊ T ⚊ ⚊ ⚊	T
F	F	⚊ ⚊ ⚊ T ⚊ ⚊ ⚊	T

Necessarily true

8.

A	B	(A → B) → [(B & A) ∨ –(B & A)]	Path
T	T	⚊ ⚊ ⚊ T ⚊ ⚊ ⚊ ⚊ ⚊ ⚊ ⚊	T
T	F	⚊ ⚊ ⚊ T ⚊ ⚊ ⚊ ⚊ ⚊ ⚊ ⚊	T
F	T	⚊ ⚊ ⚊ T ⚊ ⚊ ⚊ ⚊ ⚊ ⚊ ⚊	T
F	F	⚊ ⚊ ⚊ T ⚊ ⚊ ⚊ ⚊ ⚊ ⚊ ⚊	T

Necessarily true

10.

A	B	C	A → [A → ((A ∨ B ∨ C)]	Path
T	T	T	⚊ T ⚊ ⚊ ⚊ ⚊ ⚊ ⚊ ⚊	T
T	T	F	⚊ T ⚊ ⚊ ⚊ ⚊ ⚊ ⚊ ⚊	T
T	F	T	⚊ T ⚊ ⚊ ⚊ ⚊ ⚊ ⚊ ⚊	T
T	F	F	⚊ T ⚊ ⚊ ⚊ ⚊ ⚊ ⚊ ⚊	T
F	T	T	⚊ T ⚊ ⚊ ⚊ ⚊ ⚊ ⚊ ⚊	T
F	T	F	⚊ T ⚊ ⚊ ⚊ ⚊ ⚊ ⚊ ⚊	T
F	F	T	⚊ T ⚊ ⚊ ⚊ ⚊ ⚊ ⚊ ⚊	T
F	F	F	⚊ T ⚊ ⚊ ⚊ ⚊ ⚊ ⚊ ⚊	T

Necessarily true

Exercise 9.6 D

2. *F & –F*

F	F & –F	Path
T	T F F T	F
F	F F T F	F

Necessarily false

4. *R → R*

R	R → R	Path
T	T T T	T
F	F T F	T

Necessarily true

6. *(S ∨ A) ∨ –F*

S	A	F	(S ∨ A) ∨ –F	Path
T	T	T	T T T T F T	T
T	T	F	T T T T T F	T
T	F	T	T T F T F T	T
T	F	F	T T F T T F	T
F	T	T	F T T T F T	T
F	T	F	F T T T T F	T
F	F	T	F F F F F T	F
F	F	F	F F F T T F	T

Contingent

8. $(F \leftrightarrow -F)\ \&\ (-A\ \&\ -L)$

F	A	L	$(F \leftrightarrow - -F)\ \&\ (-A\ \&\ -L)$	Path
T	T	T	† †††† F ††††	F
T	T	F	† †††† F ††††	F
T	F	T	† †††† F ††††	F
T	F	F	† †††† T ††††	T
F	T	T	† †††† F ††††	F
F	T	F	† †††† F ††††	F
F	F	T	† †††† F ††††	F
F	F	F	† †††† T ††††	T

Contingent

10. $(H\ \&\ R) \leftrightarrow -(-H\ \&\ -R)$

H	R	$(H\ \&\ R) \leftrightarrow -(-H\ \&\ -R)$	Path
T	T	††† T †††††	T
T	F	††† F †††††	F
F	T	††† F †††††	F
F	F	††† T †††††	T

Exercise 10.1

2.

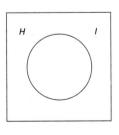

H = Happy things
I = Luisa

4.

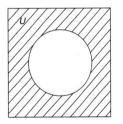

U = Ugly things

6.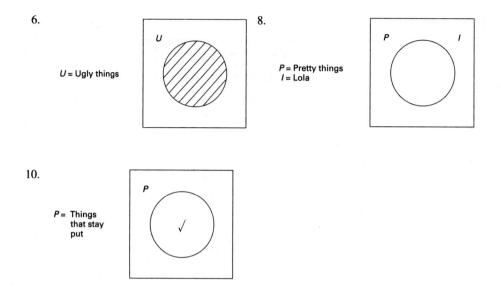

U = Ugly things

8.

P = Pretty things
I = Lola

10.

P = Things
that stay
put

Exercise 10.2A

2.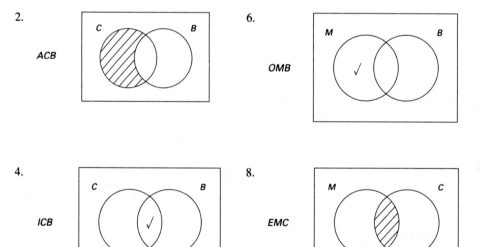

ACB

6.

OMB

4.

ICB

8.

EMC

10.

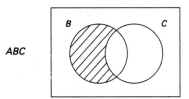

ABC

Exercise 10.2B

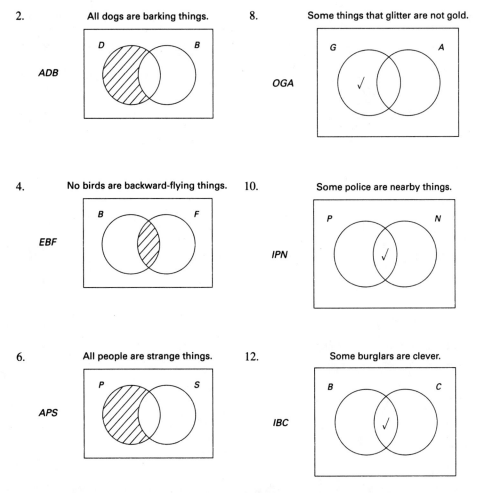

2.   All dogs are barking things.

ADB

8.   Some things that glitter are not gold.

OGA

4.   No birds are backward-flying things.

EBF

10.   Some police are nearby things.

IPN

6.   All people are strange things.

APS

12.   Some burglars are clever.

IBC

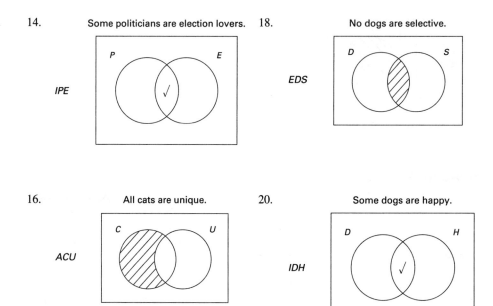

14.   Some politicians are election lovers.   18.   No dogs are selective.

IPE   [P, E Venn diagram with ✓ in overlap]

EDS   [D, S Venn diagram with overlap shaded]

16.   All cats are unique.   20.   Some dogs are happy.

ACU   [C, U Venn diagram with left region shaded]

IDH   [D, H Venn diagram with ✓ in overlap]

Exercise 10.3

2. Inconsistent   8. Inconsistent
4. Consistent   10. Inconsistent
6. Consistent

Exercise 10.4A

2. The first statement does not imply the second.
4. The first statement does imply the second.

Exercise 10.4B

2. Valid   8. Invalid
4. Valid   10. Invalid
6. Invalid

Exercise 10.4C

2. Nothing follows.   4. Nothing follows.

Exercise 10.5A

2. Equivalent

4. Not equivalent

Exercise 10.5B

2. Contraries

4. Subcontraries

Exercise 10.5C

2. Necessarily true

4. Contingent

Exercise 11.1

2. Perceiving

4. Reporting

6. Reporting

8. Sensing

10. Sensing

Exercise 11.4A

2. "Doctor" is not identified.

4. "Doctors," "studies," "universities," and "leading magazines" are all unidentified.

6. Polly Bergen is biased (since she is a member of the board of directors).

8. "Professor"/"expert" is not identified.

10. "Two prominent doctors" are not identified.

12. "National Smoker Study" is not identified.

14. "Scientific research" is not identified.

16. "Clinically proven" doesn't identify which clinic.

18. "Scientific and medical research" is not identified; "Famous lab" is not identified.

20. The gymnast is not identified as a medical doctor. "Medical evidence," "Nationwide study" are not identified.

Exercise 11.4B

2. Reasonable appeal to authority

4. Fallacious appeal to authority (authority biased and talking outside her area of expertise)

6. Reasonable appeal to authority

8. Fallacious appeal to authority (authority is not a medical doctor)

10. Fallacious appeal to authority (authority is not a certified career counselor)

Exercise 12.2A

2. Biased sample—Your mall crowd does not match the population as a whole.

4. Biased sample—Dogs kept at homes that post "BEWARE OF DOG" signs are more likely to be watchdogs, which in turn are more apt to be aggressive.

Exercise 12.2B

2. You would select a random sample of 1,500 or so American adults stratified to match the population in age, gender, ethnicity, income, and location.

4. You would randomly interview people leaving theaters showing movie x at theaters selected on a stratified basis (that is, in areas that match the population in age, gender, ethnicity, income, and location).

Exercise 12.2C

2. Question is loaded—it biases the respondent against Senator Jones.

4. Question is vague—the respondent wouldn't necessarily know what "exerted himself" means. (A president could "exert himself" by playing a lot of tennis, for example.)

Exercise 12.4

2. This is a double generalization:

   1. 96 percent (that is, 235/245) of 245 women students at Florida State University own a stuffed animal.

   ∴ Most women students own stuffed animals.

   1. 75 percent of 245 women students sampled at Florida State University talked to their stuffed animals to relieve tension or for comfort.

   ∴ Most women students talk to their stuffed animals.

   Both generalizations are hasty because the samples are unrepresentative—only Florida State students were sampled.

4. 1. One patient tried Supa Tweez, and it worked.

   ∴ Supa Tweez will work for everybody.

   Generalization is hasty because the sample consists of just one patient.

6. 1. This diet worked for the person quoted.

   ∴ This diet will work for everybody.

   Generalization is hasty because the sample consists of just one dieter.

8. 1. The mustard seed worked wonders for me.

   ∴ The mustard seed will work wonders for everybody.

   Generalization is hasty because the sample consists of only one positive case.

10. 1. I, six girls in the powder room in 1951, and my son (more recently) had lousy times at proms.

    ∴ Most people have lousy times when they go to their proms.

    Generalization hasty because the sample size is way too small (eight cases centering around one person.)

12. 1. Three-fourths of a sample of twenty-five dentists in New York, Los Angeles, Milwaukee, Dallas, and Fort Lauderdale refused to treat patients with AIDS.

    ∴ Three-fourths of all dentists won't treat patients with AIDS.

    Generalization is hasty because the sample is small, limited to big cities, and biased on a questionable interview technique—calling, saying the caller has a toothache and has AIDS, and then asking for an appointment. (Couldn't some of those dentists who refused have been all booked up? And do dentists always set their appointments, or do their office managers do so?)

14. 1. Charles Smith, an older aerospace engineer at Florida State, has not been hired as a teacher by L.A. Unified School District.

∴ L.A. Unified School District is not hiring older aerospace engineers.

Generalization is hasty because the sample is small, limited to just one person.

16. 1. Seven doctors in ten years at Vanderbilt University Medical Schools were alcoholics.

∴ Alcoholism is prevalent among doctors at medical schools.

Generalization is hasty because the sample is small and biased (just Vanderbilt University Medical School).

18. 1. The Super-Loss Diet Program worked for Pam Poco.

∴ The Super-Loss Diet Program will work for everyone.

Generalization is hasty because the sample is small—just one person.

Exercise 12.4

2. Exception: Your belly has been burned badly, and your car is equipped with air bags.

4. Exception: fresh but repellent food (such as fresh rats, roaches, and so forth)

6. Exception: You have a broken back.

8. Exception: The other person is a mass murderer who wants to make you his or her next victim.

10. Exception: Your elders are morally evil people.

Exercise 12.5

2. 1. Eighty-five percent of all people like hamburgers.
   2. Suzie is a person.

   ∴ Suzie will like hamburgers.

   Sample: Suzie
   Population: People
   Projected property: Likes hamburgers.

Does Suzie belong to any group that has food preferences that involve disliking hamburgers (for example, is she a Hindu or a vegetarian)?

4. 1. Virtually all freshmen at Cow University took Algebra in high school.
   2. Al is a freshman at Cow University.

   ∴ Probably Al took algebra in high school.

   Sample: Al
   Population: Freshmen at Cow University.
   Projected property: Took algebra in high school.

Is Al a special type of freshman less likely to take algebra?

6. 1. Seventy-eight percent of Californians intend to vote for Jones for governor.
   2. Fred is a Californian.

   ∴ Probably Fred will vote for Jones.

   Sample: Fred
   Population: Californians who are eligible voters.
   Projected property: Intend to vote for Jones for governor.

Is Fred a member of any group less likely to vote for Jones?

8. 1. Most people like cheese.
   2. Sue is a person.
   ∴ Sue will like the cheese at the party.

   Sample: Sue
   Population: People
   Projected property: Like cheese at party

Is Sue a member of any group less likely to like cheese (for example, is she lactose-intolerant?)

10. 1. Almost all dogs can't dance.
    2. Mandy is a dog.
    ∴ Probably, Mandy can't dance.

    Sample: Mandy
    Population: Dogs
    Projected property: Inability to dance

Is Mandy a special type of dog more likely to be able to dance than other dogs?

Exercise 12.6

2. Telling a child that she is terminally ill will sap her spirit, making her less likely to survive, and will make her sad. Rule does not apply in this case.

4. Guns may generally deter criminal attacks, even though with especially highly motivated attackers such as political assassins, guns may not deter.

6. Even a good hitter can't hold a bat with a broken hand.

Exercise 13.1

2. The liver is like a muscle.

4. My dog is like Einstein.

6. This evening's meal at this restaurant is like the other meals at this restaurant.

8. *A*'s latest movie is like the four movies of his that Sue watched.

10. Lorenzo is like a vacuum cleaner.

12. Reading Kepler's account of his discoveries is like watching a slow-motion film of the creative act.

14. Booing a pitcher is like giving the thumbs-down gesture in the Roman amphitheater.

16. The universe is like the skin of a balloon.

18. Belov introduces his readers to the Vologda region is like the way Turgenev introduced his readers to the Orel region.

20. The way a stone falls to Earth (and a satellite is drawn to the Earth and the Earth is drawn to the Sun) is like a straw floating on water caught in an eddy and whirled to the center of motion.

Exercise 13.2A

2. Sue concentrates like a laser.   4. The people swarmed like bees.

Exercise 13.3A

2. 1. CEOs are like movie stars, rock stars, and sports stars.
   2. We don't mind paying millions to those stars. _____
   ∴ We shouldn't mind paying CEOs millions.

4. 1. Scientific research is like prospecting for gold.
   2. Prospecting for gold is uncertain in that you can work hard but never hit a rich vein.
   ∴ Scientific research is uncertain in that hard work may not pay off.

6. 1. Science is like history in that both require practitioners to become highly specialized.
   2. We still teach history. _____
   ∴ We should still teach science.

8. 1. The world is like a man-made machine.
   2. Man-made machines are designed by the human mind. _____
   ∴ The author of Nature must have a mind similar to the human mind.

Exercise 13.3B

2. Analogy overlooks the fact that budgets in the billions are easier to shrink than budgets in the thousands.

4. Analogy overlooks the fact that a roll-on is applied directly to the skin, whereas aerosols are not.

6. Analogy overlooks the fact that the president's policies directly affect employment.

8. Analogy overlooks the fact that in our present culture, drivers are more apt to stare at a topless female than a topless male.

10. Analogy overlooks the fact that Gestapo agents shoot people, "meter maids" don't.

Exercise 13.3C

2. a. Weakens the argument because it introduces a relevant disanalogy
   b. Strengthens the argument because it introduces relevant similarities between the subject and the analogs
   c. Weakens the argument because it introduces a relevant disanalogy

4. a. Weakens the argument because it introduces a relevant disanalogy
   b. Strengthens the argument because it introduces more analogs with fewer similarities among them
   c. Weakens the argument because it introduces a relevant disanalogy

Exercise 13.4

2. *Positive analogy:* People and animals share basic biological needs and drives.
   Negative analogy: People are more intelligent, more capable of moral choice.
   Neutral analogy: People may not be able to control their impulses.

4. *Positive analogy:* Hatred and poison can both be harmful.
   Negative analogy: Hatred doesn't physically harm people, though it may make someone harm people.
   Neutral analogy: Hatred may or may not have antidotes.

6. *Positive analogy:* Life and poker have winners and losers.
   Negative analogy: Poker is a game played for amusement, life is not.
   Neutral analogy: Economic life may be a zero-sum game (as in poker).

8. *Positive analogy:* Business and war have winners and losers.
   Negative analogy: Business does not usually involve violence.
   Neutral analogy: Business may or may not require a "win-it-all" mentality.

10. *Positive analogy:* College and prison both involve certain limitations of freedom.
    Negative analogy: Being in college is voluntary (being in prison is not).
    Neutral analogy: College and prison may both make people better.

Exercise 14.1A

2. Causal
4. Not causal
6. Causal
8. Causal
10. Causal

Exercise 14.1 B

2. General
4. Particular

Exercise 14.1C

2. Remote
4. Remote

Exercise 14.1D

2. Necessary condition
4. Necessary condition

Exercise 14.1E

2. Compound
4. Compound

Exercise 14.1F

2. Deterministic
4. Statistical

Exercise 14.1G

Factors mentioned: "zero tolerance" policing; better police morale; increased police responsibility; community policing; more police; less police corruption; the "Comstat" computer software for helping police monitor crime; increased rates of imprisonment; demographic trends; social trends (cheaper prices for electronic consumer products, more burglar alarms, and so on); increasing prosperity

Factor not mentioned: increased number of states allowing law-abiding citizens to carry concealed weapons

Exercise 14.2

2. It certainly makes sense to suspect that high GPA causes increased self-esteem. It is less clear that increased self-esteem causes higher GPA—perhaps high self-esteem might make a student more patient to study hard, but it might also make the student feel he or she is so smart he or she doesn't need to study. It is also possible that something—say, genetic endowment or the right kind of upbringing—causes both high GPA and self-esteem. Because it is possible that both high GPA and self-esteem might cause each other, they could be reciprocal effects.

4. It seems reasonable that exercise would lower heart disease risk. It does not seem reasonable that higher risk of heart disease would lower the rate of exercise, even though a person with a severe case of advanced heart disease couldn't very well exercise. Nor does it seem likely that some third factor causes both a higher tendency to exercise and a lower tendency to heart disease—although it is possible. Thus, it seems unlikely that they are reciprocal effects. It is worth exploring whether exercise by itself lowers the incidence of heart disease, or whether the presence of other factors are relevant. Perhaps exercise only works when accompanied by the right genetic predisposition.

Exercise 14.3A

2. *Method of agreement:* The female monkeys given male hormones while fetuses developed into young who exhibited higher rates of aggressive play.

4. *Method of agreement:* The individuals with the guevedoce syndrome all lack a particular enzyme.

Exercise 14.4B

2. Correlation is between vocabulary size and socioeconomic status. By itself, it does not entitle you to infer the first causes the second. A better explanation for the correlation is that third factor—namely, higher education—causes both.

4. *Post hoc ergo propter hoc:* I started carrying the mustard seeds, and good things happened, so the mustard seeds caused the good things. But this could be pure coincidence, or (less likely) the carrying of a religious artifact caused an increase in self-confidence, which in turn caused the good things to happen.

6. The argument given *is* too simplistic. Other things may have caused the increase in crime since the moratorium on the death penalty—such as an increase in the population of fifteen- to twenty-five-year-old males, or an increase in violent entertainment, or a decrease in the number of police. (And why would a moratorium for a penalty for murder have an impact on other crimes, anyway?)

8. Assuming that people do indeed feel better after being touched by Diana, it doesn't follow that she cured them. They could just be experiencing a temporary psychological lift because they view her as a saint.

Exercise 15.2

2. Deterministically causal

4. Historical

6. Intentional

8. Historical

10. Intentional

Exercise 15.5

2. Hypothesis 1 is simpler—To imagine the hamster was subjected to poison gas involves imagining that some person or persons unknown broke into your house, gassed the beast, and fled.

Exercise 16.2

2. (c) is best, because (a) limits you to malls (which often have higher-priced stores), and (b) limits you to budget stores (which often sacrifice on quality).

Exercise 16.3A
Must be done by student

Exercise 16.3B

2. Overlooks the fact that knowledge comes in degrees: You can know enough about a subject to understand broadly what it studies, but know little beyond that.
4. Overlooks the option of sentencing murderers to life in prison without parole
6. Overlooks the option of studying both history (geography and so forth) *and* math/science

Exercise 16.4

2. *Goals:* Power; low cost; high reliability; more functions. *Conflicts:* Cost may be higher for more powerful or reliable systems.
4. *Goals:* High quality; low cost. *Conflicts:* Quality may cost more.

Exercise 17.4

2. Gift pitch with accenting
4. Bait and switch
6. Golden opportunity pitch
8. Assumptive pitch with puffing

10. Assumptive pitch
12. Gift pitch
14. Comparison trick (false analogy)

Exercise 18.2A

2. The comments about growing up poor, being disabled, and being wounded in battle are appeals to pity or appeals to the crowd.
4. The comment about having a widowed mother is an appeal to pity.

Exercise 18.2B

2. The question is whether Mondale will quarantine Nicaragua and how it would be done (that is, by militarily blocking incoming ships). Mondale ignores the issue by talking in generalities.
4. The issue is whether a person who can't afford to be in the U.S. Senate should run for that office. Nixon distorts the issue into whether only rich people should be senators.

6. Dole is asked two questions: (1) What could he do as president to return the nation to godly principles; (2) Does the president have the responsibility to be a good role model for young people? He "answers" question 1 by speaking in generalities about returning power to the states and people. He answers question 2 somewhat but leaves it unclear whether the private morals of a president are relevant.

8. Clinton is asked whether he would be willing to send troops to Israel or the West Bank as peacekeepers. He never answers and instead says nobody has requested troops be used there.

Exercise 18.2C

2. Nixon makes much of the fact that his opponent had his wife on the government payroll. That was a personal attack. (Nixon pretended not to be critical.)

4. Dole cites the record number of bankruptcies, high credit card debt, and loss of manufacturing jobs without any real proof that Clinton's policies caused them. False cause

6. Kennedy points out that the money spent by the Agriculture Department under his Republican opponent's eight years in office exceeded that spent in the hundred years before that. He gives no evidence that their policies caused that. False cause

8. Reagan points out that the interest rates under Mondale's vice presidency were high, without showing how Mondale's policies or actions caused them. False cause

Index